THE
DESERT
GENERALS

THE
DESERT
GENERALS

CORRELLI BARNETT

CASSELL

Cassell Military Paperbacks

Cassell & Co
Wellington House, 125 Strand
London WC2R 0BB
www.cassell.co.uk

First published in Great Britain by George Allen & Unwin in 1960
Second edition 1983
This paperback edition published in 1999

A CIP catalogue record for this book is available from the British Library

ISBN 0-304-35280-2

Printed by Guernsey Press

In Memory of
MY MOTHER
AND
FATHER
Kathleen and Douglas Barnett

AUTHOR'S PREFACE TO THE
SECOND EDITION

A book, like a battle, is the product of a particular moment and situation. *The Desert Generals* was written at a time when the Montgomery myth held almost unchallenged sway over British opinion. Indeed the myth had just reached its apogee with the publication in 1958 of the *Memoirs* of Field-Marshal The Viscount Montgomery of Alamein, K.G., and his accompanying television performances; remarkable exercises in self-praise.

According to this myth, all in the Western Desert was defeat, retreat and confusion until the War Premier, Winston Churchill, by a masterful stroke of policy replaced General Sir Claude Auchinleck as Commander-in-Chief, Middle East, by General Sir Harold Alexander, and Lieutenant-General Sir Bernard Montgomery became General Officer Commanding Eighth Army. The myth even alleged that Auchinleck was proposing to retreat from Alamein if attacked by Rommel again; and that Montgomery immediately quashed this defeatist strategy, drawing up instead with amazing speed a brilliant defensive plan for the Battle of Alam Halfa, his first success. There followed the Battle of Alamein in October 1942, which, so the myth had it, went exactly according to Montgomery's "Master Plan", demonstrated his military genius, marked the turning-point of the war and constituted one of the decisive battles of history. Churchill himself summed it all up in a phrase much quoted since: "It may almost be said [the "almost" tends to get lost in quotation]: 'Before Alamein we never had a victory. After Alamein we never had a defeat'."

Thus the Montgomery myth as it grandly stood in 1958. But my own research convinced me that it had less foundation in fact than in ambition, political convenience and personal spite.

It became clear to me that the myth unjustly neglected, indeed scorned, the achievements of the British Commonwealth forces in the Desert in the hard campaigns before Montgomery's advent. That in perpetrating it Churchill and especially Montgomery had done a grave injustice to Sir Claude Auchinleck. For their memoirs failed to acknowledge the great and gallant victory he had won in the First Battle of Alamein in July 1942, when he stopped Rommel

7

in full career for Alexandria, and so saved Egypt and the Middle East – the *true* turning-point in the Campaign. Moreover they failed to acknowledge that Montgomery's crucial first success at Alam Halfa was based on an outline strategic plan conceived by Auchinleck and fought from a defensive layout designed and largely completed before Auchinleck left the Desert.

Above all, I became convinced that Montgomery's allegation that Auchinleck planned to retreat if seriously attacked was a cruel slander without basis of fact.

I therefore wrote *The Desert Generals* in order to demolish a false but then generally accepted version of history. I wanted to remind readers that there had been three major British victories in the Desert before Montgomery's Alam Halfa and Alamein. I wanted to portray earlier Desert generals, such as Sir Richard O'Connor, whose offensive against the Italians in 1940–41 was the most daring and brilliant of all British operations in North Africa. But most of all I wanted to redress the injustice done to Sir Claude Auchinleck and to puncture the inflated Montgomery myth. Such a purpose, in the prevailing climate of opinion, accounts for the polemical sharpness of the narrative that so enraged Montgomery's fans. Were I writing the book today, with Montgomery reduced as he is to life-size, a Plumer rather than a Wellington and an eccentric rather than a genius, the tone would no doubt be cooler and more detached.

Nevertheless there is little historical analysis itself in *The Desert Generals* that I would amend or retract. Most of the book's main contentions, so outrageous in 1960, have been confirmed by later historians, including the authors of the official campaign history. Indeed the degree of uproar among Montgomery's supporters at the time indicates how close to the target was the book's fall of shot. For instance, it supplied a talking-point for the speeches of Field-Marshal Montgomery and General Sir Oliver Leese to the 1960 Alamein Reunion at the Albert Hall. And in 1961 Field-Marshal Earl Alexander of Tunis publicly acknowledged that he had decided to publish his own memoirs "almost entirely" because of *The Desert Generals*.

I have therefore thought it right in this new edition to let the original text stand without alteration as the product of its time. However, I have added at the end of each Part of the book a fresh Commentary incorporating new material from the now opened official records in the Public Record Office, and summarising the conclusions reached by the principal works on the desert war to have appeared since 1960. Without question, the most important of these is Professor F. H. Hinsley's official history, *British Intelligence in the Second World War*, which casts entirely new light on the generalship of British commanders in the Desert; above all, on that of Auchinleck and Montgomery.

Eighth Army war diaries, signals and commanders' conference papers in the Public Record Office prove beyond doubt, for example, that Auchinleck had indeed been planning to fight Rommel in the Alamein–Alam Halfa position, and not retreat as Montgomery alleged. They also prove beyond doubt that the defensive layout from which Montgomery fought his Battle of Alam Halfa had indeed been designed and largely constructed by Auchinleck. Professor Hinsley's book shows that in the First Battle of Alamein in July 1942, Auchinleck's counter-strokes were timed and placed according to *Ultra* decrypts of the German *Enigma* machine's cipher signals detailing exactly where Rommel's German and Italian units lay. This makes total nonsense of the allegations by Montgomery's latest biographer, Nigel Hamilton, that Auchinleck neglected secret intelligence and that his counterstrokes were "fantasies".

The charge levelled in the original edition of *The Desert Generals* that Montgomery was needlessly slow and cautious in his pursuit of Rommel from Alamein to Tripoli is fully borne out by new evidence that thanks to secret signals intelligence (*Sigint*) Montgomery knew exactly from day to day the extent of Rommel's weakness in men and tanks and his dearth of petrol; knew moreover Rommel's future intentions as signalled to the German high command.

In this new edition the original text of *The Desert Generals* therefore stands buttressed and vindicated by summaries of the documentary evidence opened since the book was first published two decades ago; and that text now begins with the original Author's Preface.

CORRELLI BARNETT
November 1981

AUTHOR'S PREFACE TO FIRST EDITION

The theme of this book is the struggle of individual will against circumstance. The subject matter is human character. In these five uncommon men during the Desert Campaigns, as in the condensed action of a tragedy, were displayed nobility, frailty, resolution, loyalty, indecision, vanity, fear, simplicity, selfishness, greatness and littleness. The creation of literary portraits of living men is both easier and more difficult than with the dead. Some things that are known cannot be written; other things will not be known until death has opened all private records. Yet to meet and talk with the subjects of the portraiture and with their friends and colleagues is to gain vivid and detailed impressions that no correspondence of the dead, however copious, can yield. The shaping of these various impressions into accurate pictures is a complex process. They have to be balanced against one another, against the author's own judgment of the main subjects, and against his own impression of each witness.

Apart from human character, the Desert Campaign has other fascinations. There is the pleasure of seeking out the truth; there is the excitement of watching two men fight a battle, possibly the most complete human activity, since generalship involves all the intellectual, physical and moral power in a man. Historically, the Desert Campaign constitutes the last act of the British Empire as a great independent, and united, power. It ironically epitomises the suicide of the old Europe: today neither German, Italian nor Briton controls the Middle East for which they fought so bitterly. Again the Desert Campaign reveals clearly the twentieth-century national characters and talents of Germany and Britain—and confounds accepted images. The methods of thinking, organising and fighting of each side also adumbrate their industrial and commercial methods in the post-war era.

Yet, above all, the Desert Campaign of 1940–43 is an addition to the great epics. It is the story, set in the wasteland, of how the men of ten nations strove for victory amid the mechanical tumult of a kind of battle never seen before, and likely never to be seen again.

CORRELLI BARNETT

ACKNOWLEDGMENTS

The author wishes to express his very deep gratitude to the following officers for their kindness in giving him unpublished information and comment without which this book could not have been written:

Field-Marshal Lord Harding, G.C.B., C.B.E., D.S.O., M.C.

Field-Marshal Sir Claude Auchinleck, G.C.B., G.C.I.E., C.S.I., D.S.O., O.B.E., LL.D.

General Lord Norrie, G.C.M.G., G.C.V.O., D.S.O., M.C.

General Sir Richard O'Connor, G.C.B., D.S.O., M.C.

General Sir Alan Cunningham, G.C.M.G., K.C.B., D.S.O., M.C.

General Sir Frank Messervy, K.C.S.I., K.B.E., C.B., D.S.O.

General Sir Alfred Godwin-Austen, K.C.S.I., C.B., O.B.E., M.C.

Lieutenant-General Sir Oliver Leese, K.C.B., C.B.E., D.S.O.

Lieutenant-General Sir Arthur Smith, K.C.B., K.B.E., D.S.O., M.C.

Lieutenant-General Sir Alexander Galloway, K.B.E., C.B., D.S.O., M.C.

Lieutenant-General T. W. Corbett, C.B., M.C.

Major-General W. H. Ramsden, C.B., C.B.E., D.S.O., M.C.

Major-General Sir Francis de Guingand, K.B.E., C.B., D.S.O.

Major-General Sir Michael Creagh, K.B.E., M.C.

Major-General J. M. L. Renton, C.B., D.S.O., O.B.E., J.P., D.L.

Major-General A. H. Gatehouse, D.S.O., M.C.

Major-General E. Dorman O'Gowan (Dorman-Smith), M.C.

Brigadier J. A. Caunter, C.B.E., M.C.

Brigadier E. T. (now Sir Edgar) Williams

Colonel R. N. Bruce, T.D.

The author also wishes to thank the following, who were kind enough to read all or parts of the manuscript and make valuable criticisms and comments: Field-Marshal Sir Claude Auchinleck, General Lord Norrie, Lieutenant-General Sir Arthur Smith, Sir Compton Mackenzie, Major-General Sir Michael Creagh, Major-General A. H. Gatehouse, Major-General E. Dorman O'Gowan, Brigadier Desmond Young, Captain B. H. Liddell Hart, D. A. Barnett, Esq. and Lionel Brooks, Esq.

Acknowledgments

The author is indebted to the following publishers and authors for permission to quote from books in their copyright:

Sifton Praed and Co.: *Against Great Odds* by Brigadier C. N. Barclay. Cassell and Co.: *The Second World War* by Winston S. Churchill; *Panzer Battles* by Major-General F. W. von Mellenthin; and *Jan Christian Smuts* by J. C. Smuts. Oxford University Press: *The Sidi Rezegh Battles* and *Crisis in the Desert* by J. A. I. Agar-Hamilton and L. C. F. Turner; *Infantry Brigadier* by Major-General Sir Howard Kippenberger; and *The Battle for Egypt* by J. L. Scoullar. William Collins: *The Turn of the Tide* by Sir A. Bryant; *The Rommel Papers* edited by B. H. Liddell Hart; *The Phantom Major* by Virginia Cowles; *Memoirs* by Field-Marshal Lord Montgomery; and *Rommel* by Desmond Young. Hamish Hamilton: *Montgomery* by Alan Moorehead. The Hutchinson Group: *El Alamein to the Sangro* by Field-Marshal Lord Montgomery; and *The Business of War* by Major-General Sir John Kennedy. Her Majesty's Stationery Office: *The Mediterranean and Middle East* by Major-General I. S. O. Playfair, Vols. I-III; *Despatch* by Field-Marshal Lord Alexander of Tunis; and *Despatch* by Field-Marshal Sir Claude Auchinleck. George Harrap and Co.: *Three Against Rommel* by Alexander Clifford. Heffer and Co.: *The Seventh and Three Enemies* by G. M. O. Davy. Heinemann and Co.: *Journey Among Warriors* by Eve Curie. Hodder and Stoughton: *Operation Victory* by Major-General Sir Francis de Guingand. Chatto and Windus: *Eastern Epic* by Sir Compton Mackenzie. Andre Deutsch: *Nine Rivers from Jordan* by Denis Johnston. Weidenfeld and Nicholson: *Memoirs* by Mussolini. Pavot et Cie.: *Rommel et L'Afrika-Korps* by H. G. von Esebeck. Nelson: *7th Battalion The Argyll and Sutherland Highlanders* by Ian C. Cameron. The British Broadcasting Corporation: scripts of television performances by Field-Marshal Lord Montgomery. Carroll and Nicholson: *Down Ramps* by Lampton Burn. Clowes: *History of the Royal Dragoons* by Julian Pitt-Rivers. Queen's Printer, Ottawa: *The Canadian Army* by C. P. Stacey.

Finally, the author wishes to record his immense debt to his wife for reading and criticising the draft narrative, and for bearing with him during his two and a half years of mental absence in the Western Desert.

CONTENTS

LIST OF ILLUSTRATIONS

List of Illustrations

Unless otherwise stated, photographs are reproduced by permission of the Imperial War Museum. The author wishes to record his thanks to Brigadier Young for the permission to use the photographs of General Messervy, and of the coast road; and to Major-General Dorman O'Gowan for the photograph of his diary for July 1942.

LIST OF SKETCH MAPS

List of Sketch Maps

THE FORGOTTEN VICTOR

General Sir Richard O'Connor, G.C.B., D.S.O., M.C.

> I do not think a braver gentleman,
> More active-valiant or more valiant-young,
> More daring or more bold, is now alive
> To grace this latter age with noble deeds.
>
> SHAKESPEARE: First part of *Henry IV*, v, 1.

CHAPTER ONE

WHEN Richard O'Connor took the field in a year of disastrous defeat his spectacular victories exhilarated his countrymen and astonished the enemy. Yet they have won fame not for himself but for others. The campaign which cost Mussolini an army of two hundred thousand men and an imperial province within half a year of his declaration of war is remembered as 'Wavell's offensive'. Even in that guise its lustre is now dimmed by the later victories of the war, although none of them displayed an equal genius. O'Connor deserves better remembrance.

In Jerusalem, on the 7th June 1940, Major-General R. N. O'Connor, who was then commanding the southern district of Palestine, received a signal ordering him to report immediately to Lieutenant-General H. M. Wilson, General Officer Commanding British Troops in Egypt. The signal gave no reason. O'Connor flew from Jerusalem to Cairo, and during the journey had time to speculate not merely on his personal future but on the significance of the latest news from France. The second phase of that battle had begun on June 5th with a violent German attack on the left flank of what the press and radio so foolishly dubbed 'The Weygand Line'. Already the line of the lower Somme had gone and a deep German penetration had reached Rouen; another force was on the Aisne. It seemed at best doubtful whether the disorganised French could now hold with sixty divisions a front longer than that which they had failed to hold in Flanders with a hundred.

If the French were beaten out of the war, it would reverse the balance of military power both in North Africa and the Levant; for the French were at present the senior partner in the defence against an Italian aggression that might come at any moment; British forces throughout the theatre numbered 50,000 against 500,000 Italians.

In Cairo next day, O'Connor had an interview with Wilson. The two men made a sharp contrast. 'Jumbo' Wilson was big and cumbersome, with a majestic paunch under which was strapped his pistol belt; O'Connor sat poised on the edge of his seat like a bird about to take wing, a small, self-effacing man with the shy and gentle air of a scholar. Wilson told him that he was to go up to Mersa Matruh, the railhead in the Western Desert, and take command of the Western Desert Force, with the task of protecting Egypt from Italian attack. This news O'Connor received with "surprise, and of course pride."[1] So poor was the information about the future of the French and about the intentions of the Italians, and so rudimentary was the British Middle Eastern organisation, that Wilson could give little in the way of a directive. "My recollection," O'Connor said later, "is that I was given very sketchy instructions as to policy"—which had its advantages—"I did not object really, as I don't mind being left on my own." The phrasing was characteristic of his diffidence and understatement.

Later that day he drove over Kasr-el-Nil bridge, through Gezira and along the tram route to the Pyramids, and then right on to the desert road—the 'barrel track'—to Alamein and Matruh. He arrived at his headquarters hot and dusty, and tired by the long journey over a road little smoother than the sleepers of a railway. His headquarters lay at Maaten Baggush, east of Matruh, in the dunes on the seaward side of the Matruh-Alexandria road. On the other side of this road was the headquarters airfield of the Western Desert Air Force. O'Connor found his new headquarters simple after the sophistication of Jerusalem, but comfortable enough. The headquarters offices were well dug-in beneath sandhills, and bomb-proofed. A one-storey concrete building housed the senior officers' mess; everyone slept in tents. There were two charming bays for swimming.

That evening in the mess those of his officers who were not old friends and colleagues had an opportunity of forming an opinion of their new commander. He was as small and neat as a bird. He had a fine head with an aggressive rake to it. The high, broad brow suggested great intellect; his eyes, large and deep with slightly hooded lids, powers of imagination. Command showed in the straight nose and mouth and thrusting jaw. O'Connor's voice was light and clear, with a ghost of a lisp; his manner of conversing quiet and diffident. There was little here of the façade of greatness, yet no one could talk a quarter of an hour with him without being aware of unusual qualities of character and personality.

In the thoughts of O'Connor and his officers, the question of Italy, and the three hundred thousand men across the Libyan

---

[1] In order not to encumber the text, full source references are given at the end of the book.

frontier, hung like an army's dust-cloud. A signal from Cairo two days later told them that Mussolini had answered the question by declaring war on Britain and France as from one a.m. on 11th June 1940. This news had a significance in Mersa Matruh far more immediate than in London or Paris or Cairo. For O'Connor himself it meant that he had entered the special loneliness of command of an army in the field—a small, ill-equipped army facing another ten times as great and of unknown fighting quality. The headquarters officers watched O'Connor; what would he do?

* * * * *

The desert war of 1940–43 is unique in history; it was fought like a polo game on an empty arena. With one exception, there were no roads, but as virtually the whole of the arena was good going, at least for tanks, movement was almost as free as that of a fleet. Apart from a few inhabited places along the coast there were neither towns nor villages to provide shelter or obstacles. There was almost no civilian population to get in the way of the battle. The desert campaign was therefore war in its purest form. Yet, equally, there was in this dusty arena no food and little water; all had to be imported. Supply was the major limit to free movement.

The desert of the battles is a large arena; its northern limit stretches along the Mediterranean from the salt-white dunes of Alamein, past the bald escarpments to Derna, a distance of nearly four hundred miles. Inland its limits lie at the oases of Jarabub and Siwa, a hundred and fifty miles from the coast and on the edges of the great Sand Sea, a scorching waste where only Bedouin or British can live and move. To the newcomer the desert was featureless, coverless and trackless; to the veteran, the slight swell of its rock-ocean provided useful tactical features, while maps and compasses enabled him to navigate more surely than in Britain by signposting. Ancient cisterns and ruined tombs constituted features round which major battles raged.

There is one dominating natural feature: the five-hundred-foot escarpment, facing north to the coastal plain, that leads down from the limestone plateau which is the arena of the desert battles. It is like the wall of a terrace that is broken by only a few flights of steps. It is everywhere a barrier to wheeled vehicles and in most places even to tanks. The gaps that are passable by *all* vehicles became therefore immensely important—Fuka, Halfaya and Sidi Rezegh.

As scenery the desert of the battles has little to offer; a sandy, rocky plateau patched with scrub, dun-coloured—monotony made concrete. Yet it has its beauties: the beauties of silence and solitude; dust devils whirling in the morning, and the endless gravel and scrub showing black in the long rays of the setting sun. Near the coast, spring momentarily quickens the barrenness, and bright flowers bloom along the wadis; even after the most searing dead days of summer, there is the sumptuous African night sky, the brilliant moon, and the beauty of silence etched by the tiny sounds of vipers and scorpions as they move amid the sand and rocks.

The desert became a battlefield in the Second World War because it was the western flank of the British defence of the Middle East and the Axis attack from Italian Libya had to pass over it. For the British the Middle East was only just less important to the waging of the war than their own homeland; for it contained round Mosul, in Iraq, and at the head of the Persian Gulf the oilfields without which the Royal Air Force, the Army and the Royal Navy would be paralysed. The Middle East had other strategic importances; as a support to Turkey, Russia and to action anywhere in the Mediterranean; as a half-way house to India—and Italy. However, the long campaign of 1940–43 was not fought for the Suez Canal (which bore little trans-world traffic at the time, and thus was not a 'lifeline'), but for oil.

The Western Desert was only a part of the vast responsibilities of the Commander-in-Chief, Middle East Forces. In 1940 these responsibilities were greater by far than at other times in the war; the allocated forces were of course exiguous. The ability of the commanding general had to supply the difference, and did; for the C.-in-C., M. E. in 1940 was one of the very greatest of British soldiers of any age, and certainly the greatest of the Second World War—Sir Archibald Wavell. O'Connor, Wavell—Britain was lucky that year, as she faced mortal danger almost unarmed through the lethal well-meaningness, gullibility and soft-heartedness of her people and politicians in former years.

Set up in June, 1939, Wavell's Middle East Command encompassed nine countries and parts of two continents, an area one thousand seven hundred miles by two thousand miles. To defend this theatre Wavell had, at the beginning, the un-formed equivalent of two divisions, two brigade groups, an armoured division well below strength, sixty-four field guns, and—to make up the weight— a camel corps of five hundred men. Wavell's duties were conceived on a grand scale: the government's directive enjoined him firstly to prepare war plans for the entire theatre, including arrangements for reinforcements in the case of emergency, and to share out troops and supplies among the subordinate commands. Secondly, he was to consult with the naval and air commanders-in-chief, and arrange for liaison with the French in Syria and North Africa. And thirdly, there were such things as consultation with His Majesty's ambassadors in Egypt and Iraq, the Governor General in the Sudan, the High Commissioner for Palestine and Transjordan, the Governors of Cyprus, Aden and British Somaliland, and the Political Agent in the Persian Gulf. Wavell was given a headquarters staff of five officers.

In 1939 there was no trace of the immense military base that Auchinleck was to find well on the way to completion in 1941, and Alexander to find complete in 1942. In the autumn of 1939 Wavell had a survey made of all Egyptian ports, and transport and other facilities with a view to turning Egypt into a base for an army of three hundred thousand men. This was his own idea; the Cabinet was still talking. When at last in December the politicians ordered him to begin building a base for nine divisions, Wavell's survey was already complete. The most immediate military danger was from Libya, where there was an Italian army of well over two hundred thousand men (Wavell could not be sure of their strength because the politicians would not allow spying, for fear of upsetting Mussolini). One of Wavell's first acts therefore was to instruct General Wilson, General Officer Commanding British Troops in Egypt, to prepare plans for an invasion of Italian Libya, with particular reference to the novel problem of supply in the desert. Nobody could call Wavell a pessimist.

All through the winter of 1939 Wilson worked to create an army out of the military flotsam that Wavell could spare him, using such desperate expedients as making up the transport strength of the one armoured division by stripping other formations of their trucks. By the late spring of 1940 Wilson had collected together at Mersa Matruh a force composed of 7th Armoured Division, two regiments of the Royal Horse Artillery and a screen of motorised patrols. Matruh was a little white village by a copper-sulphate sea, known before 1936 only to Greek sponge-fishers and the middle-men who handled the export trade from Siwa Oasis. But it was the terminus of the railway and the metalled road from Alexandria and now it became a base and a fortress. In 1942 it was to give its name to Rommel's most astonishing victory.

As the French Army fell back in May and June, 1940, betrayed by a decade of traditionalism, it became more and more clear that Italy was at any moment going to buy a Roman triumph at an Italian price. Along the interminable frontiers of Somaliland, the

Sudan and Kenya, Wavell posted his handful of troops. What would the Duke of Aosta, Viceroy of Ethiopia, do with his two hundred thousand men? Wavell hoped that at least he would not do it at the same time as Balbo in Libya. A commander was wanted for Western Desert Force: and the choice fell on O'Connor, who had a reputation for boldness and unorthodoxy, qualities which Wavell valued highly. Certainly mobility was O'Connor's *leitmotif* as a soldier; his formative military experiences illustrated this. "I think," he wrote later, "commanding a Brigade on the North West Frontier of India was great experience; and later commanding the southern half of Palestine during the Arab rebellion taught me a tremendous lot."

On the outbreak of the war with Italy Wavell stood on the strategic defensive everywhere; the uncertain future of the French, his ignorance of Italian capabilities and his own great weakness forced him to do so. O'Connor was therefore limited to choosing between the tactical offensive and the tactical defensive. His troops began attacking on the first day of the Italian war by cutting the frontier wire and taking seventy prisoners on Italian imperial soil. While the Italian command was mulling this over, the armoured cars of the Eleventh Hussars, together with some tanks, appeared out of the desert before Forts Capuzzo and Maddalena, white-walled evocations of Beau Geste. After R.A.F. bombers had missed the forts, the Hussars took them with the aid of a few rounds of delayed-action high-explosive shells from the 25 pounder field guns with the tanks. On the 16th June—when in France the Germans had reached Orleans, passed through Paris, and nearly reached the Swiss frontier behind the Maginot Line—an Italian column was rolling along the Bardia road in the sunshine. It included in its ranks General Lastucci, chief engineer of the Tenth Army. With the suddenness of a heart attack, the British were upon it. After a brisk action they withdrew, taking Lastucci and eighty-eight others, and leaving forty wrecked tanks.

Behind this continual skirmishing on Italian desert, O'Connor began to shape his small army. He did not make a calculated or dramatic impact in his first few days, for "I had not studied the ground . . . I made no changes until I knew a bit more about the situation." He set out to make good his knowledge on both counts. O'Connor's system of studying ground was much like Wellington's or Rommel's—a personal reconnaissance dangerously far into enemy country, with sudden alarming appearances among his own forward troops.

One night about three weeks after the first Libyan campaign commenced, while I was commanding all our forward troops beyond the frontier wire,

wrote Brigadier Caunter later,

it was reported to me by 11th Hussars that one of their forward patrols had reported that General O'Connor had, in his staff car, come on the armoured car patrol from the west, i.e. from the enemy's direction.

Brigadier Caunter commented:

I did NOT like this.

At the same time as he studied the ground, O'Connor, in his own words, "took the first opportunity of seeing the local commanders and my small divisional staff." He found the most able and thoroughly professional command and staff that any British Force enjoyed in the war, on a scale small enough to permit personal orders and an easy flexibility. The entire Western Desert Force was of regular long-service troops; the senior officers and staff officers of O'Connor's force were old personal friends. Galloway, Brigadier General Staff to General Wilson, and O'Connor had both been Staff Instructors at the Camberley Staff College; and Beresford-Peirse, 4th Indian Division, had served with Wavell's experimental motorised infantry brigade at Blackdown in 1932. Thorough training was O'Connor's principal concern:

You can't spend too much time on training. A well-trained unit pays dividends every time in the way it gets things done, and saves itself casualties. The training of formation H.Q.'s is just as important as other training: c.f. a corps headquarters.

On June 22nd, with the Compiègne Armistice, the French became neutrals: the Italian forces in Libya that had been watching the Tunisian frontier were now free to join the Tenth Army in concentrating for an offensive into Egypt. But the British forward troops continued to skirmish aggressively throughout July, achieving a moral ascendancy over the Italian army that had an effect on the coming battle.

O'Connor and his men were, in this novel business of war in a desert, explorers; they found the snags and the solutions to them; they made themselves at home in the wasteland; and those who followed in later campaigns benefited from their experience. Now O'Connor, receiving reports of wear and tear on his vehicles, learned that in the desert mobility costs dear both in terms of replacements of all kinds and in terms of supply; and he was the first desert general, British or German, to try to square the circle of finding enough trucks to feed, and move, the forward operations; the first to learn that victory depended on the three-tonner. He decided at the end of July to withdraw his tanks in order to conserve equipment for a major battle. The frontier was now to be covered by the motorised infantry and guns of 7th Armoured Division Support Group.

This expected major battle would follow the offensive now being methodically organised by Marshal Rodolpho Graziani, who had replaced Balbo—shot down by his own anti-aircraft batteries—as Governor-General and Commander-in-Chief in Libya. Graziani was a ruthless and fervent Fascist who had done well in Abyssinia in 1936, but now, faced with the British, he was in no hurry to advance. Graziani believed strongly in establishing a firm base, and all through August, while Mussolini prodded him and pointed along the road to glory, the Marshal methodically arranged himself. Graziani's idea of a firm base included a motorised brothel. No one could tell the Italians anything about mobile war. Graziani, at this time perhaps shrewder at debate than combat, suggested to Mussolini that his grand offensive should follow the expected German invasion of Britain; the disheartened British in Egypt would then offer only feeble resistance. Unfortunately for Graziani, Operation *Sealion* was postponed and postponed; and the idea began to grow in Rome that the Marshal's appetite for glory was smaller than his military discretion. On the 7th September Mussolini gave him a final order to attack within two days, *Sealion* or no *Sealion*. On 13th September, Graziani moved.

After a loud bombardment of the empty British frontier posts, the Italian Tenth Army lumbered into Egypt with four divisions and groups of tanks. As they moved along at twelve miles a day, keeping close together in a noisy Italian crowd, the British hung about their dusty flanks, stinging and disappearing. On the fourth day, Graziani halted at Sidi Barrani, sixty miles into Egypt and still eighty miles from the British army at Matruh. He spread his army into a semi-circle of defensive camps and began to build a metalled road up from the frontier, construct water-pipelines and accumulate stores well forward. He also erected a monument alongside the road in Sidi Barrani to commemorate the glorious feat of arms achieved by the Italian army in advancing sixty miles into Egypt. When this firm base was ready, Graziani proposed to move methodically on Mersa Matruh. But he was still in no hurry. He displayed rare instinct—for O'Connor had a model defensive battle ready for him:

> We hoped he would try and advance to the neighbourhood of Matruh, as we had prepared a full-dress counter-stroke with all our armour. We worked this out on the ground, and I was greatly disappointed that he never came far enough to put it into execution.

Through October and November 1940 both armies lay apart in preparation. In October the arrival of two tank regiments brought 7th Armoured Division to full strength. Next month 4th Indian Division was also at full strength. Behind Western Desert Force, in reserve between Matruh and Alexandria, were 4th New Zealand Division, consisting of one brigade, and 6th Australian Division. Most important of all accessions of strength were the fifty-seven heavy 'I' tanks of the 7th Royal Tank Regiment. This growing army now brightly reflected the qualities of its commander. It was high-spirited, alert, aggressive and full of dash. Its affection for O'Connor, its loyalty, and its confidence in him were genuine and profound. O'Connor had achieved this ascendancy without any of the advantages of what television calls 'personality'. O'Connor's expositions of his plans were modest and tentative. His plans spoke for him. In contrast to Montgomery he had not been an able lecturer at the Staff College. His public manner was always reserved, low-keyed. Comparing him with Montgomery, General Galloway, a friend of them both, wrote:

> The difference between O'Connor and Montgomery was that O'Connor detested publicity and Monty lived on it—not only lived on it, but began it: and for a very good reason.

But even the unsophisticated are more aware of the genuine quality in their leaders, whether advertised or not, than is sometimes believed in this age of contrived publicity; and O'Connor, as General Galloway put it, "had the complete confidence of the troops." For there was a subtle magnetism in this brave and gentle man. Major-General (then Brigadier) Dorman-Smith found "something boyish about him," a quality of intense life: "He was always springy and alert, even when still—always alive and vibrant."

In Cairo, Wavell was about to begin that inspired strategic juggling which by its timing and finesse was to suggest to the Italians that the same British soldiers were defeating them in simultaneous battles a thousand miles apart. The Duke of Aosta in Italian East Africa was to be his principal victim; for although that officer commanded a large and powerful army, it was a wasting one, being quite cut off from Italy. But before Wavell could concentrate his small forces against Aosta, he must deal with Graziani's threat to the Delta. On October 18th, 1940, he ordered Brigadier Dorman-Smith, Commandant of the wartime Middle East Staff College at Haifa, to visit O'Connor, spend a few days with Western Desert Force, and report on the possibility of successfully attacking Graziani in his present position. Dorman-Smith, who had a high reputation as an original military thinker, was an old colleague and friend of Wavell's, having been Brigade Major in his experimental infantry brigade in 1932. He was also an old friend of O'Connor's; they had gone on a walking tour together in the Italian Alps soon after the First World War and had been instructors together at Sandhurst. On October 22nd Dorman-Smith brought back to Wavell the opinion that an early offensive should be a success. Wavell, as usual, said nothing, but simply took out of his drawer a directive that he had just drafted to Wilson and O'Connor ordering them to prepare for attack.

The objects set out in the directive were modest: "We were simply told," wrote General O'Connor, "to carry out a five-days' raid. . . . This in fact started the campaign." Wavell suggested a plan: attacks on both Italian flanks; direct on the coast road, enveloping in the south. O'Connor and his officers sat down in the underground operations room at Baggush to consider the problem. He did not like Wavell's conception, with its turning movement round the Italian extreme right flank. "This was the obvious way from the map," wrote O'Connor, "but the ground to the south of the enemy positions was quite unsuitable for tanks, so it was not considered." Equally, he was not keen on splitting his forces as Wavell had suggested; and he considered that the separate advances might be difficult to co-ordinate. A better way must be found.

The Italian Tenth Army now lay in a series of camps echeloned in depth between Maktila, on the coast some fifteen miles east of Sidi Barrani, and the Libyan frontier. There was a forward line of camps stretching from Maktila fifty miles inland to Sofafi, garrisoned by the Group of Libyan Divisions which was estimated to contain three and a half divisions with a powerful tank group, but which in fact had three divisions with the tanks mingled with the infantry. Behind this line of camps, at Sidi Barrani, headquarters of the Group of Libyan Divisions, was a Blackshirt Division and part of another. Further back still were the 21st and 23rd Corps with five divisions between them. By a peculiar arrangement of the command, Sofafi, the camp on the extreme right flank of the forward line, did not come under the Group of Libyan Divisions, but 21st Corps. The Italian equipment was mixed in quality. The Italian tanks were so thinly armoured that even the British anti-tank rifles could penetrate them; and the heavier models had their guns in fixed casemates so that to aim the gun the tank itself had to be trained on the target. However, there was a trickle of a new type with a forty-seven millimetre gun and a machine-gun mounted in a revolving turret. But the Italian artillery, the best trained and equipped arm of the Italian service, outnumbered the British two to one.

The Italian Air Force also heavily outnumbered the British, and O'Connor had to make his plans in expectation of violent Italian air attacks on British troops in daylight. Genius makes the difficult seem easy; so it was with the British Command and the Battle of Sidi Barrani. Beforehand, however, the Italians appeared formidable enough in numbers and some forms of equipment. No one knew how a Fascist army would fight; the Italians' performance in the Spanish Civil War and Graziani's in Abyssinia suggested that they would be more dangerous than in the First World War. On the British side, it was the first offensive battle since 1918, and they were employing for the first time the untried 'I' tanks. Defeat of O'Connor's small force would have handed Egypt to Mussolini.

The Italian dispositions, which O'Connor considered extremely unsound, were curiously similar to those of Eighth Army at Gazala in the spring of 1942—a fortified and fixed forward 'line' in the desert, with a large part of the army pegged in it and at no great distance from the enemy. O'Connor, in contrast, had held his troops in loose mobile groupings well back from Graziani, protected from an Italian stroke both by distance and by a screen of covering troops. Now, looking at these Italian camps or 'boxes' each out of supporting distance of the others, O'Connor conceived a plan of attack great in imaginative boldness; one which Rommel was to copy twice, each time successfully. He would penetrate the gap between Sofafi and Nibeiwa camps, thus cutting the Italian defences in two, and, while Sofafi was masked, swing north, behind the Italian front. Part of his forces would attack Tummar and Nibeiwa camps from the rear and then Sidi Barrani; part would drive to Buq Buq on the coast, across the Italian communications.

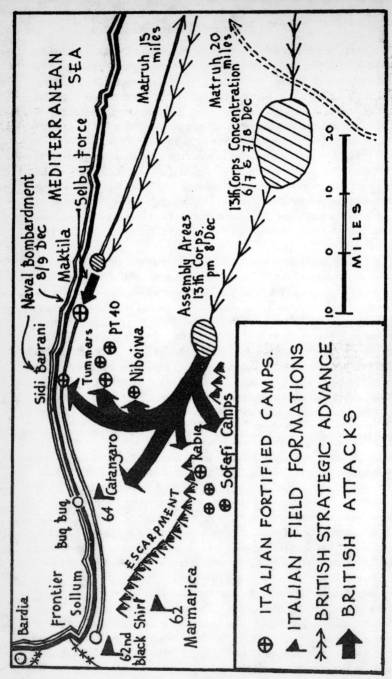

MAP 1. THE BATTLE OF SIDI BARRANI
December 1940

On November 2nd Wavell accepted this plan of battle, but his strategic intention remained a five-days' raid followed by withdrawal to Matruh.

Still wearing the Italian Silver Medal for Valour, awarded to him while fighting alongside the Italian Army in 1918, O'Connor began to plan in detail the victory of Sidi Barrani. But neither his judgment nor his resolution were softened by his continuing affection for his old comrades. He now saw beyond Wavell's directive to total victory. "I felt that they did not plan for a success," he put it with characteristic understatement, "only for mediocre results." As a planner, he was absorbed and intent: "he worried to get things right—but never showed his worry," said Galloway. Round him he had that group of officers who were so close to one another as to give almost the character of a conspiracy. There was what he called "his race of dwarfs in the desert": himself, John Harding (now Field-Marshal Lord Harding) the Brigadier General Staff, and General Michael Creagh, the Irishman who commanded 7th Armoured Division. General N. M. de la P. Beresford-Peirse, of 4th Indian Division, made up some of the weight: he was an extrovert, plain-spoken, orthodox soldier who chain-smoked Indian cheroots, which he kept in a kind of reticule. "B.P. was a very genuine personality," wrote Dorman-Smith. Brigadier Galloway, Wilson's Brigadier General Staff, who was 'lent' for the planning, was a keen, hard man; restless, quick-tempered, able, and equipped with a caustic sense of humour.

On October 30th, Mussolini invaded Greece; but the Greeks in a victorious counter-stroke established themselves in Italian Albania. This Greek victory, won before O'Connor took the field, was destined to be the ruin of his campaign.

On November 19th an important preliminary operation took place in the desert. O'Connor's strategy for the coming battle depended on the gap between Nibeiwa and Sofafi camps being neither garrisoned nor patrolled by the Italians. He therefore pushed forward the Support Group into the gap, where they fought and defeated some Italian battle-groups and established British domination of the area. On November 26th there was a full-scale rehearsal of an attack on a desert camp, planned and carried out by Beresford-Peirse and 4th Indian Division. It was a completely orthodox operation, inspired by the official pamphlet *The Division in Attack*.

After the division reached its assembly area, it waited patiently for two hours in full daylight while supporting artillery registered the enemy defences. Then, following the barrage, the infantry made a frontal assault on foot, in conjunction with the 'I' tanks. Timings had to be exact to ensure that tanks and men arrived on the Italian defences simultaneously. O'Connor held a conference to decide whether in fact this Cambrai-style attack would produce decisive results. The tank men, especially Colonel Gatehouse, second in command of 7th Armoured Brigade and chief tank umpire of the exercise, were sharply against it; so also was Dorman-Smith—sent down by Wavell to witness and comment on the exercise. They criticised the two hours' waiting time during which the entire striking force would be exposed to attack by the much larger Italian air force. They pointed out that in aerial photographs there was what looked like a minefield covering the breastwork of the camp on the front of the rehearsed attack. To succeed against superior numbers on the ground and in the air, Western Desert Force would need in their opinion all the speed and surprise that mechanised warfare made possible. Victory lay, therefore, in the unorthodox. O'Connor, though not himself a tank officer, agreed. Close re-examination of air photographs of Nibeiwa camp revealed that all vehicle tracks led into the north-west corner of the camp. This suggested absence of mines. The final and daring plan was now evolved.

The artillery would not wait to register; from the east, it would bombard the whole area of the Italian camp of Nibeiwa with the aim of causing panic and confusion rather than material destruction. Simultaneously the 'I' tanks and infantry would attack from the west, the Italian rear. The infantry would follow the tanks in their trucks and only leave their trucks for the close assault on the north-west corner of Nibeiwa. Since the British attacking force would lie in the middle of the Italian army, it would run less risk of air attack than in an advance from the east. The plan involved an approach march through the enemy's defence zone and a startline in its rear; a daring and imaginative manœuvre that broke every rule of staff college orthodoxy. It has few rivals in the history of war.

In preparing the operation O'Connor had to contend with a shortage of every kind of equipment, but especially of that specialised equipment which enabled later armies to move economically in the desert. There were no tank-transporters and no tank-towing vehicles. Tanks moved always under their own power, shortening the lives of tracks and engines. If they were stopped in action by slight damage, they could not be immediately recovered for repair. There was the question of nourishing an approach march of a considerable distance, and a battle at the end of it, in the face of a transport famine; and of transporting the troops themselves. O'Connor solved the problem by establishing magazines of petrol, food, water, and ammunition for a five-day battle in the open desert between the British and Italian armies. All transport was first devoted to stocking these magazines; and then, during the battle, to carrying the troops. It was another example of O'Connor's cool nerves and professional skill.

Yet the approach march of sixty miles, followed by a battle, would still throw a great strain on the transport and on the fighting men—too great a strain. O'Connor decided to divide the approach march into two stages. For one day and night his entire army would lie out in the open desert halfway from his base towards the Italians.

Of the complete plan for Sidi Barrani, with its litany of risks boldly accepted, and of his state of mind as the moment of action arrived, O'Connor wrote later:

> I can't describe my feelings, other than to say that I was sure it would be successful. It was a sound plan, a bit complicated perhaps, but I had every reason to rely on my commanders, their staff and the troops—all who were in very good heart.

The date of the offensive was fixed for 9th December. On November 28th, Wavell, with the astonishing military intuition that lay behind his continual silence, wrote to Wilson, O'Connor's superior:

> The difficulties, administrative and tactical, of a deep advance are fully realised. It is, however, possible that an opportunity may offer for converting the enemy's defeat into an outstanding victory . . . I do wish to make certain that if a big opportunity occurs we are prepared morally, mentally and administratively to use it to the fullest.

On 5th December, Wavell issued his formal orders to Western Desert Force for Operation *Compass*. Next day O'Connor gave his own final orders. A year of difficult and ingenious preparation and six months of training and planning had brought O'Connor's small force to a peak of professional skill and fighting dash that was never again reached by the British in the desert. The army began to gather; the routine of camp was over.

O'Connor had two divisions. Fourth Indian Infantry Division, with the fifty-seven 'I' tanks, formed the close assault force; 7th Armoured Division provided the *corps de chasse*. There was also a heterogeneous group, called 'Selby Force' after its brigadier. The entire command numbered thirty-six thousand men.

On the night of 7th December the long wait was over. The convoys rolled away through the darkness of no-man's-land, the lurching trucks full of soldiers wrapped thickly against the cold. The army had gone. O'Connor waited in the concrete ops room at Maaten Baggush as the hours of daylight on the 8th crept slowly past, wondering if his men would be discovered by Italian air or land reconnaissance as they lay out in the desert. It was a bright, cold day, with clear visibility.

During the night of December 8th/9th, 1940, the full moon, huge and white, and sharply delineated as a saucer, served for the first time as a lamp to light men into a desert battle. Beyond the shapes of trucks and tanks the desert stretched away silver, black and empty. It was bitterly cold. At last engines were started up, and the trucks and tanks lumbered off towards the rear of an army more than twice as large as the attacking force. In the doomed camp of Nibeiwa, the Italians were restless, as if they sensed the danger of which they knew nothing. Their flares flamed against the stars, but they illuminated nothing but an infinity of sand and scrub. Shots crashed out against the silence. Then the Italians quietened down.

In Baggush, O'Connor waited. It was too late for doubts now. Happily, he did not know—for Wavell had deliberately not told him—that in five days' time, whatever the state of the battle, he must relinquish half his command. For Wavell wanted 4th Indian Division for an attack on Eritrea.

CHAPTER TWO

WHEN it was full daylight on 9th December, 1940, a haze was seen lying along the desert. In the Italian camps the normal diurnal routine began. And then came the sound that no Italian or German and few Americans expected ever to be heard again—the opening salvo of a British offensive. It was the 4/7th Rajput Regiment firing on Nibeiwa from the east. Meanwhile the main assault force of infantry and 'I' tanks (of the Royal Tank Regiment) passed south of the camp, turned north in its rear, and, after the artillery bombardment by 4th Indian Division had stopped, struck without delay at the un-mined north-west corner of the camp. The Italians only realised that a formidable attack was upon their rear when they heard the growing roar of the 'I' tanks' engines. Twenty Italian medium tanks were caught outside the camp perimeter, warming their engines and quite helpless. The 'I' tanks shot these into ruin in passing, and ploughed on into the camp. Only now did the Italians begin to move, swarming madly out of tents and slit trenches.

Some immediately surrendered. Yet the Italian Army as a whole fought well. Seeing the heavily armoured 'I' tanks for the first time, they attacked them with grenades and machine-guns. The Italian gunners fought until all were killed or wounded. General Maletti, the camp commander, was shot down while firing a machine-gun in his pyjamas from the mouth of his dugout. But by half-past eight in the morning it was over. Two thousand men and thirty-five medium tanks had been captured for the loss of only fifty-six officers and men. The attack rolled on to the Tummar camps further north.

O'Connor was soon up with his forward troops.

> I remained in my headquarters until I got some information in, and then went off and saw the commanders, bringing a small staff with me. I always found this method paid me well. I left my Brigadier General Staff at my headquarters if I was out, and he knew my plans, and could prepare the administrative side.

This method of command was usual in the German panzer forces; an innovation in the British army, adopted later by Montgomery. The commanders now saw O'Connor for the first time in the role of a leader on the battlefield. The quietness, the deep thought, had given way to bristling energy and crisp decision. At the end of the campaign a senior Australian officer said to one of O'Connor's staff officers: "Do you know what we call your general? The little terrier—because he never lets go."

His tactical headquarters, so small as to have only one office truck, was established at the junction of the Enba-Sidi-Barrani tracks. From here he ranged the battlefield in his staff car, the wound-up spring that kept the battle swiftly rolling.

As the morning wore on the sky became overcast and a sand-storm began to get up slowly. By half-past one the 'I' tanks and 4th Indian Division were ready to attack Tummar West. The sand was blowing hard now and very dense. It infiltrated into eyes, noses, mouths, engines and gun-mechanisms. The field artillery fired into the whirling cloud, and the remaining twenty-two runners of the 'I' tanks lumbered into the camp via the fatal north-west corner. By twenty-past four the British were finished with Tummar West and were attacking Tummar East.

*   *   *   *   *

O'Connor drove out to the headquarters of 7th Armoured Division to see Brigadier 'Blood' Caunter, commanding the division in the place of Creagh, who had gone into hospital two days earlier with an abscess on his tongue. He ordered Caunter to push patrols beyond Sofafi on the 10th to prevent the Italians escaping. Then he swung round and drove north to see Beresford-Peirse. He reached 4th Indian Division outside Tummar East just as the one Italian counter-attack of the day was smashed by British gunfire. However, this attack saved Tummar East for a few hours; the camp did not fall until early next morning. There was a conference on the sand between O'Connor, head cocked, body taut and springy, and Beresford-Peirse, solid, red-faced, cheroot-smoking: Sidi Barrani must be taken next day. Fourth Indian Division with the eight 'I' tanks that remained runners would therefore push on during the night and be ready to attack at first light.

As all the reports came in that evening, it became clear that only Selby Force had failed to gain a resounding success. In darkness and bad going, it allowed the Italians to escape from Maktila. On the other hand, Caunter had pushed his light tanks across the coast road between Sidi Barrani and Buq Buq. O'Connor ordered him to send a brigade to destroy an enemy tank group believed by British Intelligence to be at Azzaziya. But in fact, as Caunter wrote later: "They were NOT there."

The second day of Sidi Barrani was far more loose and opportunist than the first. Beresford-Peirse started on Sidi Barrani in a dawn dust storm; it fell at 4.40 p.m. Once again the 'I' tanks of the 7th Royal Tank Regiment proved decisive. Seventh Armoured Division found no Italian tanks, but rolled further west across the Italian rear. Selby had a bad day east of Sidi Barrani in a frontal assault against prepared defences. Yet, though the troops were beginning to tire, there was no slackening in speed and pressure; O'Connor's method of fighting a battle remained, in Caunter's words, "offensive action wherever possible". He motored down to Caunter on the evening of the 10th December and told him "that pursuit was the next step". Caunter replied that he "had already ordered 7th Armoured Brigade to move in a westerly direction for forty miles an hour before dawn and then strike northwards to the coast road. The brigade was to attack any Italians found with the utmost violence".

During the night 4th Indian Division closed on the two Italian divisions encircled near Sidi Barrani. Early next morning O'Connor proposed to join Beresford-Peirse for the *coup de grâce*. Before he left his headquarters he read a signal telling him that he was to lose 4th Indian Division that day. With the conduct of a pursuit and the relinquishment of half his command on his mind, he watched Italian resistance melt. The remaining camps of Sofafi-Rabia and Khur-Samalus had been evacuated during the previous night.

On the night of 11th December, 1940, Western Desert Force camped on the field. For the first time men gazed on the scene of a desert victory: trucks and tanks abandoned or burnt, dumps of food and uniforms, guns, rifles, shells, cartridges, grenades, and, blowing in the wind, all the paper without which a twentieth-century organisation cannot live. All this sad litter resembled the aftermath of a novel kind of race meeting. Towards Matruh the Italians were marching, dirty, tired and dejected, in dense untidy columns: pawns on their way off the board.

O'Connor had more than carried out Wavell's directive. This was not a successful raid; it was a major victory. In three days' fighting O'Connor had ended the Italian threat to Egypt, smashed two Italian corps, taken thirty-eight thousand prisoners, including four generals, seventy-three tanks and two hundred and thirty-seven guns. It was achieved at the cost of six hundred and twenty-four British Commonwealth casualties, killed, wounded and missing.

O'Connor took victory quietly, without demonstration, without memorable historical asides. There was the question of 4th Indian Division. There was above all the question of whether Western Desert Force, about to be halved in size, should now fall back on Matruh according to the original intention. This was the safest thing to do. The magazines, stocked only for a five-day battle, were partly exhausted; it was difficult to see how both to replenish them *and* move the army with available trucks. The remaining Italian forces were very strong in numbers, many of them fresh formations. To advance further would be to abandon a firm base, to lose 'balance'.

That night O'Connor told his subordinate commanders that 4th Indian Division would be leaving his command; at the same time he issued fresh orders. In Brigadier Caunter's words: "He told me that he was determined to pursue the enemy with the forces he had left to him—7th Armoured Division, which I was commanding, and Selby's infantry brigade."

The five-day raid had begun to flower into a great campaign.

* * * * *

On the morrow of the battle of Sidi Barrani, O'Connor was hard after the retreating Italians—with 4th Armoured Brigade along the top of the escarpment, 7th Armoured Brigade on the coast road. Just across the Libyan frontier was the fortress of Bardia: a tiny harbour and town surrounded by modern perimeter defences, and connected with Tobruk and Benghazi by the metalled Via Balbia. In conjunction with the fortress of Tobruk, Bardia had been designed and built as the principal defence of Libya from the east. Upon this refuge the Italian Army now retreated, fighting hard at Sollum and Capuzzo against 7th Armoured Brigade. But O'Connor was already moving faster round their desert flank. He wished to reach the Via Balbia between Tobruk and Bardia before the Italians, trap them against the coast and destroy them. Swinging north for the first time across the dreary plateau of Libya, over which the war was to oscillate for two more years, 4th Armoured Brigade crossed the Trigh Capuzzo track—which lies fifteen miles south of the Via Balbia—and dashed for the coast. During the morning of 14th December men of the 11th Hussars stopped their vehicles and looked at the narrow strip of macadam that before their arrival had linked the remnants of the Tenth Army with Italy. Beside it telegraph poles marched from horizon to horizon, and, until the British cut them, the wires sang in the desert silence. Trapped, the Italians fell back into the shelter of Bardia. By 16th December the fortress was closely invested.

For O'Connor there was now the unglorious hard work and worry of organising supply between his base at Mersa Matruh and his besieging forces round Bardia: a brain-heating business of estimated minimum consumptions, capacity of available transport, distances, speeds, mechanical wear and tear. But when all had been juggled, the basic fact remained that there was a transport famine. Wavell had now given O'Connor the under-strength 6th Australian Division for the assault on Bardia; a fruit perhaps of O'Connor's daring in continuing the pursuit. As elements of it began to arrive on 18th December in the place of the departed Indians, O'Connor also had to re-organise his command.

With the lull in the fighting O'Connor and his men had time to digest Churchill's telegram of congratulation to Wavell on the victory of Sidi Barrani:

> The Army of the Nile [a propaganda name for Western Desert Force] has rendered glorious service to the Empire and to our cause and rewards are already being reaped by us in every quarter . . . Pray convey my congratulations to Longmore upon his magnificent handling of the Royal Air Force and fine co-operation with the Army . . .

The telegram thus included everything appropriate except O'Connor's name.

* * * * *

In Western Desert Force there was now a spirit of exuberance and professional self-confidence never afterwards matched by the British in the desert. It was the springtime of war. And the Army but reflected O'Connor; eager to press on, hating pauses however necessary. His was not the kind of leadership that makes of war a game of clergyman's chess; he believed in hustling the enemy, in keeping him in constant movement, in dazzling him by speed and surprise. O'Connor even tried to hustle forty-five thousand Italians and four hundred guns out of the fortress of Bardia by gunfire and a noisy demonstration by the Support Group of 7th Armoured Division. But Bardia was not to be hustled; the garrison was inspired by a message to their commander from the Duce:

> I have given you a difficult task, but one well suited to your courage and experience as an old and intrepid soldier—the task of defending Bardia to the last.

The garrison commander, General 'Electric Whiskers' Bergonzoli, had replied:

> I am aware of the honour and I have to-day repeated to my troops your message—simple and unequivocal. In Bardia we are and here we stay.

It was all splendidly Roman; and Bergonzoli, considering the strength of his position, probably thought his boast could be made good. Round the little town of Bardia and its harbour, nestling in a valley in the escarpment like a treeless white Mevagissey, was an eighteen-mile belt of modern defences. Behind a steep anti-tank ditch twelve feet wide by four feet deep, a dense barbed-wire entanglement and minefields were two lines of mutually supporting steel and concrete bunkers, about eight hundred yards apart. On the south side of the perimeter, facing Egypt, there was a second, or switch-line, defence. To hold this barrier Bergonzoli had his forty-five thousand men and four hundred guns. To attack it, O'Connor had to operate a hundred and fifty miles from his railhead with a total force smaller than Bergonzoli's and a close assault force only a third of the garrison's strength. But he was briskly confident:

> I knew I should be delayed by at least a fortnight or three weeks by (the) move of 4th Indian Division. But with the 6th Australian Division, I thought we should take Bardia all right, although of course it would require quite different tactics.

Supply was the only thing that really worried him; it absorbed much of his time, and the arrangements adopted testify to his originality and resourcefulness. Magazines like those established for Sidi Barrani were now opened along two lines from his base to Bardia, one inland and the other along the coast. There was the familiar problem of stocking these and dealing with troop movements; he partly solved it by swiftly organising captured Italian trucks into new supply units. A windfall of heavy trucks arrived from Palestine. Heavy wear and tear on the poorly surfaced coast road and pot-holed desert tracks sharpened the problem. By the end of December there was forty per cent wastage in the vehicle establishment of Western Desert Force.

On 1st January, 1941, Western Desert Force was re-named 13th Corps. At the same time the anomalous chain of command, by which General Wilson and H.Q., British Troops in Egypt, had been interposed between O'Connor and Wavell, was altered so that O'Connor came directly under the C.-in-C.'s orders. This lightened O'Connor's mind. As he wrote later:

> I don't think H.Q. BTE were really necessary, except at the start and in the early stages. I sometimes received orders from both head-quarters, which led temporarily to difficulties.

Three weeks after the victory of Sidi Barrani O'Connor felt him-self ready to attack Bardia. Seventh Armoured Division (reduced

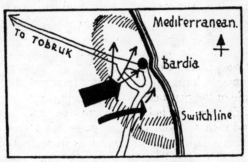

Map 2. ATTACK ON BARDIA

by wear and tear to seventy cruisers and one hundred and twenty light tanks) he reserved for pursuit; he did not consider strong fixed defences a proper object for armour. With his capacity always to see and plan a move ahead, he had already given 7th Armoured Division its orders for the pursuit; a single code-word on the fall of Bardia would set it in motion. For the assault on the fortress O'Connor employed the 6th Australian Division, one hundred and twenty guns and twenty-three 'I' tanks, all that could be got work-ing in the face of a desperate shortage of spare parts. The Australians were seriously short of all kinds of equipment; there were only two instead of three artillery regiments, of which one was equipped with 1914–18 guns; the anti-tank company had eleven instead of twenty-seven two-pounder anti-tank guns.

As at Sidi Barrani the break-in was planned round the 'I' tanks of 7th Royal Tank Regiment, but with significant differences that illustrate O'Connor's freshness of approach to each of his battles. He told Mackay, General Officer Commanding 6th Australian Division, who was to command the assault, that the tactical problem lay in passing the 'I' tanks safely through the powerful anti-tank defences. In contrast to the tactics at Nibeiwa, the infantry would have to go first in order to drive a bridgehead beyond the anti-tank ditch and minefields, bridge the ditch and clear lanes through the mines for the passage of the tanks. His mind already on the pursuit, O'Connor told Mackay to have a brigade ready on the third day of the battle to co-operate with 7th Armoured Division in a drive on Tobruk.

O'Connor placed his stroke where the enemy least expected it—on the centre of the western face of the perimeter. Once inside the fortress, tanks and infantry were to fan out to take the southern switchline in the rear.

All through the night of 2nd/3rd January, 1941, tanks with their exhaust baffles removed were kept roaring up and down outside Bardia to delude the Italians over the size of the attacking force. Soon after one o'clock in the morning of 3rd January, the Australian infantry moved forward to their assembly areas. It was a night of pitch darkness and biting cold. The men were loaded like Arab donkeys: woollen underwear and jerseys, battledress, leather jerkins and overcoats, gas masks, a hundred and fifty rounds of ammunition, grenades and three days' iron rations. At five-thirty a bombardment by every gun O'Connor could muster—as he had promised Mackay—opened the battle. To the fitful light of gun-flashes the troops moved over the desert towards Bardia, ready to deal with the barbed-wire with Bangalore torpedoes and captured Italian wire-cutters. By the last hour of darkness, the first Italian prisoners began to come out of the bunkers. By half-past six, in the grey first light, the Australians had cleared two lanes for the 'I' tanks. The infantry and tanks drove together into the heart of the fortress. There was now what Montgomery would have termed a 'dog-fight', the Italians fighting well and counter-attacking. But by eight o'clock the Australians had reached their first objectives and taken eight thousand prisoners. Meanwhile diversionary attacks had been made at either end of the perimeter.

There was now a pause in the attack, while the fleet laid a barrage and the air force bombed Italian airfields. At 11.30 a.m. the second phase opened with a brigade assault east of the Capuzzo road. Staff work here was not good; confusion slowed up progress. Yet by the end of that day the switchline had been turned by the

Australians. In the middle of next morning, an Australian brigade
led by six tanks attacked in two columns towards Bardia town and
the Tobruk road. This assault split the garrison in two; and the
fortress of Bardia fell with the resonance and suddenness of a great
tree. The water supply—with a production of four hundred tons
a day—and the harbour fell undamaged to the Australians, who took
luncheon off Italian champagne. The Italians were still fighting
sporadically in the north and south of the Bardia perimeter, but
O'Connor was already driving westward to Tobruk. On 5th January
the battle was over. While 7th Armoured Division raced via El
Adem to cut off Tobruk, the magnitude of the new victory became
apparent. The Italians had lost over forty thousand men, killed,
wounded and captured, four hundred guns, thirteen medium and
a hundred and fifteen light tanks and seven hundred and six trucks
—an especial windfall to O'Connor.

For Wavell, O'Connor's successes raised an unexpected strategic
problem. The Commander-in-Chief had to hold a balance between
his various campaigns; the development of the 'five-day raid' into
a six weeks' crescendo of victory threatened that balance. How far
should Wavell allow himself to be pulled by O'Connor's success?
Eight Italian divisions had been destroyed, seventy thousand
prisoners and a major fortress taken. But in Cyrenaica there still
remained an Italian army of nearly eighty thousand men and nine
hundred guns. In Tripolitania there were another ninety thousand,
with five hundred guns. In view of the sharpening difficulties of
supply and transport in 13th Corps and the wear and tear on
the precious tanks, there was a strong case for resting content
with a six weeks' raid. But O'Connor had already surrounded
Tobruk; and Tobruk would be a valuable supply port. And so
Wavell was drawn in behind O'Connor's advance. He gave his
approval to the extension of the campaign to the capture of
Tobruk.

But now O'Connor's victories were causing far-reaching reactions
—reactions which were to determine the course of the war in the
Middle East and Mediterranean for two years. On 11th January,
1941, a week after Bardia fell, Hitler made up his mind to send
German ground forces to Libya. Shortly afterwards it was decided
that this force of tanks, armoured cars and artillery—to be known
as the 5th Light Division—would begin their move on 15th February.
Thus unless O'Connor could destroy the Italian army in Libya in
the next month and occupy the whole province, the British would
be faced with a German invasion of North Africa. From January

11th, 1941, O'Connor and his troops, though they did not know it, were fighting in borrowed time.

A far more immediate danger, one quite well-known in Cairo, lay in the high strategy of the war cabinet in London. The Prime Minister was fascinated and deeply moved by the Greek resistance to the Italians. All through the winter of 1940–41, as the savage fighting went on in the Epirus, the British had sent what help they could. Air squadrons were diverted from support of O'Connor to support of the Greeks. However, at this time the cabinet and the C.-in-C.s, Middle East, had agreed that so far as land forces were concerned the desert came first. But on November 4th, 1940, the Fuehrer had begun to stick his fingers into the Greek affair by ordering a study of ways and means of helping the Italians from Rumania, which Germany already controlled. At this stage, London opinion had been unanimous that Turkey was more important than Greece; and that if Turkey were attacked, *Compass*—the attack on Sidi Barrani—should be abandoned and O'Connor's forces sent to help her. Wavell, with the strategic insight of genius, wrote back that he considered he would have time for *Compass* before the Germans moved in the Balkans. Next day, Hitler told Ciano that German intervention in Greece via Bulgaria could not take place earlier than March, 1941.

So far Churchill and his advisers had regarded Greece as second to the desert. Even after Sidi Barrani the Prime Minister wrote to Wavell:

> Neither of these [action in the Sudan or the Dodecanese] ought to detract from the supreme task of inflicting further defeats upon the main Italian Army.

But as evidence of German preparations in Rumania grew, the threat to Greece began to make the Prime Minister's mind wobble. Two days after the fall of Bardia, he wrote to the Chiefs of Staff:

> Although perhaps by luck and daring we may collect comparatively easily most delectable prizes on the Libyan shore, the massive importance of . . . keeping the Greek front in being must weigh hourly with us.

At this time it was only a thought set down in a minute; it was to grow until it dominated the Prime Minister's obstinate mind, was made fact against all initial advice by his formidable will; it led to two immediate military disasters; and prolonged the war in Africa by two years.

Four days later Churchill made up his mind that after Tobruk had fallen, Greece must take priority over the Desert; he would offer the Greek Government everything we could spare; that is, the troops of 13th Corps. Wavell with his cool sense of reality asked the Chiefs of Staff to consider whether the German preparations in Rumania were designed to bluff us into taking the heat off Graziani. Wavell added a judgment that events proved exactly right. He said that if the German preparations in Rumania were genuine, *nothing* we could send the Greeks could avert defeat anyway. But by now the Prime Minister was convinced of the need and possibility of building a new Balkan front against German expansion. The Greek question was settled. He replied peremptorily to Wavell through the Chiefs of Staff:

> We expect and require prompt and active compliance with our decisions for which we bear full responsibility.

But luckily for O'Connor, the Prime Minister's offer of aid was rebuffed by the Greek Government—for the time being. O'Connor could march on; but after Bardia his campaign lay under a suspended death sentence.

Meanwhile, O'Connor was briskly preparing another victory.

By 7th January, 1941, three days after the fall of Bardia, Tobruk was closely invested. By 15th January, British intelligence was able to give O'Connor the Italian garrison's order of battle. Under the command of General Petassi Manella, 22nd Corps, there were believed to be thirty-two thousand men, two hundred and twenty guns, and forty-five light and twenty medium tanks. O'Connor thought there were Italian divisions in Derna and Benghazi, and an armoured force under General Babini at Mechili. Two hundred miles from Mersa Matruh, supplied by the Via Balbia and the Trigh Capuzzo track, O'Connor was at the limit of his communications; ingenuity and improvisation could do no more. The possession of the port of Tobruk was essential to a deeper advance.

Tobruk, which was to make so many headlines in the next two years, now faced its first siege. Despite the great fame it was to acquire, Tobruk was not much of a place. There was a small harbour, a scattering of white buildings rather like a transit camp on the flat, naked, sloping ground of the coastal plain. An hotel, a restaurant and a few shops made it an urban centre. It was treeless except for some battered palms in the main square. The narrow ribbon of the Via Balbia suspended it from the hazy horizons of east and west. Round Tobruk, over the barren hinterland, ran thirty-eight miles of perimeter defences similar to those of Bardia: an anti-tank ditch—which was incomplete—dense barbed-wire, a double row of concrete bunkers each with its own ditch and wire, minefields. Tobruk seemed an easier proposition than Bardia: troops were fewer, the perimeter longer and the defences sparser.

At his headquarters at Gambut, amid continued sandstorms, O'Connor planned his assault. There was the temptation to use the armoured division as a self-contained battering ram. But O'Connor would not risk it against fixed defences; he considered it should be conserved for pursuit and mobile battle. Nevertheless he was more than usually in a hurry. He had news of fresh Italian forces landing at Tripoli; in a short time, if he allowed it, there might be four new Italian divisions and a tank group between Derna and the Gulf of

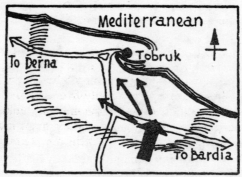

MAP 3. ATTACK ON TOBRUK

Syrte. Most worrying of all was the threat of help to Greece, which had already reduced his air support. He fixed the date of the assault on Tobruk for 20th January. His assault commanders asked for a postponement of twenty-four hours in order to work on the 'I' tanks, now reduced by the desert surface to twelve. O'Connor agreed, but ordered that in the extra time a squadron of Australian mechanised cavalry should be equipped with Italian medium tanks. His tactical employment of 'I' tanks and infantry was to be the same as at Bardia; the selected point of assault, the south-eastern sector chosen by Rommel in June, 1942.

Final preparations began on 18th January on a day of dense sand-storm and a wind that bowled petrol cans along the ground. On the 20th there was clear winter sunshine, and after dark the crystalline stars of the African night sky. The troops were in position. Seventh Armoured Division already had its orders to strike for

Mechili the moment that Creagh received the code word that Tobruk had fallen.

At five-forty on 21st January, 1941, the assault on Tobruk was opened with O'Connor's customary bombardment by concentrated artillery, and the Australian infantry charged in to the accompaniment of red Verey lights, the explosion of Bangalore torpedoes and an Australian voice bellowing:

"Go on, you bastards!"

In some places the Italians were captured before they were aware that an attack was going on. At a quarter to seven that morning the 'I' tanks lumbered through the gap in the perimeter, and infantry and tanks together began to fan out. The Italians fought bitterly all day, launching counter-attacks with tanks; when night came, their artillery was silent and General Petassi Manella was a prisoner. The long horizons of sand and scrub were lit by blazing dumps as the rest of the garrison still fought on. Dawn found them on the verge of surrender. Mackay, Australian commander of the assault, ordered a general advance; and men, tanks and carriers flowed down the naked slope into Tobruk. By early afternoon, 13th Corps was once more counting the booty while 7th Armoured Division rolled away to the west. There were twenty-five thousand prisoners, two hundred and eight guns, twenty-three medium tanks, two hundred trucks and enough canned food to have lasted the garrison two months. Though the Italians had tried to wreck the port, damage was so slight that British stores were being unloaded within three days. From O'Connor's point of view the most welcome prize was water distillation plant and wells with a capacity of forty thousand gallons a day.

He had a new base; a base which would make possible the further spring to the west that had been in his mind long before Tobruk was attacked. For O'Connor was on edge with the desire to get on, to win final victory, before Greece and German intervention broke his run of success. This anxiety bred another—the anxiety over supply and transport that nagged at him continuously. Yet, by his energy and aggression and his gift of leadership he kept the whole rickety, improvised campaign rolling forward on the heels of the demoralised Italians. It took everything he had to give. In his own words:

> There was really no time for any relaxation, other than sleeping, during this short campaign. I was constantly seeing and talking to the formation commanders, staff officers and officers of the services: talking to the fighting troops, or encouraging the administrative services to further efforts.

No one knew that he was suffering all the time from a stomach complaint. Understandably, his manner was deeply serious: "He seldom smiled," wrote Brigadier Caunter, "and I never saw him laugh." He had always taken his profession seriously. Many years before, General Godwin-Austen had taken over O'Connor's company at Sandhurst. He stayed with him one night and dined in the mess with the company. Afterwards, walking outside the New Building, Godwin-Austen saw a tent with cadets running up and down its sides. He asked O'Connor what the tent was for; O'Connor replied that it was the scorer's tent for the cricket match. At this moment the tent collapsed. Godwin-Austen remarked what a glorious game it was—he'd love to run up and down a tent. But O'Connor seemed far from amused. Later a cadet told Godwin-Austen that O'Connor had been horrified by the spectacle, and had thought it must have deeply shocked the new company commander.

After the fall of Tobruk, O'Connor's campaign entered its last phase, a finale of amazing brilliance in which great risks were daringly accepted, and the allegedly impossible triumphantly overcome. O'Connor was to drive his troops unceasingly, fretting at necessary delays, cannibalising truck parts, stealing tanks from one unit to make up another; and at last flinging the remnants of his armour across uncharted country on the last few gallons of petrol and the last few miles of life left in the tank tracks. One of the epic marches of history was about to begin.

CHAPTER THREE

ON 21st January the Chiefs of Staff had informed Wavell that the capture of Benghazi was extremely important. So O'Connor's advance received strategic sanction for yet another stage. It all had been anticipated, if not foreseen, by O'Connor as long ago as the siege of Bardia. Now, with Tobruk behind him, he advanced to destroy the remaining Italian forces in Cyrenaica and to take Benghazi—the Australians along the coast road through Gazala, the armour inland to Mechili.

He had traversed the desert of the battles now from end to end. He stood at the gates of the Jebel Achdar, the Green Mountains, a region of fertile, settled Mediterranean countryside—wide fields of grain, stony hills dotted with grey olive trees and the white cubist farmhouses of Italian settlers. Pretty modern towns with green and pleasant gardens and abundant water lay ahead of the dust-covered army, and at the back of the Jebel Achdar, Benghazi. The coastline swings north round this isolated segment of Italy or Greece, and then sharply south to the blinding sand-wastes of the Gulf of Syrte. South of the Jebel Achdar lay half a continent of desert. The Via Balbia followed the coast round the bulge of the Jebel to Syrte; the chord to this arc was supplied by un-reconnoitred desert tracks from Mechili through to Beda Fomm; going so bad that the Italians took it to be impassable to an army.

The Jebel Achdar offered better prospects of defence for the Italians than the open desert. Its hills were broken and rugged and offered little scope to armour, and its two gateways were strongly held. On the Italian left, barring the Via Balbia, was Derna, held by one division, a natural position of great strength, for it lay in a gigantic wadi that stretched twelve miles inland with nearly sheer sides up to seven hundred feet high. On the right—or desert—flank at Mechili, centre of desert track-routes south of the Jebel, was a powerful force of infantry, guns and up to seventy tanks under General Babini.

O'Connor decided to smash open these Italian defences and gain a victory before London opinion, now in favour of taking Benghazi, veered back again to Greece. By 24th January the Australians were feeling their way along the fringe of the Derna defences. They found the Italians well posted in the broken ground and full of fight. At the same time an Italian tank force near Mechili fought a brisk action with 4th Armoured Brigade. Both Italian wings thus seemed quite formidable, especially when British march wastage was considered: 7th Armoured Division was down to fewer than seventy cruisers. The Italian weakness, which O'Connor noted, lay in that their wings were too far away to help each other. O'Connor therefore decided to destroy Babini at Mechili and sweep on south of the Jebel Achdar to turn deeply the Italians at Derna and Benghazi. On 25th January he ordered Creagh to envelop Babini with the armour and then destroy him with the infantry. He pointed out to Creagh the route northwards by which Babini was most likely to retire, and suggested that if the going there was too rough for tanks, Creagh should use the Support Group. But on the night of the 26th, after the British armour was in position, Babini escaped northwest into the Jebel Achdar. It was O'Connor's first major setback, and he did not take it lightly. General Creagh wrote afterwards: "O'Connor was very disappointed and annoyed." Creagh's own explanation of the failure to block Babini's retreat is that "armour is definitely blind at night and I don't think there was sufficient active patrolling by the infantry of the leading brigade. Hence they withdrew unnoticed until daylight". Yet it was all for the best: the way was now open for O'Connor's long-meditated drive to the Gulf of Syrte. And a battle at Mechili might not have been an unclouded success. Brigadier Caunter studied the ground at Mechili after the Italian withdrawal, and found that "our maps did *not* tell us the topographical faults. The steepness of the slopes on the eastern and southern faces made tank attacks there extremely difficult, if not unsound".

O'Connor himself also made a tour of the scene of the Italian escape, like, said Dorman-Smith, "a terrier ratting".

Although the way was open, O'Connor could not march. Desert and distances were more formidable opponents than Babini. Seventh Armoured Division was down to fifty cruisers and ninety-five light tanks; and there was not enough fuel or ammunition for a long march over bad going as well as a battle. There was no alternative but to sit and wait and fret while a new magazine near Mechili was stocked and two fresh regiments arrived from 2nd Armoured

Division, newly landed in Egypt. This would take a fortnight; a time of agony for a man of O'Connor's temperament. Supposing the Italians evacuated Cyrenaica before he could move? Supposing the Commander-in-Chief stopped him or took away his army to send to Greece? While the trucks bumped their slow way from Tobruk to Mechili with the fuel, food and petrol, O'Connor sent the Australians against Derna to delude the Italians that his main attack was coming astride the coast road. Derna fell on 30th January and the Australians pushed on through the green, herb-scented landscape to Giovanni Berta. It would still be ten days before O'Connor would have the essential supplies ready for his great march in the south.

But time was running rapidly out. On February 1st, Marshal Graziani, Governor-General of Libya and Commander-in-Chief, decided to evacuate the remainder of Cyrenaica and concentrate his forces round Syrte for the defence of Tripolitania. General Gariboldi was to relinquish command in Cyrenaica in order to organise this defence, his place being taken from February 3rd by General Tellera. On 2nd February, aerial reconnaissance reports confirmed earlier intimations that, while O'Connor's field magazine was still only half stocked, his prey was slipping away.

In O'Connor's headquarters at Bomba on a bleak estuary littered with collapsed Italian aircraft there were tense discussions. It was bitterly cold except in the airfield hut where the headquarters staff lived on a balanced diet of parmesan cheese, bully and chianti. O'Connor and Harding, his Brigadier General Staff, had been joined on 29th January by Brigadier Dorman-Smith, sent down by Wavell to prepare a study of the campaign and to witness its end. The facts before them were not encouraging. The armoured reinforcements had not arrived. The existing armoured force was mechanically on its very last legs. Only fifty cruisers remained runners. This was the force which, if O'Connor decided to advance immediately, would have to make a march of a hundred and fifty miles at top speed over desert un-reconnoitred but reputed to be very bad going. When—if—the force reached its objective, it would bring to battle a greatly superior and desperate Italian army. There would be just enough fuel for the armoured division to start with full fuel tanks, enough supplies to allow it to carry its own quota of food and ammunition. A convoy of trucks could follow with two days' food, water and petrol, and two re-fills of ammunition. That was all. There was no hope of further supplies reaching the division before these were exhausted.

During every moment O'Connor spent in deciding what to do the Italians were slipping further away. But the risks spoke only too eloquently. No one could have blamed O'Connor if, with his three victories behind him, he had limited himself like Montgomery to following up the enemy retirement. Instead, a resolve to put everything to hazard swiftly took hold of O'Connor and fired his officers. O'Connor sent Dorman-Smith to Cairo by air with the battle plan in his pocket in order to ask Wavell's permission to advance. The escape of Babini still rankled; he asked Dorman-Smith to "tell the C.-in-C. how sorry I am the Italians escaped from Mechili. I'm furious about it". Wavell replied to Dorman-Smith:

"Tell General O'Connor not to fret. It is contretemps like those that add interest to that very dull business, war."

Next day Dorman-Smith was back at Bomba with Wavell's permission for an immediate advance to the Gulf of Syrte. Creagh was now there, far from well, with a very sore throat. He had arrived by accident, as he himself describes:

> There was an apparent lull for ten days whilst supplies were being brought forward. It was arranged that I myself and some of my staff should fly to Cairo for a few days' rest. We stayed for the night

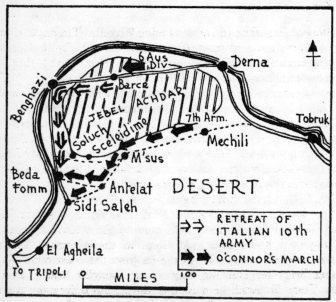

MAP 4. O'CONNOR'S MARCH TO BEDA FOMM

at O'Connor's Headquarters at Bomba. After breakfast next morning O'Connor told me that it appeared that the Italians were retreating from Cyrenaica and must be caught. We had a conference on the spot and then I returned to 7th Armoured Headquarters to lay on the battle.

O'Connor ordered Creagh to march on 4th February through Solluch to the coast road south of Benghazi. Mackay and the Australians were to hustle the Italians through the Jebel Achdar, if necessary by ferrying forward one unit at a time.

At first light on 4th February, 7th Armoured Division, with fifty cruisers and eighty light tanks, rumbled out of Mechili into the west. The going was as bad as could have been feared—strewn boulders and soft sand. But the division moved with great élan. General Creagh wrote later:

> Off we went across the unknown country in full cry. It was definitely exciting and the Division pushing on and on across the desert was a stimulating sight. Some of this desert was very rough and slowed us up; so I sent a wheeled column ahead which was faster than the tracked tanks. This column was to get on to the coast road and hold up any retreating forces until the main body of the Division could go into action.

In the evening of the 4th, after meeting Wavell at Tmimi, O'Connor followed the armour in his staff car, with Dorman-Smith as a companion. Bouncing and slewing over the terrible ground, they soon left 13th Corps headquarters (also on the move) far behind. O'Connor was determined, in Dorman-Smith's words, "to follow up 7th Armoured Division in person to ensure that it operated with the utmost energy". What O'Connor saw during the race with the retreating Italians did not reassure him that he had made the right decision: on all sides there were broken-down British tanks littered along the track. In a rare moment of revelation of his inner anxieties, he was moved to remark to Dorman-Smith:

"My God, do you think it's going to be all right?"

After the first fifty miles 7th Armoured Division struck better going, but also dust so dense that parts of the column became lost and re-joined hours later. At three in the afternoon the 11th Hussars reached Msus, still sixty miles from the coast road. In the evening Brigadier Harding flew up to Creagh's headquarters at Msus. They discussed the news that the Italian retirement was now beginning to move very fast, and decided to send a second force south-west to the coast road via Antelat as well as due west through Solluch as according to O'Connor's orders, in case the Italians passed Solluch before the British armour reached it.

At 7 a.m. Colonel Combe with a vanguard of armoured cars drove away from Msus towards Antelat. Meanwhile air reconnaissance showed that the road south of Benghazi was crammed with Italian transport driving fast southwards towards the as yet unclosed trap. O'Connor himself set off early for 7th Armoured Division headquarters in his staff car with an armoured car and another car as escort. He kept control of his racing army by wireless. One of the cars and the armoured car now broke down. O'Connor and Dorman-Smith drove on alone in the remaining car, without contact with the army, in a silence wherein anxieties could multiply. It was a long day: a day in which to wonder if Creagh had managed to close the trap in time, in which at any moment a breakdown might strand O'Connor in the open desert. But that evening his staff car drove up to Wadi Azzin, headquarters of 7th Armoured Division, and, tired and stiff, O'Connor climbed out to hear the news from Creagh. The Italians had dropped container bombs—looking like Thermos flasks—across the track, and O'Connor was greeted by the sound of rifle fire as the Free French blew them up.

Creagh had good news. Combe had entered Antelat at 10.34 that morning, found it deserted and immediately sent armoured cars on to Beda Fomm and Sidi Saleh. By noon these cars, joined by C Battery, Royal Horse Artillery, reached the coast road and blocked it. At half-past twelve the first column of Italian trucks appeared from the north. O'Connor's trap had closed with half an hour to spare. The British guns opened fire and the annihilation battle of Beda Fomm had begun. At three p.m. a column of thirty trucks tried to break through Combe's force; they were defeated and captured. At five a huge column appeared and was also captured. Meanwhile 4th Armoured Brigade had been battling over the fearsome ground and had reached Antelat at 4.30 p.m. Here Combe radioed to them that the Italians were pouring down the coast road in great strength. Creagh had instantly ordered part of his division to strike them in the flank through Beda Fomm; part to cut them off in the north at Solluch. Creagh's news delighted and relieved O'Connor.

The Armoured Division had been ordered (by me) to reach the coast, which they did splendidly. Further to the south than I originally intended, but they (Creagh and Harding) were quite right.

The dawn on 6th February, 1941, was grey and miserable with torrential rain sweeping across the coastal plain. By its dismal light the Italians made their first attempt to break through the southern British road block. It failed under the guns of the Royal Horse Artillery. O'Connor and Dorman-Smith now retraced their steps to find the corps headquarters. It lay between Mechili and Msus, out of touch with everything. O'Connor drove on to Msus to get some food and that night slept in the car without rugs. Early on the 7th, he drove back again to Antelat and Headquarters, 7th Armoured Division. As Dorman-Smith writes: "O'Connor's energy was tremendous, unsurpassed even by Rommel's."

Meanwhile the desperate Italians strove to escape. They were caught in a flat but hummocky plain between Beda Fomm and the sea along fourteen miles of road. Low north-to-south ridges gave cover to the British armour. All day on the 6th the Italians strove to knock Combe's force and the 2nd Royal Tank Regiment off their road to Tripoli. The 2nd Royal Tanks had nineteen cruisers and seven light tanks. The Italians were a *mélange* of trucks and tanks and guns, although they sometimes managed to unscramble an organised force that tried to find a way through the scattered British cordon. By midday forty Italian medium tanks had been knocked out. Yet the Italians still possessed at least fifty, against the fifteen remaining British cruisers. The only British reserve of tanks—eleven all told—lay at Antelat paralysed by want of fuel. Across the confused battle the winter rain squalls drove unceasingly. All through the afternoon the weary British pounded away at attack after attack by the desperate Italians. At last some thirty Italian tanks burst through 2nd Royal Tanks and headed south towards Combe's force, who were instantly warned. The Italians arrived after dark, but were received with vigour by Combe. Only four Italian tanks and lorries got through.

First light on 7th February found O'Connor and Dorman-Smith driving up to 7th Armoured Division Headquarters at Antelat after their cold and cramped night in the car. They breakfasted off a cold sausage each. Meanwhile the Italians were making their last violent and desperate attempt to break out. A column of trucks led by thirty tanks drove through the forward companies of the Rifle Brigade, and for a moment it seemed that the Italians were clear. Then permission was given for the British artillery to fire on them while mixed up with the Rifle Brigade. The last Italian tank was knocked out just before it reached the officers' mess-tent. It was the end of the Italian Tenth Army. Fourth Armoured Brigade rounded up another surrendering mob; the Australians, hustled by O'Connor, drove into the Italian rear, and by nine o'clock on the morning of 7th February, 1941, O'Connor had completed that rare military achievement: a victory of total annihilation.

The news of the Italian surrender reached O'Connor at Creagh's headquarters. He turned to Dorman-Smith and said:

"We'd better send a message to Archie. What shall we say?"

Dorman-Smith suggested that Wavell would appreciate a hunting metaphor: "Fox killed in the open . . ."

The full message was radioed to Cairo in clear for Mussolini's benefit. Then O'Connor said to Dorman-Smith:

"Let's go forward to see how things are."

As they drove towards the sea over the hummocky ground, herds of antelope moved in front of them, parting to let them through. They saw some bustards. The smell of the sea came strongly in through the open window of the car. Dorman-Smith asked O'Connor what it felt like to be a completely successful commander. O'Connor was silent for a moment, his calm, reflective eyes on the moving gazelle. Then he answered:

"I would never consider a commander completely successful until he had restored the situation after a serious defeat and a long retreat."

Dorman-Smith was to recall this modest and wise reply eighteen months later when he accompanied Sir Claude Auchinleck on his flight up to Maaten Baggush, O'Connor's old headquarters, to take over command of the wreckage of Eighth Army, which had retreated two hundred and sixty miles with the loss of eighty thousand men.

Now the scene of victory opened before them: the sea, the plain, the débris of an army. Along fifteen miles of road and ground this débris was piled and littered in spectacular confusion. There were hundreds of trucks either shattered by gunfire, abandoned or on their sides, derelict tanks in the dark green of the Italian army lying where they had been caught as they tried to squirm out of the trap. Field guns, sitting abandoned in a litter of ammunition cases, pointed at nothing. The plain was strewn with small arms as thickly as seaweed on a beach. And then there was the office paper blowing about the battlefield or caught in the camel thorn.

"One of the most amusing sights," in General Creagh's words, "was a bus-load of Italian ladies sitting in the middle of a battlefield powdering their noses and brewing some tea." They were protected by a lone priest in a soutane; "a highly inappropriate figure", as Dorman-Smith put it.

For the last time the booty of a victory was counted: twenty thousand prisoners, a hundred and twelve medium tanks, two hundred and sixteen guns and fifteen hundred wheeled vehicles. The commander of the 10th Army, General Tellera, had been killed, and General 'Electric Whiskers' Bergonzoli captured.

The British army, exhilarated by victory, was holding a vast celebration. O'Connor and Dorman-Smith drove down to the headquarters of the Rifle Brigade and saw the knocked-out Italian tank by the mess-tent, looking like, in Dorman-Smith's words, "a collapsed elephant". A party was in progress; it went on all day, with relays of guests for food and drink at outside trestle tables, resembling, said Colonel (later General) Renton, "badly organised catering at a point-to-point". O'Connor sipped a victory drink in his bird-like way, but his mind was already on the next advance, for which the captured Italian transport would be essential. He was worried that the Australians might seize all they could find, and he ordered Gott of the Support Group to go and halt their advance from the north. There was also the prisoners' food and welfare to organise. Later he drove to Solluch where Italian senior officer prisoners were confined to two large empty villas, guarded by vinous Free French. O'Connor pushed his way through the throng of disconsolate Italians, and asked in Italian for the senior general, who appeared in a splendid uniform, complete with spurs. O'Connor, in contrast, wore his usual campaign rig—corduroy trousers, leather jerkin, a tartan scarf and a general's red-banded cap. To the Italian general O'Connor said: "I'm sorry you are so uncomfortable. We haven't had time to make proper arrangements."

The Italian replied politely: "Thank you very much. We do realise you came here in a very great hurry."

It was O'Connor's hope that his victory of Beda Fomm would win the approval of Wavell and of London for a further advance into Tripolitania. Each of his previous victories had sucked in behind it strategic permission to march another stage; surely now even the Prime Minister would prefer to invest in success in Libya, rather than in certain failure in Greece. But speed was essential. O'Connor therefore sent Dorman-Smith to see General Wilson, who, having just been appointed Military Governor of Cyrenaica, was once more his immediate superior. Dorman-Smith found Wilson in Barce, a town full of armed but docile Italians. Wilson was in favour of asking Wavell's permission for a further advance; they drafted a message, but there were no signals in the town. So Dorman-Smith drove to Tobruk, there sent Wilson's signal to Wavell, and then drove on to

Cairo, arriving at four a.m. on 12th February. At ten a.m. he entered the map room of the Commander-in-Chief, Middle East. To his dismay he saw that all the desert maps had gone, replaced by maps of Greece. Wavell swept an arm sardonically at the new maps.

"You see, Eric," he said, "I'm starting my spring campaign."

*   *   *   *   *

On the 29th January, 1941, Metaxas, the Greek Prime Minister —or, rather, Dictator—who had spurned Churchill's offer of armed assistance, died. His successor, alarmed by the German concentration piling up in Bulgaria, was now induced by Churchill to ask the British Government what help they could furnish, should the Germans invade Greece. No appeal for aid against Germany ever failed to touch the heart of the Prime Minister. For emotion was the drug that equally stimulated his tremendous primeval force, and sometimes distorted his judgment. Therefore Churchill added this rider to his telegram congratulating Wavell on O'Connor's victory at Beda Fomm:

> We are delighted that you have got this prize [Benghazi] three weeks ahead of expectation, but this does not alter, indeed it rather confirms, our previous directive, namely that your major effort must now be to aid Greece and/or Turkey. This rules out any serious effort against Tripoli . . . You should therefore make yourself secure in Benghazi and concentrate all available forces in the Delta in preparation for a move to Europe . . . Therefore it would seem that we should try to get in a position to offer the Greeks the transfer to Greece of the fighting portion of the Army which has hitherto defended Egypt [that is O'Connor's 13th Corps].

The Prime Minister's advisers had done their best to induce him to look objectively at the strategic implications of intervention in Greece. As long ago as 13th December, 1940, General Kennedy, Director of Military Operations at the War Office, had written in a minute:

> Though the defence of Salonika is important, it would be dangerous to attempt it with less than twenty divisions, which cannot now be made available.

On 11th February, 1941, General Dill, the Chief of the Imperial General Staff, told Churchill that all troops in the Middle East were fully occupied and none was available for Greece. Churchill replied: "What you need out there is a Court Martial and a firing squad..." This was four days after Beda Fomm. On 16th February, a general staff minute drawn up by Kennedy stated:

Nothing we can do can make the Greek business a sound military proposition . . . In the Middle East we must not throw away our power of offensive action by adopting an unsound strategy in Greece . . .

But Churchill was now determined to attempt a Balkan front. Intervention in Greece became a fact: O'Connor's advance was stopped and his magnificent army disbanded. The results of this attempt to succour the Greeks were to be just as predicted by the Prime Minister's advisers. The Greek army collapsed swiftly: the British expeditionary force reached its allotted line only to retreat immediately to its ships. We lost precious equipment, some warships, and had an army thrown into complete disorganisation. We neither helped the Greeks nor embarrassed the Germans. Field Marshal Lord Alanbrooke summed it up:

I have, however, always considered from the very start that our participation in the operations in Greece was a definite strategic blunder. Our hands were more than full at the time in the Middle East, and Greece could only result in the most dangerous disposal of force.

Churchill was unrepentant:

If Hitler had been able, with hardly any fighting, to bring Greece to her knees and the whole of the Balkans into her system . . . might he not have had terms with the Soviets upon the conquest and partition of these vast regions and postponed his ultimate, inevitable quarrel with them to a later part of his programme? Or, as is more likely, would he not have been able to attack Russia in greater strength at an earlier date?

In fact, the timing of the German attack on Russia was not affected at all by the British expeditionary force to Greece, but seriously upset by the unconnected event of the sudden change of régime in Yugoslavia, which changed peaceful occupation into desperate war. The Greek question was a major crisis in grand strategy; by his decision to intervene, the Prime Minister showed for the first time in the war that although he was a Churchill, he was not a Marlborough. Instead of his ancestor's cold and long-sighted sagacity,

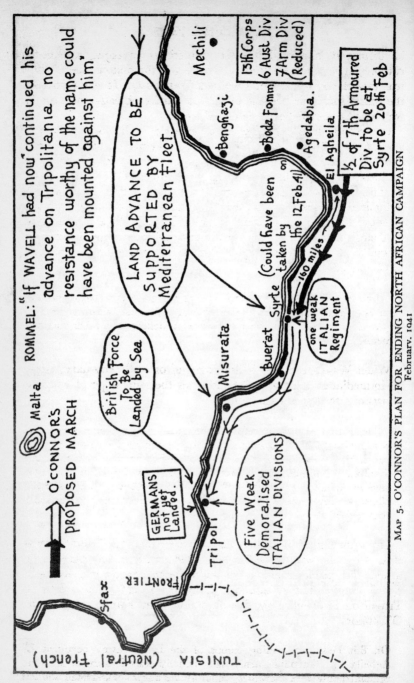

MAP 5. O'CONNOR'S PLAN FOR ENDING NORTH AFRICAN CAMPAIGN February. 1941

ROMMEL: "If WAVELL had now continued his advance on Tripolitania no resistance worthy of the name could have been mounted against him"

O'CONNOR'S PROPOSED MARCH

Malta

British Force To Be Landed by Sea

LAND ADVANCE TO BE SUPPORTED BY Mediterranean Fleet.

GERMANS not yet Landed.

Five Weak Demoralised ITALIAN DIVISIONS

Tripoli

Misurata

Buerat

Syrte (Could have been taken by the 12 Feb 41)

one weak ITALIAN Regiment

160 miles

El Agheila

Agedabia.

Beda Fomm

Benghazi

Mechili

13th Corps
6 Aust Div
7 Arm Div
(Reduced)

½ of 7th Armoured Div to be at Syrte 20th Feb

TUNISIA (neutral French)

Sfax

FRONTIER

62

he displayed emotional impulse; sometimes generous, sometimes ruthless, always overwhelming. Greece was the first occasion in the war that these impulses had worked disastrously. It was a mistake the more disastrous because of the alternative objective of Tripoli, which O'Connor believed he could attain.

He proposed to take Syrte immediately with armoured cars, artillery and the Support Group. On 20th February, backed by the entire available Middle East air strength and the Royal Navy, as well as by all the military and supply resources of the Middle East, an armoured striking force—made up from cruiser tanks of 7th Armoured Division and the newly arrived 2nd Armoured Division —would have advanced from Syrte on Tripoli. At the same time O'Connor had in mind that an infantry brigade might have been landed from the sea at Tripoli. Speed of execution was essential. O'Connor later stated:

> In my opinion the operation would not only have been possible, but would have had every chance of success provided all three Services gave their maximum support and were not deflected by other commitments.

When Wavell received Wilson's signal on 10th February, 1941, he immediately telegraphed London in the vain hope of winning a last-minute stay of execution.

> The extent of Italian defeat at Benghazi seems to me to make it possible that TRIPOLI might yield to small force if despatched without delay. I . . . hesitate to advance further in view of the Balkan situation. But you may think the capture of Tripoli might have favourable effect on attitude of French North Africa . . . I will make plans for capture of Syrte which must be the next step. Please cable your views . . .

On 13th Churchill replied that Greece ruled out Tripoli (see p. 60). After the war Wavell loyally made an excellent case (as he would) for pronouncing a further advance beyond our strength, Greek intervention or no. But Rommel himself, who arrived in Tripoli on 12th February, five days after Beda Fomm, agreed with O'Connor:

> On 8th February leading troops of the British army occupied El Agheila . . . Graziani's army had virtually ceased to exist. All that remained of it were a few lorry columns and hordes of unarmed soldiers

in full flight to the west. If Wavell (sic) had now continued his advance into Tripolitania no resistance worthy of the name could be mounted against him.

Thus the Greek episode lengthened the campaign in North Africa by two years—a campaign that sucked in the major ground efforts of the British Commonwealth, and left the Far East almost undefended against the Japanese.

On 13th February, 1941, the day following Lieutenant-General Rommel's arrival in Africa, O'Connor learned after six days of silence and anxiety that his campaign was dead. This was a moment of great anguish—a moment when so many men would have given way to bitterness and recrimination as they totalled up the prizes of which they (and their country) had been robbed, as they bleakly considered the nature of the Greek adventure.

The temptation was there to advance without orders, present the *fait accompli* of a victory, and force the Cabinet into support. There have been generals who, when convinced they are right, have not balked at covert disobedience. It was repugnant both to O'Connor's character and his sense of public duty. Suppressing his deep feelings in the matter, he obeyed with outward composure. Even after the war O'Connor refused to proclaim that he had been right. On the contrary: "Suffice to say," he wrote, "that I was sorry for our own selfish reasons that the Greek Campaign had been decided on."

He had therefore to rest content with the ten-weeks' campaign in which he had advanced over five hundred miles, destroyed an Italian army of ten divisions, taken a hundred and thirty thousand prisoners, four hundred tanks, one thousand two hundred and ninety guns, and two major fortresses, all for the cost of four hundred and seventy-six killed, one thousand two hundred and twenty-five wounded and forty-three missing. It was a model campaign, opening with a set-piece battle of great originality and faultless execution, continuing with a relentless pursuit with improvised supply services, and ending with a daring strategic march and a battle of annihilation. Sidi Barrani, Bardia, Tobruk and Beda Fomm—their brilliance sparkles against the darkest setting of the war; hardly rivalled, never surpassed.

*   *   *   *   *

Now, on the morrow of Beda Fomm, the apparatus of O'Connor's victories, and their effects, vanished with the suddenness and completeness of a phantom at first light. It is a sad story, quickly told. Thirteenth Corps was disbanded and a static area command was set up—Cyrenaica Command. The personnel of Seventh Armoured Division were scattered through Egypt on miscellaneous duties, thus destroying a well-knit and experienced team. O'Connor, still with stomach trouble, became General Officer Commanding, British Troops in Egypt. Standing on the defensive under General Neame, Cyrenaica Command, was an Australian Brigade Group and one of the armoured brigades of the green 2nd Armoured Division, partly armed with captured Italian tanks. Wavell saw no danger in this: British intelligence considered that the newly-arrived Rommel and his fledgeling Italo-German force could not be ready to advance before May, or at the very earliest, mid-April. This, by normal standards, was a sound estimate, for Hitler had in fact ordered Rommel only to prepare plans by April 20th for the re-conquest of Cyrenaica, and not to move beyond Agedabia before the arrival of 15th Panzer Division. But Rommel, like O'Connor, was a man who considered the enemy's sound estimate of the possible as the main ingredient of his own success. He attacked on March 31st, 1941. He came on cautiously at first; then he found there was nothing very coherent or dangerous in front of him and began to hustle. Pushed about by Rommel in a hurry, the inexperienced Neame, his static command and his raw troops fell into confusion. Rommel drove forward in three columns: along the coast road through Benghazi, along O'Connor's route of Msus-Mechili, and further south on Mechili-Derna. As the news reached Wavell, he sent O'Connor back to Libya to advise Neame. O'Connor arrived on 3rd April. On 6th, in a car with Neame, he lost his way in the dark and ran into a German detachment behind our forces. Both were captured. This tragic accident robbed the British of the greatest of all their desert generals and inflicted on the eager, ardent little commander the gnawing frustration of the prison camp. The most fascinating of desert encounters—O'Connor versus Rommel—would never take place.

COMMENTARY: PART ONE

CHAPTER ONE

Thanks to Professor Hinsley's Official History *British Intelligence in the Second World War*, Volume One, we now know that O'Connor and his staff devised the plan for *Operation Compass* and its deception measures on the basis of copious and accurate information about Italian strength and dispositions in North Africa. This information derived mostly from Italian Air Force ciphers, for even its high-grade cipher was 80 per cent readable until 31st December 1940, when it was changed, and again readable from the beginning of the fourth week of January 1941. Luftwaffe *Enigma* signals, decrypted by the *Ultra* organisation at Bletchley Park, also proved useful by making clear that no movements of German forces to North Africa were then in the offing. However, although Italian army ciphers had been broken as well, the crucial information about the gap in the minefields covering Nibeiwa Camp was discovered by a patrol of the 2nd Rifle Brigade on the night of 7th/8th December, 1940, while air reconnaissance spotted the gap in the Tummar West defences. O'Connor's decisive opening victory of Sidi Barrani thus displays him making creative use of secret intelligence in the formulation of a daring and unorthodox operational plan.

CHAPTER TWO

During O'Connor's subsequent advance through Cyrenaica decrypts of Italian tactical signals available to him included the reports to the Italian High Command from the commander of Bardia fortress, as well as the strength of the garrison of the Tobruk fortress—material help in assessing the problems of attacking these fortresses. Later in the campaign decrypts giving details of the Italian withdrawal from Benghazi towards Tripolitania played a key part in O'Connor's decision to launch his mobile troops through Msus to Beda Fomm in order to cut off the Italian retreat, which led to his triumph in the Battle of Beda Fomm.

By the end of December 1940 the British knew from Luftwaffe *Enigma* decrypts and other sources that Germany was preparing a major offensive in the Balkans, probably southwards against Greece. On 9th January 1941 the Defence Committee in London became convinced from the latest decrypts that the German offensive would be launched on 20th January. Next day the Committee ordered

General Wavell, the Commander-in-Chief, Middle East, and Air Chief Marshal Longmore, the Air Officer Commanding-in-Chief, to fly to Athens in order to offer British forces to the Greek Government. With O'Connor now besieging Tobruk and with every prospect of further victories in Libya, Wavell questioned these instructions and also the evidence for an early German attack in the Balkans. As it happened the Greeks refused British aid, so enabling O'Connor's offensive to roll on to its climactic victory at Beda Fomm on 7th February 1941. No German attack in the Balkans in fact took place until April.

CHAPTER THREE

While O'Connor was advancing beyond Tobruk, further decrypts of Luftwaffe *Enigma* signals and also of the German railway administration *Enigma*, coupled with the breaking of the *Abwehr* hand ciphers, convinced the Director of Military Intelligence in London that the Germans now had twenty-three divisions in Rumania; in fact, the true figure was nine. The British Embassy in Bucharest reported that the Germans would invade Bulgaria on 17th February. The DMI now estimated that the enemy would reach the Greek frontier with five divisions on 12th March, Salonika a week later, and Athens (with ten divisions) between mid-April and mid-May. The Defence Committee therefore concluded that there would be time for a British expeditionary force to install itself in northern Greece before the enemy attacked, and on 11th February 1941 took the decision to instruct Wavell that aid to Greece must rule out an advance on Tripoli.

Although the whole Greek project was later reconsidered, and reconfirmed by the War Cabinet on 24th February with Wavell's professional support, following Eden's visit to Athens and Ankara, it was the decision of 11th February that was crucial. For the opportunity of advancing to Tripoli against slight opposition was but fleeting: the German general Rommel arrived in Tripoli on 12th February and by the 16th the first (though small) German fighting units had been deployed west of Syrte. By the time of the Eden mission to Greece, all chance of taking Tripoli easily had vanished.

Professor Hinsley's account makes plain that the fateful decision of 11th February was not warranted by the top-secret intelligence available to the Cabinet Defence Committee. The estimate of German strength available to attack Greece, at five divisions rising to ten, was reasonably accurate, since in the event ten divisions (three of them armoured) invaded Greece across the Bulgarian frontier, and five reached southern Greece by the middle of April. Yet at most only three British Commonwealth infantry divisions and a single armoured brigade could be found for Greece. Indeed, since British intelligence greatly exaggerated the total strength of German forces then in Rumania, the British decision of 11th February was made in the face of apparent odds much more adverse than in reality. How then did the Defence Committee convince itself that so heavily outnumbered a British force could sustain a successful defence? The answer lies in the high hopes placed in the resisting power of the Greek and Yugoslav armies, even though British information about these armies was scantier than about the German. Professor Hinsley remarks that it is "clear that Whitehall's hopes of co-operation from these countries were based on wishful thinking". A fortnight later, on 24th February, when the fleeting opportunity of advancing to Tripoli had already gone, the Director of Military Intelligence was warning that "we must be prepared to face the loss of all forces sent to Greece . . ."

Thus the hitherto closed information about top-secret intelligence presented by Professor Hinsley only serves to confirm that the first and crucial decision of 11th February 1941 to halt O'Connor and send an expeditionary force to Greece instead was, as *The Desert Generals* argued, a disastrous mistake; and one for which the War Premier, as the Chairman and dominating figure of the Defence Committee, and personally wedded to the fantasy of a "Balkan Front", bore principal responsibility.

Although the German Army *Enigma* was not extensively broken until September 1941 and not read regularly until April 1942, British intelligence was able to build up a fairly full picture of Rommel's strength and deployment before his first Desert Offensive (31st March 1941) through the Luftwaffe *Enigma*. This source of information led Wavell to appreciate on 2nd March that Rommel would not be strong enough to attack before mid-summer, and as late as 27th March Wavell and his Director of Military Intelligence still believed that Rommel remained too weak to launch an offensive before the middle of May. On the basis of orthodox calculations, they were quite correct: their view was shared by the German High Command. Unfortunately, Rommel was not an orthodox general. Here was an early illustration of the pitfall of good intelligence: it is one thing to have accurate information, but it is another to draw from it the correct operational conclusions.

PART TWO

THE BLUNT BATTLEAXE

An Interlude

THE BLUNT BATTLEAXE

THE unique opportunity of winning final victory in North Africa had gone. The Prime Minister was to spend eighteen months attempting to retrieve it by egging on his commanders-in-chief in the Middle East to premature desert offensives. The cool reaction of Wavell and later Auchinleck to these demands lost both generals their reputations with him; to Churchill their closely reasoned replies proclaimed tiredness and defeatism. Nevertheless, they did, at the risk of their reputations, generally resist the Prime Minister's desire for premature battle—except in one case, Operation *Battleaxe*, in June, 1941.

On 6th April, 1941, with O'Connor and Neame captured, the British forces in what had so recently been the quiet backwater of Cyrenaica were now headless as well as disjointed. Benghazi and the Jebel Achdar had fallen; Tobruk formed a precarious rock amid the rising German tide. On the 9th April Wavell decided that the best way of checking Rommel's progress towards Egypt was to hold Tobruk. He ordered his temporary Director of Military Operations, Brigadier Dorman-Smith, to fly to headquarters, Cyrenaica Command, believed to be now in Tobruk, to hand over this order. On 10th April Dorman-Smith flew up in a Lysander. Tobruk was totally obscured by a dust-storm but the pilot made a perfect landing, although he could not even see the airfield buildings. Dorman-Smith saw Brigadier John Harding and General Morshead (1st Australian Division) and handed over Wavell's written order. Both, it seemed to Dorman-Smith, were quite unconcerned and well in control of the situation. That afternoon Dorman-Smith, on his way back to Cairo, passed low over what looked like Afrika Korps troops on the Bardia road near and to east of Tobruk. It is therefore possible that there was no alternative but to hold out in the fortress. On 13th and 14th April, Rommel, who perfectly well appreciated the effects on his advance of a major fortress on his lines of communication, tried to storm Tobruk and was beaten off by Morshead's Australians. He failed again on 16th and 17th April. Meanwhile his troops drove on towards Egypt; the frontier was reached on 28th April, and Sollum, at the base of the escarpment, and Fort Capuzzo were captured. From 30th April to 4th May, 1941, Rommel made a carefully prepared assault on Tobruk, and again was beaten off. The Axis forces on the frontier, running out of fuel, could advance no further, and the desert war was in equilibrium. The lull was broken only by an abortive British attack, well-named *Brevity*, under General 'Strafer' Gott, in the middle of May.

This quiet in Cyrenaica was very badly needed by Sir Archibald Wavell, the speed and intensity of whose strategic juggling was now working to a climax. On 29th April we had been thrown out of Greece with a loss of a fifth of our expeditionary force. On May 5th a pro-German revolution broke out in Iraq under Rashid Ali, who seized control of most of the country. On May 20th the Germans attacked Crete in the greatest airborne operation of the war. Meanwhile German infiltration into Vichy-French Syria had apparently become so dangerous—though post-war research shows it to have been exaggerated—that it had been decided to invade that country, and Wavell was deep in planning how so to do with smaller forces than the Vichy French. The invasion of Syria began on June 8th.

It was while Wavell was coping with this welter of lost battles and new dangers that Churchill pressed him to attack Rommel in the desert. Before the Greek adventure was even over, the Prime Minister's supreme object had become "a victory in the Western Desert to destroy Rommel's army. . . . This would at least save our situation in Egypt from the wreck." The telegrams began to flow. On 12th May he asked Wavell for the date when the three hundred assorted tanks sent round the Cape, and only just arriving in Egypt, would be used in battle. He told Wavell that "Our first object must be to gain a decisive military success in the Western Desert." On the same day however Wavell telegraphed to the CIGS that it would be at least June 7th before an attacking force could be cobbled together, and "I think it right to inform you that the measure of success which will attend this operation is in my opinion doubtful." His reasons for doubt lay in the mechanical unreliability of British cruiser tanks, the vulnerability of the 'I' tanks to German anti-tank guns and a calculated inferiority of numbers. Three days later Wavell put off *Battleaxe* until 15th June, 1941. At home Churchill displayed, in his wife's words, "terrible anxiety and even anger" at the delays.

Battleaxe began on 15th June, 1941. The operation had been planned by General Beresford-Peirse, commander 13th Corps, and

Brigadiers Harding and Galloway—all of whom had been with O'Connor at Sidi Barrani. The force included twenty-five thousand men and about a hundred and eighty mixed cruisers and 'I' tanks. Creagh commanded 7th Armoured Division, General Frank Messervy 4th Indian Division. Seventh Armoured Division was not the thoroughly-trained, highly-experienced and well-run-in machine of O'Connor's campaign; it had been stripped of its equipment when it was withdrawn from Cyrenaica and re-equipped piece-meal and in haste. Its personnel had been completely dispersed, and then re-assembled. In General Creagh's words: "The position in the Division as a whole showed a serious shortage of M.T., a lack of trained personnel in the 'I' brigade and some disorganization in the matter of spares." There were two armoured brigades in the divi-

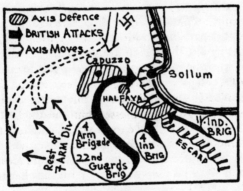

MAP 6. BATTLEAXE
Phase A

sion: 7th, equipped with A.15 cruiser tanks straight off the ships— which were capable of twenty-six m.p.h.; and 4th, equipped with 'I' tanks borrowed from army tank battalions, which could only manage eight m.p.h.

In planning the attack, little was known of enemy dispositions, partly owing to a shortage of cameras for air reconnaissance. British intelligence thought there were about seventy German tanks on the frontier supporting the powerful German fixed defences round the Halfaya Pass up the escarpment; and the rest of the German and Italian armour (a hundred and thirty tanks) eighty miles away at Tobruk. Creagh thought that the Germans on the frontier were much stronger—two complete regiments. This matter was important, for the whole British plan depended on a temporary local

British superiority in the forward area leading to a German defeat in detail.

Beresford-Peirse, as his mock-attack on a desert camp before Sidi Barrani had shown, was completely orthodox and unimaginative. He had never commanded armour. The final plan for *Battleaxe* consisted of a frontal approach to the well-sited German frontier defences, with the main body of the armour and part of the infantry swinging left-handed towards Capuzzo. Halfaya Pass—according to Rommel "the crucial position in this battle"—where the coast road climbed from the sea to the top of the escarpment, was to be assaulted frontally by two separate forces, one on the escarpment and one below it. When the Axis defences had been carried by this infantry and 'I' tank attack, and 7th Armoured Division had defeated the forward German armour, the success was to have been exploited, in conjunction with the Tobruk garrison, as far as the line Derna-Mechili. The plan of *Battleaxe*, in its directness of approach and in its general disposition, resembles Montgomery's plan at El Agheila in December, 1942. But the essential ingredients of success in frontal assaults—overwhelming artillery and air support and superiority of numbers—were completely lacking in June, 1941. The fearsome haste with which the operation had been prepared dimmed what little hope the equipment, the commander and the battle plan provided. It was only on 29th May that Creagh had received the operation instruction; the date of attack was given as not later than 10th June. It was put back to June 15th because Creagh pointed out the unreadiness of his division. As regards the chances of success, Creagh wrote later:

> An answer was difficult since it depended on which side could reinforce the quicker—though we could concentrate on undoubted initial superiority, the Germans could reinforce with their second Armoured Division from Tobruk, only eighty miles distant, while as far as I knew we had no means of reinforcement at all.

All was thus set for defeat. As if to emphasise the unprepared, amateurish quality of the whole enterprise, some of the new tanks had to calibrate their guns on the way to the startline. The frontal attack on the Halfaya Pass on June 15th broke down completely. The 22nd Guards Brigade and the 4th Armoured Brigade ('I' tanks) took Capuzzo but were stopped west of Sollum. The 4th Armoured Brigade ran into serious trouble. Beresford-Peirse had ordered the tanks to 'rally forward'—that is to leaguer in front of the infantry and guns. Brigadier (now General) Gatehouse, of 4th Armoured

Brigade, thinking that the Corps Commander, out of his ignorance of tank warfare, had confused the well-understood tank order to 'forward rally'—leaguer *behind* the infantry and guns, ready to support them, but protected while essential repairs were made—questioned this order, which would expose the tanks to enemy gun-fire or capture while immobile. Beresford-Peirse, in the sudden flaring anger of the man in command caught out in ignorance, had replied:

"You have your orders, Gatehouse—carry them out!"

In the course of *Battleaxe*, Gatehouse lost ninety-nine out of a hundred and four tanks—many of them only slightly damaged, but, because of Beresford-Peirse's order, irrecoverable.

It had been intended that when the infantry had taken the Halfaya

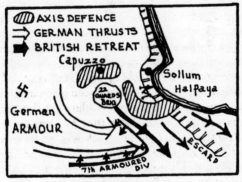

MAP 7. BATTLEAXE
Phase B

defences, 4th Armoured Brigade should abandon its role of infantry co-operation and re-join Creagh for the armoured battle. Creagh planned, in his own words, "to lead the German tanks on to the 'I' tanks (of 4th Armoured Brigade) situated in a hull-down position. But the plan never materialised as the 'I' brigade could not be released from their role of infantry support." On the second day of the battle, renewed frontal attack of Halfaya failed, owing, according to General Messervy, to the first appearance of the 88 mm. gun in an anti-tank role, with the consequent surprise. Yet its use in this role had been noted in the War Office during the Spanish Civil War. Fourth Armoured Brigade therefore remained caught up in the infantry battle. The Germans had now had plenty of time to react: a large force of tanks forced Creagh's remaining armoured brigade and the support group back from Sidi Omar. On 17th June Rommel, all his armour up, attacked the left flank of 4th Armoured Brigade, while another force, in a manoeuvre typical of Rommel, felt more deeply for the British rear. The British command was in a real dilemma: Creagh could not effectively counter-attack unless Messervy released 4th Armoured Brigade, and this Messervy could not do without exposing his own flank. This day Wavell came up from Cairo to see how the battle was going, visited Beresford-Peirse, who was well behind the front and out of touch, and concluded that success depended on Creagh's tanks. He therefore flew out to 7th Armoured Division headquarters. Meanwhile, Messervy, who considered that his entire infantry division was seriously threatened by Rommel's operations against his flank and rear after Creagh's withdrawal the night before, ordered a retirement on his own responsibility. The armour had to conform. It was the ignominious end of *Battleaxe*'s swing; and far from being cleaved to the marrow, Rommel was hardly dented.

But in fact the battle was already lost on the first day when 13th Corps had failed to gain an immediate and decisive success over the portion of the Axis forces posted round Halfaya. In all respects *Battleaxe* is the reverse of Sidi Barrani; it deserves attention as an example of what happens to an army when there is no great commander to animate its limbs and supply its brain; when mediocre minds plod narrowly along a precedent. Yet all its shortcomings— in equipment, skill, training, leadership, strategy and tactics—are really traceable to one cause: the hurriedness of preparation.

Churchill was bitterly disappointed with the failure. But he did not see that *Battleaxe* had been hopelessly premature; and therefore its lesson was forever lost on him. By an amazing injustice, however, the failure of *Battleaxe* caused the Prime Minister to decide to relieve Wavell of his command. He blamed the collapse of O'Connor's conquests not on himself for his decision over Greece, but on Wavell. And so on 21st June, 1941, he telegraphed Wavell that he was to be relieved by Sir Claude Auchinleck, Commander-in-Chief in India.

There was no valid case for relieving Wavell. In his two years in the Middle East he had built a base and a command structure from nothing. He had conquered the whole of Italian East Africa, had captured two hundred thousand prisoners, including the Duke of Aosta, Viceroy of Ethiopia. Under his strategic aegis, O'Connor had taken Cyrenaica and another two hundred thousand prisoners. Between February and June 1941 he had conducted six major campaigns, never less than three at a time, and in May five at a time.

No other British soldier of the day had the strategic grasp, the sagacity, the cool nerves and the immense powers of leadership to do all these things and steer a course free of total disaster. Certainly Wavell's career had been latterly clouded by defeat—Greece, Cyrenaica, Crete. Yet Greece and Cyrenaica, the most serious of the three, were the Prime Minister's responsibility.

Dismissal of Wavell, in fact if not in intention, made him a scapegoat for Churchill's own mistakes. Now the Commander-in-Chief was going, Churchill could recognise that he had asked too much of him, and could ease the responsibilities of his successor:

> It was only after the disasters had occurred in Cyrenaica, in Crete, and in the Desert that I realised how overloaded and under-sustained General Wavell's organisation was. Wavell tried his best; but the handling machine at his disposal was too weak to enable him to cope with the vast mass of business which four or five simultaneous campaigns imposed upon him.

As first fruits of the Prime Minister's belated recognition, Oliver Lyttelton was appointed Minister of State in the Middle East to shoulder the political responsibilities, and General Haining was made Intendant-General to look after rearward administration and supply.

Auchinleck arrived in the Middle East on July 2nd and formally assumed the command on the 5th. Though Churchill alleged that Wavell was tired, Auchinleck did not receive this impression:

> Wavell showed no signs of tiredness at all. He was always the same. I think he was first class; in spite of his silences, he made a tremendous impact on the troops. I have a very great admiration for him . . . but he was given impossible tasks.

Sir Claude Auchinleck was an able and strong-minded officer always ready to attempt the bold and novel course. In northern Norway in June, 1940, for example, after allied evacuation had been ordered, he had attacked and taken Narvik in order to deceive the Germans into thinking that the allies meant to stay. The deception was successful; not a man was lost during the subsequent evacuation, although the Germans had command of the air. However, Auchinleck brought to his new post two shortcomings that were not his fault: he was an Indian soldier and he knew little about armoured warfare. The Indian Army and the British Army, though they served together in India, formed two professional worlds separated by mutual pride. The British service looked down on the

Indians—'frontier soldiers'—and the Indians resented this because in their view India had the men and the space for proper training and preparation for war, while Britain had neither. Whatever the justice of these attitudes, the result was that Auchinleck, late professional head of the Indian service, knew very few of the officers of the British service and was not aware of the comparative reputations of its rising men. He was therefore handicapped in making a sound choice of subordinates from the British service. In his practical ignorance of armour, however, Auchinleck was joined by every senior officer of both the British and Indian armies.

Settling in amid the peace-time luxury of Cairo—Egypt was not at war—Auchinleck received, rather like Macbeth from the witches, a sombre warning from the Chief of the Imperial General Staff, General Dill, about Cabinet pressure for premature battle. It was Auchinleck's first acquaintance with that special anxiety which dwarfed all the other mammoth anxieties of the Middle East Command. Auchinleck was not as diplomatic a man as Wavell; his instinct was to oppose the Prime Minister's interference bluntly and resolutely. The battle between them was soon under way. Before Auchinleck had even formally taken up his command Churchill was asking him about a renewed offensive in the Western Desert. Auchinleck replied that there should certainly be another offensive—but with adequate forces, which he put at two, possibly three armoured divisions and a motor division, and after adequate time for thorough training. He decided that he could not be properly prepared for at least three months. But Churchill continued to question him about this and even about his placing of a certain division in Cyprus. Auchinleck determined to stop this interference at once. He told the Prime Minister apropos the Cyprus division:

If you wish I can send you detailed reasons which actuated me and which appeared to me incontestable. I hope you will leave me complete discretion concerning dispositions of this kind.

He was equally austere on the topic of an early offensive:

To launch an offensive with the inadequate means at present at our disposal is not, in my opinion, a justifiable operation of war . . . To gain results risks must be run, and I am ready to run them if they are reasonably justifiable.

Churchill did not like this and asked Auchinleck to come to England for consultation. In London, Auchinleck refused to budge from his decision not to launch an offensive—which was code-named *Crusader*—earlier than November 1st. Of Auchinleck's visit Churchill observed later: "He [Auchinleck] certainly shook my military advisers with all the detailed argument he produced. *I was myself unconvinced*" (Author's italics).

Auchinleck returned to Cairo resolved never to expose himself again to the ruthless personal pressure employed by the Prime Minister to get his way in default of rational exposition. Thus within a month Churchill was already dissatisfied with his new broom; like those in *The Sorcerer's Apprentice* it had a life of its own instead of passively obeying the Prime Ministerial directions. Auchinleck took back to Cairo agreement on November 1st, 1941, as D-Day for *Crusader*. He also took back concurrence with another crucial decision of his: General Alan Cunningham to command the battle, rather than General Wilson, who, being associated by the Prime Minister with O'Connor's successes, had been London's preference. It was the beginning of a tragedy.

COMMENTARY: PART TWO

The decisions to launch the abortive British offensives codenamed *Brevity* (15th May 1941) and *Battleaxe* (15th/17th June) rested on unsound deductions from *Enigma* intelligence. By 4th May cumulative decrypts from the Luftwaffe *Enigma* had revealed that Rommel had been ordered to stand on the defensive, undertaking no further advance without OKH (*Oberkommando des Heeres*) permission, and that his troops were exhausted. This convinced the British War Premier that the time was ripe for a British offensive. But the *Enigma* decrypts could not reveal the qualitative superiority of German equipment and training, nor did it reveal the number of available German tanks, which in the case of *Battleaxe* proved twice what the British expected. Poor British field intelligence failed to fill in these gaps left by *Ultra's* partial decrypting of *Enigma*. Thus a crude and superficial reading of *Ultra* information on Churchill's part provided the key factor in his insistence that Wavell should launch what *The Desert Generals* describes as "hopelessly premature" offensives, and lends extra weight to the charge that Churchill's decision finally to sack Wavell because of the failure of *Battleaxe* was "an amazing injustice".

PART THREE

THE PRICE OF DUTY

General Sir Alan Cunningham, G.C.M.G., K.C.B.,
D.S.O., M.C.

> O God of battles! steel my soldiers' hearts;
> Possess them not with fear: take from them now
> The sense of reckoning, if th' opposed numbers
> Pluck their hearts from them!
>
> SHAKESPEARE, *Henry V*, iv, 1.

CHAPTER ONE

IN THE summer of 1941 General Alan Cunningham enjoyed far greater fame than O'Connor. On February 10th, 1941, he had advanced from Kenya into Italian Somaliland with four infantry brigade groups and fought a battle on 22nd against six brigades of Italians and some local levies at Jelib, north of the Juba river. In Cunningham's words, "The Italians in front of me broke." In the next three days he covered two hundred miles to capture Mogadishu, capital of Italian Somaliland. There was still nothing in front of him. He decided to march the seven hundred and forty miles to Jijiga in Abyssinia, thus threatening the rear of the Italian forces opposing our invasion of Eritrea. Wavell consented, and after a halt of only three days Cunningham set out on March 17th. March 26th brought him to Harrar and March 29th to Diredawa. On April 6th Cunningham entered Addis Ababa, capital of Abyssinia. In eight weeks he seemed to have marched half across Africa; his speed and dash delighted the British public. His success was taken as complementary to O'Connor's victories in Libya. But whereas O'Connor had had only a few brief mentions by Press and Prime Minister, Cunningham now became well known.

Sir Claude Auchinleck, the new Commander-in-Chief in the Middle East, had also been deeply struck by this performance. He decided to appoint him to command the new army forming in the desert—Eighth Army.

> I asked for Cunningham [he wrote later] as I was impressed by his rapid and vigorous command in Abyssinia and his obvious leaning towards swift mobile action. I wanted to get away from the idea, which seemed to be prevalent, of clinging to the coastal strip, and to move freely and widely against the enemy's flank and communications.

In July 1941 Cunningham had rounded off his astonishing successes in East Africa by placing Haile Selassie, Lion of Judah and King of Kings, on that throne from which the Italians had driven him in 1936. Then he flew to Nairobi, where he received Auchinleck's letter of appointment. It marked his great professional opportunity; the letter made him, as he said later, "extremely proud and hopeful". Cunningham travelled by air down the Nile valley to Cairo, saw Auchinleck, a stern and formidable figure, and joined his as yet unformed army. He was now in the centre of the British Commonwealth's war. He commanded the only British land forces in contact with the enemy, and the best-equipped. He enjoyed the support of both a strong air force under the command of Air Vice-Marshal Coningham, and of the Mediterranean Fleet, under the command of his own elder brother, Andrew, the great sailor. At his back in Egypt he had the resources of what had now become a great military base—a miniature war economy. As the implications of his new surroundings sank in, the greatness of his opportunity became more clear to him. So did the greatness of his problems and responsibilities:

> I arrived in August and was told that there would be an offensive in November. I therefore had two months only in which to form and train an army. Some of the divisions were not there. Apart from 4th Indian Division and 7th Armoured Division, most of the troops were quite untrained. Time was so short. That was my trouble.

He made a good first impression on his new command; his personality lived up to his East African reputation as a commander. As Brigadier (now Major-General) Gatehouse put it, "Cunningham was a magnificent-looking chap. I thought, this is the man. . . ." Like O'Connor, Cunningham was small, but unlike O'Connor, he gave an immediate impression of energy and decision. He was a handsome man, with a high-coloured, high-nosed face, and flashing blue eyes. He talked easily and well. He was charming, in a jovial way; but he was also, in General Godwin-Austen's words, "somewhat choleric"—this touchiness of temper was noted—"he would weigh everything you told him, very carefully, and though he might 'blow up' at first, would never do so after calm reflection."

Cunningham never had much opportunity with Eighth Army for calm reflection.

The assembly of forces for *Crusader* were already under way when Cunningham arrived in the Desert. He had therefore the task of leaping into the saddle of a moving horse and taking control of it. It was far from easy for him. In the first place there was the desert itself, which he had never seen before, with its agoraphobic vastness, and emptiness and sameness; an arena as naked and overwhelming as a bare stage to a green actor. To a newcomer, it was so much more than a strange kind of topography. It made a deep impression on Cunningham: "The terrain was so different from that of East Africa, where we had to make use of tracks through bush country —the desert was all the same, and just nothing, with navigation as if you were at sea." He had only two months in which to get so used to the desert that he could handle an army in its spaces with easy confidence.

Cunningham was also somewhat overwhelmed by the vast scale of military operations in Egypt. "In East Africa, we had almost nothing at all—everything was improvised." For supply he had depended on the Royal Navy's kindness in landing small stores along the Somaliland coast. His command had never been larger than four brigades of infantry. In Eighth Army he had two army corps, including three armoured brigades and more than two divisions of infantry. The size and complexity of command and staff organisation were equally new to him. He was rather like the successful owner of a village shop suddenly put in charge of a London department store.

He faced a further difficulty. He knew little about armour and had never commanded it. This was true of all British officers of his rank. But whereas O'Connor had had six months of relative quiet in which to learn about it, Cunningham had two at a time of frantic preparation and rapid expansion. He was to control a swiftly moving armoured battle against Germans who had been practising tank warfare in the field since 1936; yet when he first reached the desert he so little understood radio-telephony that he is remembered fumbling helplessly with a radio-telephone, trying to use it like an ordinary telephone. Sureness of command depends on professional knowledge and experience. However great the qualities of leadership in a man, he cannot make use of them unless he is a master of the technical details of his profession—unless he knows his subordinates' jobs at least as well as they. Otherwise his orders, made in partial ignorance, must be given and received with underlying diffidence. In the desert, in command of a large tank army, Cunningham was the green newcomer, the outsider, in the presence of many officers to whom the desert was a familiar thing, a friend; who had seen Western Desert Force grow into Eighth Army; and whose military mind had grown with it. Slight though their knowledge might be, it was yet more than that of their army commander. Thus, though it was no fault of his, Cunningham found himself in a difficult and embarrassing position of learning and at the same time giving orders to his teachers. The result was a weakening of his authority and, personally, an added emotional strain. As General Godwin-Austen, who served under Cunningham both in East Africa and the Desert, wrote later: "I felt he was not as happy in Egypt ... he did not dominate conferences as he had in East Africa."

As Brigadier General Staff, Cunningham had Galloway; and daily association with him could only bring home constantly to Cunningham his own inexperience. Galloway himself was a forceful personality, crisp in speech, impatient, and, like his Army Commander, inclined to short temper. Though he supplied some of the knowledge of desert warfare that Cunningham lacked, he was hardly the man to make Cunningham feel any more easy and comfortable in his headquarters. Yet Cunningham was fortunate in not having to assert himself over a larger number of senior desert veterans; Creagh had gone back to England after *Battleaxe* and Caunter was in India. By the end of October, Morshead too had left the Desert. The general lack in Eighth Army of familiarity both with the desert and with command in tank warfare was sharpened by a tragic loss. The corps commander designate of the armour, Pope, a tank officer with long experience, had been killed with some of his headquarters staff in an air crash, and was replaced by General Willoughby Norrie, a cavalryman who had been commanding 1st Armoured Division in England. The infantry corps was to be commanded by General Godwin-Austen, who, like Cunningham, was fresh from East Africa.

The formation of Eighth Army therefore marked in not altogether a happy sense a fresh start in the history of the British desert forces. To most observers in and out of the army, however, the summer and autumn of 1941 marked a fresh start of the right kind. Trucks, tanks and aircraft were flowing into Egypt in quantities that seemed prodigal to veterans of O'Connor's make-do-and-mend campaign or of the money-starved peacetime army. It was clear that at last British and American war production had caught the Germans up; and that at last the British too were putting in the field a superb modern tank army. Soon a British-made blitzkrieg would revenge on the Germans their easy successes of Norway, France and Greece. A new confidence—more, an elation—seized all ranks as they hastily learned to handle this magnificent and copious new equipment. There was a mood of eagerness and novelty never seen again in the desert, yet different from the earlier professional élan of Western Desert Force. A contemporary piece of public relations copy catches it well:

Libya is full of our troops. It is grand. Everywhere there are eager faces: convoy commanders sitting up aloft their trucks like sunburned gods—their sun compasses pointing a black sliver of shadow towards the Boche; despatch riders bumping incredibly through the sandy, rutted tracks; officers in groups, their maps on their knees, listening to their orders; lorried infantry, waiting, waiting, waiting; guns, their dust covers off, marching through the infantry and off to a flank in majestic indifference.

But when Cunningham set up his headquarters in the desert on September 9th, 1941, all these troops and equipment had still to be organised into an army and trained. At the same time Cunningham had to invent a plan for a battle that was scheduled to begin in eleven weeks' time. First came the organisation of what was to be Eighth Army, strong in armour. There were no British precedents for the functional combination of tanks, guns and infantry in a panzer army. Instead there was either the orthodox 1914–18 concept of an army's organisation which had been official doctrine until 1940, or there was the pre-war theory of thwarted and embittered British armoured experts such as Hobart. The first was plainly inapplicable in the desert, though in the next two years some devoted efforts were made to apply it; the second was strongly urged by British armoured officers in the desert. Before the war, Hobart, finding that the decisive importance of the tank was rejected by the cavalry- and infantry-dominated army, had in his turn rejected all other arms and proclaimed that tanks could and would win battles (and the war) by themselves alone. Tank would kill tank with its gun and then massacre the infantry and artillery. The decision lay therefore in the clash of tank battlefleets. Cunningham's organisation of Eighth Army closely reflected these views:

I formed an infantry corps (13th) and an armoured corps (30th) with the idea of using the armour [on its own] as a corps.

Seventh Armoured Division was to consist of three armoured brigades (more than equal to the tank strength of both Rommel's panzer divisions together) and a Support Group of guns and lorried infantry. Thus though 30th Corps did not quite fulfil Hobart's ideal of a striking force composed of nothing but tanks, the tanks and infantry were kept segregated. The infantry corps (1st New Zealand Division, 4th Indian and 1st Guards Brigade) also contained tanks—two hundred and twenty-five 'I' tanks, which, by that departmentalism of the British mind, had been designed only for co-operation with infantry and, though a powerful weapon, had not the speed for a battle of manœuvre and could not take part in the decisive tank action.

Cunningham did have second thoughts about the separation of infantry corps from tank corps, and therefore the division of the offensive into two battles:

> I sometimes wondered if it were the right formation. The alternative would have been mixed groups.

This was in fact the German system.

On 2nd September Auchinleck issued his first directive to Cunningham, on the planning of *Crusader*, by which he was to work out in detail two alternative plans: the first for a wide turning movement through Jalo and Jarabub and the second for a direct blow along the coast, with feints in the centre and on the left. Cunningham did not like the Jalo plan at all; in his view, "it was hitting at nothing". Nor did he accept Auchinleck's alternative. During September he worked out his own plan in consultation with Galloway. At midnight on 26th September the Eighth Army was officially born. Two days later Cunningham submitted to the Commander-in-Chief his plan for Eighth Army's first offensive. In its final form it was, in his words, "entirely mine". However, there are signs that others, especially Galloway, had an important share in it.

The theory of armoured warfare that dictated Cunningham's organisation of the Army, also determined the plan of the offensive. It was based on seeking and winning a decisive tank battle. Tobruk, the relief of which had been in Auchinleck's plans both the object and the occasion of battle, was seen as only incidental. Thirtieth Corps under Willoughby Norrie would swing round the right of the German frontier defences that ran from Bardia through Sollum to Sidi Omar, and occupy the area about Gabr Saleh. Here Rommel was expected to meet Norrie's three armoured brigades with all his armour in the decisive encounter. Meanwhile 13th Corps would envelop the frontier defences, but would remain passive and inactive until the tank battle had been won. Only then, and in conjunction with 30th Corps, would it fight its own battle against the Axis infantry in the frontier defences and round Tobruk.

Cunningham himself saw that in this plan the distance between his tank and his infantry wings could be dangerous if Rommel struck with his armour through the gap on to the left flank of his infantry; it was a possibility that the infantry commanders appreciated very keenly. He therefore compromised the purity of his dispositions by reserving one of the three armoured brigades (4th) as a flank guard to 13th Corps. Eighth Army would thus advance on three divergent axes. However, once it was clear that Rommel was not threatening 13th Corps, 4th Armoured Brigade would be released for the decisive tank battle.

Auchinleck accepted his Army Commander's plan. On 6th and 21st October Cunningham explained his intentions to his corps commanders and heard their views. Norrie was strongly critical of the dispositions. He considered the use of 4th Armoured Brigade as a flank guard to 13th Corps was a dangerous dispersal of effort and intention when a decisive tank battle was being sought. In his view, the presence of 30th Corps itself was a sufficient flank guard. He could not see why Gabr Saleh had been chosen as the objective that our armour was to reach, halt at and await German reaction: it had no military significance to the Germans and there was no reason to suppose our occupation of it would force a decisive action. He suggested that the British armour should drive straight for Tobruk; Rommel would then be forced to fight us.

Godwin-Austen insisted on specific flank protection. Though infantry divisions were equipped with anti-tank guns and field artillery, the infantry also believed the Hobartian doctrine that only tanks could fight tanks; and throughout the battle there were to be constant local pleas on the infantry's part for armoured escort. Cunningham listened to the arguments of each corps commander, and said that the use of 4th Armoured Brigade as a specific flank guard to 13th Corps would stand. But he emphasised that "it was a temporary arrangement, until the direction of Rommel's main movement was known". Cunningham also refused to substitute Tobruk for Gabr Saleh as an objective for 30th Corps: "Gabr Saleh was chosen because Rommel was bound to pass it, north or south." Our presence in this central position would force Rommel to concentrate in order to defend either his siege of Tobruk or the frontier defences; or even to split his forces up. Should he divide his command, Cunningham explained, we could divide ours. This was an odd and novel military principle. But the oddest aspect of the *Crusader* plan lay in the vagueness with which the results of it were visualised. We were to advance to Gabr Saleh—and then? Cunningham's answer seemed to hand the attacker's perquisite, the initiative, to the defender. For, he told Norrie and Godwin-Austen, by Rommel's reaction to our approach march "we should know what he meant to do; by the first evening his intentions would be known, and a decision could be taken".

Though the corps commanders issued their own orders for this plan on November 8th, and 7th Armoured Division held a war game rehearsal in Norrie's and Cunningham's presence on the 9th, Norrie remained unconvinced. He returned to the old point. The whole elaborate and rigid plan depended on the premise that the Germans would fight at Gabr Saleh. Why? We should drive, rather, straight for Sidi Rezegh, the key to Tobruk. Exposed to Norrie's able reasoning, Cunningham began himself to wonder. Perhaps Rommel would not oblige by fighting at Gabr Saleh. Yet this was the basic premise of the plan. It was far too late now to undo his and Galloway's month of work, invent a new conception and issue fresh orders. The present plan would have to serve; but his faith in it was shaken. He decided therefore "to travel with Willoughby Norrie for the first few days. We did not know what Rommel's reactions would be". If Rommel did not react at Gabr Saleh on the first day, he himself would decide whether the tanks should push on further and in which direction. He was still worried about 13th Corps: "I thought Rommel would attack the infantry."

Thus after two months of exhausting work, and of the emotional strain of trying to establish personal ascendancy over more experienced men, in a strange and over-aweing environment, Cunningham found himself on the eve of battle with a compromised plan that seemed quite likely to produce no desired results, but instead a wide choice of unpleasant possibilities. It was not a situation conducive to buoyant confidence or calm resolution. It was aggravated for Cunningham by a personal matter. He had always been a very heavy pipe smoker; but he had recently stopped smoking altogether, because he had slight trouble with one of his eyes, said by his occulist to be caused by smoking. But he concealed his anxieties; General Freyberg even thought him over-confident. In his eve-of-battle press conference his voice was hoarse, perhaps with strain, but his talk was resolute enough: "I am going to seek old Rommel out and destroy him and his armour."

Yet despite Cunningham's and Norrie's doubts, the army was throughout its ranks cock-a-hoop with optimism. It was the lavish quantity of new equipment that had convinced them that for the first time they were to meet the German on equal terms. In particular the tank commanders and their men had no doubt that when they had found Rommel's armour they would be able to destroy it. But to those with deeper perceptions and greater knowledge, the picture was not so full of sunshine. The Crusader tanks, for example, that looked so squatly powerful, had come off the ships with nuts and bolts hand-tight. Even when properly assembled they were, in Cunningham's words, "extremely unsound mechanically". Above all, this mechanised equipment which seemed so abundant to the uninformed was in truth dangerously scarce.

Auchinleck had told the Prime Minister that he would require for the battle fifty per cent reserves in strength: twenty-five per cent to cover those in workshops, and twenty-five per cent to replace battle casualties. On this requirement, which in view of our tanks' mechanical unreliability was only moderate, Churchill's comment was: "Generals only enjoy such comforts in heaven." Auchinleck had hoped to put in the field three armoured divisions; instead there was only 7th Armoured Division with its tank strength augmented to equal one and a half British armoured divisions (a British armoured division at this time contained six battalions of tanks, a German two). One of its three armoured brigades (22nd), which had been expected to arrive in Egypt between 13th and 20th September, actually completed its disembarkation only by 14th October. This forced Auchinleck to postpone D-Day for *Crusader* from 1st November to 15th; but even then this brigade had no more than four weeks in which to train and become desert-worthy. It was composed of highly inexperienced territorials. The delay "vexed" Churchill, who telegraphed to Auchinleck that "It is impossible to explain to Parliament and the nation how it is our Middle East armies have had to stand for four and a half months without engaging the enemy." But Auchinleck had to order a further delay of three days as, in his own words, "the 1st South African Division, which was to play an important part in the initial operations, had not had enough time to train for a mobile role owing to the late arrival of the bulk of its vehicles". Even with its total postponement of eighteen days, the offensive was a gamble. "We were working to very close margins as regards equipment and training," wrote Auchinleck later. "The same conditions applied to the building up of supplies and the construction of pipelines and railways." All this was hidden from the rank-and-file of the army and its war correspondents, who could see, but not count, the fresh troops and new equipment. But the Commander-in-Chief was thus far from wild optimism about Cunningham's chances: "I thought the quality and quantity [of troops and equipment] was just adequate, and gave a reasonable chance of success."

By the evening of November 15th, the forward concentration of

Eighth Army was complete. There was a pause of silence and still-
ness between the frenzy of preparation and the agony of battle.

Cunningham now had actually with 7th Armoured Division four
hundred and fifty-three gun-armed cruiser tanks, of which a hundred
and sixty-six were American 'Honeys' or Stuarts (in 4th Armoured
Brigade) and the rest Crusaders. The Stuarts, powered by a Pratt
and Whitney radial aero-engine, were reliable, and faster, at 36
m.p.h., than any other tank in Africa. But because of their aviation
petrol, they had a tendency to flare up easily. They mounted a 37-
mm. high-velocity gun that had a slightly better power of pene-
tration than the two-pounders of the Crusaders; their armour was
thinner. *Battleaxe* had confirmed British confidence in the solid-shot
two-pounder, which formed both their anti-tank artillery and their
principal tank-gun. British intelligence calculated German tank
strength at two hundred and seventy-two tanks, of which ninety-six
were Mark II light tanks and unfit for battle; and Italian strength
as a hundred and thirty-eight gun-armed tanks. This gave Cun-
ningham an apparent superiority for the decisive clash of more than
four to three over the combined German and Italian battleworthy
armour and more than two to one over the Germans alone. There-
fore, in Cunningham's words, "the armoured commanders were
quite confident of themselves and their equipment before battle".

That a British offensive was impending was well known to Rom-
mel; it placed him in a dilemma, for he himself was preparing a
grand assault on Tobruk with both his panzer divisions. It was to
take place on or after 20th November, in the new moon. It was
tempting to Auchinleck and Cunningham, who were aware of this
impending attack, to delay *Crusader* until Rommel was fully em-
broiled in Tobruk, and then strike him in the back; but, in view of
the Prime Minister's impatience, it was impossible. As knowledge
of British preparation grew, Rommel decided not to commit 21st
Panzer Division against Tobruk, but to place it south of Gambut.
Even 15th Panzer was ordered to make its plans so that at twenty-
four hours' notice it could break off and join 21st Panzer. As a
forward defence against the British, Rommel had prepared the
twenty-five-mile line from Bardia to Omar, thickly mined and garri-
soned by the Italian Savona division and German anti-tank guns;
and far to the south, the Italian Ariete armoured division well dug-in
at Bir Gubi, on the flank of a British march towards Tobruk. These
dispositions were known to Cunningham.

Throughout the night before the battle there was pelting rain,
with thunder and brilliant lightning: nature imitating the art of

war. Generals and privates waited for the morning with dry mouths and queasy stomachs. They were all aware of the crucial importance in the war of their offensive; it had been pointed home to them by a message from the Prime Minister:

> For the first time British and Empire troops will meet the Germans with an ample supply of equipment in modern weapons of all kinds [sic]. The battle itself will affect the whole course of the war. Now is the time to strike the hardest blow yet struck for final victory, home and freedom. The Desert Army may add a page to history which will rank with Blenheim and Waterloo. The eyes of all nations are upon you. All our hearts are with you. May God uphold the right!

But for Cunningham this revelation of how much now hung upon the coming battle constituted another tremendous anxiety at a moment when, after an exacting period both emotionally and physically, he was suffering from the first-night nerves common to all soldiers before a battle. The long night of 17th November, 1941 was a time of loneliness and self-awareness, a time to think with heated and beating brain: there were old questions—supposing the Germans did not fight at Gabr Saleh? Supposing Rommel attacked Godwin-Austen's infantry? There was the new realisation of responsibility —responsibility for the precious first products of allied war production, for the lives of hurriedly raised, hurriedly trained soldiers, for the British reputation before the eyes of the world, for bringing back a victory as great as Blenheim. The rain swept over trucks and tanks and bivouacs, beating in squalls against the steel sides of Cunningham's caravan. The thunder reverberated, a constant reminder of battle. In the desert there was no refuge, not even in sleep.

CHAPTER TWO

CUNNINGHAM, it now seems clear, was not fit enough to bear the weight of commanding a major battle. Since February he had been under pressure almost without a pause. This pressure had culminated in ten weeks of over-work and emotional strain. His physical strength, his nerves and his capacity for clear judgment and decision had all suffered. On the eve of *Crusader* he seems to have already reached that stage of mental and physical fatigue when even ordinary tasks and decisions loom immense and daunting to a man. Yet Cunningham would never admit it, not even to himself; his duty lay in leading Eighth Army into battle, as it was his brother's duty to lead the Fleet; he could not go sick on the eve of action. While the army marched into Libya, therefore, Cunningham fought a private battle against the effects of over-strain.

On the morning of 18th November, 1941, he rose early and, while it was still pitch dark, drove away from his own headquarters to join Willoughby Norrie. It was an unfortunate journey over ground made miry by the heavy rain: the Army Commander's car got stuck in the mud and Cunningham had to wait while it was pulled clear. He joined Norrie an hour later at Alam Abu Ngeira, thirty miles on the Egyptian side of the frontier wire. Daylight illuminated a depressing waste of gravel and scrub under a low sky of racing storm clouds. At six o'clock Eighth Army began to roll towards the German rear in an enormous column of transport led by the armour. *Crusader* had begun.

For the lower ranks of the army there were plenty of tasks, plenty of orders to give in the course of the long mechanised advance of a hundred thousand men. For Norrie and Godwin-Austen—above all, for Cunningham—there was nothing to do but look at the unchanging waste, the crawling tanks and the bumping trucks. There was a halt in the middle of the morning while the armoured brigades refuelled. The armoured cars reported a screen of German armoured cars and tanks in front of them covering the Trigh el Abd. The

British armour rolled on again and by last light the German cars had withdrawn, leaving Cunningham in possession of his objective of Gabr Saleh and the surrounding desert. The British had apparently achieved complete surprise. At six o'clock in the evening orders for the next day were issued: to make secure the pre-arranged battle positions and push out strong reconnaissance forces towards Bir Gubi and the Trigh Capuzzo. These colourless orders reflected Cunningham's and Norrie's puzzlement; the entire Eighth Army had marched all day into Rommel's rear without causing noticeable reaction on his part. There had been no hardening resistance, and no local counter-attacks. So far as British information went, there had been no re-grouping of the German panzer divisions in preparation for a major counter-stroke.

Though this was only the first day, its events seemed to bear out Norrie's prediction that occupation of Gabr Saleh would not force Rommel to accept battle. The silence and stillness in the German part of the desert induced a sense of unease. The troops were not bothered by such things, however: leaguers of vehicles pointing in every direction peopled the desert with villages, in which men strolled about, cooked on little flaring petrol fires, or even played football amid the camel thorn.

There was a reason for the failure of the Axis forces to regroup to face the British advance. The commander of *Panzergruppe Afrika* still had no idea that a major British offensive was rolling up from the south. His armoured cars had reported a reconnaissance in force, and Rommel was far too interested in his own impending attacks on Tobruk to worry about reconnaissance troops. General Cruewell, commanding the Afrika Korps, pressed him to send a battle group south towards Gabr Saleh: Rommel, irritated and reluctant, agreed, but otherwise reserved his forces for Tobruk.

In the morning (19th November) at 30th Corps H.Q. there was still no news of German reaction upon which Cunningham could base tactical decisions; instead there was an uncanny absence of signs of movement that suggested the stalking wild animal. Norrie seemed finally to have been proved right about Gabr Saleh; and there was nothing else to do but push on deeper into Rommel's rear. Yet with the German armour's situation and intentions a mystery despite air reconnaissance, Cunningham did not feel he could release 4th Armoured Brigade—as he had hoped to do by now—from its special role as left flank guard to 13th Corps. Therefore the further north-westwards advance of 30th Corps was limited to two of its three armoured brigades. But now, as with Hougoumont at Waterloo, a local action was to draw in a disproportionate strength of the attacking forces; a dispersal of armour that wrecked Cunningham's new plan.

About eleven in the morning of 19th November tanks of 22nd Armoured Brigade found Italian tanks near Bir Gubi, on the left flank of the British advance. It was known that Bir Gubi was occupied by Ariete Division. Gradually a battle flared up between Ariete and 22nd Armoured Brigade, a battle which moved to Gubi

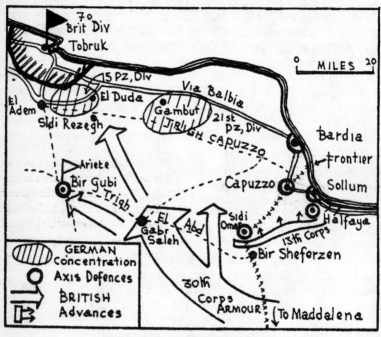

MAP 8. THE 'CRUSADER' BATTLE
Phase A, November 1941

itself, where the Italians were strongly posted with anti-tank guns. General Gott, commanding 7th Armoured Division, seemed to think this action offered an opportunity for the comparatively easy destruction of an Italian armoured division and the securing of Bir Gubi, on our flank, as a defended locality to be held by 1st South African Division.

With Gott's approval, the whole of 22nd Armoured Brigade was now drawn into this action, and away from the northward advance ordered by Cunningham. It was the beginning of a process of disintegration in the control of the British offensive. The first that Norrie and Cunningham heard of the battle at Bir Gubi was in the evening, when news came in that the green territorial troops of 22nd Armoured Brigade, only a month in Egypt, had charged home on the dug-in Italians as if on a fox, and had been beaten off with the loss of fifty-two tanks. The principal northward advance had thus been made by 7th Armoured Brigade alone, a third of the British strength; this brigade now occupied the Sidi Rezegh area, with Axis forces on every side but the south. By nightfall on 19th November, therefore, one of the British armoured brigades had been defeated with heavy losses, and one was in a dangerously exposed situation far out of supporting distance of the rest of the army. Only 4th Armoured Brigade remained in the old battle positions at Gabr Saleh.

Here it was attacked, just as Cunningham might have hoped, by the battle group that Cruewell had prised out of Rommel. But of course the Germans now encountered only a single brigade instead of three; however, they withdrew eastwards after an indecisive action, 4th Armoured Brigade following them. After forty-eight hours, Cunningham had still not brought the main body of the German armour to battle. Intelligence reports were scanty and gave no real lead. It remained a most uneasy situation, aggravated for Cunningham by his inability to act, and by the long blank hours of waiting at Norrie's headquarters. In his state of health, an immediate general action might have had a better effect than this agonising dalliance.

By nightfall on 19th November Cunningham desperately wanted Rommel to declare his main direction of attack. Seventh Armoured Division's orders for the 20th (whether ultimately derived from Cunningham, Norrie or the divisional commander himself) therefore reflect a commander groping for a principle of action: 4th Armoured Brigade to return to its original battle positions, still to cover the left flank of 13th Corps and the right of 30th, 7th Armoured Brigade merely to make reconnaissance to the north, 22nd Armoured Brigade not to join 7th until Bir Gubi had been captured by the South Africans, Support Group to join 7th Armoured Brigade.

Rommel however had now in fact begun to react—and exactly as intended in the original *Crusader* plan. Cruewell was ordered to use both panzer divisions "to destroy the enemy battle groups in the Bardia-Tobruk-Sidi-Omar area before they can offer any serious threat to Tobruk."

That night (19th/20th November) a wireless breakdown in Eighth Army added to the general uncertainty: Cunningham could receive no news from his own headquarters, and could transmit no orders to it. He was like a man already blind who felt himself going deaf and dumb. He decided to fly back to his H.Q. first thing in the morning.

When he left Norrie he had still not been able to give him free control of 4th Armoured Brigade, his principal reason for travelling with him at all. Galloway greeted Cunningham with a letter setting out what was known at Eighth Army Headquarters: nothing, except that air reconnaissance had seen much German transport heading westwards. Again this obscurity and negativeness instead of the violent armoured shock that the British had visualised and for which they had nerved themselves. Cunningham spent another cold, grey morning in an operations caravan worrying and waiting; for a change it was in his own headquarters at Maddalena and with Galloway's brisk company instead of Norrie's.

Then at last events began to move with unpleasant speed—as Cruewell, with two panzer divisions at his back, carried out Rommel's orders of the previous night. He had problems similar to those of Cunningham; his knowledge of British dispositions was confused and incomplete, and he could not decide which of Cunningham's scattered armoured brigades constituted the main British attack. All morning Cruewell ranged up and down the Trigh Capuzzo looking for British armour that had never been there, until 21st Panzer ran out of fuel. He then analysed his information again and concluded that the British main thrust was aimed at relieving Tobruk. Cruewell could now choose between attacking the British troops nearest Tobruk—7th Armoured Brigade at Sidi Rezegh—or smashing the forces that covered the hub of the British wheel into Libya and protected its dumps and supply lines.

In the afternoon of the 20th, Cruewell, with 15th Panzer Division, advanced southwards towards 4th Armoured Brigade, which was now in the strength of a hundred and twenty-three Stuarts. In the operations caravan at Eighth Army headquarters at Maddalena, Cunningham watched Cruewell move down the battle-map. Here at last, after two and a half days, was German acceptance of battle at Gabr Saleh. But instead of relief, the news caused consternation. There were no longer three armoured brigades grouped there in readiness for a major action, but a single brigade fettered by its obligations to the infantry of 13th Corps. If it were beaten, 13th Corps would be massacred by 15th Panzer Division. Time, of which there had recently seemed such a surplus, now became desperately short.

Cunningham ordered Norrie to send 22nd Armoured Brigade

from Bir Gubi east to Gabr Saleh to join 4th Armoured Brigade. It was a belated attempt to rebuild his lost concentration; was it soon enough? From twelve noon until about three in the afternoon, Cunningham lived in suspense. Godwin-Austen, of 13th Corps, suggested that he should support 4th Armoured Brigade with the New Zealand Division and its heavy 'I' tanks. Cunningham turned this down: 30th Corps alone was the instrument of decision. It was an example of the rigidity and departmentalism of the British mind. Cunningham's hopes and worries remained on the race between 15th Panzer and 22nd Armoured Brigade. Cruewell and 15th Panzer got there first. Throughout the late afternoon Gatehouse and his brigade of light Stuarts fought a savage battle against the heavier German armour. Twenty-second Armoured Brigade was now ordered to drive into the German right flank. Not until half-past six did part of this brigade get into action; Gatehouse had already been forced away to the south. As night fell the fighting died, with the Germans, as was their custom, camping on the battlefield, and the British, as was theirs, withdrawing from it.

For Cunningham, however, the outcome of 20th November had been immensely heartening. Cruewell had not destroyed 4th Armoured Brigade, nor made any dangerous advance towards Eighth Army's communications: he was believed to have lost thirty-four tanks. On the other hand, Cunningham now had two of his armoured brigades concentrated near Gabr Saleh. He believed that the decisive tank action had taken place, and that he had won it. After the worry and disappointment of the first two days of the offensive, a wave of success buoyed him up. His orders for the 21st November verged on a general chase: 4th and 22nd Armoured Brigades to attack the German armour as soon as possible after first light, and pursue it relentlessly if it withdrew, the Tobruk garrison to break out through El Duda to make a junction with 7th Armoured Brigade at Sidi Rezegh, 5th South African Brigade to advance in support to Sidi Rezegh.

On the German side, the battle was still being conducted by Cruewell, because Rommel was unwilling to admit that his own attack on Tobruk was defunct, and refused to turn his thoughts to the unwelcome reality of a major British offensive. Cruewell suggested that 21st Panzer (now refuelled) should join 15th Panzer by a night march, and that both should move north and west—along the original British axis of advance—to take 7th Armoured Brigade in the rear. This movement exactly dovetailed into Cunningham's intentions for 21st November. Soon after first light both Panzer divisions set off to destroy 7th Armoured Brigade, pursued only distantly by 4th and 22nd Armoured Brigades, who jubilantly reported that the German armour was in full retreat. Norrie reported this tremendous news to Cunningham at a quarter to nine in the morning. Here was a moment of great relief and pleasure. Cunningham had gained his victory after all. He rang up Godwin-Austen of 13th Corps and told him that he could advance if and when he wished. Godwin-Austen immediately ordered the New Zealand Division with two hundred 'I' tanks to advance along the Trigh Capuzzo towards Sidi Rezegh and Tobruk and the 4th Indian Division to take the fortified Axis positions round Sidi and Libyan Omar. The whole of the Eighth Army was set in motion after the 'beaten' enemy.

In Cairo, by a conspiracy of foolishness between press and public relations, the 'victory' was announced to the world with vulgar flamboyance. Since the beginning of the offensive the press had destroyed more German tanks than Rommel had ever possessed— three times heavier losses than those of Cunningham. There were stories of forty thousand men being encircled south of Tobruk.

The resolution of the battle into clear terms, and favourable ones, displayed Cunningham as he had been in East Africa: energetic, thrusting and impatient. When he heard from Norrie that 30th Corps could do nothing to help the sortie of the Tobruk garrison until the next day, and that none of the South Africans had yet reached the Sidi Rezegh area, he sharply pointed out the necessity for speed; that if the Tobruk sortie reached Duda, a junction with it "would appear to involve only a short night march". Cunningham went further: if a firm junction was not made with the Tobruk garrison he would "certainly require to see the Corps Commander tomorrow". He also spurred on his other corps by telling Godwin-Austen's Brigadier General Staff, Harding, that 13th Corps could advance according to their initiative "and need not refer unnecessarily to the Army Commander. At the same time, the Commander 13th Corps was not to take unnecessary risks."

Tobruk remained all day his chief anxiety. In the evening he ordered Godwin-Austen to send the New Zealanders westwards as fast as possible.

The illusion of victory became hour by hour more lovely. That night a liaison officer from G.H.Q. arrived at Cunningham's headquarters with news that a hundred and seventy German tanks had been hit during the day, and that the German armour, in fragments, was running westwards with the British armour striving to cut it off.

Four hours later Cunningham read an Eighth Army situation report which said that sixty German tanks were surrounded at Sidi Rezegh.

In fact the major events of the day had been that Rommel had personally stopped the sortie of the Tobruk garrison with a scratch force, and that 7th Armoured Brigade at Sidi Rezegh, attacked by two panzer divisions, had been reduced to twenty-eight tanks.

Next day, the 22nd November, 1941, was the fulcrum of a swift transformation scene that substituted disaster for victory. A dispersed, murderous and uncontrolled battle smouldered round Sidi Rezegh all day long, as Rommel (now in active command) and his two panzer divisions strove to clinch the destruction of 7th Armoured Brigade by forcing it and the guns and infantry of the Support Group off the Sidi Rezegh aerodrome. The British clung stubbornly to this naked and flattened piece of desert. It was the sort of battle that suited the national temperament. "Half-naked, weary, dust-begrimed gunners of all regiments," said a Royal Artillery account, "repulsed attack after attack. Shelled, battered from the air, and machine-gunned by infantry, they steadily fought on." The gunners of the Support Group earned a German tribute: "The British artillery was the best trained and best commanded element in the British army, and the quality of these gunners was fully proved in the desperate fighting round Sidi Rezegh . . ."

Meanwhile the British armour was coming up to the rescue. But instead of both 4th and 22nd Armoured Brigades being launched together in a properly conceived attack, they joined the fighting one an hour and a quarter after the other, and with no more coherent purpose than to shoot it out with any German tanks they might see through the smoke and the dust. There was great confusion. Twenty-second Armoured Brigade lost heavily to German anti-tank guns before 4th Armoured Brigade came up. As the light faded, the British were forced backwards to the south, and Sidi Rezegh aerodrome fell to Rommel. According to the Royal Artillery Commemoration Book:

> The final scene was awe-inspiring enough. In the light of burning vehicles and dumps our guns slipped out of action, leaving the field to a relentlessly advancing enemy, who loomed in large, fantastic shapes out of the shadows into the glare of bursting shells.

Only forty-five tanks remained to 22nd Armoured Brigade out of the seventy-nine with which they had begun the action. Gatehouse's 4th Armoured Brigade with a hundred Stuarts was the only large British tank force left. Now, in the bad luck of war, its head-quarters was overrun by 15th Panzer Division as it plunged through the confusion and darkness.

In the flaring light of burning tanks, the Germans captured most of the headquarters personnel and the wireless links; they had smashed the brain of the brigade and for twenty-four hours its hundred tanks were out of the battle. The result was to be disastrous. Gatehouse, on his way back from a conference, escaped. None of this was yet known to Cunningham at Eighth Army Headquarters.

Rommel judged that the fighting of the 22nd November was a German victory, and that he now held the initiative. With an accuracy that contrasted with the fantasy of British estimates of German tank losses, he calculated that he had destroyed two hundred and seven British tanks. He proposed to clinch his success by attack-ing the remnants of the British armour on 23rd November con-centrically.

At Maddalena Cunningham remained cut off from the facts of the forward battle by the delays and inaccuracies of situation reports. In particular he did not know that General Gott (7th Armoured Division), working desperately to sort out the wreckage of the armour, had now decided that "with present forces, no further advance appeared possible without assistance", and had gone over to the defensive. On the contrary, Cunningham's thoughts were busy on the re-grouping of his army for the continued pursuit and destruction of the beaten enemy. At half-past six in the morning of the 23rd November, he took off in his personal aircraft to visit Godwin-Austen (13th Corps). It was "a bright, sunny morning. White racing clouds made moving islands of shadow on the desert surface." He explained to Godwin-Austen his new grouping: 13th Corps now to include the South Africans and the Tobruk garrison and to be responsible for operations to relieve that fortress, 30th Corps to protect the left flank of 13th Corps and the army's com-munications, and to destroy the enemy's armour.

Cunningham then flew back to Maddalena, having, as he thought, completed his arrangements for the consummation of victory. It was turning colder and showery. Within a few moments of re-entering his headquarters he learned that far from consummating a victory, he was in the midst of a disaster.

Reports of yesterday's defeats had at last reached Eighth Army: Cunningham read for himself that 7th Armoured Brigade, which had begun the battle with a hundred and twenty-nine tanks, had not a single runner, that 22nd Armoured Brigade (originally a hundred and fifty-eight tanks) had only thirty, and that nothing was known of 4th Armoured Brigade, whose headquarters had been destroyed. He had in fact lost the decisive armoured battle that was the basis of the *Crusader* plan.

In Cunningham's own words,

the main thing was to destroy Rommel's armour. One entered the battle with that object and then found one hadn't the means. One night the tank state showed forty-four runners.

However, there was in this crisis of November 23rd, 1941, a much more profound meaning than the miscarriage of a particular battle. The unfortunate Cunningham had picked up the bill for twenty years of military decadence.

It is generally true that an army is an extension of society; military disaster is often national decline exposed by the violence of a battle. Examples are Imperial Russia and Austria-Hungary in the First World War, France in the Second. Any army thus reflects in sharp focus the social structure, the state of technological progress and the creative vigour of a society. The opposing armies at Crécy illustrate this general rule. However, the British army in the Second World War is an exception, perhaps the only one in history. Although the army of a twentieth-century social democracy and a first-class industrial power, it was nevertheless spiritually a peasant levy led by the gentry and aristocracy. Its habits of mind and work, its mental and emotional life were those of the social order based on birth and lands that had passed from supremacy in the national life by the end of the nineteenth century. Few poor men of great ability chose the army as a rewarding outlet for their talents—pay for all ranks was less than an income. Purchase had died with Cardwell, but its soul went marching on. Men of great ability did of course make their careers in the army, but because it was a tradition of their caste and because they enjoyed private means. Therefore in a true sense most regular officers of the British Army were amateurs as well as gentlemen. Born into the gentry or the aristocracy, spending their lives in the last sanctuary of privilege in Europe, their mental characteristics and morality were not surprisingly very different from those of the managers, the scientists and technicians of industry. Cleverness, push, ruthlessness, self-interest and ambition were considerably less prized than modesty, good manners, courage, a sense of duty, chivalry and a certain affectation of easy-going non-professionalism. There was therefore in the British professional soldier little identification with the world of twentieth-century tech-nocracy and little sympathy. They rightly judged it sordid and barbarous. But this did not help them prepare for its wars.

Within the army's own structure this nineteenth or even eigh-teenth century mentality was reflected by the veneration for the regiment, which had long ceased to be a functional unit on the battle-field, and by the amazing prestige and pre-eminence of the cavalry. The regimental system was of course limited to the infantry and the cavalry. The artillery, engineers, supply and technical services formed single arms of the service in much the same way as cavalry and infantry in the American, Russian and German armies. These branches were, significantly, quite ready for and equal to their task in modern war. Functional reality had by 1941 almost disappeared from the regiment: the Scottish regiments were full of English, West Country regiments salted with Yorkshiremen, the cavalry regiments amalgamated in pairs. To allow training and reinforcement with the scale and flexibility necessary in modern war while retaining the eighteenth-century regiment, elaborate compromises had to be worked out. Yet for the regular British soldier—officer or private —the regiment was a tremendous emotional reality, a focus for all his military pride and loyalty. Memories of ancient battles and the practice of peculiar customs kept alive this heartfelt parochialism. As a result the real organisations of a modern army—the division, the branches of the service, the army itself—were denied the cor-porate spirit that they so badly needed to give them cohesion.

In this spiritually eighteenth-century army, the cavalry, as the arm of fashion and aristocracy, was the haughty queen. Over its stiff-necked elegance and pride the heroes of the past—Uxbridge, Lucan, Cardigan and Haig—nodded approval; approval of a mili-tary code based not on technical competence, but on high birth, an esoteric way of life, and veneration for the horse. To these lancers and dragoons and hussars—each regiment of each species jealously guarding its separatist pride—was to be given the oily, smelly, clank-ing product of a technical society: the tank. And with it they were to be invited to fight a homogeneous German panzer arm composed of twentieth-century men of all social classes, who were more interested in sprockets than spurs.

The result between 1918 and 1939 of the natural conservatism of the British officer, of the preservation of the regiment and of the pre-eminence of the cavalry, was the stultification of development of an army in Britain as modern in equipment and thought as the Royal Air Force. This stultification was sharpened by the use of the British army in peace-time as an imperial gendarmerie. Development of tanks and of a theory of tank warfare suffered particularly.

After the First World War, few officers thought there would be another major war; the concept of tank warfare, which by 1918 had progressed as far as deep break-throughs, seem irrelevant. One or two radical theorists such as Liddell Hart and Fuller proclaimed that the future army should be based on the tank as the decisive weapon and consequently completely mechanised. But this was so costly a conception, and the army was so needed battalion by battalion for police duties in far-flung colonies, that such a revolutionary and comprehensive re-organisation seemed out of the question to conservative, easy-going minds. In the late 1920's the army did progress as far as experimenting with a mobile, semi-armoured force on Salisbury Plain, that hearth-rug of a manœuvre ground. Early in 1930 a similar formation was devised for the infantry: 6th (Experimental) Infantry Brigade at Blackdown, with Archibald Wavell as Brigadier and Dorman-Smith as Brigade Major.

Throughout the year 1935, when the new German army was in bud and about to bloom, the future of the British army was at hazard. Army and Royal Air Force fought a bitter battle for the limited amount of money allotted for defence, the R.A.F. arguing *au fond* that an army was no longer necessary; the overseas defence of Britain could be entrusted to an Independent Bomber Force with a small fighter component. Far from being re-organised and mechanised, the army, in the view of the R.A.F., could be reduced to a gendarmerie without tanks or medium artillery. The Air Force, at a time when the Germans were developing the close-support dive-bomber, also refused to develop any specialised army co-operation aircraft, except the string-bag Lysander. While this battle for the army's survival was going on, the army's own radicals, several ranks from the top, were trying to get revolutionary changes past the World War One veterans in high places. Dorman-Smith, whose reputation for original military thinking was extremely high, was now on the staff of a section of the War Office, S.D.2., that was charged with experimentation and the preparation of the army for modern war; it also prepared the army estimates. S.D.2. set about producing plans for complete mechanisation of the army along the lines of the experimental brigades—for the elimination of the horse, which at that time not only formed the instrument of reconnaissance and of exploitation of break-throughs, but also pulled guns and transport. But Dorman-Smith and his colleagues balked at destroying the cavalry regiment, although this was the logical consequence of abolishing the horse. Even slavering revolutionaries must have some sense of the possible, and the cavalry was too well protected by its influence in high military and political circles to give the smallest hope that a plan for its destruction would ever mature. There was also the emotional pull, the veneration that ancient regiments exercised even over British military radicals. The problem was solved by sliding easily along a fallacious analogy. A modern armoured corps performed the same function as an antique cavalry corps—reconnaissance, shock action, mobile exploitation. The existing cavalry had been trained in these roles. Therefore it was obvious that the cavalry should be converted to armour; objections would be loud about the loss of the horses, but not so loud as about the loss of the regiments.

There had existed since the First World War the Royal Tank Corps. Although larger than a cavalry regiment (eight battalions instead of one), it was far short of being an arm of the service like the artillery—or the cavalry. It therefore had no influence, and its officers no high seniority in the army. It contained of course all those who really believed in the future of armour, and who understood and loved mechanical things. The alternative in the 1930's to armour-plating the cavalry lay in creating a mass, technical panzer arm, like that of the Wehrmacht and analogous to the Royal Artillery, and based on the nucleus of the Royal Tank Corps. Recruited freely from all classes of an industrial country, mentally free from irrelevant traditions, the Royal Tank Corps had in fact worked out by 1934 the tactics, strategy and mechanical techniques of armoured warfare with revolutionary thoroughness. These were borrowed by Guderian for his panzer arm. The Royal Tank Corps could, like that arm, have become a new mass *corps d'élite* completely of the twentieth century, based on a central system of depots and reinforcements and with the division as a focus of loyalty. In the German army the creation of such a corps was not only possible, it became the instrument of victory; in the British, it had no more chance than universal suffrage in 1815. For two effects of the class structure of the British army were that in fact the cavalry officer did display greater powers of leadership than the tank officer, and also that British soldiers preferred to be commanded by 'gentlemen' than by able men of their own class.

Nevertheless, by 1936 the mechanisation of the army and the conversion of the cavalry to armour had been accepted; it was some mercy. The mentality of the army's senior and rising officers could not be similarly converted by decree to suit mobile armoured warfare. The stiff, positional war of the Western Front between 1914 and 1918 was the only modifying influence in a world of polo, the social round, and the close life of the regiment. Though the 1936 Field Service Regulations, written by Wavell, emphasised mechanised mobility, the current Infantry Training Regulations had been written by Montgomery before modernisation.

Meanwhile the neglect of the tank and the low seniority in the army of the tank officers, however able, had a pernicious reaction within the Royal Tank Regiment. Like a persecuted minority sect, it became bitterly extremist. Tank men now began to proclaim that the tank alone would decide the battles of the future; infantry and artillery were useless encumbrances to be mopped up by the victors of a tank-to-tank battle. For them—particularly for their plain-spoken and prickly leader, General Hobart—an armoured division consisted entirely of tanks, and the battle was decided by the guns of the tanks.

Thus as the British armoured forces began to take shape, there had been no such fundamental thinking and no such fundamental agreement about their role and organisation as Guderian had fostered in Germany; on the contrary there was the uneasy marriage of the 'tank-alone' school of the Royal Tank Corps, and the 'armour-is-cavalry' school of the cavalry. To this want of intellectual preparedness was added want of operational experience owing to the lateness of British re-armament. The Germans tried out and modified their conceptions of armoured warfare in the Spanish Civil War in 1936–39. They attempted their first major mechanised advance in the peaceful march to Vienna in 1938; it was a muddle that taught them much. *Crusader* was the first British operation of this size. The Germans refined their technique in the advance into Czecho-slovakia in 1939, and perfected it in the brilliant campaigns of Poland and France.

Meanwhile, in their half-baked British way, the British were still cobbling together with empiricism and pragmatism a panzer arm. Only in 1940 was the Cavalry Division in Palestine converted (with reluctant emotions) to armour; its units fought with O'Connor and in *Crusader*. The War Office, fearful of "tanks alone" extremism, gave the command of 7th Armoured Division to Creagh, a cavalry-man, instead of Hobart. The holy odour of the horse clung to the British armour. In *Crusader*, the G.O.C. 7th Armoured Division commanded from his 'charger' (a tank or armoured car); supply trucks went to a rendezvous on the order "Lead horses". Only much later in the war did the cavalry become armoured in mind as well as fact: and then the class tradition of leadership of the cavalry officer vindicated itself.

O'Connor's victories did not really test the armour; *Battleaxe* was the first encounter with the veteran German panzer troops. *Battleaxe* and the five months that followed offered the British a belated opportunity to think hard and deep about such basic matters as the organisation and tactics of an armoured division, and to evolve a coherent theory. The lessons of *Battleaxe* were apparently noted. In a lecture on the battle, General Creagh said: "When on the defensive his [the German] policy was to draw our tanks on to his guns, and then to counter-attack with tanks." Middle East Headquarters issued *Notes on Enemy Tactics and Training*, showing that the Germans used mobile artillery as an offensive weapon; that they attacked by pushing forward a mixed force and then fighting defensively on the ground occupied. In September, 1941, a Training Memorandum was issued on the conduct of the next battle; it suggested tactics very like the German. But the officers and men of the British armoured brigades were as generally untouched by these warnings as road-hogs by road safety propaganda. A coherent system of tactics and training was neither evolved nor practised. An exception however lay in 4th Armoured Brigade, trained and led in the German style by Brigadier A. H. Gatehouse—a tank officer. General Gott, General Officer Commanding 7th Armoured Division in *Crusader* (by supreme British inconsequence, a light-infantry-man) himself summed up the state of British theory of armour on the eve of the battle, when he told his men: "This will be a tank commander's battle. No tank-commander will go far wrong if he places his gun within hitting range of an enemy."

The Germans, on the other hand, had spent the five months since *Crusader* adapting their excellent and proven general system of armoured warfare to the particular circumstances of the desert. In their thorough, serious, clever German way, they not only perfected their operational handling and such battlefield services as tank-recovery, they also practised them over and over again on the ground. As a result, in the words of a German staff officer:

A German panzer division was a highly flexible formation of all arms, which always relied on artillery in attack or defence. In contrast the British regarded the anti-tank gun as a defensive weapon, and they failed to make adequate use of their powerful field artillery, which should have been taught to eliminate our [the German] anti-tank guns.

After the *Crusader* battle was over, Gott wrote in his secret report on the operations of his division:

> The German will not commit himself to tank versus tank battle as such. In every phase of battle he co-ordinates the action of his anti-tank guns, Field Artillery and Infantry with his tanks and he will not be drawn from this policy.

All this could—should—have been foreseen before the battle; before the war.

There was a last adverse factor: the quality of British equipment. Post-war researches have indicated that in guns and armour-plate the British tanks of 1941 were much on a par with the Germans. However, the latest armour-plate on some German tanks could only be pierced by capped two-pounder shot—which the British did not have. And the British-built cruisers, mass-produced straight from the drawing-board, were greatly inferior to the German in mechanical design and reliability. Moreover there is no doubt about German superiority in two crucial things—telescopic sights and anti-tank artillery, in particular the 88 mm. gun, though subsequent research has shown that its relative importance was exaggerated in wartime. This magnificent German weapon had been designed as an anti-aircraft gun, but the Germans had found that it was far superior in hitting tanks to their own new 50 mm. anti-tank gun, which was arriving just before *Crusader*, and itself more powerful than the two-pounder. The 88 mm. was so dangerous that four of them could stop an armoured brigade. General Messervy considered the surprise of their first appearance in *Battleaxe* was a major cause of the failure of that operation. Yet its possible influence on *Crusader* does not seem to have been appreciated or countered. The tragedy however lay in that the British also had a magnificent anti-aircraft gun, the 3.7-inch, no more of a conspicuous target than the 88 mm., and of even greater penetrative power. In November 1941 there were in North Africa more 3.7's than 88's. But the British never used them in an anti-tank role, either in *Crusader* or in later desert battles. It was a depressing example of a streak of conservatism, rigidity and de-partmentalism in the twentieth-century British mind. The 3.7 was an anti-aircraft gun. It was to be used therefore to shoot at aircraft. The two-pounder was supplied to shoot tanks. And that was that.

When *Crusader* opened, the British thus advanced to battle with an armoured corps trained and organised according to a haphazard set of wrong principles, led by officers who had never commanded armour in battle before, and who were not tank men—Gott, Norrie, Cunningham—and with defective equipment. During the engagements which led up to the crisis of 23rd November, the British phalanxes of tanks had tried to get at the German armour, ensconced amid its lorried infantry and artillery, in a series of 'cavalry' charges (if a cavalry unit) or 'tank *v*. tank' (if Royal Tank Regiment) actions. They had been shot to a standstill by the German anti-tank artillery ("I did not myself know," said Cunningham later, "that the Germans had rearmed with 50-mm. guns. Though it appeared in a Middle East intelligence summary, nobody pointed it out to me") and they had broken down through mechanical weakness.

The cumulative and accelerating effects of twenty years of military decadence were thus on the morning of 23rd November, 1941, presented to the over-strained Cunningham as a situation of immediate and terrible danger. The suddenness and force of the shock overwhelmed him. The facts of the matter allowed only one deduction: we had lost the battle and must break it off. Out of four hundred and fifty cruiser tanks, Eighth Army had lost already at least three hundred. In yesterday's battle alone the British losses had been almost sixty. If Rommel pressed home his attack today against our weakened and disorganised forces, we might easily lose another sixty. In two days we might have no cruiser tanks at all—with Godwin-Austen's infantry spread out over Cyrenaica and the Axis Halfaya defences between them and Egypt. And beyond the immediate danger to Eighth Army there was the broader threat to Egypt and the Middle East.

For Cunningham there were other disquieting implications in the morning's news. It was now revealed how little control—or indeed knowledge—was enjoyed by Eighth Army headquarters in regard to the forward operations: and one of the most terrifying of emotions is a sense of impotence in the presence of unfolding disaster, an awareness that events are slipping beyond the limits of one's technique.

Cunningham now sent an "urgent request" to the Commander-in-Chief, General Auchinleck, to fly up at once to discuss the situation; or, in plain terms, to decide whether the offensive should go on, or whether Eighth Army should re-group for defence. Cunningham's own inclinations were clear to his staff, who were far from agreeing with him. But they were without Cunningham's responsibilities; there was no emotional pressure on them. It is easy to offer cool and resolute counsel about another man's troubles. Brigadier Galloway, Brigadier General Staff Eighth Army, now went to Norrie's headquarters to acquaint him (and Godwin-Austen who came over specially) with the morning's news of disaster and solicit opinions as to future action.

The meeting began at 12.15 p.m. Norrie, fully immersed in battle, was represented by Major R. M. P. Carver. This meeting witnessed the beginning of a movement of morale that was to transform the *Crusader* battle. In this movement, the gentlemen who led the British army displayed those virtues which were as much a part of their social and intellectual order as the shortcomings that had got them into the present mess. They had defied reason in the inter-war years; they defied it now with an instinctive faith that the right thing to do was the most dangerous and difficult. They had been bred to provide leadership; they prized bravery and resolution above any kind of cleverness and expertise; and they were to fight their way out of catastrophe, as had their country in 1940, by treating facts as less real than willpower.

Galloway explained in his blunt, vigorous manner the army's situation and Cunningham's reactions to it. Godwin-Austen, a solid, robust, eighteenth-century kind of general, formed the impression from Galloway that Cunningham was already thinking of breaking off the battle. Galloway asked him his opinion of a retreat into Egypt. Godwin-Austen was horrified. He replied in his renowned fog-horn voice:

"I couldn't possibly ask Freyberg and the New Zealand Division to call off their attacks—it is absolutely unthinkable."

Cunningham's state of mind was not altogether a surprise to Godwin-Austen: when they had met earlier in the battle Cunningham had not been happy about his tremendous responsibility in view of the Prime Minister's valedictory telegram and the general focus of interest on *Crusader*. Godwin-Austen had gained the impression too that Cunningham personally did not feel happy or at home in his headquarters.

Galloway returned to Maddalena after the meeting, and Godwin-Austen conferred with his brother corps commander, Norrie, on the telephone. It is difficult to resist the impression that Galloway had set out to canvass a solid opinion in favour of going on with the battle. He certainly succeeded. Godwin-Austen found Norrie calm and easy. He assured Godwin-Austen that he could hold on at least for a day. Godwin-Austen then wrote to Freyberg to say:

> I heard the question of withdrawal mentioned today, but refuse to consider it while our prospects on the whole are so rosy by comparison with the enemy's, whose mobile German forces are so small . . .

All now depended on the Commander-in-Chief. Some strange events occurred to keep the army in place until he arrived: tents and caravans at Eighth Army headquarters took an astonishing time to be struck, telephone lines were cut so that orders to retire or cease advancing, should they be issued, could not be received. For Cunningham was a spent man: with that determination which Godwin-Austen considered his most outstanding characteristic, he had driven himself beyond the limit.

More tidings of disaster now came in: of the state of 4th Armoured Brigade's disorganisation, and of the annihilation of 5th South African Brigade by German armour. In the evening Auchinleck arrived, a tall, big-shouldered man whose austere manner suggested moral strength. The grimness of his visage was accentuated by the jut of his jaw, by the stare of fierce blue eyes. In Galloway's caravan, he heard Cunningham set out the facts of defeat, and draw the logical conclusion that prompt disengagement while some armour remained was the only course that might save the army and Egypt. Auchinleck wrote later:

> Cunningham was obviously worried by the collapse and disintegration of his armoured formations. He had every reason to be so— I should have been in his place. He did not strike me as emotionally disturbed but obviously under great strain—again very naturally— as the battle had not gone according to plan and the change in it had been kaleidoscopic. He said that if we went on as we had been, we might be left without tanks, while the Germans might still have some; in which case, Egypt would be in danger.

Auchinleck had no doubts about the reality of the danger, nor illusions about the possible consequences of either retreat or continued attack. Auchinleck and Cunningham had no large reserves of armour and men to pour into the battle. But Auchinleck, with the intuition that is the mark of a great general, saw—or felt— beyond the facts on the Sitreps, the tank-states and the battle-map, beyond the confusion of the disintegrating battle into Rommel's own situation:

> My opinion was different from Cunningham's. I thought Rommel was probably in as bad a shape as we were, especially with Tobruk un-vanquished behind him, and I ordered the offensive to continue. I certainly gambled [in fact, by going on, we might have lost all] and Cunningham might very well have been proved to be right and I wrong!

On the evening of 23rd November, 1941, the course of the history of the war in the Middle East, perhaps world history, thus turned on the character of a single man. "This," wrote a German staff officer, "was certainly one of the great decisions of the war: Auchinleck's fighting spirit and shrewd strategic insight had saved the *Crusader* battle and much else besides." The Prime Minister wrote: "By his personal action Auchinleck thus saved the battle and proved his outstanding qualities as a commander in the field."

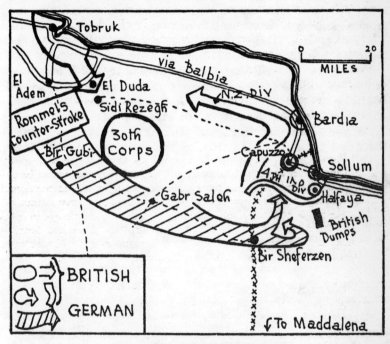

MAP 9. THE 'CRUSADER' BATTLE
Phase B, November 1941

Auchinleck's intuition about Rommel's weakness was correct: on the evening of 23rd November Rommel was down to a hundred tanks, and his army was in wild confusion. "The wide area south of Sidi Rezegh," wrote General Bayerlein, "had become a sea of dust, haze and smoke." When darkness fell, "hundreds of burning vehicles, tanks and guns lit up the field". But Rommel also was a great general, and he too had sensed intuitively the mind of the man who faced him distantly across the tumult—Cunningham, though; not Auchinleck. He now decided to lead his entire armoured force off the Sidi Rezegh battlefield, and on to Cunningham's communications with Egypt in the area of the Omars. By academic military principles this tangential move from the centre of the battle was wildly unsound; psychologically it was a sure success, for it was in fact the one manœuvre that Cunningham feared above all. At ten-thirty in the morning of 24th November, Rommel left his Ia, Colonel Westphal, in charge of *Panzergruppe Afrika* headquarters, and led the Afrika Korps towards Egypt in a column forty miles long. His route took him in succession through the headquarters of 30th Corps, 7th Armoured Division, 1st South African Division, 7th Support Group and 7th Armoured Brigade, mostly caught basking in the sunshine of a brilliantly fine and warm day.

Half an hour before Rommel began this rampage, Godwin-Austen arrived at 30th Corps headquarters to discuss plans with Norrie. Norrie was twelve miles away with Gott, but they spoke on the field telephone. Between them it was decided that 13th Corps should drive with all its strength towards Tobruk and Sidi Rezegh along the Trigh Capuzzo. Then Godwin-Austen returned to his corps. Soon afterwards Cunningham arrived by air at 30th Corps, found Norrie absent, and motored over to see him. He clearly did not in his own mind believe that Auchinleck's orders were feasible, for he told Norrie, in Norrie's words, "that things had not gone according to plan and at the back of my mind I should think how my troops would withdraw back to where we had started, should such an order be given".

While this talk was going on, Rommel was storming towards them on a direct course. First there were reports of his approach, then shells. Norrie thought that the Army Commander should leave. He was therefore driven, accelerator to floorboards, across country to the air strip amid shell and tracer and a thickening mob of fleeing transport. Cunningham climbed on board the revving Blenheim, which instantly took off, clearing a three-tonner by inches.

It was now 11.45 a.m. What General Norrie christened 'The Matruh Stakes' had officially started. All the soft transport of 30th Corps pounded to the east, half a length in front of Rommel, with at least one officer, caught sponging himself down, driving stark naked. But the fighting troops stayed put.

When Cunningham after his exciting morning arrived back at Maddalena, Auchinleck handed him a directive setting out in detail Auchinleck's reading of the situation and his orders for a continued battle. His conclusion re-affirmed his decision of the night before:

> You will therefore continue to attack the enemy relentlessly using all your resources even to the last tank.

Auchinleck saw firm possession of the Rezegh-Duda ridge by 13th Corps and the Tobruk garrison as the key to the battle.

The Commander-in-Chief, the Army Commander, and Galloway, discussed this directive. To Cunningham, after his morning's excursion, it did not appear entirely seasonable. Auchinleck was disturbed

> by what seemed to be excessive anxiety on his part lest the enemy should break through in force to our rear areas and dislocate our vulnerable supply and repair organization east of the frontier. His anxiety undoubtedly grew when the enemy swiftly followed up his recent success by a powerful counterstroke with that very intention.

In the afternoon Cunningham had another exciting flight:

> After lunch I went out by plane to Godwin-Austen, and then back to my headquarters at a hundred feet. As we were flying along the [frontier] wire, I looked down and saw a tank battle going on. When I got back to H.Q., the staff could hardly believe me. Rommel was in the right direction for my base—water and supplies. This rather shook me. He stopped fifteen miles short—he didn't know the base was there. Four divisions were depending on that water.

Auchinleck was unruffled. Eve Curie, the war correspondent, was taken to see Air Vice-Marshal Coningham in his caravan, and found herself in the presence of another commander,

> a strong sun-burned man with light-brown hair and blue eyes, who sat . . . in almost complete silence . . . The silent officer was no other than the Commander-in-Chief in the Middle East, General Sir Claude John Eyre Auchinleck . . . He sipped his drink quietly and listened— or perhaps did *not* listen—to our conversation.

After a while he referred to the question in everybody's mind— Rommel's advance:

> 'He is making a desperate effort, but he will not get very far. That column of tanks simply cannot get supplies. I am sure of this.'

Auchinleck was right. The Afrika Korps milled inconclusively about the Omars throughout 24th and 25th November, its units periodically paralysed through want of fuel, and its men more concerned in foraging for petrol and supplies than carrying out Rommel's orders. The 4th Indian Division, in the Omars, beat off German attacks with heavy losses. Rommel's tremendous counter-stroke had guttered out in a military vacuum, for, with Auchinleck at Eighth Army, the psychological principle behind it no longer applied. But a surface panic still agitated Eighth Army. In the morning the Germans were only twenty-eight miles from Mad-dalena, and it was feared that their armour was heading for Eighth Army headquarters. Until noon the military phenomenon of a 'flap' made H.Q. hearts flutter. In Auchinleck's words: "There was a scare that German tanks were moving on 8th Army H.Q. This made Cunningham naturally very anxious and insistent to get me, the C.-in-C., out of danger and further to the rear—not himself but me." Before Auchinleck was hurried into his aircraft, he gave Cunningham a message to him and his army for general publication:

> During three days, at your Advanced Headquarters, I have seen and heard enough to convince me, though I did not need convincing, that the determination to beat the enemy of your commanders and troops could NOT be greater, and I have NO doubt whatever that he will be beaten. His position is desperate, and he is trying by lashing out in all directions to distract us from our object, which is to destroy him utterly. We will NOT be distracted and he WILL be destroyed. You have got your teeth into him. Hang on and bite deeper and deeper and hang on till he is finished. Give him NO rest. The general situation in NORTH AFRICA is EXCELLENT. There is only one order: ATTACK AND PURSUE. ALL OUT EVERYONE.
>
> *C. Auchinleck.*
> *General C.-in-C.*

Auchinleck flew back to Cairo resolved to relieve Cunningham who, it was plain to all observers, was mentally and physically exhausted with battle-fatigue. It was not an easy decision and one which Auchinleck only implemented after long thought, and dis-cussion with the Minister of State in the Middle East, Oliver Lyttelton (now Lord Chandos).

To remove Cunningham [wrote Auchinleck later] was a very serious step. It might have adversely affected the morale of the Eighth Army very greatly. It would certainly encourage the enemy, who would count the removal as a confession of defeat. It would lower our prestige and morale everywhere, not only in Egypt, because it was a confession of failure. Therefore it was a difficult decision but it did not worry me once I had decided it had to be done—rightly or wrongly.

Meanwhile the scattered troops of 30th Corps south of Sidi Rezegh were making good use of the lull in the battle caused by Rommel's disappearance into the east. The formations began to regain cohesion: 4th and 22nd Armoured Brigade repaired its tanks and scrounged the quiet battlefields for potential runners. Most important perhaps of all was the rest accorded to the men after five days of constant fighting. As the British refreshed themselves, the Germans, behind Rommel, were still at full stretch. The 25th November was, however, far from being a day of complete peace round Sidi Rezegh. The 1st South African Brigade was attacked at Taieb el Esem by Ariete and rescued by Gatehouse and 4th Armoured Brigade. Gatehouse led his brigade sitting with tartan rug across his knees in an armchair strapped to the top of a tank. "What else could I do?" he remarked later. "I had no head-quarters."

The New Zealanders reached Sidi Rezegh. At *Panzergruppe Afrika* headquarters, Colonel Westphal frantically signalled Rommel to come back to the centre of the battle.

In the morning of 26th November, 1941, David Stirling, of the Special Air Service, was asked to see Cunningham, who wished to hear what traffic Stirling had seen on the Gazala-Tobruk road during his recent raid. Stirling was taken to a small tent in the headquarters at Maddalena; Cunningham was sitting at his desk. He questioned Stirling for five minutes. Stirling "was struck by the strain and fatigue on the general's face".

In the afternoon General Sir Arthur Smith, Chief of the General Staff, Middle East Command, arrived by air with Major-General Neil Ritchie, lately Deputy Chief of the General Staff, who was to replace Cunningham. Smith handed Cunningham a letter from Auchinleck to the effect that he had most reluctantly decided to relieve him of his command because he had begun to think defen-sively. However, Cunningham's relief was not announced publicly until 11th December. When Cunningham's personal gear was ready, he and Smith climbed on board the aircraft and flew back to the luxury and peace of the Delta. It was a painful journey for both officers. Smith was moved both to sympathy and admiration for Cunningham. "He was," said Smith, "a grand chap. How sad it was that at this critical time and because of his health he lost grip. He was not himself—he was not Cunningham." Even now, with the Army's battle fading behind him, Cunningham did not give up his own battle with himself. "He was absolutely tired," said Sir Arthur Smith, "but was fighting against it with tremendous courage. I had great difficulty in persuading him to enter hospital for a check-up." After Cunningham had been in hospital some days, his doctors found that he was suffering from severe over-strain.

It was now nearly four months since Cunningham had arrived in the desert; he had fought his private battle to the last round.

COMMENTARY: PART THREE

CHAPTER ONE

In planning the *Crusader* offensive (launched 18th November 1941) the new Commander-in-Chief in the Middle East, General Sir Claude Auchinleck, and his Eighth Army Commander, Lieutenant-General Sir Alan Cunningham, enjoyed improved but still far from complete or regular top-secret German intelligence from *Ultra* decrypts of *Enigma*. A direct service of decrypts to the Middle East was opened on 13th March 1941, with a forward link to the Western Desert from September. The German Army *Enigma* was read with difficulty from September onwards, but not rapidly and in quantity until May 1942. Nevertheless *Ultra* broke the Luftwaffe *Enigma* cipher virtually every day with little delay, as well as the ciphers of *Fliegerkorps X* and *Fliegerführer Afrika*, while Middle-East Intelligence succeeded in breaking the German Army's medium-grade cipher in July 1941. From these sources the British command learned of the arrival of 90th Light Division in Libya; the extent of Rommel's supply difficulties, especially his shortage of 88 mm. gun ammunition; and identified and located major enemy formations, such as the presence of *Ariete* at Bir Gubi on 13th November. It also was able to compute an accurate figure of the enemy tank strength. However, such intelligence sources could not and did not cast light on the qualitative superiority of German equipment, such as the improved Mark III and Mark IV tanks, or the use of the high-velocity 88 mm. anti-aircraft gun in an anti-tank role.

CHAPTER TWO

According to Professor Hinsley, the role of high-grade signals intelligence (*Sigint*) during the *Crusader* battle itself was helpful but not decisive, partly because tactical information was still not being read and communicated quickly enough to be of use in a fast-moving battle. While it was known, for example, that Rommel had fielded his entire strength to meet the initial British thrust, and that he faced a fuel shortage, no reliable intelligence about German tank losses was received before 23rd November. Lack of such reliable information provided, of course, an important element in Cunningham's mental crisis on 23rd November, when figures indicated that his own army had already lost three hundred out of four hundred and fifty cruiser tanks.

Early on 24th November came a foretaste of what *Ultra* would in the future provide regularly and swiftly: prior warning of the enemy's battle plans, in this case of Rommel's "dash to the wire". Unfortunately the information did not reach the Desert in time for the Eighth Army to be redeployed accordingly. However, it may be inferred that this clear revelation of Rommel's intentions, and the danger thereby to the Eighth Army's supply dumps, coming on top of Rommel's rampaging early progress on the ground, helped to produce that "defensive" state of mind in Cunningham so evident to Auchinleck when he flew up to confer with him that same day.

On the question of Auchinleck's subsequent decision to relieve Cunningham of his command, the only fresh information to appear since the original publication of this book consists of a medical report on Cunningham and private and confidential letters to him from Auchinleck quoted in, of all places, Nigel Hamilton's official biography of Montgomery, *Monty: The Making of a General 1887–1942*. Hamilton writes that Montgomery "seems to have purloined the War Office file [or a copy of it] when he later became CIGS." According to this file, Auchinleck, in a personal letter accompanying his formal letter of dismissal, asked Cunningham to go into hospital, not because he was ill, "but in the public interest". He therefore entered No. 64 General Hospital, Alexandria, on 26th November under an assumed name. His brother, Admiral Cunningham, insisted that he be examined by a consultant physician, who reported, according to Hamilton, that there was no question of a "nervous breakdown". Auchinleck wrote to Cunningham in hospital on 27th November to thank him "for the way you accepted my decision, and for your very great loyalty and public spirit in agreeing to go into hospital secretly and against your will. I ask your forgiveness in having inflicted this indignity on you, and I know very well how you disliked having to pretend that you are sick when you are not."

While it appears that in hospital Cunningham recovered his poise within a few days, and while noting the opinion of the consultant physician that he had not suffered a nervous breakdown (whatever the clinical definition of that may be), there is still absolutely no question from the oral evidence given to me by General Galloway and others of Cunningham's senior subordinates partially cited in this book that in non-medical terms Cunningham by 24th November was a spent man, incapable of decision and resolute leadership. I therefore interpret Auchinleck's letter to Cunningham in hospital as a white lie proceeding from Auchinleck's characteristic kindness and humanity.

PART FOUR

THE IMAGE OF A GENERAL

General Sir Neil Ritchie, G.B.E., K.C.B., D.S.O., M.C.

Be sure yourself and your own reach to know,
How far your genius, taste, and learning go;
Launch not beyond your depth; but be discreet,
And mark that point where sense and dulness meet.

ALEXANDER POPE,
An Essay on Criticism.

CHAPTER ONE

MAJOR-GENERAL NEIL M. RITCHIE, the Deputy Chief of the General Staff in Cairo in November, 1941, was an officer for whom life had apparently unrolled a red and softly piled carpet. He seemed surely destined for professional success because of his talents and not less because of his connections. He was rich; and he had served as Brigadier General Staff to General Alan Brooke in Second Corps in Flanders in 1939–40. Alan Brooke had found him an able and cool-headed staff officer. Personally Alan Brooke had become "devoted to Neil". Later in 1940 Ritchie had been Brigadier General Staff to Auchinleck as G.O.C. Southern Command. To Auchinleck Ritchie was no less impressive than to Brooke. He was vigorous and thorough. His personality and appearance made him the image of a British general. Ritchie was very tall and very big. He was handsome and authoritative; good-humoured in a slightly heavy manner. There was a bovine strength about him. Yet his brain was good. He was liked and trusted. His immediate superior in Cairo, General Sir Arthur Smith, said of him later: "He was straight-forward and absolutely honest. If one could criticise him, he was a little slow—but caution is often better than being too slick."

To Auchinleck, returning to Cairo on 25th November from Cunningham's headquarters, Ritchie appeared the best possible candidate for the command of Eighth Army. The choice was limited. There was no time for a new Army Commander to fly out from England; Cunningham must be replaced in a matter of hours. Among Middle East generals, Norrie or Godwin-Austen would have been the most obvious choice. Auchinleck rejected it. The present confused battle was being directed more from the two Corps headquarters than from army headquarters. Moving a corps commander would upset the entire command structure; bringing in an army commander from outside would leave Eighth Army's organisation undisturbed. The army was morally shaken. It needed a strong, unflustered, self-confident commander. Ritchie seemed therefore on all counts just the man. However, he was only a staff officer; his last command in the field had been of a battalion in France in the First World War. He was junior to both Norrie and Godwin-Austen. For these reasons Auchinleck viewed his appointment as temporary, to last until the present battle crisis was resolved and a permanent army commander could be flown out from England. His want of experience in command Auchinleck intended to supply himself; he wrote afterwards:

> Ritchie was perforce pitch-forked into a command at a desperate moment [really desperate], knowing little or nothing of his subordinate commanders or troops and told to retrieve an apparently lost battle. I, therefore, thought it only right to 'hold his hand' and make myself very readily available for consultation at short notice. I had not done this with Cunningham, who had formed and trained the 8th Army and was fully equipped to act on his own. This relationship continued to the end.

Ritchie, when told of the appointment, was ready and eager to go up to Eighth Army. It was a unique, a wonderful opportunity for a junior major-general who four years before had been a major. Self-doubt did not seem to trouble him. He was always, in General Godwin-Austen's words, "very full of himself and very self-assured —was prepared to occupy any position and quite confident he could do the job". When Smith and Cunningham flew back to Cairo and left him experiencing for the first time the peculiar loneliness that consists in command of an army, he seemed quite at home. David Stirling, who had seen Cunningham before lunch that day, saw Ritchie in the afternoon and found him genial, smiling and confident. A public relations officer was most impressed: "huge, handsome man, most extraordinarily smartly turned out and fairly oozing energy and vigour."

But his appointment had no great moral effect on the army. "When one heard that he was taking Cunningham's place there was no general reaction," said General Godwin-Austen later. "The fact was that neither Cunningham nor Ritchie were generally known to 8th Army." The events of the battle were equally indifferent to Ritchie's arrival. *Crusader* had reached a stage of confusion and dispersal never before seen in warfare, with British and Axis formations intermingled inextricably from the Omars to El Duda. Effective and realistic control could only be exercised by officers much nearer events than the Army Commander, whose information was late and unreliable, who was new to the battle and who had no reserve. On neither German nor British side was there now a coherent plan; only a purpose, expressed in a hundred vicious engagements. Yet in the forty-eight hours between Auchinleck's departure from Eighth Army headquarters and Ritchie's arrival, the balance had tilted away from the Axis and towards the British. Rommel's own hand had moved the balance by his raid into Egypt, which had given the exhausted and shaken British time to collect themselves.

On the first night of Ritchie's command, Freyberg and the New Zealanders, by Godwin-Austen's order, had passed Sidi Rezegh, captured Belhammed and joined hands with the Tobruk garrison, who had broken out over the El Duda escarpment. On his return to the main battlefield on 27th November, 1941, Rommel therefore found the British once more holding the vital ground from which he had so painfully expelled them on 24th November. On 28th November there was a lull while Rommel considered his prospects. On 29th he struck again at Sidi Rezegh and after two days' fighting won a second tactical victory on this unpleasant stretch of gravel. The New Zealanders, South Africans and the British armour had been driven away to the south and Tobruk isolated once more. "But the price paid had been too heavy," wrote a senior German staff officer, "the *Panzergruppe* had been worn down, and it soon became clear that only one course remained—a general retreat from Cyrenaica." With characteristic obstinacy and persistence, Rommel refused to recognise this.

Auchinleck had joined Ritchie at Maddalena; he was to remain at his headquarters for ten days. In fact Auchinleck commanded the British battle with Ritchie as his deputy. It was their old relationship of commander-in-chief and staff officer translated to new circumstances. As Churchill put it in the House of Commons,

> behind all this process working out at so many different points and in so many separate combats has been the persisting will-power of the Commander-in-Chief, General Auchinleck. Without that will-power we might very easily have subsided to the defensive . . .

Placed therefore between the authority of the Commander-in-Chief and the seniority of his corps commanders, Ritchie found himself in a situation difficult both militarily and personally. He did his best to cope with it and at the same time seize hold of a kaleidoscopic battle, so different from any of his own experience or of the tradition in which he had been trained as a staff officer. In the words of a German account: "The situation was now extremely complicated and confused, and both sides were almost at the end of their tether. The conditions were very severe; the troops were fighting in waterless country where the normal water supply had virtually broken down." Ritchie flew up to see Norrie (30th Corps) and Gott (7th Armoured Division); they were elsewhere, immersed in battle.

When Ritchie did meet Norrie, he made some semi-apologetic, semi-humorous reference to his getting the army command before his senior. On December 2nd, he visited Tobruk, where Godwin-Austen (13th Corps) now had his headquarters. Godwin-Austen found him "a very confident fellow—thought he was the goods. But universal agreement [about this] was doubtful". However, the anomalies of Ritchie's character and of his position did not seem important to senior officers of the Eighth Army at this busy time: Auchinleck was directing the battle; Ritchie's appointment was temporary, and in the meantime he was admirably acting the part of a bluff army commander.

His efforts to interpret and influence the tail-end of somebody else's battle displayed the optimism, perhaps complacency, that dominated his mind and temperament. Blended with Auchinleck's own energy and aggressiveness, it found expression in orders to attack and pursue a supposedly broken enemy. Though a premature and over-coloured estimate of Rommel's weakness, it was in the right spirit, and better by far than a too-sober caution.

The days between 1st and 4th December, 1941, witnessed the passing of the final decision in *Crusader* to the dogged British and their greater reserves of tanks. Rommel in his refusal to admit defeat planned yet another dash to the frontier wire. At the same time Ritchie ordered Norrie to advance through Bir Gubi on El Adem. This attack was repulsed by the Italians in Bir Gubi, but it caused Rommel not only to cancel his own operation but to order the Italians to evacuate their siege lines on the eastern perimeter of Tobruk. Hour by hour, imperceptibly, the battle now quietened down and melted into a German retirement. On 4th December an Italian officer arrived at Rommel's headquarters from Rome with the news that the *Panzergruppe* would get no more bulk supplies until the end of December, when aircraft of the Luftwaffe would be installed in Sicily and able to give air cover over the central Mediterranean sea routes. For Rommel, aware of the prostration of his men and of acute shortages in supplies, and harassed by British mobile 'Jock' columns at El Adem and round his own headquarters, this news was decisive. He began to issue orders for a retirement on Gazala; he feared it might even have to be on El Agheila.

A report that the Germans might be going reached Ritchie, who ordered Norrie to resume the advance to El Adem. But British and Axis troops had now fought themselves out: not all the sanguine and aggressive generals in history could have stirred them into another hard fight. The advance on El Adem simply did not take place. On the night of 7th/8th December, 1941, Rommel began to go. The *Crusader* battle was over, and Eighth Army had won it. In terms of courage and resolution, *Crusader* was the greatest achievement of British Commonwealth soldiers in the desert. "This battle," said General Sir Frank Messervy afterwards, "was an epic of British doggedness and optimism in adversity."

Yet the adversity that they had met so resolutely need never have existed in view of their quantitative superiority. The British blamed their difficulties on their equipment. This half of the truth enabled them to ignore the other half—that except in courage they themselves had been found wanting. They had failed intellectually over the theory of modern war, and they had failed operationally in the techniques of mobile organisation and command. Nevertheless in muddling through to victory, the Eighth Army had inflicted damage on the *Panzergruppe* almost as severe as in Second Alamein a year later. A third of Rommel's command had been destroyed. The same number of prisoners had been taken as in Second Alamein: thirty-six thousand. They had reduced the German tank strength to thirty, as against twenty-two at Second Alamein. Yet this equal victory had been won by an army incomparably weaker than the Eighth Army in October, 1942—one hundred and eighteen thousand men as against two hundred and twenty thousand. And Rommel's forces, by contrast, were stronger in *Crusader* than in Second Alamein: a hundred thousand men against ninety-six thousand, and with adequate supplies of fuel and munitions instead of paralysing shortages. Eighth Army in *Crusader* suffered eighteen thousand casualties in three weeks as against thirteen thousand five hundred in the twelve days of Second Alamein.

In spite of the British achievement in *Crusader*, the officers and men who won this the Eighth Army's first victory are not entitled to the figure "8" on the ribbon of the Africa Star. The principle behind this official ruling has never been disclosed.

*　　*　　*　　*　　*

There followed three weeks of anti-climax, as Rommel fell back steadily behind skilful rearguards with the British close behind him. At Gazala Rommel deployed and offered battle. Between 11th and

15th December Ritchie attacked him in front with 4th Indian Division while 4th Armoured Brigade felt their way over difficult ground past the Axis right flank. Finding himself turned, with his ammunition scarce and the Italians shaky, Rommel decided to retire on El Agheila. Behind his anti-tank guns, he retreated with deliberation and was never in serious difficulty, except through heavy attack by the Royal Air Force. He feared a repetition of O'Connor's march to Beda Fomm, and therefore kept the main body of his armour south of the Jebel Achdar. An attempt by British armour to cut the coast road west of Antelat was beaten in detail by 15th Panzer on 23rd December. On Christmas Eve, 1941, Benghazi fell, a ruined and empty white town under the winter clouds, a painting by Chirico. On 26th December Rommel stood at Agedabia reinforced to seventy tanks. In the nineteen days since he had begun to retreat from Sidi Rezegh he had received forty new tanks as against only thirteen in the equivalent period after Second Alamein.

Auchinleck and Ritchie now considered whether to risk an immediate attack with the forces available in the forward area. If successful it would force Rommel in disorder through his fortified bottleneck at El Agheila, a·position which in British hands would serve either as a sally-port for a renewed offensive into Tripolitania or as a barbican for captured Cyrenaica. However, the remaining tanks were almost worn out, and manned largely by green replacement crews. The risks were obvious. Like those that faced O'Connor they were accepted with spirit. But the courage of Auchinleck and Ritchie was rewarded by a minor disaster. A frontal attack by the Guards Brigade was repulsed. The flanking manœuvre of 22nd Armoured Brigade met a German counter-stroke that destroyed sixty-five British tanks. On 5th/6th January, 1942, Rommel retreated to El Agheila and the second British Libyan offensive came to a halt, but only, it was hoped, for rest and reinforcement. On 17th January the surrender of the last Axis garrison in the Egyptian frontier defences ended the long epilogue of the *Crusader* battle.

*   *   *   *   *

The Commander-in-Chief, Middle East, General Sir Claude Auchinleck, now found himself caught in a series of interlocking dilemmas. Like O'Connor a year before, and Montgomery a year after, he recognised that to drive the enemy to Agheila was only a partial and unstable success. True victory lay at the end of a second march, in Tripoli. But Auchinleck faced O'Connor's difficulties without Montgomery's advantages. In O'Connor's time it had been

Greece that had bled the desert forces into weakness and into the
defensive on indefensible ground. Now it was the Far East. On
8th December, 1941, Britain had declared war on Japan. On 12th
December, while Rommel was still standing stubbornly at Gazala,
the Prime Minister had informed Auchinleck that reinforcements
of two divisions, four light-bomber squadrons and a consignment
of anti-tank guns destined for him must be diverted to the Far
East. At the same time as Auchinleck was thus weakened, his
command was extended to include Iraq and Persia and the troops
already there; he was now responsible for the northern defence of
the Persian Gulf oil fields in the event of a Russian collapse in the
Caucasus. Two days after Eighth Army entered Benghazi, Auchin-
leck had learned from the Prime Minister that he was also to lose
four fighter squadrons to the Far East; he was asked to send a
hundred Stuart tanks. The Commander-in-Chief, with an Indian
soldier's appreciation of the dangers of Japanese success, offered fifty
light tanks and a hundred and ten Stuarts, organised and manned as
a complete armoured brigade group. Auchinleck's loss of strength
went on: 6th and 7th Australian Divisions were despatched hastily
eastwards, while some tanks had to go to Malta where invasion was
now expected.

For Auchinleck therefore in January, 1942, the prospects for a
renewed offensive against Rommel and into Tripolitania were
dubious. There were neither troops nor transport to prepare for a
fresh advance and at the same time establish a firm base and
balanced dispositions for the repulse of a German counter-stroke.
However, the elimination of the Axis from North Africa was a
tremendous strategic prize, opening the way either for a blow at
Italy or for massive reinforcement of the Far East. Auchinleck was
not afraid of risk; like Wavell he commanded at a time when there
were no certainties for a soldier. His intelligence staff in Cairo were
absolutely sure that no reinforcements had reached or could reach
Rommel in time for him to anticipate our renewed offensive.
Auchinleck therefore decided to attack Rommel at El Agheila as
soon as possible.

There remained for him the matter of the command of Eighth
Army. The *Crusader* battle being over, it was time to end Ritchie's
temporary appointment and ask for an army commander of appro-
priate talents and seniority from England. But this was now not
so easy. When the Prime Minister had announced Ritchie's appoint-
ment on December 11th, 1941, he did not say that it was temporary.
Ritchie was thus accepted by press and public as the new *permanent*

British desert leader; the man who had carried *Crusader* to a triumphant conclusion. How could Auchinleck now send him back to Cairo without serious effects on morale and on public opinion? Even on strictly military grounds, Ritchie seemed well-established and successful. Of his conduct of the second half of *Crusader*, Auchinleck wrote later, "I was satisfied with Ritchie." He had shown the vigour, self-confidence and emotional stability required for high command; his record on the staff was good. It might be better to leave him where he was. He had, after all, experienced corps commanders to advise him, and in the event of real difficulty, the Commander-in-Chief himself could intervene.

So Ritchie stayed on. There was, perhaps, a subtler, personal reason for Auchinleck's decision. He had enjoyed his ten days of battle during *Crusader*; pitting his wits and will against an enemy in the field was a richer professional experience than the military diplomacy that was the lot of modern commanders-in-chief. With Ritchie, his old staff officer, as a kind of proxy he could retain a close interest and control in the Western Desert battles while commanding in chief in Cairo. This arrangement had worked well in the closing stages of *Crusader*; why not in the future?

The decision to retain Ritchie as Eighth Army commander after *Crusader* was Auchinleck's second great error of judgment in the Middle East. Like his first—the appointment of Cunningham—it stemmed, in General Galloway's words, "from his inability coldly to consider whether a man was really up to the job". Auchinleck's judgments of professional ability were too often coloured by his personal liking for the person concerned. His warm-heartedness and his sense of loyalty as a man sometimes betrayed him as a general.

For Ritchie himself the real test—and opportunity—lay ahead; *Crusader*, after all, had been another man's battle. He set to work to prepare Eighth Army for an offensive into Tripolitania; magazines and workshops in the forward area, supply routes from Benghazi and Tobruk. He was strongly advised to prepare a defence system at Gazala in case Rommel should move first. Resting on the categorical assurances of G.H.Q. intelligence that Rommel was not being reinforced, Ritchie refused.

I was told [said General Sir Frank Messervy, now temporarily commanding 1st Armoured Division before El Agheila, in the place of Lumsden, who had been wounded] that my role was to reconnoitre and make every sort of preparation possible for a further major offensive. General Headquarters wouldn't believe there were large German tank reinforcements—which infuriated the forward troops who had actually seen them. That was why we were on the wrong foot when he advanced.

These reinforcements had arrived in two convoys escorted by Italian battleships, which had been able to move freely in the Central Mediterranean since the British Force K, based on Malta, had been sunk in mid-December. On 12th January, 1941, Rommel held a conference at his headquarters on the possibility of an early counter-stroke. German intelligence, through wireless intercepts, was able to give him an accurate account of the British order of battle in Cyrenaica. In the forward area was 1st Armoured Division, trained under Alan Brooke's direction as C.-in-C. Home Forces and fresh from England (the British seemed to fight the war with relays of green troops); near Benghazi was the 4th Indian Division; 7th Armoured Division was as far away as Tobruk. The whereabouts of 1st South African, 2nd New Zealand and 70th British divisions were not known, except that they were out of the forward area. Rommel could put in the field a hundred and seventeen German tanks (including light tanks) and seventy-nine Italian, against a hundred and fifty gun-armed tanks in 1st Armoured Division.

In the evening of 21st January, 1941, he began one of his most brilliant displays of military agility and opportunism. He advanced in two columns, one on the Via Balbia and one inland through the desert. British forward troops fell back or were over-run. Wireless intercepts informed Rommel correctly that the bulk of 1st Armoured Division under Messervy lay east of Agedabia. He decided to shift his weight to the coast road, drive through Agedabia and get between Messervy and Benghazi. Many of Rommel's tanks were now stranded through lack of fuel, but as usual he used time as a weapon with which to belabour the slow British. He personally led the remaining mobile group of his command, Group Marcks, on a race into Agedabia (taken on 22nd January) and on towards Antelat and Saunnu.

To Ritchie, in his headquarters at Tmimi, Rommel's advance presented itself as a reconnaissance in strength that would be followed by retirement next day. However, Antelat and Saunnu fell; Rommel now issued orders for the complete encirclement of 1st Armoured Division. The attempt, made on 23rd January, failed because of a "serious lapse of staff work" at Afrika Korps Headquarters by which 21st Panzer did not occupy the Saunnu area until some time after Group Marcks had moved away to close the ring

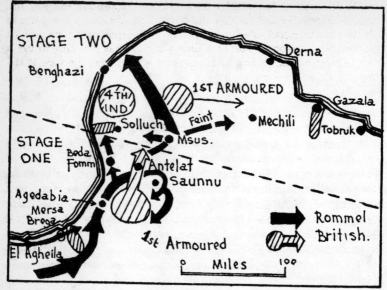

MAP 10. ROMMEL RETAKES WESTERN CYRENAICA
January–February 1942

round 1st Armoured on the east. The bulk of 1st Armoured retreated through this gap at Saunnu in some disorder and not without heavy loss. "There were petrol echelons, workshops, supply lorries of all kinds streaming past at full speed in disorderly array like a hunting field," said a British account.

The rout worsened next day as Rommel swept on with matchless dynamism. Six miles north of Saunnu he smashed a large force of British tanks; in the words of a German staff officer:

> These were overwhelmed by Panzer Regiment 8, closely supported by anti-tank guns and artillery; it soon became apparent that the British tank units had no battle experience and they were completely demoralised by the onslaught of 15th Panzer. At times the pursuit attained a speed of fifteen miles an hour, and the British fled madly over the desert in one of the most extraordinary routs of the war.

By the end of the day Rommel was in Msus, and considering a leap to Mechili. First Armoured Division had disintegrated. It said little for their training in England. Ritchie received this flabbergasting news with a combination of stubbornness and indecision. In General Messervy's words,

Ritchie was all haywire by then. All for counter-attacking in this direction one day and another the next. Optimistic and trying not to believe that we had taken a knock. When I reported the state of 1st Armoured Division to him at a time when he was planning to use it for counter-attack, he flew to see me and almost took the view that I was being subversive.

It was Ritchie's first battle crisis and it had occurred only a month after he had been 'pitchforked' into his first command for twenty years. He was not properly equipped to cope with it. He understood now the difference between coolly working out appreciations for other men to act upon, and thinking on your feet at Rommel's speed while your army waited for its orders. It was the difference between walking a plank placed on a drawing-room carpet, and the same plank placed over a two-hundred-foot crevasse. It is not surprising that General Godwin-Austen, 13th Corps, which included both 1st Armoured and 4th Indian Divisions, noted that Ritchie had "a great air of decisiveness, yet was really rather indecisive".

Upon receiving reports of Rommel's advance Auchinleck flew up to "hold Ritchie's hand". Although he now provided sureness of control, Auchinleck also was outwitted by the brilliance of Rommel's manœuvres, which here raised the German commander to the level of Marlborough or Napoleon. Rommel lay at Msus, where he equally threatened Benghazi or, through Mechili and Gazala, Eighth Army's communications with Egypt. Which way would he go? This was one question. There was another: the true strengths of the opposing forces. Remembering the early days of *Crusader* both Ritchie and Auchinleck were inclined to doubt the stories of rout and disintegration that reached them, and to underestimate Axis strength. Godwin-Austen, on the other hand, who was the last man to become flustered or alarmed, had no doubt that if we were to extricate ourselves from a fast-closing trap, both divisions of his corps must fall back on Derna, 4th Indian on the coast from Benghazi through Barce, 1st Armoured Division (now a wreck) via Mechili. When asked by Ritchie for advice, he therefore recommended a general withdrawal. Ritchie consented, and Godwin-Austen issued orders accordingly. Nevertheless, in Godwin-Austen's words, Ritchie "had a tendency to ask your advice and having received it act in the opposite way". In another flush of optimism he decided to fight for Benghazi, countermanded Godwin-Austen's orders and began to issue tactical orders directly to 4th Indian Division. "I approved of this change of plan," wrote Auchinleck later. Ritchie now tried to prepare a counter-stroke by both divisions of 13th Corps against the Germans at Msus.

On the map it was the right thing to do, but the balance of forces made it quite unreal. It was anticipated by a further display of brilliant manœuvre by Rommel. On 27th January he feinted towards Mechili, and tricked both Ritchie and Auchinleck into moving their armour to the east, thus uncovering Benghazi and 4th Indian Division. With his characteristic agility Rommel changed his direction, lunged to the coast and cut off the Indians. Gallantry, as so often in the history of British arms, redeemed error; and the Indians cut their way out, with insignificant loss. Benghazi fell on 29th January with the enormous quantities of stores and petrol built up for the British invasion of Tripolitania. As Rommel entered the ruined town he received Mussolini's signal authorising him to advance to it. At last convinced of the reality of the danger, Auchinleck and Ritchie led Eighth Army back to Gazala, reached on 4th February. For a time, a retreat to the Egyptian frontier seemed to them a possibility. Rommel, now a Colonel-General, followed with light forces, having outrun his supplies.

The uncertainty of Ritchie's leadership in the last fortnight led to one further result: Godwin-Austen asked Auchinleck to relieve him of his command, "as he felt," in Auchinleck's words, "that General Ritchie had displayed a lack of confidence in him by issuing orders directly to his subordinate commanders". Auchinleck, as he had to do, upheld his army commander, and Eighth Army lost an able, strong general and a much-loved man.

The campaign had once more come to rest. Eighth Army at Gazala and *Panzergruppe Afrika* round Tmimi settled down to a long period of tedious preparation and training. It was time for Auchinleck to think again about Ritchie's continuance as Eighth Army commander. He had his doubts now. He ordered Brigadier Dorman-Smith, who had remained commandant of the Haifa Staff College since Wavell's time, to visit Eighth Army, ostensibly to check on staff techniques, but actually to take the pulse of the Army and to sound divisional commanders as to their opinions about recent operations. On 16th February, Dorman-Smith arrived at Eighth Army and began his tour. He found general dissatisfaction among higher commanders at Ritchie's leadership, and a loose and amateurish approach to organisation and tactics in which slang words like 'swanning', 'boxes' and 'jock-cols' had become charged with tactical significance. On his return to Cairo, Dorman-Smith talked also to Godwin-Austen and learned fully what had lain behind his request for relief.

Auchinleck invited Dorman-Smith to join him in a picnic on the shores of Lake Fayoum, where they could talk freely and privately. They were old intimates. Dorman-Smith had been Director of Military Training in India when Auchinleck was Deputy Chief of the General Staff. They had worked very closely together on the modernisation of the Indian Army.

Upon the results of this picnic for two depended the course of the next six months of the war in the Middle East. It took place on 1st March, 1942. The day was cold and the scene depressing: the large, sluggish lake overlooked from the north by a line of desert cliffs, and bordered on the south by the allotments and ditches of the Egyptian countryside. Here the cars were stopped. Dorman-Smith told Auchinleck exactly what he had found in Eighth Army. He said that Ritchie was "not sufficiently quick-witted or imaginative enough for that command". He strongly recommended to Auchinleck that Ritchie should be replaced. Dorman-Smith therefore suggested that Ritchie should return to Cairo as Deputy Chief of the General Staff, and London should be asked to find a successor. Auchinleck was deeply perturbed. He replied to Dorman-Smith:

"I have already sacked one army commander. To sack another within three months would have effects on morale."

Personal motives, partly unconscious, distorted Auchinleck's sight of the bleak prospect of public interest. He was a simple man with old-fashioned principles of straightforwardness and plain-dealing. He liked subordinates who appeared to him open and trustworthy. These qualities he knew Ritchie to have. What kind of an army commander would London send him? He had had experience in England of unprincipled intrigue by ambitious subordinates. When the next battle in the desert opened, he could reason, Ritchie would have had time to settle in and master his job; so far as tactics and organisation were concerned he, Auchinleck, could supervise him closely.

So Ritchie stayed on. This decision, proceeding from a flaw in the character of a great man, was to prove a disaster to Auchinleck, Ritchie and Dorman-Smith, and nearly so to the Middle East.

CHAPTER TWO

From February to May, 1942, the armies rested motionless in the gravel wastes of Gazala. For the troops the long days stretched full of boredom and discomfort. There was nothing to interest the eye but the blank swell of the brown desert; nothing to do but lay mines, dig fox-holes and uncoil wire under a sun that grew ever more fierce; nowhere to go but the sea, in a bouncing three-tonner full of whirling sand, for a weekly bathe. A gallon of water a man per day served for drinking—connoisseurs alleged they would tell the difference between Buq Buq or Sidi Barrani or Bardia water—making tea and washing. Petrol was therefore often used for laundry. Sweat and dust permanently stifled the skin, and started desert sores. The flies clung in dense, lazy constellations. The coolest place was inside a tank. Behind the army, the three-tonners pitched perpetually in line ahead from horizon to horizon as they brought up petrol, food, ammunition, cigarettes, mail and Naafi stores. Although on the move, it was not much more enlivening to be a truck driver: day after day they sat over their hot engines, driving for twelve hours in second gear over the vacant desert, naked feet pressing the accelerator to the floorboard.

While the army made the best of its boredom, its senior commanders were digesting the lessons of the mobile battles of the winter. They had apparently learned much, not only from the Germans, but from their own mistakes. General Gott's report on 7th Armoured Division operations in *Crusader* stated that

> tanks require the support of Field Artillery, Anti-Tank guns, and Motor Infantry. The higher proportion of these supporting arms to actual tanks in his Panzer Divisions gave the German a distinct advantage—To our own tanks, the value of good support from 25-pounders was demonstrated time and time again—Therefore, it would appear that in the future the Armoured Brigade Group should take the place of the Armoured Brigade.

The Commander-in-Chief, General Auchinleck, agreed that the basic ideas and organisation of our armour in *Crusader* had been proved unsound: and he set about a radical re-organisation of the British armoured forces for which he has never received general credit.

> It seemed to me [he wrote later] that our pre-war divisional organisation was too rigid and lacking in flexibility to be really adaptable to the conditions of modern quick-moving warfare in the Desert, or even elsewhere . . .

In particular the British practice of large armoured divisions strong in tanks and weak in infantry and other arms was wrong; it encouraged the idea that the armour was an 'army-within-an-army'. He was also worried by the parochialism of spirit caused by the ancient prides of regimental tradition. Auchinleck therefore broke down the division (whether armoured, motorised or infantry) into self-contained brigade groups with their own artillery and engineers. These groups remained under the command of the divisional general. In the case of the armoured divisions, he replaced the two armoured brigades and a support group by a single armoured brigade group and two lorried infantry brigade groups. This organisation (with one lorried infantry brigade) later became standard throughout the British army.

These changes were intended to coerce the separate arms of the British service into thinking and working together in the German style. They were reinforced by a radical overhaul of the training system in the Middle East: Auchinleck created the post of Director of Military Training, and appointed to it Major-General Harding (now Field Marshal Lord Harding), who had been O'Connor's Brigadier General Staff. Thus, between one battle and another, Auchinleck attempted to repair the reckless conservatism of twenty years. But was there time to change the habits of minds long trained to the static and rigid?

* * * * *

On 26th February, the Prime Minister was writing again: what were Auchinleck's intentions in the Desert? A detailed memorandum gave the answer; Auchinleck was determined not to embark on another ill-prepared offensive like *Crusader*, with poor equipment and an untrained army thrown hastily together. He would attack when his reforms in training, organisation and tactics had been thoroughly completed, and when he had a superiority of three to two over the Germans in armour. This superiority he considered was the minimum necessary to make up for the Germans' greater experience and superior equipment. Given his commitments to the Northern Front (Turkey, Iraq, Persia, the Caucasus), Auchinleck did not think he could launch an offensive until 1st May, 1942 at the earliest.

Auchinleck also informed London that in the event of a German offensive:

> I was determined not to allow Tobruk to be besieged a second time ... I did not consider I could afford to lock up one and a half divisions in a fortress. Admiral Cunningham agreed, particularly since the siege had proved so costly in ships, and so did Air Chief Marshal Tedder, who doubted whether he had sufficient aircraft to provide aircover.

Auchinleck later hinted that the offensive might be postponed because of delays in completing the railhead and dump at Bel-hammed.

Churchill was not satisfied; telegrams rained on Cairo throughout March, April and May.

> The P.M. for the biggest possible political reasons

said Auchinleck later with a reverberating reticence

> realised the tremendous desirability of beating Rommel at the earliest possible moment. The Command in the Middle East realised it just as much, but it was their duty to relate this to the resources available.

The new Director of Military Intelligence in Cairo, Brigadier de Guingand, considered "that in this case the Commander-in-Chief was pressed too hard, and as one who was in daily and intimate contact with him, I noticed that he was feeling the strain of fighting this battle in order to give his own troops a fair chance". The battle culminated in a letter from Churchill to Auchinleck on May 10th ordering him to attack in June, or resign. The Prime Minister also suggested that Auchinleck should take personal command of Eighth Army during the coming battle; this Auchinleck was unable to do because of his responsibility as C.-in-C. for the whole of the Middle East and especially the threatened northern front.

On the German side, Rommel had political troubles of an exactly opposite kind. Conscious of the superiority of his troops and equipment, he wished to seek a great victory in North Africa; but he needed extra troops and air support. The German High Command however was not interested in North Africa, it was interested in Russia. When Rommel flew to the Fuehrer's headquarters in March, it was agreed that there should be a combined German and Italian invasion of Malta during the first June full-moon period, after heavy Luftwaffe bombing. At the end of April there was another meeting, at Obersalzburg, between Hitler, Mussolini, Rommel, Kesselring (German Commander-in-Chief, South) and Cavallero, chief of the Italian *Commando Supremo*. Rommel argued in favour of an offensive in Libya in May with the object of taking Tobruk. If the attack on Malta could not take place before June, he wanted his own offensive to come first. He pointed out that the British were preparing their own desert offensive. Hitler and Mussolini agreed to allow Rommel to advance in May, but once Tobruk had fallen, he was to stand on the defensive and release air support in favour of the attack on Malta.

Between February and May 1942 Ritchie had been developing the Gazala area both as the springboard of an offensive and as the defence of Tobruk and Eastern Cyrenaica. This ambivalence was to prove damaging in the defensive battles that followed, for the presence of the huge dumps at Belhammed and Tobruk cramped the mental and physical freedom of manoeuvre of the British armour. When in mid-May Ritchie learned that his offensive was certain to be anticipated by Rommel, he concentrated his efforts solely on the preparation of his army and the Gazala defences for a defensive battle. His final dispositions betray alike his own unoriginality and the inadequacy of the military tradition in which he had been trained. These were, in brief, an attempt to set down in the desert a linear fixed defence (in some depth) full of infantry and guns, with a reserve of armour held behind it, just as if Eighth Army were fighting in France amid rivers and other natural features, and with another army on its flank.

From Gazala on the coast to Bir Hacheim there was a continuous 'mine marsh', within which were 'boxes' or independent strongholds of guns and infantry. The right flank of this line, on the coast, was held by 1st South African Division and 50th (British) Division (Major-General W. H. Ramsden), whose front extended as far south as the Sidi Muftah box. In Tobruk itself (now of course a fortress in dereliction) was 2nd South African Division. These troops were grouped under 13th Corps (General W. H. E. Gott). The left flank of the Gazala line, including the fortress of Bir Hacheim (Koenig's

Free French Brigade) and the armoured mass of manoeuvre was commanded by Lieutenant-General Willoughby Norrie (30th Corps). Some depth was given to these defences by further isolated boxes at Knightsbridge, Acroma, El Adem and Bir Gubi.

The organisation and layout of Eighth Army showed little understanding of the nature of mobile, mechanised desert war; an imperfect appreciation of the lessons of two campaigns. They marked a regression of twenty years from O'Connor's defensive dispositions at

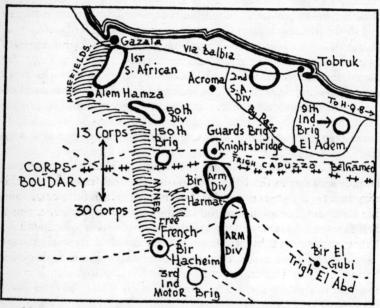

MAP 11. RITCHIE'S FORWARD AND DISPERSED DISPOSITIONS
26 May 1942

Mersa Matruh against Graziani. O'Connor had held his forces sixty miles behind the line of his forward patrols, protected thereby from surprise and sudden shock. His men were not pegged out on the ground in any kind of fixed defence, but kept on wheels and tracks so that they could manoeuvre freely in any direction. They were organised in loose, fluid, flexible groups. There was no attempt to form a front to the enemy. Ritchie on the other hand had placed the main bulk of his army in his forward area, wrapped up as gifts to Rommel in those 'boxes.' The first sixty miles of a German advance through the desert south of Bir Hacheim would take Rommel deep into Ritchie's rear: Ritchie thus invited surprise and an early decisive clash. He also repeated the error of the *Crusader* plan whereby the army fought in two halves: the mobile armour, and the static infantry and guns. The infantry would watch helplessly from their boxes while the armour won—or lost—its encounter battle with Rommel.

The static and rigid cast of mind of the Eighth Army command is particularly demonstrated by the division of responsibility between the two corps. Given Ritchie's compartmental conception of a fixed defence zone and a mobile mass of manoeuvre, it would have seemed that the logical division of responsibility was to allot all the fixed defences and infantry to 13th Corps and the mobile forces and armour to 30th Corps. This is what Auchinleck strongly recommended to him. Ritchie however simply drew a corps boundary along the map and allotted the Gazala defences north of it to Gott and south of it to Norrie, who in addition commanded all the armour. This was the orthodox way, the way in which Ritchie and all his contemporaries had been trained, the static rather than the dynamic; to extemporise other solutions required the creative genius of a man like O'Connor.

There were, however, serious weaknesses in Ritchie's dispositions considered even in the light of old-fashioned and 'non-desert' military practice. Between Sidi-Muftah, on the British left centre, and Bir Hacheim, the anchor of the left flank of the Gazala line, was a stretch of mine-marsh twenty miles long that was not defended by boxes, nor covered by gun-fire. Ritchie believed the mines were enough. His other major error lay in the failure to concentrate his mobile forces. Thirtieth Corps lay stretched all over the desert between Knightsbridge, Bir Hacheim and Bir Gubi. To the south of Bir Hacheim were 7th Motor Brigade and 3rd Indian Motor Brigade, not together. These formations were too strong for reconnaissance, too weak for an effective delaying action. Fourth Armoured Brigade lay east of Bir Hacheim; 22nd Armoured Brigade by Knightsbridge. There was a danger therefore that a swift advance by German armour would plough successively through each scattered brigade of 30th Corps.

In Cairo, Auchinleck saw this danger and wrote to Ritchie about it on 20th May. He advised him to place both British armoured divisions (7th and 1st) well concentrated and well northwards astride the Trigh Capuzzo. British intelligence staff (in Cairo) strongly believed that Rommel would attack the Gazala line frontally between the coast road and the Trigh Capuzzo in an attempt to break through straight on Tobruk. An alternative, which intelligence considered highly unlikely, lay in a flanking movement south of Bir Hacheim: *Crusader* in reverse. Auchinleck's suggested placing of the armour would either cover a direct attack on Tobruk, or, should Rommel march by Bir Hacheim, would force the Germans to come a long way for a decisive battle, thus giving Eighth Army ample guard against surprise and straining the German supply system. Auchinleck emphasised to Ritchie that the British armour must not fight in bits and pieces:

> They have been trained to fight as divisions, I hope, and fight as divisions they should. Norrie must handle them as a Corps Commander, and thus be able to take advantage of the flexibility which the fact of having two formations gives him.

This sound advice was not implemented by Ritchie, with the result, in the words of a German account, that "his armoured brigades were committed to battle one after the other, and neither corps nor divisional headquarters had any control over the fighting." The reason for Ritchie's disdain for Auchinleck's freely proffered advice perhaps lay in his personal situation as Army Commander.

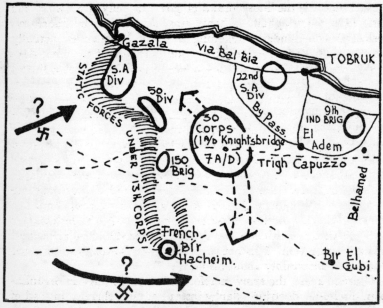

MAP 12. DISPOSITIONS SUGGESTED BY AUCHINLECK IN LETTER OF 20 MAY 1942

He had now, in May, 1942, held the post for six months. However, his reputation with the army and especially its senior commanders had risen no higher, and his grip both of policy and of his subordinates was still very uncertain. Under Ritchie, Eighth Army was presided over, not led. He remained a paradox—an impressive man who impressed very few. General W. H. Ramsden, commanding 50th Division, found him "a fine robust-looking man with charm and manner; but no aurora". General Messervy, now commanding 7th Armoured Division, noted like Godwin-Austen months earlier that he was "confident and decisive in his speech, but one did not always feel he was quite so confident and decisive in his mind". This profound doubt as to Ritchie's intellectual and personal grasp of war in the desert did not prevent his subordinates liking and admiring him as a man. Messervy summed up the general feeling:

> He was an absolutely honest, downright soldier who was put into a position which at the time was beyond his capacity. Although he had leadership and powers of command, he was thrown into a very difficult position before he had had time to develop methods of command.

This was exact and just. Ritchie did his best, but, as the French proverb has it, the most beautiful girl can only give what she has. Like Cunningham, Ritchie was surrounded by more experienced commanders, including a corps commander actually senior to him. There was Gott, the lone survivor of the great days of Western Desert Force, already a legend in the desert as a British 'Rommel' tirelessly roaming the battlefield to rally and drive on shaken troops, a man of immense prestige. There was Willoughby Norrie, who had been commanding an armoured division when Ritchie was a colonel, and who had behind him the experience of fighting the *Crusader* battle. His knowledge of armour, lately acquired though it was, far outstripped Ritchie's. His too was a strong personality: urbane, cool, easy, he wore his ability, as a gentleman should, slightly carelessly. If he proffered advice on the placing or handling of armour, it might be difficult for a green army commander to refuse it. Caught therefore between Norrie, Gott, Auchinleck and his own inexperience, Ritchie was delicately placed and independence was not easily won. It is not surprising that Dorman-Smith noted "an air of uncertainty about his face".

Courage apart, the army therefore suffered. It was—in organisation, discipline, doctrine—flabby instead of taut, sluggish instead of agile. There was a tendency to plan, and later to fight, private battles. For example, Ritchie himself considered that Rommel might attack in one of three directions: along the coast road, along the Trigh Capuzzo, or round Bir Hacheim, with Tobruk as the objective in each case. Two of these possibilities fell in the 30th Corps area. But Norrie believed there was a third possibility on his front: an attack through the twenty-mile gap (mined) between Sidi Muftah and Bir Hacheim. He therefore planned for this as well. Yet Ritchie never knew it.

In fact, Rommel intended to pass all his mobile forces round Bir Hacheim, fight and win a battle, and drive on Tobruk. It was the *Crusader* plan in reverse; but in other senses than geographical. Whereas *Crusader* had been planned in great detail, in the British manner, Rommel took Moltke's view that "no plan survives contact with the enemy". If his plan got him into battle, it was enough. After that, Rommel would fight by ear and eye and tactical sense, like a duellist. He entered the Gazala battle with a total of five hundred and sixty-one German and Italian tanks of all kinds. But his principal weapon lay in his two hundred and eighty German medium tanks. However, except for nineteen Mark III Specials, these were completely outclassed in guns and armour by the one hundred and sixty-seven American Grants that now formed the back-bone of the British armour, which numbered altogether some eight hundred and fifty tanks. The Grants carried their magnificent 75 mm. gun in the hull of the tank: the gun had therefore a very limited traverse, and could not fire from a hull-down position. Apart from the Grants, the British possessed a mixture of British-made 2-pounder Crusaders and American Stuarts. The British apparently enjoyed a qualitative as well as a quantitive superiority on the basis of armour and guns alone. But the British-made tanks forming the majority of Eighth Army's equipment were unreliable, partly owing to poor maintenance, and had a short track mileage. This was a major worry to Ritchie, because it limited training. In anti-tank artillery, which the Germans used as an offensive weapon, Rommel had a crushing superiority, for both his 50 mm. and the new, captured Russian 76 mm. guns were better than the British 2-pounders, whose solid shot could not pierce the armour of the latest German tanks. New 6-pounder anti-tank guns were on their way to the Middle East, but so far Eighth Army had received only enough to equip the lorried infantry brigades and motor battalions, and not in time to allow training in their use. Rommel also had his magnificent 88's; the British still would not use their 3.7-inch anti-aircraft gun in an anti-tank role.

During the latter half of May, 1942, G.H.Q. Cairo intelligence had warned Eighth Army that a German attack was imminent. In view of the proven wild inaccuracy of G.H.Q. intelligence over the past eighteen months, this information, in the absence of evidence from patrols, was widely disbelieved. However, there was now a new Director of Military Intelligence (de Guingand) and a new, reliable source of information in the Axis camp.

On 26th May, 1942, about half-past three in the afternoon, Eighth Army armoured cars reported by wireless a forward movement of much German transport. This information was passed by 7th Motor Brigade to 7th Armoured Division and 30th Corps by telephone. Thereafter the armoured cars radioed back Rommel's positions and strength at half-hourly intervals: fifty-two messages between 1530 hours on 26th May and 0700 hours next morning. At 2130 hours on 26th May, the presence of panzer divisions had been identified. None of this information reached the various units of 30th Corps, because a constant wireless watch was not ordered either by 7th Armoured Division or 30th Corps—that is, the subordinate formations were not ordered to listen to the armoured cars' radio messages. The information, sent on by 7th Motor Brigade by telephone, apparently only reached 30th Corps and 7th Armoured headquarters. Later, when 7th Motor Brigade had to retire before Rommel's advance and itself use wireless instead of telephone, a constant wireless watch was still not ordered, and Eighth Army still lay in ignorance.

Ritchie himself remained as ignorant as the units spreadeagled in Rommel's path. He concluded in the middle of the afternoon of 26th May that the German offensive was under way, but had no idea of its direction.

Under brilliant moonlight, in a planetary silence, *Panzerarmee Afrika* rolled towards Bir Hacheim, lit now by Luftwaffe flares. Brigadier (now General) Renton of 7th Motor Brigade went on trying to rouse his division and corps. During that night he gained the impression that they thought he was "a bit panicky in reporting the enemy advance and withdrawing before it, as they were both convinced the attack was going to come in from the North".

General Messervy, of 7th Armoured Division, now avers that in fact he was not so convinced:

At a 30th Corps conference with Norrie [some time previously], we were all asked our opinions as to the direction of Rommel's coming offensive. I gave it as mine that Rommel would come round our left flank, and that therefore we should dispose the armour to fight as a corps and not piecemeal. Lumsden (1st Armoured Division), Ritchie and Gott thought it was impossible to come round the left flank; he would try and break through our centre. Therefore the eventual disposition was 7th Armoured Division on the left and the other armoured division miles away on the northern flank—the idea being that when Rommel did attack, and his direction known, there would be time to concentrate.

Messervy therefore accepted Renton's messages as proof of a major German attack:

> I reported them to corps, asking permission to take up our battle stations which had been planned in case of an attack from the left flank. But this was refused by Norrie, who wanted to wait until Rommel's main blow was known. By morning it was too late . . .

In the small hours of 26th/27th May, 1942, therefore, voices were raised in urgent argument along the British field telephone wires as Rommel, with five hundred tanks behind his armoured car, drove towards Bir Hacheim. But the arguments accomplished nothing: Eighth Army did not move.

At half-past six in the morning of 27th May the *Panzerarmee* was level with Bir Hacheim and beginning to swing north towards Tobruk. The next intimation of Rommel's advance received by Eighth Army was more urgent than a radio report. In the unfinished Retma box the garrison breakfasted late and leisurely among piles of unlaid mines, enjoying a glorious May morning. A few days before it had been rumoured that a *British* offensive was in the offing but that it was unlikely that Rommel would attack. Between Retma box and 7th Armoured Division H.Q. there was a direct telephone line, but no message came down it about the German advance. An air of pleasant relaxation held the Retma garrison.

> Then [in the words of an eye-witness] some gunner started banging away like mad. Thinking it was trigger-happiness, I was about to have it stopped, when we saw something moving in the desert away to the south, about four miles off. It was the whole of Rommel's command in full cry straight for us.

Bir Gubi, east of Retma, was the rallying or pivoting point of Renton's 7th Motor Brigade. When he arrived there he found that 7th Armoured Division headquarters had given permission for half the garrison to go to Tobruk for a swim. There were not enough of them left to fire all the guns.

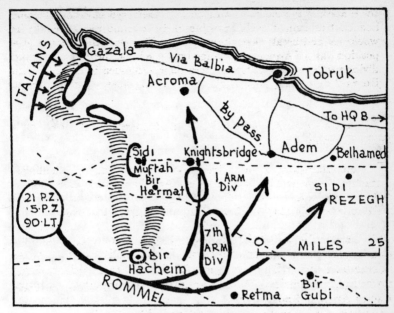

MAP 13. GAZALA BATTLES 1942
Phase A, 27–28 May

Rommel swept on and over and through 7th Motor Brigade and 3rd Indian Motor Brigade. Next in his path, like a township in line for a tornado, was 4th Armoured Brigade.

News of the massacre of 3rd Indian Motor Brigade and the scattering of 7th Motor Brigade now reached Ritchie at Gambut and told him, with a shock like a sudden blow in the kidneys, that the great German offensive had already arrived, from the wrong direction, and before Ritchie's army had been alerted and posted in its battle stations. Now Norrie too was convinced about Rommel's intentions. All over the sunlit morning desert the units of 30th Corps scrambled to get themselves on wheels and tracks. But it was now too late to concentrate in the prepared defensive stations, and as General Messervy put it, "it became an awful muck of a battle. The armour never really recovered its poise."

Fourth Armoured Brigade was caught by 15th Panzer while still readying itself for a move; it lost heavily in tanks and its command organisation was wrecked. Rommel drove on to the north. General Messervy himself was surprised by the headlong speed of Rommel's advance: he and his divisional headquarters were caught, overrun and scattered by the Afrika Korps. Messervy was taken prisoner. By mid-morning of 27th May, 1942, 7th Armoured Division was no longer a coherent fighting force. Its men fought as they had in *Crusader*, blindly and instinctively; shooting Germans wherever they could. Norrie and 30th Corps knew nothing of the disaster to 7th Armoured Division, for with the capture of its headquarters there was no one to tell him. A silence walled him—and Ritchie—off from events at the battlefront. Rommel was clearly moving at some speed, however, and Norrie and 30th Corps headquarters removed to the shelter of the El Adem box; this move, made in haste, further loosened the cohesion of the corps. Norrie ordered 22nd Armoured Brigade to drive southwards to support 4th Armoured Brigade; he did not know that the 4th had been already shattered. Before 22nd Armoured Brigade could move Rommel drove into it in a whirling cloud of dust and gunfire. The brigade, surprised, was also thrown into disorder. However, it fought hard all the way back to Knightsbridge, the box behind the centre of the Gazala line that controlled the cross-roads of important tracks.

In the Gazala defences, news of Rommel's storming advance behind them had now arrived. General 'Strafer' Gott rang up Ramsden (50th Division) and said: "There's bad news on the blower from the south." It was Ramsden's first knowledge that any kind of German advance was under way. He went out to the rear of his position and through glasses saw packed German transport near Knightsbridge.

At Gambut, Ritchie spent a hot and anxious time. In the absence of accurate up-to-date reports he was not merely unable to control the battle, he was unable even to picture clearly what was going on. Meanwhile the instinctive courage of the British troops saved the day. Without any very definite plan, they closed through the smoke, dust and heat haze on to Rommel's columns and fought them to a standstill. The heavy Grants, in battle for the first time, shook the German tank crews. Fresh armoured brigades unknown to German intelligence joined the fight. Rommel and his commanders began to be anxious; the British armour, supposedly destroyed in the morning, was fighting with a violence never seen before. Their blind advances were now falling into a wide gap that existed between Rommel's armour at Knightsbridge and his supply trucks at Bir el Harmat. When night fell, Rommel's as well as Ritchie's battle was slipping out of control. He had achieved none of his objectives and he lay almost out of petrol far behind the British defences open to a counter-stroke. If the British armour had received him in their ordained battle stations, as a corps, Rommel would undoubtedly have been as decisively beaten that day as he was to be at Alam Halfa. Even now prudence suggested that he should retreat to secure his communications. Characteristically he opted for another attempt to break through to Tobruk.

It was the moment for a prompt rupturing British counter-stroke. However, it was only on the morning of 28th May, when such a counter-stroke should have been under way, that Ritchie learned of the wreck of 7th Armoured Division and the dislocation of 30th Corps. For a time he could not believe the accuracy of the reports: it was the first example in this battle of his stubborn optimism. With Ritchie's knowledge twenty-four hours behind events no swift British counter-action could be expected, especially in view of the state of 30th Corps.

During another day of fragmentary fighting, Rommel pushed on further into danger: Afrika Korps beyond Knightsbridge towards the coast, 90th Light Division near El Adem. Far behind at Bir el Harmat lay the Italian 20th Corps and all Rommel's supply echelons. Already, however, superiority of German skill, training and anti-tank artillery was beginning to tell in a way devastating to the morale of British troops. Once again the British found their equipment wanting. "On the second day of the battle," said General Renton afterwards, "the German armour was scattered all over the desert immobilised for want of petrol, a sitting target. But our 2-pounder anti-tank guns could not damage them."

On the third day of the battle Rommel saved his army by his personal leadership. During a *khamsin* he himself led his supply trucks up from Bir el Harmat through a gap in the British forces. By nightfall the *Panzerarmee* was concentrated and supplied. Ritchie, who by the rigid systems of British command was sitting remote from the battle in Gambut, had missed his first opportunity of winning a great victory.

Rommel now abandoned his plan of driving to the sea at Tobruk; his forces were too shaken and the long supply lines round Bir Hacheim, still held by the French, were too vulnerable. He must consolidate and re-group. His method illustrated the originality of his genius. He proposed to break through the British minefields between Sidi Muftah and Bir Hacheim from the eastern or British side in order to shorten his communications, and pull his army back into a bridge-head at the east of the gap.

This moment of disengagement and retreat was highly dangerous, but the British made no significant or co-ordinated effort to interfere.

By nightfall Rommel was in a safer position inside British minefields, in the shelter of anti-tank guns and with two cleared corridors behind him for his supply trucks. He held a bridgehead through the left centre of the Gazala line. This move was interpreted by Ritchie as a crushing German defeat. How should it be exploited?

There now began a series of wearisome and indecisive conferences between Eighth Army commanders; a series that lasted throughout the Gazala battles. "Ritchie," recalled General Messervy (who had escaped twelve hours after capture and re-joined Eighth Army), "was rather stupidly optimistic in remarks and demeanour, but uncertain beneath it all. He was always saying 'Ah, now we've got him', when it was clear we hadn't." While the British talked, Rommel was all driving energy and singleness of purpose, preparing for a second sally towards Tobruk; while the British talked, the British 150th Brigade box, controlling one of Rommel's supply corridors, was taken against bitter resistance. No real attempt was made by the British to save this commanding position. "Relief of the 150th Brigade locality (Sidi Muftah) failed because of piecemeal efforts and disorganisation of armour," wrote General Ramsden (50th Division). General Messervy said: "150th Brigade was down and out before Ritchie realised it."

Rommel now controlled the centre of the Gazala line. Bir Hacheim was completely isolated and under furious land and air attack. During 1st, 2nd and 3rd June Rommel lay in his bridgehead —'The Cauldron'—preparing his army for further attack and untroubled by the British in any way. For neither Ritchie nor his committee of senior commanders could make up their minds what to do. They could agree however that Rommel was beaten. Lumsden for example believed that Rommel's bridgehead was in fact a gap. Ritchie wrote to Auchinleck: "I am much distressed over the loss of 150th Brigade after so gallant a fight, but still consider the situation favourable to us and getting better daily." Various plans for counter-attack were pressed on Ritchie in the long, hot committee meetings: by 1st South African Division out of the Gazala line along the coast; by Briggs' 5th Indian Division round Bir Hacheim on Rommel's communications; by the armour and infantry straight on to Rommel's bridgehead. The uncertainty and slowness of British policy began to creep paralysingly through the veins of the army: General Ramsden recalls Gott returning from the conferences and saying: "I *think* Ritchie is going to do this or that."

Eventually Ritchie agreed to Briggs' idea of a drive (with motorised infantry) on to Rommel's communications. After Ritchie had left this particular meeting to go on a visit the plan was attacked, especially on administrative grounds. Another gained general acceptance—direct assault on the German bridgehead by 5th Indian Division and 22nd Armoured Brigade (Stuarts), with an army tank brigade ('I' tanks) coming in from the north. "I was put in joint command of it with Briggs," said General Messervy afterwards. "It would more normally have been under a corps commander." So much for Auchinleck's warning that Norrie must use his armour as a corps commander. General Messervy adds: "I accepted the idea (of the Cauldron attack) and thought it might come off." When Ritchie returned, the new plan was presented to him. He consented and wrote to Auchinleck: "I have decided I must crush (the enemy) in the Cauldron . . ."

This operation was the first planned and concerted move undertaken by Eighth Army in a battle now eight days old; it would be launched when Rommel had been snug in his gap in the minefields for four days. It was organised and led, not by the Army Commander, not by a corps commander, but by two divisional commanders exercising alternate control. It was delayed for further preparation for twenty-four hours.

Everyone was confident that German resistance would be easily overcome. Norrie reported to Ritchie that Messervy and Briggs "were full of beans, and happy". However the techniques of combined operations by tanks and infantry had been lost since O'Connor's time. Operation *Aberdeen* proved a shambles. The infantry went in first, at three in the morning of 5th June, 1942, under cover of darkness. They made an encouraging advance. After daylight, 22nd Armoured Brigade not having come up, the infantry were furiously counter-attacked. Then the hundred and fifty-six Stuarts (the lightest of Eighth Army tanks) of 22nd Armoured Brigade advanced three miles beyond the British infantry and were fired upon by Rommel's concentrated army artillery. They fell back behind the infantry, who were now attacked by German combined groups of all arms and massacred.

It had taken Eighth Army four days to think up *Aberdeen*; it took Rommel half a day to plan and launch a counter-stroke against *Aberdeen*'s left flank, which rested on an uncovered minefield. The German attack routed the British assault forces and captured Messervy and his headquarters for the second time. Meanwhile the northern British attack on the Cauldron was struck in the flank by 21st Panzer Division and driven into a German minefield covered by furious anti-tank fire. On the first day of *Aberdeen*, Ritchie had

lost a hundred and ten tanks. Eighth Army signalled Auchinleck
that while the operation had not been "wholly successful", there
were "signs that the enemy (was) not entirely happy."

Next day, 6th June, Messervy—who had escaped again—tried
to rescue the British forces still marooned in the Cauldron. It was
another day of marching, waiting, orders, counter-orders, cancelled
orders and piecemeal effort, ruthlessly exploited by clever German
tactics. When at last Ritchie's counter-stroke had been written off,
it had cost a hundred and sixty-eight cruiser tanks, fifty 'I' tanks,

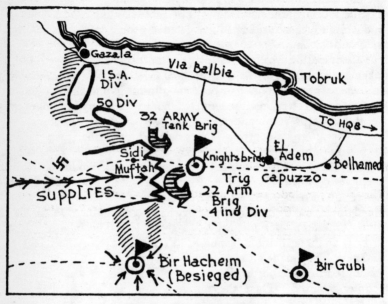

MAP 14. GAZALA BATTLES
Phase B, 31 May—5 June 1942

four regiments of artillery, an Indian brigade and 7th Armoured
Division Support Group. Yet Ritchie signalled Auchinleck that
night that, in his belief, the enemy had "suffered considerable
losses" and that "the enemy's position is not too easy".

What is the explanation of Eighth Army's apparent combination
of smugness and inertia? Strafer Gott, of 13th Corps, considered
for example that "6th June has been a profitable day". Norrie,
of 30th Corps, was responsible for the forward battle; he was
undoubtedly cool and experienced and able; but had he the driving
energy, the ruthless killing urge that the situation demanded?

Had Whiteley, the Brigadier General Staff, Eighth Army, the quick, creative intellect needed at the head of the staff? Messervy, a great likeable Airedale of a man, was dashing and brave enough; but was he—was any Eighth Army commander—the cold professional, the clever military scientist that could be found among Rommel's officers?

It was the turn of Bir Hacheim. This fortress, once the left flank peg of the Gazala defences, was the last impediment to Rommel's resumed drive on Tobruk. For ten days under fierce attack, it now was assaulted by a major part of the *Panzerarmee* and the Luftwaffe. Once Bir Hacheim fell, Rommel would be able to roll up the Gazala line as far as Knightsbridge; Eighth Army would have to form a front parallel to its communications. Rommel therefore pushed on the attack in person. On the British side, nothing decisive was done either to relieve the fortress or evacuate it. This inactivity stemmed from the usual reason; the committee could not make up its mind.

There was endless shilly-shallying over Bir Hacheim,

later said General Messervy, whose own exercise of command was by no means always fortunate:

They were put under us—an absurd thing, a static fortress under an armoured commander. Bir Hacheim fell because Ritchie had not really made up his mind what his main plan was going to be. There was a token advance towards Bir Hacheim, but it was too far away.

Meanwhile the men of the Free French garrison continued a magnificent but futile resistance. General Koenig, the garrison commander, however, was so much in favour of evacuation that he refused to accept supplies. While the German attack grew closer and closer to the web of foxholes, barbed wire and mines, and the French soldiers, stunned by endless bombardment and lack of sleep, fought on, the indecision continued. Koenig pleaded that he had no water or ammunition; finally Ritchie ordered the garrison to break out on the night of 10th/11th June.

It was the end of the Gazala line. It was the end of Ritchie's chances of victory.

CHAPTER THREE

AFTER the fall of Bir Hacheim Ritchie pulled his left flank back to the line of the Trigh Capuzzo, parallel with the Mediterranean coast and at right angles to the remaining half of the Gazala line. This new left flank position was also parallel, and close, to the Eighth Army's main lines of communication.

It was a situation pregnant with disaster. If Rommel broke through again, the Eighth Army might easily be pinned against the coast between Gazala and Tobruk and annihilated. Ritchie, however, preserved his robust optimism; he believed he could halt Rommel on his new line; and halting an offensive is a victory. The line was tactically strong. There were the heavily fortified boxes of Knightsbridge and El Adem, and from north of Knightsbridge to the 69th Brigade box in the Gazala line were minefields and more defences. The decayed perimeter of Tobruk supplied a further, if feeble, guard to the left flank. Ritchie had been able to make up a good deal of his losses in tanks from the large British reserves. In the shelter of the Trigh Capuzzo defences was an armoured force of two hundred and fifty cruisers and eighty 'I' tanks. To Rommel now remained only a hundred and sixty German tanks and seventy Italian.

However, the British armour, though strong in numbers, had weathered the battle far more heavily in terms of skill and cohesion than the German. As units were diluted with fresh crews, or amalgamated with other units, the shallowness of British experience and training, and the unsuitability of the ancient cavalry regiments as a basis of organisation and replacement were revealed once more. The performance of the British armour in the battles for the Trigh Capuzzo line was therefore much poorer than in the early days of Rommel's offensive, though not less courageous. The German armour, more skilled at the start, began now to achieve a dangerous ascendancy. General Messervy of 7th Armoured Division wrote afterwards of the Gazala battles:

His (the German) handling of armour, anti-tank guns and mechanised formations in co-operation was, with the *schwerpunkt* idea, much better than our rather dispersed idea of fighting . . . We were given area commands, not functional commands—which kept fluctuating. We never fought as a division—always getting different brigades, trained in different ways.

Ritchie himself continued to display that curious personal blend of complacency and indecision. The remains of the Gazala line, held by 1st South African Division and 50th Division, was a deeply turned salient; he looked upon it as a bastion. He still could not hit upon a basic battle plan, and this want of purpose began to be appreciated more and more widely in the ranks of Eighth Army, with damaging effects on morale.

One felt there was no real theme in the battle,

said General Messervy later.

It seemed to us at the time that after Bir Hacheim fell we should have fallen back immediately to a strong position El Adam–Bir Gubi. But Ritchie's intentions were not very evident to us.

About this time Messervy met Renton in the desert. Renton asked his superior: "What is the main idea in the battle now?"

Messervy answered: "I wish I knew—the only real order is to fight Germans wherever you see them."

On 11th June, 1942, the German dust-clouds were seen moving north again, and the second act of the Gazala battles had opened. Rommel sent 21st Panzer and Ariete against the British centre north of the Cauldron, 15th Panzer, 90th Light and Trieste towards the British left flank at El Adem. As always, Rommel was feeling for the communications of the flank-conscious British. Rommel in attack never worried about his own flanks: a punch protects itself.

On the eve of the renewed battle, disagreement was arising in Eighth Army over the handling of armour. Headquarters Eighth Army issued an instruction that our tanks must fight from the cover of their artillery and infantry in the Trigh Capuzzo defences; there must be no more rash attacks in the open. However, subordinate commanders, tired of waiting for guidance that rarely came, had by now taken to acting very much on their own initiative. Thus both Messervy (7th Armoured Division) and Norrie (30th Corps) separately and unknown to each other conceived plans and issued orders for the 12th June.

Messervy wished to get the armour out of the Trigh Capuzzo defences and grouped in the open desert to the south-east, near El Gubi. He saw his two brigadiers, gave his orders, and then went off to confer with the Army Commander before the move was made. However, Messervy ran into 90th Light and spent the day in a dry well.

Norrie meanwhile had issued his own orders for the armour to attack southwards directly into 15th Panzer Division. The only common factor in Norrie's and Messervy's orders was contradiction of the Eighth Army instruction on the handling of armour. Norrie now learned that Messervy had disappeared. Meanwhile Rommel, who knew of Messervy's plan through wireless intercepts, had laid an ambush for it. At noon Norrie placed 7th Armoured Division under the command of General Lumsden, of 1st Armoured Division, and instructed him to attack 15th Panzer Division immediately. Almost simultaneously Rommel ordered 21st Panzer Division to drive into 7th Armoured Division's rear. This division, caught waiting for orders and unprepared for battle, melted into a confused mass of vehicles ringed by German anti-tank guns and tanks.

Lumsden now arrived with his own division (1st Armoured) to take 7th under his command. It seemed to him an unpropitious moment to mount a joint attack to the south and he told Norrie so. Norrie disagreed; the British armour must break through 15th Panzer to the south; not, as Lumsden wished, fall back to the shelter of the Knightsbridge box.

During that sweltering afternoon, with vehicles and black smoke shimmering in the haze, the British armour, attacked from all sides, suffered the greatest defeat of its history. At the end of the day Rommel had driven its wreckage beyond Knightsbridge like paper before a gale. As night fell Rommel was through the Trigh Capuzzo line between Knightsbridge and El Adem, was holding in strength the escarpment north of it, and was across the by-pass road round Tobruk. The only land link between Egypt and the mass of troops pinned in the old Gazala line was now the Via Balbia, picking its congested way through Tobruk. The unfortunate Lumsden tried to get further orders from 30th Corps, failed to speak to it, and finally was told that he had been placed under 13th Corps. Owing to the general chaos he was to have no contact with that headquarters for twelve hours.

During 11th and 12th June, 1942, Eighth Army had lost two hundred cruisers and sixty 'I' tanks.

On 12th June Auchinleck paid Ritchie a visit. He found "the

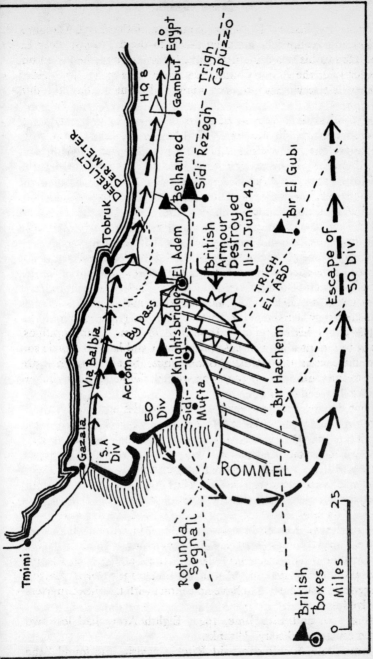

Map 15. GAZALA BATTLES, LAST STAGE
11 June–14 June 1942

Tmimi
Gazala
Via Balbia
I.S.A Div
Acroma
50 Div
Sidi Mufta
DERELICT PERIMETER
Tobruk
By Pass
El Adem
Knightsbridge
Belhamed
Sidi Rezegh – Trigh Capuzzo
HQ 8
To Egypt
Gambut
British Armour Destroyed
11-12 June 42
Bir El Gubi
TRIGH EL ABD
Bir Hacheim
ROMMEL
Escape of 50 Div
Rotunda Segnali
British Boxes
Miles
0   25

atmosphere here good. No undue optimism and realities of situation are being faced calmly and resolutely". In Eighth Army head-quarters it was believed that the tank battle of the day had not been conclusive, although apparently the British losses had been heavier. Auchinleck and Ritchie therefore agreed that further battle should be offered on the line Gazala – El Adem. Orders were issued accordingly, together with another warning, again to be unheeded, that the armour must fight defensively under our own guns.

Next day Rommel wrecked this plan by isolating Knightsbridge, whose garrison was got away safely after dark. The danger that the whole of Eighth Army, pressed nearer and nearer the coast, might be cut off was now acute.

This was a time of complete chaos on the ground, in the command structure, in men's minds. Telephone lines carried a dense traffic of anxious consultation. Ritchie, who had tried earlier to display his independence of Auchinleck's continual flow of advice, now felt the need of the Commander-in-Chief's support; Auchinleck, on his part, began to take a closer and closer hand in events in the desert as he sensed the battle slipping away from Ritchie. His signals gradually alter from general advice to specific recommendations that are almost orders.

At 10.30 in the morning of 14th June, Ritchie sent a signal to Auchinleck outlining his new plans. He proposed that the garrisons of the Gazala defences should be immediately evacuated, while a new mobile force of armour and infantry was built up west of the Egyptian frontier defences. He did not tell Auchinleck that Gott of 13th Corps had been *already* ordered to send the Gazala garrisons straight back to the frontier. He intended, Ritchie said, to hold in the meantime a line from the western perimeter of Tobruk through El Adem to Belhammed. Tobruk had a month's supplies and might be cut off for a time. He therefore asked Auchinleck if they should risk a temporary siege, or evacuate Tobruk and draw the entire army back on the frontier.

It seems clear from the terms of this signal and of Gott's orders that Ritchie had now decided on falling back to the frontier defences, with or without Tobruk as an isolated fortress. That is one crucial point; the other is that the idea of ever again holding Tobruk in isolation had been specifically abandoned in January by the three Commanders-in-Chief in the Middle East, and the decision communicated to London.

Now, however, on the same day as this signal of Ritchie's, came one from the Prime Minister:

Presume there is no question in any case of giving up Tobruk. As long as Tobruk is held no serious enemy advance into Egypt is possible . . .

The situation was already complicated enough, with half-understandings and misunderstandings developing between Ritchie and Auchinleck; but this signal, contradicting policy long agreed, marks the true cause and beginning of the resounding disaster of Tobruk. While Eighth Army scrambled out of the Gazala line and Rommel's dust clouds swept nearer and nearer Tobruk's ruined perimeter, a three-cornered correspondence raged between Ritchie and Auchinleck, and Auchinleck and the Prime Minister, in which firm statements of policy were gradually transformed by qualification into opposites.

Auchinleck's own plan was clear-cut. He rejected equally Ritchie's alternatives of evacuating Tobruk or allowing it to be besieged; he also ruled out a retreat to the frontier (which was by then, unknown to him, already in progress). He instructed Ritchie:

Tobruk must be held and the enemy must not be allowed to invest it . . . Eighth Army must hold the line Acroma – El Adem – and southwards and resist any enemy attempt to pass it . . . If you feel you cannot accept the responsibility of holding this position you must say so . . .

This of course was highly embarrassing to Ritchie. He consulted Gott; another drawn-out conference. Gott was sure that the army must make for the frontier; if Tobruk were held at all, it must be in isolation. Torn between Gott and Auchinleck, Ritchie hit on a British compromise, the reality to satisfy Gott, who was on the spot, and the words to satisfy Auchinleck, who was not. At eight o'clock in the evening (14th June, 1942) Ritchie signalled the Commander-in-Chief that he

had ordered Eighth Army to deny to the enemy the Western and Southern perimeter of Tobruk, the Tobruk – El Adem road and El Adem to the South. You may rely on us to do our utmost to achieve this . . .

Auchinleck could not know that 1st South African and 50th Division, the only fresh and intact formations, were en route for the frontier, and that the new line was to be only thinly held by the wreckage of earlier defeats. As regards the investment of Tobruk, Ritchie was also disingenuous. He summed up his policy in two alternatives: to fight alongside Tobruk to prevent its investment, or, if that failed, to allow it to be temporarily invested rather than risk a hasty evacuation. "If this is a correct interpretation of your orders," he concluded, "I accept responsibility."

Meanwhile Auchinleck had been considering Churchill's telegram. The centre of the drama now moved from Ritchie's headquarters to G.H.Q. Cairo, where all important decisions were henceforth made. Throughout 14th June there was a conference of intense anxiety in the long, bright, map-walled war-room. It was a very hot Cairo day. Auchinleck discussed the telegram with Corbett (his Chief of Staff), de Guingand (his Director of Military Intelligence), and Dorman-Smith (Deputy Chief of the General Staff). Should they flatly disobey the Prime Minister's orders, reminding him of the January decision, with which London had never disagreed? Discipline ruled this out. Should Tobruk be held in isolation after all? This would invite disaster. Its defences were in ruins, the minefields partly cleared—for our own convenience—the artillery control system dismantled. It was no longer a fortress at all. Perhaps the complete answer to Churchill and to the military problem lay in holding Tobruk as part of a line, as Auchinleck had already ordered Ritchie —if Ritchie carried the order out.

At 1.55 in the morning of 15th June the meeting at last broke up. Corbett was ordered to carry personally to Ritchie uncompromising and reinforcing orders that Rommel must be kept west of a line Tobruk-Acroma-El Adem-Bir Gubi.

Corbett flew up to Eighth Army headquarters and, in Ritchie's caravan, gave Ritchie the Commander-in-Chief's orders. This was a bad moment for Ritchie, who knew that there was no hope of the sketchy forces left south-west of Tobruk offering serious battle. The best he could do, he told Corbett, was to hold the old perimeter of Tobruk, with Indian infantry in El Adem and the armour to the south—the bulk of the army was already partly in motion to the frontier. Corbett reiterated Auchinleck's cast-iron orders. Jolted at last out of his calm, Ritchie grew red and angry, banged the table and said of offering battle on the line Tobruk-El Adem: "I'm damned if I will!"

Corbett too grew angry: "We thumped the desk and shouted at each other. It was most unpleasant."

That evening (15th June) Corbett returned to Cairo and reported to Auchinleck and his staff. Meanwhile, Churchill, who had received from Auchinleck a summary of his orders to Ritchie, had despatched another peremptory telegram about Tobruk:

We are glad to have your assurance that you have no intention of giving up Tobruk. War Cabinet interpret your telegram to mean that, if the need arises, General Ritchie would leave as many troops in Tobruk as are necessary to hold the place for certain.

This of course was an order, and Auchinleck obeyed it. Corbett's report had shown that in fact Tobruk could now either be invested or evacuated, but not held for long as part of a general line. Auchinleck therefore replied to Churchill on 16th June in language that curiously recalls the disingenuous signals he himself had received from Ritchie:

War Cabinet interpretation is correct. General Ritchie is putting into Tobruk what he considers an adequate force to hold it even should it be temporarily isolated by the enemy . . . Basis of immediate future action by Eighth Army is to hold El Adem . . . and to use all available mobile forces to prevent enemy establishing itself east of Tobruk.

Thus Churchill had his wish, and paved the way for one of the greatest single disasters ever suffered by the British in the Middle East and Mediterranean in the Second World War. He attempted later to shift the blame from himself to Auchinleck with a disingenuousness only qualified by the weakness of his argument:

We did not however know the conditions prevailing in Tobruk. Considering that Auchinleck's plan had been to await an attack, and remembering all the months that had passed, it was inconceivable that the already well-proved fortifications of Tobruk should not have been maintained in the highest efficiency, and indeed strengthened.

Elsewhere he stated:

At home we had no inkling that the evacuation of Tobruk had ever entered into the plan or thoughts of the commanders.

However, London had been informed by a copy of Auchinleck's Operation Instruction No. 110, dated 19th January, 1942, that:

It is NOT my intention to try to hold, permanently, Tobruk, or any other locality west of the frontier.

This instruction was sent on by General Kennedy, Director of Military Operations at the War Office, to General Alan Brooke, Chief of the Imperial General Staff, on 6th February with a note agreeing with Auchinleck's intention: "In my opinion, it would be right to avoid such detachments in the future."

It is impossible therefore to believe that Churchill was never told of this decision—neither at that time nor when the question of Tobruk came up in June. Given that all in London had known and accepted that Tobruk was never again to be used as a fortress, it is highly illogical and unjust to suggest that Auchinleck ought to have diverted men, weapons and materials to fortifying it.

The Prime Minister's last-minute reversal of policy long accepted by the three Middle East C.-in-C.s and the C.I.G.S. was perhaps partly for reasons of home morale, partly the product of another of his waves of patriotic emotion, caused this time by Tobruk's legendary fame. There is a curious reference in *Jan Christian Smuts*, by Smuts' son. The author, in dealing with the effects of the loss of Tobruk and its South African garrison on public opinion in South Africa, refers to demands for an inquiry into the reasons for its fall:

> It was common knowledge that we would not again commit the dangerous error of trying to hold this [Tobruk] or any other isolated strong-point. The minefields and other defences of Tobruk were therefore never properly prepared for a siege. It was therefore obvious to all on the spot that Tobruk could never be held. The last-minute decision by the highest authority to hold it came as a complete surprise to us. The decision must either have come from Mr. Churchill or some other very high body. *The fact that my father, while opposed to the decision, never pressed the enquiry, may perhaps be significant.* [Author's italics.]

While the fate of Tobruk was being decided, the troops in the Gazala line had begun on 14th June to try to escape from Rommel's closing trap, a process known at the time as the 'Gazala Gallop'. Their sole eastward route was the Via Balbia, and all that stood between it and Rommel was a line of small boxes hastily manned and supported by bits and pieces of 1st Armoured Division and 32nd Army Tank Brigade. Against this thin, desperate line, so true to British military traditions, Rommel personally drove the Afrika Korps. All the day, as the South Africans slipped away along the Via Balbia, the line stood firm and, when at last at nightfall Rommel broke it, his troops were so exhausted they lay down in the breach and slept. Rommel watched helplessly as the rest of the South Africans escaped under the muzzles of his silent guns.

The 50th British Infantry Division was placed too far south in the Gazala defences for it to escape by the Via Balbia, even if that narrow road could have carried the volume of traffic. The division—under

General W. H. Ramsden—therefore broke out westwards into open desert and motored right round Bir Hacheim, behind Rommel. "The journey back to the frontier was calm," said General Ramsden afterwards. "We stopped in the desert for a brew-up." In the afternoon Ramsden reported to Ritchie at Maddalena, whence Eighth Army headquarters had now removed. They sat in a car and Ritchie explained the situation and how Tobruk was to hold out as a hinge for a countermove, after re-organisation of the army. Despite the fast flowing current of rout and confusion, Ritchie remained "calm and collected".

"At that moment," said Ramsden, "I really admired him."

Four days later Eighth Army headquarters was back to Sollum. Here Ritchie was visited by Auchinleck and Dorman-Smith. "There was a general optimism and belief that Rommel would take his time over Tobruk, and that we had leisure to re-arm and re-group," recollected Dorman-Smith. "Ritchie still said he would not allow Tobruk to be invested. Auchinleck was disturbed by this atmosphere; he thought it was not yet the moment to relax."

Ritchie's character was thus sustaining magnificently the cumulative disappointments and dangers. He was perhaps mentally protected in defeat by that very lack of imagination that had denied him victory. But intellectually he was done. His mind could no longer cope with the speed and complexity of events. His indecision displayed itself, for example, over the defence of El Adem, which in Auchinleck's opinion (strongly expressed) was the 'decisive spot'.

> Twenty-ninth Brigade was in El Adem,

recounts General Messervy.

> I got via Corps an order: on no account was El Adem to be evacuated —they were to fight it out to the last. It was already surrounded. I was told by Norrie that these were the Army Commander's personal orders. Then I had a message: It might be evacuated if I thought it couldn't be held. I said I was quite sure it could not be held for long; then I was told to pass this message on to 29th Brigade. Then I got another order—the Army Commander says it must be held. Then yet another: that it was to be evacuated if the brigade could get out. I passed this on to Denis Reid (the Brigadier), and they got out. This was an example of what was happening all the time.

The bulk of Eighth Army was now behind the Egyptian frontier; although Ritchie and Auchinleck were still exchanging signals about the firm holding of Tobruk-El Adem-Bir Gubi line, it was in fact held by a weak screen of disorganised remnants. The only significant British force left in Libya was the thirty-three thousand men mustering in the rusty perimeter of Tobruk: 2nd South African Division, 11th Indian Brigade, 201st Guards Brigade, 32nd Army Tank Brigade, 268 Medium Regiment Royal Artillery.

To Gott (13th Corps) and Major-General Klopper, now fortress commander, the problem of organising the defence of Tobruk in a matter of hours was horrifying. The Italian anti-tank ditch had partly filled with sand, partly been filled, for convenience, by the British; "it would hardly have interfered with the progress of a garden roller". The minefields had been breached on the south-eastern side during the British sorties in *Crusader*. Inside the perimeter were scattered uncharted minefields of every nationality. The inner perimeter defences had disappeared. Organisation of command, of fields of fire and of signals was derelict.

The survival of the garrison depended, as Auchinleck knew and Ritchie had promised, on a powerful force operating in its support in the area El Adem–Belhammed. But on 17th June occurred another disastrous tank action which ended hope of supporting Tobruk from the outside. With cavalry pennants fluttering in the breeze, as they had at Balaclava, 4th Armoured Brigade (under Messervy's orders), drove westward towards the German concentration between Sidi Rezegh and El Adem. It was the last charge of the British armour in the Gazala battles, ninety assorted tanks and crews, new to each other, though not to battle. They met the two panzer divisions of the Africa Korps, and when they had lost thirty-two tanks they went back to Egypt. Eighth Army no longer possessed a battleworthy tank arm.

This defeat, which rendered Eighth Army quite helpless, caused Ritchie to relieve Messervy of command of 7th Armoured Division. In telling Messervy of this decision, Ritchie displayed amid all his worries the courtesy and generosity that formed so strong a part of his personal character: "Well, Frank, I'm afraid I've lost confidence in you—you seem to be out of luck. Nothing seems to be going right with you."

On 18th June, 1942, Rommel's forces closed the ring round Tobruk.

Inside the fortress there was an atmosphere of doom. Klopper, the fortress commander, had been a general for a month only; his recent military experience had been in the administration of training in South Africa. The headquarters staff of his division (2nd South African) were also green. As subordinate commanders, Klopper had two highly experienced brigadiers, Willison and Johnson. He never established his personal ascendancy; Tobruk was commanded, in the current British manner, by a debating society. The troops were in every stage of disorganisation. Maps were hopeless: Willison's showed him minefields he himself had lifted a year ago; Klopper's was a captured German one dating from November, 1941.

By nightfall on 19th June, Rommel had completed the preparations for his attack. The assault force was made up of 21st and 15th Panzer, Ariete and Trieste. Ninetieth Light Division would fend off British attempts at relief. Rommel chose as his point of entry the same sector of the perimeter as O'Connor: the south-eastern. This was also where Rommel had intended to attack in November, 1941, had he not been anticipated by *Crusader*.

In the small hours of the night before the assault, Klopper received a secret signal from Ritchie outlining Eighth Army's plans to help Tobruk and giving Klopper general guidance. Ritchie considered that Rommel would attack Tobruk as soon as he was ready; but on the other hand he might attack the Egyptian frontier defences instead. Ritchie would risk this, and form a striking force of guns and tanks which could attack towards El Adem, on to the rear of a German assault on Tobruk. If Rommel should march straight on the frontier, Tobruk garrison would make a sortie behind him.

This was Klopper's last word from the Army Commander before the German assault. It was heartening: powerful Eighth Army forces would be operating against the rear of the besiegers.

Ritchie, after signalling Klopper, had signalled Auchinleck in similar terms; but he added an extra piece of information. This was that the creation of the striking force of guns and tanks would be a slow business. Rommel's troops were then readying themselves on their startlines. The Commander-in-Chief replied with sharp urgency:

> I am perturbed by the apparently deliberate nature of your preparations though I realise the difficulties. Crisis may arise in matter of hours not days and you must therefore put in everything you can raise.

There can have been no conscious intention to deceive in Ritchie's signal to Klopper: his personal honesty rules it out. The explanation lay in his utter inability to think and act at Rommel's speed, or even to imagine Rommel's speed. Grappling with that tempestuous commander, Ritchie with his stolid British virtues was as baffled as a two-dimensional being in a three-dimensional world.

The dawn of 20th June, 1942, lightened the sky along the bleak escarpment; the night mists lifted. Then the German barrage fell upon the bunkers of the Tobruk perimeter; the desert burst apart in dust and thunder. The Stukas came with the early morning sun. Orange smoke rolled up against the blue sky as the German engineers signalled their gunners to lengthen the range so that they could move in to breach the minefields and anti-tank defences. Just before seven o'clock the German infantry followed. Before eight, the *Panzerarmee* was one and a half miles inside the Tobruk perimeter.

Within the falling fortress there were the too-familiar decisions and counter-decisions and time-wasting exchanges of visits between commanders. A counter-attack was ordered: the tanks arrived without the infantry two and a half hours after the German break-through. Only then did the infantry begin to move. By now, two German panzer divisions were driving for King's Cross, where the Via Balbia and the El Adem road met.

Outside Tobruk Ritchie was visiting his corps commanders: at mid-day he learned that "some enemy activity" was in progress, "apparently against Tobruk". He immediately ordered 30th Corps to attack through Sidi Rezegh with all available armour and mobile forces. This move achieved nothing: in Axis war diaries it is hardly noticed.

Inside Tobruk, the defence was disintegrating in scenes of apocalyptic confusion and doom. By four in the afternoon the Germans were on the eastern airfield, and driving straight for the town of Tobruk, with all its stores and installations prepared for the intended British summer offensive. Under heavy German gunfire, demolition charges were blown in petrol, water, refrigerations and naval ammunition stores. A dark column of smoke towered through the sunshine into the blue Mediterranean sky.

At seven in the evening 21st Panzer had captured the town. Germans swarmed everywhere through the confusion and noise, performing the housewifely function of mopping-up. Some British units held out for a time, others were quickly overwhelmed.

As the debris of his garrison poured past his headquarters, Klopper signalled and signalled Eighth Army. There was no answer. At five o'clock the desperate Klopper had telephoned Brigadier Thompson, the Area Commander, that fortress headquarters was about to disperse, German tanks being close. In the hope of speaking to Eighth Army Klopper nevertheless held on until half-past six, when his headquarters started to pack up.

Now at last came a personal signal from Ritchie:

> . . . You are having a very tough fight today and I see this afternoon
> some enemy tanks have got through the outer perimeter. But I feel
> quite confident of your ability to put them out after destroying as many
> as possible. I am doing all I can from outside to relieve the pressure
> on you and our power to help you from outside will increase daily.
> The turn of the tide will come and feel quite sure of inflicting a crushing
> defeat on the enemy . . . All good fortune to you personally and the
> whole of your grand command.

Dusk fell, and men from broken formations crowded wearily into
the precarious security of the western half of the perimeter. In their
nostrils was the ubiquitous smell of burning; in their mouths the sour,
familiar taste of defeat. Klopper himself had joined 2nd South
African Brigade, where he tried to speak to Ritchie on the Army Com-
mander's personal radio-telephone link. But Ritchie was away from
his headquarters. Klopper spoke to Whiteley, his Brigadier General
Staff, and conveyed the state of the fortress. Whiteley got in touch with
Ritchie, then passed on to Klopper the Army Commander's orders
to break out tomorrow night; an escape route would be held open.

While Klopper's officers talked and talked endlessly round the
questions of whether, and how, to break out, the men settled down
to wait with that patient resignation of the soldier, and Klopper
himself tried again and again to speak to Ritchie. Midnight passed.
At two in the morning of 21st June, Klopper gave Ritchie up, and
signalled Eighth Army:

> Am sending mobile troops out tonight. Not possible to hold until
> tomorrow. Mobile troops nearly nought. Enemy captured vehicles.
> Will resist to last man and last round.

At three that morning Ritchie returned to his headquarters,
immediately telephoned Tobruk and found he could not get through
to Klopper. Now it was Ritchie's turn to endure anxiety and
frustration before a silent telephone. As dawn crept palely up the
sky, he paced up and down outside his caravan, waiting. At last he
and Klopper talked. Ritchie gave Klopper leave to capitulate if the
local situation warranted it. Klopper told him that "he was doing
the worst". Ritchie ended the conversation with a characteristically
generous message:

> Whole of Eighth Army has watched with admiration your gallant
> fight. You are an example to us all and I know South Africa will be

proud of you. God bless you and may fortune favour your efforts wherever you may be . . .

That morning, 21st June, 1942, a white flag was hauled up over Klopper's new headquarters. It was Sir Claude Auchinleck's fifty-eighth birthday.

*   *   *   *   *

At a quarter to ten, amid the shambles of surrendering troops and burning equipment, Rommel imperiously signalled the *Panzerarmee*:

> Fortress of Tobruk has capitulated. All units will re-assemble and prepare for further advance.

It was Ritchie's turn again.

Since the evacuation of the Gazala line, Ritchie had been re-organising his army in the field defences along the Egyptian frontier. These were similar to those of Gazala—a series of boxes, minefields and wire, stretching thirty miles inland and ending in a wide-open flank. Since there no longer existed a British armoured force capable of offering battle, these positions could be turned by Rommel without difficulty: the result of staying there would be a second Gazala, a second Tobruk.

On 22nd June, Auchinleck and Dorman-Smith flew up to Ritchie's headquarters, now in O'Connor's old camp at Maaten Baggush. Ritchie was still personally unaffected by events, unalarmed by the progressive dissolution of the fighting power of his army and the nearness of final catastrophe. But his remaining military intention indicated a dearth of ideas. Rightly arguing that the frontier defences were, in the circumstances, indefensible, he said that he must "put distance" between himself and Rommel in order to gain time to re-organise. He proposed therefore to retire at the utmost speed on Mersa Matruh, where he would offer a final battle for Egypt. The New Zealand Division from Syria would garrison the Matruh box together with 5th South African Brigade, with 10th Indian Division further back along the coast at Baggush.

Auchinleck agreed that Eighth Army was not strong enough to defend the frontier, and he therefore sanctioned retirement on Matruh. However, he pointed out to Ritchie that the considerations that made the frontier indefensible also applied to Matruh. Auchinleck also agreed that only infantry with transport should remain in the field. The process was now under way of forming battlegroups of lorried infantry and guns.

The 'Gazala Gallop' was therefore resumed. Auchinleck himself arranged for Norrie and 30th Corps headquarters, as well as 1st South African Division, to go back even further, to El Alamein, there to re-organise, and for 10th Corps (from Syria) to hold Mersa Matruh.

On 22nd June, Rommel, now a Field-Marshal, was up to the frontier. On the 23rd he drove south of the frontier defences in a wide sweep towards Sidi Barrani; he reached the coast east of that place at nightfall on 24th June, having covered a hundred miles in twenty-four hours. Eighth Army retreated in a final state of rout and dissolution; one observer said he did not see a formed unit of any kind. Eighth Army losses in the Gazala battles had now reached about eighty thousand, mostly in prisoners.

By nightfall on 25th June, Rommel was in front of the Matruh defences. Ritchie had failed to 'put distance' between himself and the *Panzerarmee*. The final battle for the Middle East was at hand.

The Mersa Matruh defences had not been garrisoned or maintained since November 1940. They were more derelict than those of Tobruk: "Most of the dug positions," wrote a New Zealand brigadier, "had caved in or filled with sand, much of the wire was

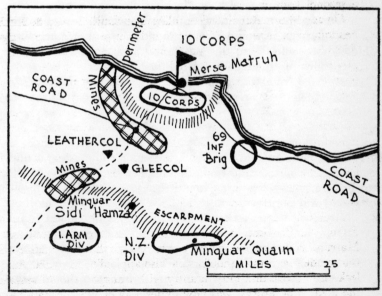

Map. 16. RITCHIE'S DISPOSITIONS AT MERSA MATRUH
25 June 1942

on the ground, minefields were badly marked, communications non-existent, and the whole plan of defence obscure." There was the fortified perimeter round Matruh itself, another belt of defences to the west, and an unfinished box at Minquar Sidi Hamza el Gharbi, some thirty miles inland. The whole complex was protected by minefields in two sections separated by a six-mile gap in which were thinly scattered on 25th June fresh mines.

Ritchie's dispositions for this last battle were curious: he had no centre, but two widely separated wings facing north and south. Holmes of 10th Corps, with 10th Indian Division and 50th Division, lay in Matruh, with his back to the sea; Gott of 13th Corps (now the mobile and 'offensive' wing), lay along the east-west escarpment nine miles to the south, with 29th Indian Brigade in the Sidi Hamza box and Freyberg's New Zealanders—Freyberg had refused point-blank to be shut up in Matruh—ten miles to the *east* at Minquar Quaim. In the empty centre were two tiny battle-groups, Gleecol and Leathercol. In the open desert south of Minquar Quaim was First Armoured Division, now, owing to Auchinleck's energy in rustling up reinforcements from all over the Middle East, formidable again in numbers: a hundred and fifty-nine tanks, including sixty Grants. But numbers did not make a team.

Ritchie now awaited, without flinching, the final action. There was to be no more retreat. Eighth Army would stay at Mersa Matruh alive, or it would stay there dead. If dead, the entire Middle East would fall to the Axis. But that was not the affair of a commander of the Eighth Army. As June 25th slowly passed, Ritchie waited amid the sand dunes for Rommel. Late in the afternoon Auchinleck arrived from Cairo and relieved him of his command.

*   *   *   *   *

Ritchie epitomised the cherished and admired qualities of the British Establishment: he was stolid, thorough, rather slow, honest, conventional, courteous, brave and unimaginative. Even if he had had Rommel's experience, he would therefore still have been out-generalled and beaten—unless he had also enjoyed the good fortune of Montgomery in the way of overwhelming numbers and equipment. As it was, he was far too junior an officer for his command, as all but Auchinleck recognised. Placed in an impossible position, he did his duty as best he could, never losing heart, never (except once) losing his self-command and courtesy, never imputing blame to others for the defeats of Eighth Army. Ritchie far from lost personal stature in the course of his military failure in the desert.

And the failure itself was not decisive for him. Auchinleck wrote an enthusiastic report on his qualities—though with the recommendation that he was not suited for independent command; Brooke retained his high opinion of him; and when Ritchie returned to England in August he was invited to Buckingham Palace for an audience of the King. In 1944 he was to be a corps commander—and a successful one—under Montgomery in north-west Europe. For a man who in 1937 had been only a major, this was professional success indeed.

COMMENTARY: PART FOUR

CHAPTER ONE

According to Professor Hinsley, *Enigma* decrypts played no important part in the latter stages of the *Crusader* battle and Rommel's withdrawal to El Agheila. Nor did it provide warning of Rommel's counter-stroke in January 1942, since the German Army *Enigma* was no longer being broken and the *Luftwaffe Enigma* yielded only one signal that offered a possible clue to Rommel's intentions.

In Professor Hinsley's judgement, it was only after Brigadier F. de Guingand replaced Brigadier J. Shearer as Director of Military Intelligence in the Middle East that G.H.Q. really began to integrate secret intelligence with operational planning and decision; an interesting judgement since some historians seem to believe that such integration began only under Montgomery. It is also note-worthy that de Guingand, an outstanding staff officer, was selected as D.M.I. and later as Brigadier General Staff of the Eighth Army by Auchinleck, whom critics have dubbed a poor picker of men.

CHAPTER TWO

In the long-running argument in spring 1942 between London and Cairo or, more particularly, between Churchill and Auchinleck, about the merits of an early British offensive in Libya, *Enigma* decrypts played a significant part by repeatedly providing accurate information about Rommel's tank strength. On 11th March 1942 *Ultra* provided the first *Enigma* decrypt since the previous November giving the number of Axis tanks in the forward area; the figure came closer to Cairo's estimate than London's. On 10th April the *Ultra* organisation succeeded in breaking the German North Africa command *Enigma* again, and on 21st and 22nd April this yielded further tank states, the second of which gave German strength at two hundred and sixty-four and Italian at a hundred and fifty-one. On 6th May *Enigma* provided yet another tank state, and it was four days later that Churchill signalled Auchinleck to attack in June or resign. However, the essential difference between London and Cairo lay in the operational lesson to be drawn from the figures of tanks revealed by these decrypts. To Churchill, ever prone to count the forces available on each side rather than to judge their fighting capability, and even to Brooke, the C.I.G.S., comparison of overall strengths indicated a comfortable British margin of superiority that fully justified the early offensive so urgently demanded by wider strategic and political factors. To Auchinleck, conscious of the mechanical and design weaknesses of his British-made tanks and of the need for time to prepare his new American "Grants" for the field and train their crews—conscious too of the shortcomings in training, leadership, organisation and doctrine of his hastily-raised and heterogeneous army—the total of enemy tanks revealed through *Enigma* suggested a need for an ample margin of numerical superiority before he launched an offensive, as well as adequate time for training.

In any event, from 19th April onwards decrypts of the German Army *Enigma* gave warnings of an impending German offensive aimed at Tobruk; and by 2nd May London had become convinced that Rommel would attack sometime between 20th May and the end of the month. On 25th May further *Ultra* intelligence led to 30th Corps being brought to four hours' readiness; and on 26th May, the day Rommel's forces began their long march round Bir Hacheim, British army "Y" intelligence intercepted the Axis operation codename "Venezia". Nevertheless, no information about Rommel's actual plan of attack was revealed by *Ultra* decrypts or other intelligence sources; it remained for the British command to make its own guess in traditional fashion.

*　*　*　*　*

The Desert Generals contended that Auchinleck offered sound advice to Ritchie in his letter of 20th May 1942 when he suggested concentrating both armoured divisions astride the Trigh Capuzzo track, where they would be equally well placed to meet either a frontal attack through the centre of the Gazala Line or a flanking manoeuvre round Bir Hacheim. The book criticised Ritchie for disregarding this advice and posting 7th Armoured Division away to the south of 1st Armoured and, moreover, with its units dispersed rather than concentrated, so that Rommel was able to surprise it and overrun it piecemeal. However, Field-Marshal Lord Carver, in a letter to *The Times* on 31st March 1981, took the view "that it was well that Ritchie did not accept Auchinleck's advice" because, according to Lord Carver, this advice was based on a "quite wrong" forecast that Rommel would try to break through the centre of the Gazala position; and Ritchie guessed better in being concerned about his open flank. Lord Carver regards Ritchie's final deployment as being "perfectly reasonable", and describes various last-minute regroupings by which both armoured divisions could have been concentrated to meet a German attack either through the centre or round Bir Hacheim. He considers that there should have been enough time to have effected these last-minute regroupings, and blames Norrie, the commander of 30th Corps, and Messervy, commander of 7th Armoured Division, for the failure to concentrate in time. He goes further, and lays the final blame on Auchinleck by arguing that in their reluctance to believe that Rommel's move round Bir Hacheim was the real attack and not a mere feint, they "were all undoubtedly influenced by Auchinleck's prediction" that Rommel would feint in the south and attack in the centre.

Lord Carver's authority is weighty, but his arguments less so. In the first place Ritchie was the Army Commander; it will not really do to attribute blame for his army's surprise to his superior and his subordinates. In the second place Auchinleck's letter to Ritchie of 20th May 1942 does not bear the construction put on it by Lord Carver. Auchinleck did *not* write, as Lord Carver alleged in his *Times* letter, simply "forecasting that [Rommel] would try and break through the centre of the Gazala line, while making a feint round the south of Bir Hacheim". Instead he wrote at equal length to suggest *two* alternatives that Rommel might adopt, the first being an envelopment of the British southern flank, and the second being the one cited by Lord Carver. Auchinleck's letter to Ritchie then proceeds:

> I feel myself that the second course is the one he will adopt, and that it is certainly the most dangerous for us, as if it succeeds, it will cut our forces in half and probably result in the destruction of the northern part of them. *We must of course be ready to deal with the enemy should he adopt the first course, and in either event you must of course be most careful not to commit your armoured striking force until you know beyond reasonable doubt where the main body of his armour is thrusting* . . . [present author's italics].

Moreover, in suggesting to Ritchie that he should concentrate both armoured divisions astride the Trigh Capuzzo in order to meet a possible direct breakthrough attempt against the British centre, Auchinleck added:

> It does not look from the map as if this would be too far north to meet the main attack, should it come round the southern flank, instead of against the centre as I anticipate. Your covering troops should give you good warning of any main enveloping movement on your left, even if you do not hear of it before it starts.

It is therefore evident that Auchinleck in no way excluded the southern option. No matter what errors of judgement were committed by Norrie, Messervy and Lumsden on the first day of Rommel's offensive, the primary reason for 7th Armoured Division being surprised by Rommel while itself dispersed and while separated from 1st Armoured lay in Ritchie's failure to heed Auchinleck's advice to concentrate both divisions on the Trigh Capuzzo behind the British centre. As Lord Carver himself summed it up in his book *El Alamein*, Rommel's advance caught "Norrie's 30th Corps unbalanced, its three armoured brigades separated by considerable distances, and 7th Armoured Division, east of Bir Hacheim, still out of its battle positions."

Professor Hinsley casts important new light on the disastrous British counter-strokes of 1st June and 5th June against the German bridgehead through the British minefields known as "the Cauldron". *Enigma* signals of 31st May, decrypted and received in the Middle East next day, gave away the German strategy, which was to break up the British counterstroke with a powerful anti-tank defence and then launch a fresh offensive. Before the second British "Cauldron" attack was launched on 5th June, *Enigma* decrypts revealed that the enemy was expecting it. Nonetheless the Eighth Army still proceeded with its plan, Operation *Aberdeen*, counting on the preliminary bombardment to neutralise the German anti-tank guns which, falling short of those guns owing to inadequate reconnaissance, it failed to do. Thus the incompetence of the Eighth Army Command in the "Cauldron" battle was actually greater than alleged in this book, triumphing even over accurate top-secret intelligence about the enemy's plans and his expectations of British attack.

CHAPTER THREE

From early June 1942 onwards there was a dramatic and permanent improvement in all kinds of British intelligence. In particular the German Army *Enigma*, which hitherto had taken about a week to break, was now being read with an average delay of only twenty-four hours, and more completely than before. Moreover, the tactical *Enigma* links between field formations had also now been broken, along with the *Enigma* of Luftwaffe liaison officers with army units. The latter provided better current tactical intelligence than any other *Enigma* key, according to Professor Hinsley. From the middle of June onwards G.H.Q. Middle East was receiving Rommel's own daily report to the German high command at twenty-four hours' delay. British Army "Y" intelligence was also now much improved.

Thus on the morning of 12th June 1942 the Eighth Army received the *Enigma* decrypt of Rommel's orders the previous day for a renewed offensive north-east towards Tobruk. But such was now the confusion within the British command structure that this intelligence could not avert the mishandling of the battle on 12th June which led to the virtual destruction of the British armour.

On 22nd June, the day after the fall of Tobruk, *Enigma* decrypts provided information about Rommel's intention to outflank the Egyptian frontier defences, and on 23rd/24th June further decrypts suggested that Rommel was now proposing to drive deep into Egypt. It may be surmised that this revelation played its part in Auchinleck's decision on 24th June to relieve Ritchie and take personal command of the Eighth Army.

Lieutenant-General R. N. O'Connor
Western Desert Force and Thirteenth Corps, June 1940 to February 1941

General "Electric Whiskers" Bergonzoli, captured at the Battle of Beda Fomm, February, 1941.

Marshal Rodolpho Graziani, Governor-General and Commander-in-Chief in Libya, 1940–41.

ove left: Brigadier A. Galloway, Brigadier General Staff, Eighth Army in *Crusader*, November–December 1941.

ove right: Lieutenant-General N. de la P. Beresford-Peirse. Commanded *Battleaxe* operation, June 1941.

Below: Tobruk, 1941. A view from the harbour.

Above left: Lieutenant-General Godwin-Austen, 13th Corps.
Above right: Major-General von Ravenstein, 21st Panzer Division.

CRUSADER, NOVEMBER–DECEMBER, 1941

Below: The battlefield near Sidi Rezegh.

LIEUTENANT-GENERAL ALAN CUNNINGHAM
EIGHTH ARMY, AUGUST–NOVEMBER, 1941.

Above left: General Cruewell, commander of Afrika Korps.
Above right: Major-General Bernard Freyberg, New Zealand Division.

CRUSADER COMMANDERS

Below left: Major-General "Strafer" Gott, 7th Armoured Division.
Below right: Lieutenant-General Willoughby Norrie, 30th Corps.

LIEUTENANT-GENERAL NEIL RITCHIE
EIGHTH ARMY, NOVEMBER 1941 TO JUNE 1942.

Above left: Major-General Frank Messervy, commander 7th Armoured Division in Gazala battles, June 1942.

Above right: General Navarrini, commander Italian 21st Corps.

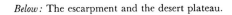

Below: The escarpment and the desert plateau.

BATTLE CONFERENCES
GAZALA, 1942.

Right: Colonel-General Rommel, Panzerarmee Afrika, and General Nehring, commander Afrika Korps.

Below: (left to right) Lieutenant-General Norrie, 30th Corps, Lieutenant-General Ritchie, Eighth Army, and Lieutenant-General Gott, 13th Corps.

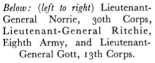

Mon. 29 21 ~~~~~ Quejil

Quejid.
06.45

Tues. 30 (26)
Two park said.
13 in 21 Gus. Canal.

Wed.
1 JULY Battle of El Alamein

Battle of El ALAMEIN.
Thur.
2   E 19.
B5e. 21. u.s. (27)

Fri.
3 Battle of El Alamein

Sat.
4 Battle of El Alamein
"Kwill battle do ?   ?
Germans surrender ...? (28)
NZ. Night Attack.

Sun. 5th after Trinity
5 Battle of El Alamein

443225.. New HQS.

Memo.

Above: Major-General Dorman-Smith's diary—first written reference to a "Battle of El Alamein" two months before Montgomery's arrival in Egypt.

Below: The coast road.

GENERAL SIR CLAUDE AUCHINLECK, COMMANDER-IN-CHIEF, MIDDLE EAST, 1941–42, ACTING EIGHTH ARMY COMMANDER, JUNE–AUGUST 1942.

Major-General E. Dorman-Smith, acting Chief-of-Staff, Eighth Army, during First Battle of Alamein, July 1942.

Major-General Morshead, commander 9th Australian Division during First Battle of Alamein, July 1942.

LIEUTENANT-GENERAL B. L. MONTGOMERY
EIGHTH ARMY, FROM AUGUST 15TH, 1942.

Above left: Lieutenant-General Brian Horrocks, commanded 13th Corps at Alam Halfa and Second Alamein.

Above right: Lieutenant-General Oliver Leese, commanded 30th Corps at Second Alamein, October–November 1942.

CORPS COMMANDERS, EIGHTH ARMY

Below (centre): Lieutenant-General W. H. Ramsden, commanded 30th Corps at First Alamein, July 1942 and Alam Halfa, August–September 1942.

Above left: Major-General John Harding, 7th Armoured Division.
Above right: General Ritter von Thoma, Afrika Korps.

SECOND ALAMEIN COMMANDERS

Below left: Major-General A. H. Gatehouse, 10th Armoured Division.
Below right: Lieutenant-General Herbert Lumsden, 10th Corps.

Generalfeldmarschall Erwir Rommel, Oberbefehlshaber der Panzerarmee Afrikas.

The desert of the battles British tanks assembling on the plain of Duda, 2nd December 1941.

PART FIVE

THE VICTOR OF ALAMEIN

Field-Marshal Sir Claude J. E. Auchinleck, G.C.B.,
G.C.I.E., C.S.I., D.S.O., O.B.E., LL.D.

Of General Auchinleck I will only say that he is an officer
of the greatest distinction, and of a character of singular
elevation.

WINSTON CHURCHILL.

CHAPTER ONE

As he flew back to Cairo from Ritchie's headquarters on 22nd June, 1942, the Commander-in-Chief, General Sir Claude Auchinleck, faced a situation more desperate than any other British commander confronted during the Second World War. It was made worse for him by strong feelings of personal loyalty to Ritchie, and perhaps of culpability. He knew he had to decide—and quickly—whether to replace Ritchie. It would be the second time he had relieved an army commander in the middle of a crisis; this sort of thing did not come more easily with habit. But his visit to Eighth Army headquarters at Maaten Baggush no longer allowed him to deceive himself.

Ritchie had seemed to him surprisingly calm and clear-headed in the face of cumulative disaster. But he—and the rest of his headquarters—seemed to suffer from a numbness of the will. Defeat hung over them like smoke above a burning town. Ritchie now proposed to stake everything in a final battle at Mersa Matruh, almost as though he wanted it all to be over and done with. If he had in fact ceased to believe in the possibility of victory, what hope was there that he would find the generalship to win?

As Auchinleck weighed the consequences of Ritchie's losing the battle of Mersa Matruh and the last field army in the Middle East, the more catastrophic they seemed. The Middle East Command formed the connecting cog round which revolved the great wheels of the allied coalition. It joined Britain to India and the Far East; British and American factories (through Persia) with the soldiers of the Red Army; Africa and Asia. It was Russia's southern flank; it was the moral and physical prop that kept wobbling Turkey out of the Axis and, neutral, protecting both Russia and ourselves. And, above all, in Iraq and Persia, it contained the oilfields without which the British armed forces would be paralysed.

The Eighth Army once finally destroyed, the Germans would hold the magnificent Delta base within a week. The Mediterranean fleet would have to escape southwards through the Suez Canal;

Palestine and Syria, bereft of troops, would fall in a few days; and then—within a month at Rommel's pace—the oilfields of the Persian Gulf would be wrecked or producing for the Axis. Turkey would be unable to resist German pressure to enter the war, and with Anatolia and Persia in German hands, the Red Army's extreme left flank would be uncovered. The second German summer offensive in Russia was already a few days old and moving fast. Sevastopol was falling to von Manstein; Kupiansk, some three hundred miles west of Stalingrad, was being smashed from Russian hands by von Weich's army group.

India too might be exposed to attack by a German force from Persia while the Japanese tried in Assam to repeat the easy triumphs of Rangoon and Singapore.

In one sad and bloody encounter at Mersa Matruh Ritchie could lose the war.

And Ritchie was certain to be beaten; that was the obvious truth that Auchinleck had to accept. In this defeat, and the total disaster which would follow, Auchinleck felt himself deeply involved. Ritchie had been his choice; he had left him in command despite advice earlier in the year.

Should he send up another army commander to fight the battle in place of Ritchie and perhaps to save everything by winning it? Should he go himself? Amid all his anxieties, one thing, dictated by his sense of honour, was immediately clear; he must take the blame. And so, in his house by the Pyramids at Mena, on 23rd June, 1942, he wrote to the Chief of the General Staff in London, accepting full responsibility for all that had occurred, offering to vacate the post of C.-in-C. if the C.I.G.S. wished it, and suggesting Alexander as his successor:

> The unfavourable course of the recent battle in Cyrenaica culminating in the disastrous fall of Tobruk impels me to ask you seriously to consider the advisability of retaining me in my command. No doubt you are already considering this and quite rightly, but I want you to know that I also realize the probable effects of the past month's fighting. Personally I feel fit to carry on and reasonably confident of being able to turn the tables on the enemy in time. All the same there is no doubt that in a situation like the present, fresh blood and new ideas at the top may make all the difference between success and stalemate . . . After steeping oneself for months in the same subject all day and every day one is apt to get into a groove and to lose originality. For this theatre originality is essential and a change is quite probably desirable on this account alone, apart from all other considerations such as loss of

influence due to lack of success, absence of luck and all the other things which affect the morale of an army. It occurred to me that you might want to use Alexander who is due here in a day or two. Personally I do not think Wilson could do it now, but he might. I have thought over this a lot and feel I must tell you what I think."

Next day he wrote a letter to the Prime Minister which did credit to his magnanimity as well as his integrity:

I thank you personally and most sincerely for all your help and support during the past year, and deeply regret the failures and setbacks for the past month, for which I accept the fullest responsibility.

The Prime Minister telegraphed assuring him of his complete confidence.

These letters written, part of Auchinleck's mind returned to rest, and he was able to consider more clearly the command of Eighth Army.

Ritchie, of course, must go. "The danger of complete catastrophe," Auchinleck wrote afterwards, "was too great for me to leave the responsibility with a subordinate already subjected for several weeks to extraordinary strain." But even then it was not an easy decision for a man with Auchinleck's sense of loyalty, for Ritchie was, in Auchinleck's words, "a trusted friend and subordinate".

Auchinleck's choice of a new army commander fell for a time on 24th June on General T. W. Corbett, his Chief of the General Staff, and fellow officer of the Indian Army. But then he decided that no subordinate could be asked to preside over the coming disaster. He must go himself.

Corbett was to remain at G.H.Q. to transact all routine business of the office of Commander-in-Chief and to prepare for the defence of the Delta. Because Auchinleck felt that the Eighth Army Staff were tired by battle and mentally vitiated, he decided to take with him a close adviser and personal staff officer, but his choice did not fall on any of the obvious men who had already served him in high staff appointments.

He chose instead his Deputy Chief of the General Staff, Major-General E. Dorman-Smith. It was, and is, a highly controversial appointment; and it had a crucial bearing on the outcome of the most dangerous three weeks of the war.

Dorman-Smith was an Irishman of great charm and high intellectual powers. To these abilities were unfortunately added a fatal gift for wit and a short patience with the stupid. Before the war he had enjoyed a reputation in the British Army as an advanced military thinker; he had played an important part in the struggle to mechanise the army. Dorman-Smith had later been associated with O'Connor and Galloway in planning the highly unorthodox battle of Sidi Barrani. He had been Commandant of the Haifa Staff College from 1940 to December, 1941, and Deputy Chief of the General Staff in Cairo since June, 1942.

Auchinleck had first met him in India before the war when Auchinleck, as Deputy Chief of the General Staff, and Dorman-Smith, as Director of Military Training, had radically re-shaped the Indian Army for a mechanised war. Despite his record and the high opinion of such men as O'Connor and Wavell, Dorman-Smith was by now suspected by the orthodox, who regarded him as 'brilliant but unsound'. But it was because of his unorthodoxy that Auchinleck turned to him in a moment of impending ruin:

> I took Dorman-Smith because I knew he had a most fertile, active and a very good brain. I wanted him because I knew he was a man I could talk to—a fresh mind. I remembered him from our time together in India, when we walked every morning before breakfast in the Simla hills.

In fact, Auchinleck and Dorman-Smith constituted a formidable combination: great powers of leadership united with a brilliant and original intellect. Want of either would have lost us the Middle East.

The prospect of personal command in the field did not exhilarate Auchinleck: "The problem was much too grim and the future much too uncertain for anything of that sort." At 10 a.m. on 25th June, 1942, Dorman-Smith reported to Auchinleck's office in Cairo. The Commander-in-Chief told him that he was going up to take over Eighth Army and that Dorman-Smith was to accompany him. Auchinleck's mood was sombre, but lightened when Dorman-Smith suggested that they should have a final good lunch at the Mehemet Ali Club. At two in the afternoon they climbed aboard an empty bomber. Rommel's advance guards were already beginning to run blind fingers over the face of the Matruh positions.

It was now, sitting on the floor of the aircraft during the flight to Maaten Baggush and amid the roar of the engines, that Auchinleck and Dorman-Smith talked out the strategy and tactics that were to save Egypt and the oil. To help them there was the valuable information received that day from the Prime Minister in Washington: according to the President's informants in Rome, Rommel was expected to delay his attack on Matruh for three or four weeks, but the Prime Minister's own guess was that the delay might be greater.

Auchinleck was clear that the army must not be pinned to the ground at Mersa Matruh; that battle was already compromised. The army must, if there were time, fall back to El Alamein, where it could be disposed for battle according to Auchinleck's own wishes. But even here there was to be no question of a last stand, because at all costs the army must be preserved in being, even if it meant retreating into the Delta, or up the Nile on Port Sudan. For the Persian Gulf oilfield, not Egypt, was the object he must protect to the last. Supplied through Port Sudan he could lie on the flank of a German advance from Egypt towards Iraq and eventually launch a counterstroke.

This strategy has since been strongly condemned. It is said that he should have issued an order of "No retreat" and staked everything on a last battle at the gates of Egypt—as in fact Ritchie had intended. It is difficult in the circumstances of June 1942 to see much merit in the criticism, which Auchinleck himself regards as nonsense; heroic gestures were more opportune in August when all was over.

The aircraft flew on towards Baggush. Dorman-Smith suggested to Auchinleck that their counter-attacks should be aimed at the Italians. To rally them Rommel would have to use his Germans and so disperse his own striking force. This idea Auchinleck accepted. He also agreed that the army artillery should be placed under central control.

In the course of the long flight Auchinleck's mood changed. The sense of defeat that had gripped him on the previous day faded; it had been quite foreign to his character, a stealthy intruder in a moment when all the cumulative pressures had pushed him under.

Early in the evening the aircraft landed on the Royal Air Force field at Maaten Baggush. The sun was throwing long shadows across the salt-sparkling dunes of the coast as the Commander-in-Chief and Dorman-Smith climbed into a dusty yellow staff car and were driven to Eighth Army Headquarters. It had been in these headquarters that O'Connor had planned the destruction of Graziani and his two hundred thousand men two years ago; it was thus familiar ground to Dorman-Smith.

Auchinleck stepped out of the car and on to the sand and officers saluted. They watched the tall, bull-shouldered figure of the Commander-in-Chief as he strode alone towards Ritchie's caravan.

Inside, the two big men—Ritchie was actually the taller—faced each other. Ritchie still showed no outward sign of fatigue or strain; he was, as Auchinleck said, "a strong and stolid fellow", and Auchinleck found him, as he was to find the rest of his headquarters, "surprisingly normal".

No time was wasted.

> I told Ritchie that the situation was such that nobody but I could be saddled with the responsibility and that therefore I was taking over from him.

Ritchie took the news calmly: did he not take everything calmly? There was no tension, no recrimination. The efficient staff officer once again, Ritchie described what he knew of the situation, which, in Auchinleck's words, "wasn't much".

The brief conversation over, Ritchie came out of the caravan alone, got straight into a car and drove away towards the Delta. Then Auchinleck, now in command of Eighth Army, went down into that underground operations room that O'Connor had used, and which had remained unoccupied for eighteen months.

Auchinleck was not a fresh man. He had borne the responsibilities of commanding-in-chief in the Middle East—and the ceaseless, ignorant goading of the Prime Minister—for twelve months. The double burden he could never share and only momentarily forget. But others sometimes glimpsed his intense desire to get some sort of relief from the constant mental pressure. General Galloway recalled that the C.-in-C.:

> might look out of his window and see his ADC's playing some game with a ball in the garden, and would join in. Then he would really enjoy himself, even if only for a few minutes—you and he would forget that he was the Commander-in-Chief.

As Auchinleck entered, Dorman-Smith and the staff looked at him. There were always the others watching—to see whether the chief was tired or angry or despondent or, more rarely, if he had good news. But at G.H.Q. this watching was in a context of wall-map generalities. Here in the shadow of the prison camp and the operating table was the reality of war and, for a general, the reality of command.

Lonely in Cairo, Auchinleck would now be lonelier still, for he had become the leader of desperate and defeated men. It was his job to do the worrying so that every man in the army, from corps commander to private, could sleep easy in his blankets, knowing that defeat would not bear his signature. And here in the desert, the strain of command would be sharpened by want of privacy; there was no secluded commander-in-chief's house where Auchinleck could relax safe from watching eyes for a time in each day; eating and sleeping in the open amid the men, he would have to act out the role of bluff confidence every moment he was awake.

Auchinleck's years spent in small expeditions had given him a very close sense of community with the men in the ranks. This sense was to refresh and strengthen him in the coming battles. He felt strongly that no man must die unnecessarily; the lists of killed and wounded were to lie heavily against his will to continue the fight. It was this true and uncontrived kinship with his soldiers—which he shared with Rommel—that made him seem a warrior of the ancient kind who stood on the field with a pile of enemy dead under his sword and his retainers round him. And in fact his magnificent figure, which wore modern uniform so well, seemed made for armour; the blue eyes for glaring through a visored helmet.

On the evening of 25th June, 1942, he felt, as well as the weight of his new anxieties, a sense of "relief at being in command, with the soldiers and doing something; at being at last personally responsible". He had stepped into a crisis within the general crisis. General Holmes (10th Corps, in Mersa Matruh) drove in to report to the new army commander and receive his orders. He told Auchinleck that Rommel was certain to attack the Eighth Army early on the morrow; this news made it certain that the compromised battle of Matruh would have to be fought after all. The prospects for the battle were gloomy. In Auchinleck's words, "nobody knew where anything was. I was desperately afraid that the troops in Matruh would be surrounded". Auchinleck therefore made clear to Holmes that in no circumstances was he to allow himself to be bottled up in Matruh; Ritchie's order to stand and fight to a finish was revoked. If the battle of Mersa Matruh went badly, Eighth Army would fall back towards El Alamein. Holmes went back to his headquarters "alert and confident", but then he was new to defeat.

There was no time for Auchinleck to alter Ritchie's dispositions; there was no reserve; and Auchinleck's ability to control the battle was further blunted by the distance between his two corps in Mersa Matruh and round Minquar Quaim. He realised that he could be hardly more than an onlooker. But in the few hours that remained he could at least impress on his subordinates the style of warfare he expected.

He was an Indian soldier. All his experience was of empty plains and hills; his natural bent was for mobility and manœuvre. In the First World War he had taken part in the vain attempts to relieve the fortress of Kut-el-Amara in Mesopotamia; it made a permanent mark: "The Turks should have been manœuvred out of their positions—not frontally attacked." Of the great campaigns in history, Stonewall Jackson's Shenandoah campaign with its deception and manœuvre had made a deep impression on him. As a staff college instructor, as a field force commander on the Frontier, and as Deputy Chief of the General Staff in India during the modernisation of the Indian Army, mobility and manœuvre remained his theme, "as opposed to anything based on the battles in France in the First World War". On the evening of 25th June, 1942, he issued to Eighth Army a series of instructions and orders which constitute his written testament as a desert general, and which foreshadow the revolution he tried to bring about during the July battles at Alamein.

He insisted that the army must keep its mobility. It must work as a team, with units co-operating with each other and co-ordinating their efforts. Rigid corps and divisional autonomy was outmoded at the present time; Auchinleck sharply reminded the proudly separatist arms of the British service that they all belonged to the same army. He went on to tell his commanders how they were to deal with German penetrations of the ancient Matruh minefields.

> He will be at once engaged with all available artillery by the division or divisions nearest the threatened spot. Other divisions, while continuing to watch their own allotted flank and fronts, will move at once to the threatened front and attack the enemy boldly and quickly with all available artillery, this movement being co-ordinated by Corps Commanders.

Auchinleck was particularly concerned about the quality of leadership in Eighth Army manifested during the summer campaign. Now, a few hours before battle, he tried to infuse into his commanders something of the initiative and energy shown by their German rivals. He instructed them:

> An essential part of [my] method of defence is the close control and co-ordination of the action of battle groups by divisional commanders who must make their presence felt on the battlefield. It is their duty to supply the driving power . . . The Corps Commanders must be in the closest possible touch so as to ensure that if one Corps or part of it has to give ground the other is immediately able to take advantage of the situation by rapidly and boldly attacking the enemy in the flank.

His conception of war in the desert, as he pointed out with some-what acid emphasis, "called for the maximum of mobility on the part of the troops concerned and the greatest alertness and quickness of decision on the part of all commanders".

All this was revolutionary and long overdue, but it had no effect on the battle of Mersa Matruh. The old, slow habits of the eighteen months since O'Connor had been captured and the ingrained rigidity and orthodoxy of pre-war British military doctrine could not be eradicated in a few hours; it required a long period of repose, wherein the army could be taken apart and remade. The advantage of such a period was to be bought by Auchinleck in the coming battles, but to be enjoyed by his successor.

That night Auchinleck lay in a sleeping-bag on the sand. He slept well, for although he knew that tomorrow's battle was really out of his control, the oriental fatalism he had absorbed in India gave him peace of mind. Early in the morning, as the bright sun beckoned to Rommel from the East and the desert snails crawled up the camel thorn to drink the dew "like", as Dorman-Smith expressed it, "lazy soldiers getting out of their blankets", Auchinleck was awakened, as was to be his habit, with the latest situation report.

All over the desert men stirred, boiled tea over petrol fires and prepared for a day of battle. When the sun was high the *Panzer-armee* came on over the stony ground, dark columns of transport led by squat, white-crossed tanks with gun muzzles nosing left and right for targets. From the shallow weapon pits of the British, they appeared to dissolve and float in the shimmering heat haze.

Rommel's plan for the battle of Mersa Matruh was that of O'Connor for Sidi Barrani; and it was to be as successful. In forty-eight hours Rommel, with sixty tanks and two thousand five hundred German infantry, was to rout two British army corps, with a hundred and fifty tanks, and fling them again along the bitter road to the Nile. But Rommel's plan was more daring in theory than it proved to be in fact. His intelligence placed the tanks of 1st Armoured Division in the British centre, which was in fact virtually empty, and he proposed to drive through this division with the twenty tanks and six hundred men of 21st Panzer Division, together with 90th Light Division. When well in the British rear he would fan out in a double envelopment of the British wings at Mersa Matruh and Minquar Quaim.

British intelligence, no more accurate than the German, credited Rommel with twenty-five thousand Germans and a hundred tanks. For the Panzer Army it was an unexpectedly easy day. In the centre 21st Panzer and 90th Light flicked aside Gleecol and Leathercol, lost in those spaces, and rolled on to the east between 10th and 13th Corps. This was the moment for Gott and 13th Corps to drive into the extended German flank and smash 21st Panzer and 90th Light against 10th Corps in Matruh, in accordance with Auchinleck's orders. But Gott's corps did not move; as in all the battles of the summer British formations who were not under attack were the interested but inactive spectators of those who were. The tanks of the 1st Armoured Division, upon whom the outcome of the battle depended, spent the day by Gott's orders so far out of touch to the south of Sidi Hamza that they did not even meet Rommel's feinting force, 15th Panzer Division, as it drove eastwards along the escarpment south of Minquar Quaim.

Night fell on this scene of British passivity and German progress; Rommel was now ready to sweep north and south in his double envelopment. Yet Rommel's advance constituted only a fantastic imposture; he was so outnumbered by the British that by his manoeuvre he had really put his head through an open door which might slam at any time on his ears. He himself lay with his main body between Holmes and Gott. Far away to the south the twenty tanks of 15th Panzer Division risked collision with the one hundred and fifty of 1st Armoured Division. But Rommel's moral ascendancy over Gott and other Eighth Army commanders was now such that he convinced them it was they who were in terrible danger. On 27th June, he and 21st Panzer Division 'surrounded' the New Zealanders, who remained quite still on the ridge of Minquar Quaim as the Germans worked round them. Rommel then went by car across the empty British centre to 90th Light Division; a brief conference, and 90th Light drove east and north to the coast behind Matruh. Now Holmes too was 'surrounded'.

Rommel's shadow of an army had passed deeper still into a trap; but a trap that would never be sprung because the trappers were held frozen in an hypnotic trance. Ninetieth Light lay on the wrong side of a 'fortress' held by five full-strength, semi-mobile brigades; 21st Panzer Division, now in a strength of fourteen tanks and six hundred men, lay scattered round the full strength and fresh New Zealand Division.

A concise account of the battle suggests an exactitude and tidiness that did not exist. Neither Eighth Army intelligence nor the outgoing army commander had been able to give Auchinleck more than the vaguest picture of his new command—of its dispositions, its numerical strength, its moral state or its equipment. Reports coming through to Auchinleck's headquarters at Baggush during the battle added fresh obscurity to what was already confused; it was impossible for Auchinleck to tell what was really happening. It was thus pointless and even dangerous for him to issue fresh orders. Nor was it possible for him to go up to one of the corps himself, because Ritchie's dispositions had so separated them that once there he would lose all power of decision over the rest of the army.

Therefore, like a calm man lost in the fog, Auchinleck listened to the reports and considered the proper battle he was going to fight at Alamein. Perhaps his principal regret was that he had not been able to meet Gott as well as Holmes beforehand to impress on him personally how the battle was to be fought and to put some backbone into him. But Gott had been unobtainable, roaming as usual somewhere out in the desert in the semi-independent way to which he had become accustomed. And now, though happily Auchinleck did not know it, Gott was losing the battle of Mersa Matruh.

Gott at this time had supped too long on disaster; his optimistic energy had turned into an energetic pessimism. The advance of 21st Panzer Division to the east of the New Zealanders had convinced him that the battle was lost. At a time when Auchinleck expected him to order the combined blow of 1st Armoured Division and the New Zealand Division to the north that would crush Rommel against Holmes' corps, Gott was in fact telling General Freyberg of the New Zealanders that he could withdraw if he so wished. Later in the day, having motored to another part of the field, he had doleful and utterly untrue news for General Lumsden of 1st Armoured Division. Lumsden wanted to move his division up close to the New Zealanders, a manœuvre which might have saved the battle; but Gott shook his head. The New Zealanders, he told Lumsden, "did not exist". He followed this with a formal order to Lumsden to fall back. When Freyberg next spoke to Lumsden by telephone, he therefore learnt that the armour was already leaving him high and dry on Minquar Quaim. Gott's leadership that afternoon had certainly led to mobility, but hardly of the sort intended by Auchinleck.

The news that his left flank had melted eventually reached Auchinleck in the operations room at Maaten Baggush, and told him that the battle was lost. He signalled Holmes in Matruh that Gott had gone and ordered him also to fall back on Alamein. This done, Auchinleck climbed into a covered station wagon and went back himself. This station wagon, with a hole in the roof through which the Commander-in-Chief could stand and talk to his men on the road, was for a few days Eighth Army headquarters; Auchinleck was accompanied by a signals truck and a small staff. Dorman-Smith had left for Fuka the day before in order to prepare for the C.-in-C.'s arrival.

After an unpleasant journey over rough going and under German air attack, Auchinleck and his party bivouacked in the desert. The night spent under the stars, the sleeping-bag laid over a scooped-out body-shaped cavity in the sand, the tea brewed over a petrol fire—these things brought Auchinleck back from the lofty splendour of commanding-in-chief to the kind of soldiering he liked best. In the morning his party found themselves and their vehicles the centre of an empty circle described by the low desert horizon. They set up their wireless; and this was combined headquarters of Eighth Army and Middle East Forces. During the day the Luftwaffe found some targets to bomb in their piece of the desert.

But if the battle of Mersa Matruh was over so far as Auchinleck knew, it was in fact only just beginning for Freyberg and Holmes. Because of confusion in Eighth Army signals, Holmes did not get Auchinleck's order to fall back to Alamein until twelve hours after Gott's corps had begun their retreat. And because of this signals delay, Holmes launched his own break-out when Gott had already abandoned the battle. On the night of 27/28th June, under a bright moon, 10th Corps drove southwards in a dense and conspicuous column of guns and transport. Soon the characteristic lofty profiles of the British trucks stood out starkly in the light of flares and tracer as the Germans poured fire into this easy target. Naked on that open desert, Holmes' inexperienced corps fell back routed into Mersa Matruh. It was on the following morning, while sorting out his force, that Holmes learned that they had been left by Gott surrounded and alone.

That night of the full moon had seen another stirring action as Gott's other victims, the New Zealanders, broke out from Minquar Quaim. With the bayonet they hacked a hole in 21st Panzer Division through which they charged in column, men clinging to every kind of vehicle. As they bucked through moonlight seamed with tracer and splashed with gun flashes, their general, Freyberg, wounded and in bandages, stood in front of a truck shouting:

"By God, another Balaclava!"

It was on the following day, 28th June, that the last bloody encounter of the Matruh battle was fought out between 10th Corps and *Panzerarmee Afrika*. In the white glare of late afternoon Rommel began attacking the surrounded British in Mersa Matruh; but, when night fell, he still lay outside the perimeter. In the utter darkness before the moon rose, 10th Corps prepared for escape. At nine o'clock 10th Corps charged blindly into its besiegers. It was a night of chaos. The British trampled through the headquarters of 90th Light; Rommel's own headquarters were surrounded by burning trucks, which as the only objects to be seen in the pitch dark attracted everybody's fire; the Royal Air Force bombed British troops; and the Germans fired on each other. And then 10th Corps were out in the open, bumping along the escarpment towards Fuka and the passes down to the coast road which Auchinleck had ordered Gott to hold open. But Gott was still elusive, still running a private war without reference to orders; and so when 10th Corps reached the head of the passes, they were greeted not by 13th Corps but by *Panzerarmee Afrika*. There was another brisk action before four-fifths of the corps were able to reach El Alamein. Meanwhile Rommel gathered in six thousand prisoners, forty tanks and many guns in Mersa Matruh.

The Battle of Mersa Matruh, Rommel's most astonishing victory, the battle Auchinleck never meant to accept, was over.

It marked the consummation of a colossal moral ascendancy of the *Panzerarmee Afrika* over the Eighth Army; a matter far more alarming to Auchinleck than the mere fact of defeat. Scattered now between Fuka and El Alamein was the wreckage of two British corps, while close behind them, and sometimes in front of them, came the *Panzerarmee*. It seemed like the last disaster. The Cairo stock exchange and Strafer Gott agreed upon fearing the worst, and all over Egypt panic began to flap its quivering wings. 'Groppi's Horse' and 'Shepheard's Short Range Desert Group' began a highly mobile retirement to the King David Hotel in Jerusalem. In this sliding, melting world of rout and defeatism Auchinleck stood a lonely and defiant figure, and the troops rallied to him.

Perhaps the most disconcerting factor for Auchinleck was his continued ignorance of the state of his army, for Eighth Army headquarters could tell him nothing.

> No one [he wrote later] least of all I—could say whether the Army could be rallied and re-formed soon enough to hold Rommel and save Egypt. This remained in doubt for at least a fortnight.

Therefore, while the race to El Alamein was still going hard, he left his headquarters—now at Ommayid—and drove back towards the enemy, against the current of retreat, to Daba on the coast road.

First he superintended the destruction of the immense stores in Daba. Then he went out on to the coast road, because "I wanted to see what the general state of morale and discipline was among the troops coming back".

The road stretched away from him through the flat, scrubby desert, a black and shimmering tape, two vehicles wide; fifteen hundred miles away through Sollum, Tobruk and Benghazi was Tripoli. Auchinleck stood in the sand by the roadside, bare-headed, and watched his beaten army stream past him towards El Alamein. It came radiator to tailboard: tanks on transporters; supply trucks; troop carriers; towed bombers without wings, like monstrous maimed insects; trucks loaded with mess and Naafi stores and furniture; guns. A yellow-painted travelling fun-fair on the move to the next ground. As a scene of disastrous retreat, it was incongruous: instead of the starvation and frostbite that Corunna, Moscow and Valley Forge have made the traditional trappings, there was the travel agent's sunshine, the Mediterranean's copper sulphate blue between the white dunes. Their faces dried and brown as biscuit, the men passed by him in trucks powdered thickly with dust and hung about with bed-rolls and billy-cans.

> The troops were bewildered [Auchinleck recollected later] but completely unconcerned. There were no signs of panic, such as people trying to pass each other. The spectacle was encouraging from the point of view of morale, but there was terrible disorganization, and I could see the army would need re-fitting.

Yet there was an aspect of the choked traffic on the coast road which surprised, appalled and angered the Commander-in-Chief; it was the superfluous clutter the army was carrying with it in its retreat—the trucks loaded with Naafi stores and furniture and all the other hamper of welfare. It had not been necessary—it would have been impossible—to take all this comfort up the passes of the North-West Frontier; and to Auchinleck it was another aspect of the softness and luxury that he had hated in Cairo. In his anger at the sight he resolved to strip the army down to what it needed for battle; and he, the Commander-in-Chief, would set the example in his own headquarters. "I think," he said long afterwards, "that we are inclined to carry too much about. We are too luxurious. In Mesopotamia in 1914–18 we lived much more simply."

His vigil on the roadside had served another purpose: "I also wanted to show myself a bit, and talk to one or two of the chaps." Either there, or while standing up hatless in his car, he chatted to

as many as he could, from as many different formations as possible—
to British, to Indians, to Commonwealth soldiers. If his men impressed Auchinleck, 'The Auk' equally impressed his men. He looked a fighter, big and burly, with a fighter's pugnacious chin and mouth; and they could tell from the way he talked to them that he was a real chap—no tricks, none of 'the old flannel', the 'bull' through which the British soldier can instantly see.

For Auchinleck was a simple, genuine man, brought up by his mother—whom he admired and loved—in an old-fashioned code of manners and principles. Men had always loved the Auk. "He sometimes appeared severe and formidable," as General Galloway put it, "but he had great charm and innate kindness."

Auchinleck drove back to Ommayid again to prepare for the desperate action that would be under way in a few hours. Yet there was on that day, 29th June, 1942, a fair chance that there would be no such action, for Rommel was trying with all his relentless energy to sweep the British in shreds through the Alamein 'bottleneck' without giving them a pause in which they might recover themselves. The exhausted *Panzerarmee*, dreaming of sleep and of swimming in the creamy breakers that curled endlessly along the coast of Egypt, toiled on through the heat and sand clouds. Above them the sky now belonged to the Royal Air Force, which had at last abandoned distant strategic targets and was dropping a moving curtain of bombs between Eighth Army and its pursuers. With their petrol and ammunition trucks burning, the starved panzers began to slow down.

During the 29th and 30th June, 1942, the war in the desert—the war between Britain and Germany—moved to its climax, as both armies raced each other over the last few miles to Alamein. No moment in the war had been or was to be as mouth-drying as this.

Back in the Delta the British were affording an example of British phlegm that could be remembered by the Egyptians with advantage in the future. Behind a smoke-screen of burning paper, the 'Gabardine Swine' (as Auchinleck recollects that base personnel were dubbed) moved out of harm's way with a speed that would have impressed Rommel. The Royal Navy, without bothering to inform the Army, weighed anchor and sailed from Alexandria with such despatch that the White Ensign was still flying over the deserted camp at Sidi Bishr while Egyptians looted it at leisure. In the Alamein defences the racket of road-drills gave an imitation of the noise of battle as the troops employed the last hours in drilling new weapon pits in the hard rock.

From the open desert the last British stragglers were coming in. Among these was 1st Armoured Division, which had hoped for a peaceful journey but which had instead bumped into two Italian divisions once and into the Afrika Korps twice. During the morning of 30th June, 10th Corps was still streaming east along the coast road past El Alamein and through 1st South African Division, which held the coastal flank. But the stream of vehicles at last dried up; the road stretched empty into the haze before the eyes of the Eighth Army gunners, and somewhere beyond was Rommel.

Auchinleck had now moved from his temporary headquarters at Ommayid to the place behind the Ruweisat Ridge from which he was to direct the battle. To his soldiers he issued a calm and characteristically untheatrical order of the day:

> The enemy is stretching to his limit and thinks we are a broken army . . . He hopes to take Egypt by bluff. Show him where he gets off.

Auchinleck's own personal recovery from the terrible depression and sense of failure of June 23–25 was now complete.

"The British pride themselves on being good losers," he remarked to Dorman Smith. "I'm a damn bad loser. I'm going to win."

About noon visibility grew worse as a sandstorm rose. Whirling dust filled eyes and nostrils and choked the mechanisms of guns— thick as a London fog, but oven-hot. Eighth Army peered into the billowing murk, waiting for it to form into the shapes of tanks crawling on towards Alexandria.

Then something moved out there—tanks, trucks and guns in the blowing sand. It was 90th Light. A salvo crashed out from a battery of British field artillery, the first shots in the First Battle of Alamein.

But no more Germans were seen that day.

CHAPTER TWO

At this time, the British Broadcasting Corporation and the British press were telling their public that the Eighth Army had retreated into 'The Alamein Line', which apparently stretched like a desert Maginot from the Mediterranean forty miles to the salt marshes of the Quattara Depression. Here, alone in the desert arena, it appeared that there were no open flanks for Rommel to turn with his armour. It is the way of wartime propaganda, manufactured from hour to hour to keep up home morale, to form in the public's mind lasting and false impressions; impressions which over the years become national myths. But the oddest thing about the dream world of propaganda is its influence on the real world of battle. Hitler and Stalingrad is one case of this; Churchill and Tobruk another; the B.B.C. and Alamein a third. On 29th and 30th June, 1942, the British broadcasts about the Alamein Line reached two unexpected audiences. The first was the troops of the Eighth Army, who heard it on the way back from Matruh, and who were surprised to find that the line was just the same old empty desert. The second was Rommel, who believed in it and, because he believed in it, delayed his attack twenty-four hours in order to prepare more thoroughly, and so gave Auchinleck what he needed more than tanks—time.

In fact, neither under Auchinleck nor Montgomery was the British front at Alamein a continuous web of defences right across the bottleneck. There was always an open flank; at first because the troops were so thin on the ground it was impossible to hold the entire forty-mile front, and later because Auchinleck preferred to leave the southern sector open in order to tempt Rommel on to the British refused left flank along the Alam Halfa Ridge. What defences there were on 30th June, 1942, had been constructed by Auchinleck's orders after June, 1941, and improved in haste by Norrie in the last few days.

Between the Mediterranean at El Alamein and the seven-hundred-foot cliffs that line the northern edge of the Quattara Depression

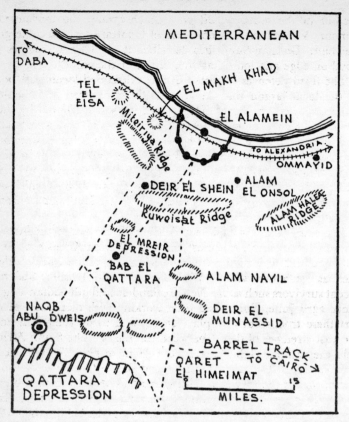

Map 17. GENERAL MAP TO ILLUSTRATE FIRST BATTLE OF
ALAMEIN
July 1942

was a stretch of various desert as wide as the distance between
Croydon and Brighton—about forty miles. This can hardly be called
a bottleneck. The northern half was so featureless that almost
imperceptible rises in the ground became of great tactical import-
ance. South of these ridges—Miteiriya, Ruweisat—there were
abrupt escarpments and bad going that became worse and worse
until the Quattara Depression was reached. Auchinleck in 1941
had chosen this unpleasant piece of country as the final defence of
Egypt for two reasons: firstly, if the forty-mile-wide neck were held
in proper strength (two full-strength infantry divisions and a large
armoured force), it could not be turned; and secondly, the jagged

ground in the south would very much cramp the movement of armour. West of the Alamein-Bab el Quattara track too the going was bad: Dorman-Smith has described it as "large flat stones that stood on edge and looked at you, one after the other".

The fixed defences consisted of three defended localities ('boxes' in the local jargon that Auchinleck hated) placed at fifteen-mile intervals across the neck. The right flank was anchored by the El Alamein locality, which blocked the railway and the coast road; it had been intended as a corps headquarters. Its defences were much like Tobruk's, but with a perimeter shorter by half. In the centre was the locality of Bab el Quattara, in fine defensive country full of cliffs; and in the south was the locality of Abu Dweiss which commanded a way down the cliffs to a track in the Quattara Depression that could be used by cars.

Into these positions had been drifting for the last fortnight troops from all over the Middle East Command: fresh troops such as the 18th Indian Brigade from Iraq; the wreckage of the Gazala defeats, such as 1st South African Division and 50th Division; and more recent survivors such as the New Zealanders and 9th Indian Brigade. Since 23rd June, Norrie had been working with desperate speed to sort these troops out and place them; and to do something to fill the vast stretches of desert between the boxes. The South Africans held the extreme right flank, in the Alamein box. A new box had been established between Alamein and Bab el Quattara, at Deir El Shein, west of the Ruweisat Ridge, and had been garrisoned by 18th Indian Brigade. Bab el Quattara was held by the 6th New Zealand Brigade, with 4th and 5th New Zealand Brigades behind them to the east. Far out to the south was 9th Indian Brigade, lacking both a water supply and artillery.

In the breathing space accorded him by Rommel, Auchinleck continued the radical changes in battle technique laid down in his operations instructions before Matruh. It was clear to him that the immobile infantry in the Alamein defences would be as helpless and ineffective as those in the Gazala boxes. Auchinleck therefore thinned them out so that no more remained in the line than could be carried by allocated transport. He also broke down the divisional organization into the flexible 'battle group' system that Rommel had used with such success for eighteen months. Auchinleck's battle groups, extemporized in a time of scarcity of equipment, consisted of lorry-borne infantry surrounding nuclei of 25-pounders. They could do two things in the desert that a British infantry division could not do—move and hit. In particular, Auchinleck took two brigade groups from the South Africans in the Alamein perimeter and placed them in the open desert north of the Ruweisat Ridge. Hence the box was almost empty. But its presence was a psychological factor forcing avoidance on Rommel.

Auchinleck's efforts to cure the arthritis of the traditional fifteen-thousand-men British division have aroused enduring controversy. Orthodoxy alleged it was a 'penny packets' policy. But Auchinleck is convinced he is right:

> The "Battle Group Controversy" is rubbish. In the circumstances existing there was no other way. Infantry and artillery in solid divisional lumps were not and could not be any match for armour, until and unless they were dug in with unturnable flanks. Even so the enemy armour could penetrate and play hell behind unless opposed by our armour, which was not there—to begin with.

Auchinleck further considered that

> swift turning movements are the essence of desert warfare. To do this you must be strong in "armour", stronger than the enemy or at least as strong. If this requirement is absent you have had it—infantry and artillery are helpless in the Desert without armour, however brave they are—useless mouths who can be outflanked, surrounded and mopped up at will . . .

Auchinleck had his supporters. The New Zealand Brigadier Kippenberger, a hard critic of British command, wrote that "The brigade group organization had many advantages for desert warfare, particularly in mobility and quick readiness for action." Since the Second World War, the American, British, French and German armies have all replaced the division as a basic unit by some form of the brigade group.

At Dorman-Smith's suggestion, Auchinleck had now had all the artillery re-grouped under his own command as an equivalent of Rommel's army artillery. For the first time in the desert since O'Connor the British were to defend and to attack under the cover of mass gunfire. Auchinleck also formed a new kind of armoured brigade—4th Light Armoured Brigade—composed entirely of armoured cars and intended to exploit break-throughs at a speed impossible for tracked vehicles.

The armour remained the greatest of Auchinleck's anxieties. He had a hundred and fifty tanks in 1st Armoured Division, commanded by General Lumsden, but of them only two squadrons were Grants, which were now believed by the British command to be the only British tanks at all fit for battle. The morale of officers and men was shaken after a month of heavy losses and continuous defeat. This was no reflection on the courage of British tank men, but they had seen too many knocked-out tanks with charred objects still sitting in the crew's places, had experienced too often the warm and odorous horror of a comrade's intestines spread over them in the hot imprisonment of the tank. Shaky nerves extended to Lumsden himself. For example, four days after the battle at Alamein began, there was a sharp exchange between him and his corps commander, Norrie, in Norrie's caravan on the Ruweisat Ridge, witnessed by Dorman-Smith. Lumsden pleaded hysterically the strain of battle on his division and "in terms almost insultingly insubordinate" demanded that the armour should be stationed further to the rear. The meeting might have ended in a furious row; but Norrie, himself a cavalryman and an officer of great coolness and balance, handled Lumsden with patience and sympathy, and the armour stayed where it was. But Auchinleck intended to use it 'close-hauled' under the cover of his artillery.

In the last two days before the battle began, Auchinleck, Norrie, Dorman-Smith and the staff worked without a break in the heat and flies of the operations caravan. In the absence of an H.Q. mess, sandwiches filled with oily butter and 'desert chicken' and mugs of tea were brought to them from time to time. There was no question, in those flying, crowded hours, of preparing a tidy, copy-book array. In Auchinleck's words,

> The Eighth Army was rebuilt as far as could be done with the forces available and having regard to the standard of training of newly arrived troops. It was not and could not be a reasoned, measured process.

At the same time he had to prepare against possible defeat. On 30th June he ordered Holmes of 10th Corps to go back and organize the defences of the Delta; next day he issued orders for the conduct of a retreat from Alamein, should that be necessary. For Auchinleck's view was—and is—that to issue a "No retreat" order at Alamein in the circumstances of the time would have been "bloody stupid". He was, after all, Commander-in-Chief as well as Eighth Army commander, and he had to consider the safety of his entire command. Eighth Army must be kept in being, because he recognized, as did the Chief of the Imperial General Staff, that the oil of the Persian Gulf was more important to the war than Egypt. In fact, to stand and fight at all at Alamein was a decision of enormous courage; Wavell, for example, had accepted a staff study in 1941 which recommended that if the Axis forces got east of Matruh, then Egypt would have to be evacuated.

His army placed, Auchinleck waited in his headquarters behind the Ruweisat Ridge, close to the front, for Rommel to attack. He had made his guess as to Rommel's plans: he signalled London on the evening of 30th June that he expected the enemy to make his main effort between Alamein and Bab el Quattara. The British army was therefore disposed to meet an attack on its right centre. He signalled his army at the same time that

the Army Commander appreciates that as the enemy has not attacked this evening he will attack at a very early hour tomorrow morning . . . all troops to expect attack from midnight onwards.

The time for attack in fact given in the *Panzerarmee*'s operations orders was 0300 hours.

Auchinleck proposed to defeat any attempt by Rommel to pass round the El Alamein box to the sea by blocking it or taking it in the flank with the South African battle groups. The German force making the expected main blow on his right centre would be struck from the south by New Zealand battle groups—especially at night when the exhausted German armour leaguered—and from the north by 1st Armoured Division from its assembly area at the western end of Ruweisat Ridge.

Rommel proposed to hustle the British into a fresh retreat by bluff and dazzling manœuvre. Of the great army that had rolled round Bir Hacheim in the bright morning of 26th May, only fifteen hundred German infantry and some sixty tanks remained, together with thirty Italian tanks and about five thousand men of that Italian infantry which was useless in an offensive battle. So starved was Rommel of essential supplies and equipment by the ships of the Royal Navy and the stupidity of the German Supreme Command that four out of five of his soldiers had travelled up from the frontier in captured British trucks. The German Command just could not be made to see what a colossal strategic success might be won in the Middle East by sending Rommel one of the twenty-odd panzer divisions swallowed up in Russia. However, Eighth Army Intelligence credited Rommel with at least a hundred German tanks and twenty-five thousand Germans; bluff was in fact his most hopeful weapon. Therefore Rommel planned to repeat Matruh: 90th Light Division

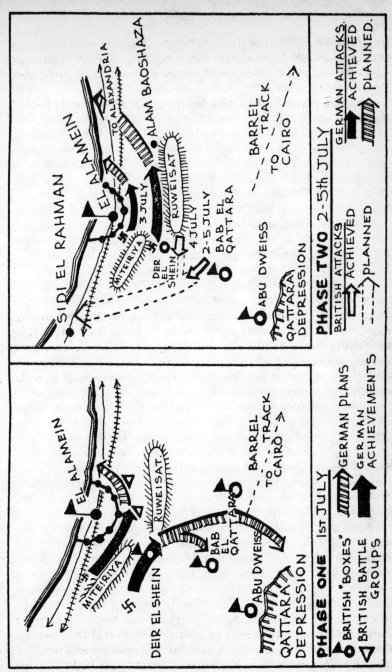

MAP 18. FIRST BATTLE OF ALAMEIN
July 1942, Phases One and Two

PHASE ONE 1st JULY

EL ALAMEIN

SIDI EL RAHMAN

MITEIRIYA

DEIR EL SHEIN

RUWEISAT

BAB EL QATTARA

ABU DWEISS

QATTARA DEPRESSION

BARREL TRACK TO CAIRO ─>

BRITISH "BOXES"
BRITISH BATTLE GROUPS
GERMAN PLANS
GERMAN ACHIEVEMENTS

PHASE TWO 2-5th JULY

SIDI EL RAHMAN

EL ALAMEIN

TO ALEXANDRIA

ALAM BAOSHAZA

MITEIRIYA

3 JULY

DER EL SHEIN

RUWEISAT

4 JULY

2-5 JULY

BAB EL QATTARA

ABU DWEISS

QATTARA DEPRESSION

BARREL TRACK TO CAIRO ─>

BRITISH ATTACKS: ACHIEVED PLANNED
GERMAN ATTACKS: ACHIEVED PLANNED

and the Afrika Korps would drive through the British right centre, between the Alamein and Deir el Shein boxes; and then, while 90th Light turned north to the sea and cut off the troops in Alamein— which German intelligence thought consisted of the remnants of 50th Division—the Afrika Korps would sweep far to the south behind the British centre and left flank to attack them from the rear. It was exactly as Auchinleck had guessed.

Rommel expected his men to move at a brisk pace: Afrika Korps, for example, was to cover thirty miles through the British defences at ten miles an hour. A sign of growing German weakness was the employment of Italians, who had not been used at all at Matruh. A part of them was to line the western face of the Alamein box, part to hold the Ruweisat Ridge when it had been captured. The Italian 20th Corps (*Corpo Armata de Manovra*) would accompany the Afrika Korps and attack the New Zealanders at Bab el Quattara.

The battle plan was typical of Rommel: hasty, reckless, unrealistic and based on poor information. But he counted as always on the moral factor to make nonsense of rational calculation; once he was behind the enemy, the British Command, fearful for its communications, would again lose its nerve and bolt. He did not know yet that he now faced the man who had called his bluff in November, 1941.

If there were a moment during the desert campaigns when, as before Valmy, destiny seemed to hold its breath, it was on the night of 30th June/1st July, 1942. This night, the eve of the battle that, with the defence of Stalingrad, marked the turn of the Second World War, was fine and decked with stars. Later the moon rose, and turned the desert and its waiting armies to black and tarnished silver. By its sad and fatal light the two veteran divisions of the Afrika Korps set out on their approach march, and became deeply entangled in the course of climbing up and down unexpected and deeply shadowed escarpments. As was the Germans' custom when in confusion, they sent up a magnificent display of Very lights of every colour to indicate to each other where they lay. For the watching British outposts it was an odd diversion. The Afrika Korps arrived on their startline three hours late; things had already begun to go wrong with Rommel's battle. When it was light enough on the morning of 1st July, 1942, for airmen to discern targets on the ground, the Royal Air Force savagely bombed the Afrika Korps and threw it into more confusion. At last, and very late, the Panzer Army, with a squealing clatter of tank tracks, began to advance.

Afrika Korps (21st and 15th Panzer Division) on Auchinleck's right centre ran immediately into heavy fire from the Indians in the Deir el Shein box and the South African battle groups further east. This was a check and a shock: German intelligence had placed these troops much further to the east, out of their way. Rommel's tired men therefore had to endure heavy fighting instead of the expected morning's motoring. As they struggled towards the east, the fire grew hotter and the whole of the day was spent by both panzer divisions, led in person by the corps commander, General Nehring, in dealing with the Indians in Deir el Shein, in the face of whose stubborn defence the southern German envelopment thus completely broke down.

The northern envelopment did no better. 90th Light Division wheeled round the Alamein box as expected by Auchinleck and was caught in the converging fire of the South African brigade groups on Auchinleck's right flank. Ninetieth Light struggled on through soft sand and shell-bursts; and by midday its attack seemed more promising to Rommel than that of Afrika Korps, stuck at Deir el Shein. He switched his few reserves to their support and in the afternoon he and Bayerlein went up in person to drive on the attack. With Rommel behind them, 90th Light managed to move a little further to the east of Alamein. The desert about them continually erupted in plumes of sand and lumps of rock as Auchinleck's newly re-grouped army-controlled artillery shelled them furiously from all sides. By the late afternoon even Rommel was stuck; he and Bayerlein lay out on the ground with his troops under this fire, unable to move, unable to give an order.

These were the hours when the tactical initiative began to pass from Rommel to Auchinleck. While the Panzer Army and its chief were paralysed, the British commander was preparing orders for counter-attack.

That night, as 90th Light lay panting in its salient, and Afrika Korps were discovering that their eventual capture of Deir el Shein had cost them eighteen out of fifty-five remaining runners, Strafer Gott at last came into Auchinleck's headquarters. There was a conference in Auchinleck's operations caravan—Gott, tired and stained with defeat; Norrie, cool and able, but carrying his own memories of defeat; Auchinleck, new from Cairo, vigorous and belligerent.

Auchinleck reviewed the day's fighting. It had gone well. Rommel had achieved nothing of his strategic design. His only success had been the destruction of the Indians at Deir el Shein at the price of Afrika Korps' standstill; and Auchinleck took the loss calmly. It might have opened a dangerous breach in his right centre, but the slowness of its fall had given him time to muster fresh forces, and Afrika Korps now faced an even harder task on the morrow.

A greater cause for anxiety was the state of the British armour. This had been intended by Auchinleck to fall upon the Germans investing Deir el Shein and destroy them: it would have been a major success. Instead, one British armoured brigade became hopelessly stuck in soft sand and the other, with eighteen runners, did not get into action until the box was about to fall. This brigade skirmished with 21st Panzer Division and then, by a mistake, was ordered home again.

Auchinleck explained his orders for the following day. It was essential that Eighth Army recover the tactical initiative—strategic defence depended on tactical attack—in order that Rommel should be thrown off his stride. Therefore Eighth Army would launch a counter-stroke on the morrow. The plan, as Auchinleck expounded it in his deep, big man's voice, was bold. While 30th Corps held Rommel's attacks, as it had done all that day, 13th Corps, with the armour, would drive into and round Rommel's right flank, across his communications and on to the coast road at Sidi Rahman. The object of the manoeuvre was Rommel's complete destruction.

This conference with Gott and Norrie on the evening of 1st July, 1942, ended the drift and confusion in Eighth Army. It established Auchinleck's personal authority over his corps commanders; this was specially important in the case of Gott, who had been so disheartened. It opened the resolute and clever fighting by which Rommel's will to victory was bent, at first slowly, then more and more quickly until finally it was broken.

The oppressive awareness of being mastered by a superior will and superior forces would come to Rommel gradually through the dense medium of a confused battle, with its clash of isolated units, its false and true reports, its small defeats and little victories. But on the evening of 1st July and despite the setbacks of the day Rommel was still buoyant and sanguine. He signalled to Rome and Berlin that he had won a great victory and that he was on the road to Alexandria. There only remained the task of turning this lie into fact.

During those night hours when exhausted men hunger desperately for sleep, he tried to drive his divisions along their original thrust lines, but in vain. The Afrika Korps, on Auchinleck's right centre, could not move because the Royal Air Force had bombed their convoys of supply trucks to a standstill. It was quiet in 90th Light's part of the desert, but the division did not move either. Its men wanted sleep more than victory, more than food; and because it was a quiet night, they slept. Towards dawn they returned reluctantly from the womb of sleep to the cold white sand of Egypt and began again to struggle towards the east, round the Alamein box. Out of the darkness came the murderous concentric fire from Auchinleck's army artillery, the tracer curving towards them, and 90th Light were stuck again.

By first light on 2nd July, Rommel had had to submit a little to Auchinleck: he had abandoned his plan of a double envelopment. Instead Afrika Korps was to join 90th Light in a single envelopment of the El Alamein box. Subsequent reports that both German panzer divisions were concentrating about Deir el Shein gave Auchinleck hope that his own plans for the day would bring a decisive victory, for Rommel's concentration towards the north had exposed his right flank.

The day—the endless day of a battle—slowly passed in the tiny army headquarters behind the Ruweisat Ridge. Distantly the smoke rose and drifted across the brassy sky.

From the west, where the mirage turned desert and crawling armies to a glittering liquid, sounded the iron rattle, the dull violence of a major action. The reports came in, the flags moved on the map in the baking metal oven of the operations caravan; did they truly represent what was happening out there beyond the mirage?

There were other doubts for the C.-in-C. Would his troops and their officers remain steady in the face of a dangerous encirclement of the Alamein box? Most of the men on his right flank were South Africans under Pienaar, who was under pressure from his own government to avoid white South African losses. If they should give way, the army would be in great danger. And how was his own attack going? Gott had seemed very tired last night; was he driving the attack as hard as he should? If it were successful, the danger to the Middle East might be over before nightfall.

The day died at last, and gradually the truth began to shape itself as the reports were sifted. Auchinleck's counter-stroke had failed; yet, not so much failed as never been made. To prepare and launch such a stroke in a few hours had proved beyond the powers of British staff work and leadership alike. Instead of a sudden terrible blow coming out of the desert, there was a slow and laborious accumulation of pressure. The New Zealand Division, which provided most of the infantry, was commanded by a young brigadier instead of the wounded Freyberg, "that tremendous dynamo", as Auchinleck expressed it. Gott, the corps commander, could not find the bounding energy of leadership the bold plan required. The armour, instead of passing to the south of the German armour, met it head-on along the Ruweisat Ridge, and in that collision both Rommel's and Auchinleck's plans were smashed.

Yet, with the road to the Delta still barred, the day was Auchinleck's; and German war diaries after six weeks of triumphant reporting became competitive essays in tear-jerking. They were fluent and moving on such topics as battle fatigue, the incessant British air attacks, and the universally powerful British defences. Rommel himself sensed the change in the climate of the battle:

> General Auchinleck, who had meanwhile taken over command himself at Alamein, was handling his forces with very considerable skill . . . He seemed to view the situation with decided coolness, for he was not allowing himself to be rushed into accepting a "second best" solution by any moves we made.

A tank state informed Rommel that he had only twenty-six runners. His supply lines, stretched to Benghazi and Tripoli, were dislocated by bombing. His men, he knew, were exhausted, and British resistance, instead of collapsing, was sharpening.

He gave himself one more day in which to gain a victory, failing which the Panzer Army would have to pass to the defensive.

Auchinleck on the other hand was still thinking in terms of a massive counter-stroke to Rommel's rear. Having forced Rommel to commit all his Germans on the coastal flank, he now felt himself able to bring the New Zealanders at Bab el Quattara and the Indians at Abu Dweiss in to his centre; instead of a curtain of troops across the Alamein neck, he would now have his army concentrated closely under his hand. There was a mass of manoeuvre at last.

Next day Rommel struck again. The panzer divisions struggled on, calling upon each other for help, shelled, bombed, and disgruntled. The fruit of all their efforts still lay just beyond their reach, on the other side of the unexpectedly revived British: modern cities and ancient vices, hot baths and white beds, the pleasure of women, final victory. It was therefore with the energy of desperation that Rommel, cursing and exhorting, and his *Panzerarmee* strove to split the British and motor the last few miles into Alexandria. At ten to one in the afternoon Rommel signalled:

I demand energetic attack by the whole of DAK.

At twenty-past he was up in person to inform them that "the Commander-in-Chief orders that the attack must be carried out with the utmost energy". The Panzer Army fought their way eastwards along both sides of the Ruweisat Ridge and by late afternoon, with the sun behind them, had reached Alam Baoshaza, well to the south-east of Alamein.

On the map in Auchinleck's caravan this might appear a deep and dangerous penetration, but the Auk was unmoved. It had, he knew, been made against the bitter and deliberately mobile defence of his battle groups and of 1st Armoured Division; his sense of the battlefield told him that the Panzer Army had little left to give. At the end of the day the Germans had stopped in a paralysis of exhaustion, and Auchinleck was still between them and victory.

Meanwhile the Italians in the south had suffered a bloody reverse. As Ariete Division tried to outflank the New Zealanders (who had not yet moved north from Bab el Quattara), it was struck from the east by tanks of 1st Armoured Division and from the south by the New Zealanders. By midday Ariete had lost almost all its artillery and all but five tank runners.

At four minutes to eleven p.m. on the 3rd July, 1942, Rommel acknowledged temporary defeat by ordering his army to dig in and await a British counter-stroke.

Auchinleck sent an encouraging signal to his men that evening:

> From C-in-C to all ranks 8 Army. Well done everybody. A very good day. Stick to it.

It was on this day when the Panzer Army was panting in prostration under Auchinleck's guns, that the Prime Minister in London chose to attack Auchinleck and his men to the Chief of the Imperial General Staff. Of this, Brooke wrote later:

> I had an uphill task defending him and pointing out the difficulties of his present position. Also the fact that any rash move on his part at the present time would very quickly lose us Egypt. However, P.M. was in one of his unpleasant moods, going back over old ground, and asking where the 750,000 men in the Middle East were, what they were doing, and why they were not fighting.

It was still, as Wellington would have said, a near-run thing. As Auchinleck went among his troops in the lulls of the battle to revive the offensive, optimistic spirit in them and their officers, he was conscious that he stood almost alone against a drifting current of defeatism that was perhaps as dangerous to the Army's defence of Egypt as Rommel. An anecdote illuminates this loneliness. On 1st July, the Afrika Korps radio had jubilantly warned the ladies of Cairo and Alexandria to "make ready to receive them to-night". Dorman-Smith thought he would use this news item to amuse the Auk and take his mind off his anxieties. He went to Auchinleck's caravan and said:

"Sir, I'm afraid we are attempting the impossible."

Auchinleck rounded on him, grim and surprised.

"What do you mean?" His voice was thick with sudden anger. "Do you say this? I always thought you believed we could pull this thing off."

Dorman-Smith went on to explain about the Afrika Korps' message to the ladies of Alexandria and to suggest that for Eighth Army to try to defend *their* honour was a hopeless task since they hadn't any. Auchinleck was mollified, but not amused:

"Don't be a damn fool, Chink."

As well as conducting a touch-and-go battle, and rallying and re-forming his army in the middle of it, he had his continued vast responsibilities as Commander-in-Chief, Middle East, not made easier by a lack of consistent advice from London on strategic priorities. There was for example the news from Russia, worse every day and heavy with impending threat to Auchinleck's northern front. Kupiansk had fallen on the day Auchinleck had arrived at Eighth Army; then another gigantic German blow was struck from the region of Kursk; and on 1st July the 2nd Panzer Army smashed a gap in the Russian defences through which the whole of von Weich's army group began to roll towards the Don. Next day the third German attack was launched by von Bock with three armies and three panzer armies between Byelgorod and Kharkov. The Russian front in the Ukraine had thus broken like glass under a hammer; and for Auchinleck, who knew that Persia and Iraq—with their essential oilfields—were held by troops hardly numerous enough to assure civil order, the news of this developing threat to his rear was deeply disturbing. It was not less so to the higher direction of the war in London: the Chief of the Imperial General Staff and his staff were busy working on plans for dealing with a German arrival at the head of the Persian Gulf.

Yet despite his double burden, Auchinleck outwardly retained his cool nerve and his big-man's calm. He had settled in now at his tiny headquarters behind the Ruweisat Ridge. Here, in an area of featureless and unpleasant desert, were the caravans of the

Commander-in-Chief, his operations and communications staff, an operations room, a mess lorry (but no mess) and some slit trenches. Auchinleck's caravan had a let-down lean-to shelter; beneath this, in sleeping bags on the desert ground, slept the Commander-in-Chief and Dorman-Smith, his Chief of Staff—the first in the history of the British Army.

It was not every man's idea of an army headquarters. Some of the staff and the press bitterly criticised its austerity and discomfort, its distance from anywhere but the front, the number of its flies and the scarcity of its headquarters staff and equipment. For the first time since Auchinleck and Tedder had established in 1941 very close co-operation of army and air force through a combined headquarters, the Eighth Army and the Desert Air Force headquarters were apart; the Air Force had gone back to Burg el Arab on the coast. It was an amicable arrangement: Tedder felt he could not risk his elaborate communications network in a place so near the fighting, while Auchinleck had equally valid military reasons for staying there. He wrote later:

> In the conditions prevailing and the desperate nature of the situation, it seemed to me essential that the Commander should be as close behind the line as he could be without risking dislocation by capture or bombardment. Ruweisat Ridge was in my opinion the key to the whole position.

He was only half a mile from Willoughby Norrie's 30th Corps headquarters; it was easy to confer without either of them being taken far from home.

Auchinleck also had a characteristic personal reason for not joining the air force:

> To have gone to Burg el Arab would have taken me out of the atmosphere in which I wish to live, for the sake of my own and the army's morale.

The critics especially disliked Auchinleck's headquarters' exposure to air attack; there was one air raid in which Auchinleck and Dorman-Smith fell out of a caravan into a slit trench a few seconds before a German cannon shell tore a hole in the floor where the Commander-in-Chief had been standing.

If there were valid reasons for siting the Army H.Q. behind Ruweisat, there were others, springing deep from Auchinleck's character, for making it so austere. The memory of the circus on the

Daba road remained with him; and he, the Commander-in-Chief, would set the army an example of plain living. His headquarters staff had the same water ration as the troops; he himself had a basin wash once a week. He wished also to regain that sense of kinship with his men he had known in the hills of India; to draw strength from the awareness that he was no longer a uniformed diplomat, but a soldier again. He wrote later of the simplicity of his headquarters:

> It had an effect on me. If I had been sleeping in a bed I would not have felt the same. As it was, I felt a sense of community with the chaps.

Amid the unceasing worries of the battle Auchinleck left undisturbed the anomalous situation in regard to Brigadier Whiteley, Brigadier General Staff of the Eighth Army, and General Dorman-Smith. Dorman-Smith was in the first place the channel through which Auchinleck transacted business as C.-in-C.; but he also acted, as Auchinleck intended, as his closest adviser on the battle; as *de facto* Chief of Staff. Whiteley was tired by the long summer battle and Auchinleck suspected that he and the rest of the Eighth Army staff, with their placidity and conventional minds, had had a share in the slowness and clumsiness of British reaction and action. Auchinleck therefore began to issue orders through Dorman-Smith rather than through Whiteley; and this developed into a custom. This duplication was bound to lead to bad feeling within the army, especially as Dorman-Smith had no official post. In retrospect it seems clear that Auchinleck should have faced the implications of his temporary arrangement, and recognised Dorman-Smith's functions by appointing him formally Chief of Staff, as was de Guingand later. But Auchinleck was immersed in the crowded events of a battle and he left the arrangement alone. In his own words, "It worked."

On 4th July, 1942, as the Americans celebrated their first wartime Independence Day and the British had been fighting in the desert for over two years, the stillness of perfect balance held the Alamein battlefield. Rommel, checked in his first rush, was preparing to deploy the *Panzerarmee* again for a fresh attempt on the last sixty miles to Alexandria; Auchinleck was preparing another counter-stroke. In the evening he had Norrie and Gott in to hear his orders; it gave him a fresh opportunity of judging Gott, that romantic legend of the desert. He was not as impressed as some: "A very curious character. He was a tradition in the Army, especially with the junior officers. I thought he was tired at that time."

As Gott and Norrie listened, Auchinleck expounded his plans:

> Our task remains to destroy the enemy as far east as possible and not
> let him get away as a force in being. This can best be achieved by
> containing the enemy's eastern and southern flank and attacking his
> rear. It is important that the enemy should be given no rest . . . Eighth
> Army will attack and destroy the enemy in his present positions.

He added: "Speed of action is essential."

His plan was simple: the whole of Gott's 13th Corps and 7th Motor
Brigade, 4th Light Armoured Brigade (newly formed out of spare
armoured-car units) and a squadron of Stuarts would drive into
Rommel's right rear and roll *Panzerarmee Afrika* up towards the coast
at Ghazal and Sidi Rahman.

It was a more hopeful conference than his first. That morning
Dorman-Smith had been down to see the first German prisoners—
they were "absolutely whacked". And in fact the German morale
was the main object of Auchinleck's manoeuvres:

> The whole idea was to get Rommel over to the defensive—upon
> troops so long victorious and on the verge of Alexandria, the moral
> effect would be disproportionately great.

Auchinleck had piped a lively tune for 5th July, but Eighth Army
could not manage more than a bear-like shuffle. It was beyond the
compass of the military doctrine, the training and the mental agility
of the Eighth Army, exhausted by battle, to organize in the course
of a night an attack imbued with the Commander-in-Chief's offen-
sive energy. What Auchinleck had conceived as a killing blow
became in fact a slow tightening in pressure between 5th and 9th
July, as 13th Corps felt its way cautiously round Rommel's right
flank.

Among some of the Commonwealth troops that formed the
majority of Eighth Army, there was at this time a sullen reluctance
to move. In the New Zealand Division, one brigadier's opinion of
the plan for 13th Corps was that "it doesn't look real". The same
brigadier described as 'fanciful' an attack by ninety-nine tanks and
an infantry brigade on the fifteen German tanks of 15th Panzer
Division. Thus it was that this officer was able to describe 6th July,
when his division and the rest of 13th Corps should have been driving
hard for the coast, as "a really quiet day".

The only gleam of light in this scene of inertia was shed by the
flashing advance of 4th Light Armoured Brigade. Its armoured cars

broke right through the German defences and wheeled north-westwards towards Daba, far in Rommel's rear and a nodal point in his precarious supply lines. The cars were taken to be tanks, and because the Germans had no anti-tank or other shells left, a shiver of alarm went through the *Panzerarmee*. But with the mass of 13th Corps inert behind it, the dash of 4th Light Armoured Brigade was a gesture in the air; and Auchinleck's second counter-stroke had failed.

Yet the failure was only relative. The pressure of 13th Corps on Rommel's southern flank was enough to alarm the German commander and make him bring 90th Light to the south from its salient by El Alamein. At the same time Rommel was being forced to deploy Italian infantry for the first time since the beginning of the battle of Gazala. Therefore Auchinleck had succeeded in pulling the tactical initiative further out of his opponent's hands. But Rommel was still confident that Egypt would be his. Reinforcements would reach him soon: 164th Infantry Division from Crete, and a shipment of two hundred and sixty tanks. On 8th July, having stood on the defensive for four days, Rommel decided that his best hope lay in attacking the New Zealanders at Bab el Quattara, taking their box and driving far to the east towards the Delta, while Auchinleck was left in the air at Alamein.

But Auchinleck too was planning another stroke. It was now his policy to gain and keep the tactical initiative by a series of attacks upon different parts of Rommel's army—like a tennis player placing the ball so that his opponent is constantly running for it. This time he was going to use his personal reserve, the newly arrived and fresh 9th Australian Division, to break through the German defences on the coast road, west of El Alamein, and force the *Panzerarmee* off its communications into the desert. To draw Rommel's attention from the coast, Auchinleck therefore pulled back 13th Corps and evacuated the Bab el Quattara box—a manoeuvre that by the odd coincidence of war exactly fitted into Rommel's own plan. Jubilantly the German commander congratulated himself on 9th July on the success of his new offensive which had opened with a British retreat and the 'capture' of a magnificent box; the road to Cairo, he thought, was at last open.

That night, as Rommel slept in a concrete shelter in the Quattara defences, wrapped in impending triumph, the massed guns of Auchinleck's army artillery shook and tore the German positions west of Alamein; it was, so one German officer said, like a barrage of the First World War. In the morning, the Australians went in.

The Italians of the Sabratha Division broke and bolted, discarding all impediments to mobility, such as their armament. The hill of Tel el Eisa, which commanded the western approach to El Alamein and which was to be immensely important to Montgomery, was taken. Almost all Sabratha's divisional artillery was captured. The Australians and light armour drove on towards the larger objectives given them by Auchinleck—Daba and the Sidi el Rahman track.

This was a moment when Rommel was near disaster. In his own words "the enemy was now in hot pursuit westwards after the fleeing Italians and there was a serious danger they would break through, and destroy our supplies". It was the finish of Rommel's own ambitions in the south; his plans cancelled, he hurried north with part of 15th Panzer Division in time to help a scratch force from the *Panzerarmee* Headquarters stop the Australians. Since Auchinleck had no reserves with which to maintain the momentum of the attack, Rommel was able to prevent catastrophe—but by using German troops earmarked for an offensive. This had been the first of those blows on Italians that Auchinleck and Dorman-Smith had discussed during the flight from Cairo to Baggush.

Two days later Auchinleck attacked again, and this time the Trieste Division was routed; once more Rommel prevented a complete break-through only by draining Germans from his southern flank. He counter-attacked the Australians in the Tel el Eisa salient, and saw his men fail in a choking sand-storm and heavy gunfire on 13th July. Both sides now made up the accounts of war. Auchinleck's claims were modest: fifteen guns and over a thousand prisoners. The failure to achieve a general break-through was a disappointment, but hardly a surprise in view of his complete want of reserves. But he preferred to give large rather than limited objectives, "to keep the troops going". In his opinion orthodox British doctrine of attack placed too much emphasis on the attainment of certain linear objectives upon which the attacking force then halted for fresh orders; he preferred Liddell Hart's concept (taken over by the Germans) of the *Schwerpunkt*, or drive without limits along a given axis.

Rommel's estimate of the results of the battle of Tel el Eisa was gloomy: "This British drive along the coast had brought about the destruction of the bulk of Sabratha and a large part of Trieste, and important sectors of the country had fallen into enemy hands." He now had utterly to abandon his own proposed offensive in the south because, with the unsteadiness of the Italians, "... the situation was beginning to take on crisis proportions".

A growing sense of impotence and frustration began now to tell on the spirits of German commander and soldier alike. Rommel confided his bitter disappointment to his wife in his letters, and awarded Auchinleck a tribute: "During the past few days the British Command has been showing considerable enterprise and audacity." On the British side there was a sense of easing tension which showed itself in small things, such as the permanent mess, with tables and chairs, that was installed at Auchinleck's head-quarters.

The improvement was even sensed in London, for the Prime Minister, who had fallen silent in the face of catastrophe, now began again to send Auchinleck exhortatory and minatory telegrams. They did not help; they were, in Auchinleck's words, "a cause of consider-able anxiety, an added burden". General Ramsden, who took over from Norrie at 30th Corps on 7th July, noted that "Auchinleck was obviously labouring under pressure from the P.M.". But Auchinleck impressed the newcomer by his strength and coolness: "He inspired confidence even in the most precarious circumstances." He slept well at night. The only hint of concealed strain that his colleagues noted was sudden and formidable outbursts of anger; but these quickly subsided into his usual gruff charm.

The climax in the long and wavering battle at Alamein for the control of Egypt and the Middle East was now at hand. In the next four days, between 13th July and 17th July, 1942, Auchinleck defeated Rommel's last attempt to crown his Gazala victories with the conquest of Egypt; and forced him back on to the general defensive. On 13th and 14th July the Germans came slowly on with the white glare of the afternoon sun behind them and the massed guns of the Eighth Army before them; 21st Panzer Division against the Alamein box, while their comrades at Deir el Shein waited for its fall before beginning their postponed drive on Cairo. When night fell on the 14th July, 21st Panzer Division had failed, and it was time for Auchinleck's next blow at the Italians.

It was a cold and dark night, the Ruweisat Ridge like the back of a great beast stretched under the stars. It was quiet, and men snuggled gratefully into their blankets. Then the night exploded in flares and tracer as the New Zealanders and 5th Indian Brigade attacked along the Ridge with the bayonet. At the glint of steel, the Italians of the Brescia Division broke.

The whole of the Ruweisat Ridge fell to Auchinleck's troops, who now cut into the rear of the Brescia and Pavia Divisions and (accord-ing to Rommel) took most of them prisoner.

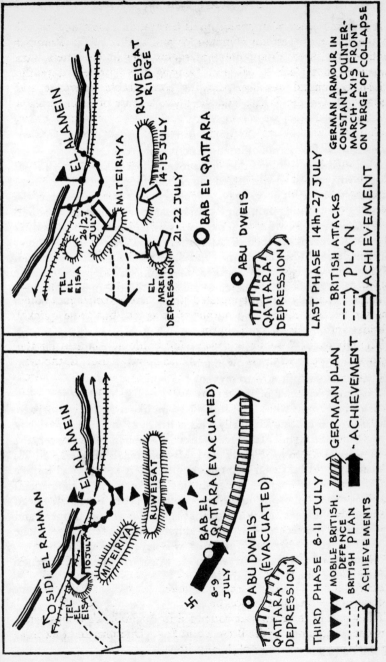

THIRD PHASE 8-11 JULY

▼▼▼ MOBILE BRITISH. IIII⟩ GERMAN PLAN

◄ DEFENCE   ▶ - ACHIEVEMENT

---- BRITISH PLAN

⟹ ACHIEVEMENTS

LAST PHASE 14h-27 JULY

GERMAN ARMOUR IN CONSTANT COUNTER-MARCH. AXIS FRONT ON VERGE OF COLLAPSE

BRITISH ATTACKS

⟹ PLAN

⟹ ACHIEVEMENT

Map 19. FIRST BATTLE OF ALAMEIN
July 1942, Third and Last Phases

South-east of Deir el Shein the Axis line also collapsed, as the British overran German anti-aircraft batteries and broke into the Deir el Shein box itself. Brought yet again to the edge of rout by a blow on his Italians, Rommel saved himself yet again by using his Germans to patch the front. Twenty-first Panzer Division abandoned for good its attack on El Alamein, came down to Deir el Shein and retook some of the lost ground.

A battle between evenly matched opponents is like a tug-of-war. At first there is a period of intense and prolonged effort during which the knotted handkerchief does not move. Then it begins to shift; at first slowly, and then with increasing ease and speed until the moment of victory. By 16th July, 1942, Auchinleck was giving the easy, the assured, the winning pull, and Rommel was moving helplessly with it.

By Auchinleck's wish rather than his own, Rommel now had all the Afrika Korps grouped in his centre, round Deir el Shein; therefore he decided to attack in the centre and recapture his lost ground. But he was anticipated by another of Auchinleck's night attacks; the Australians drove along the coast road to take the important ridge of El Makh-Khad. Next day they trampled through the Trieste and Trento Divisions and began to roll up Rommel's front like a ceremonial carpet, north to south. Rommel hurried northwards with every last German reserve in his army. He managed to prevent a general rout; but from now on his mind turned not on how to achieve victory, but how to prevent retreat.

His great summer offensive was over, and it had failed.

He wrote to his wife: ". . . it can't go on like it for long, otherwise the front will crack. Militarily, this is the most difficult period I've ever been through." In three weeks at Alamein he had seen the triumphs of Gazala, Tobruk and Matruh made bootless; all his straining effort had won him only empty desert and a cruel mirage of victory parades amid the fountains of Cairo. This moment of sudden defeat following upon easy triumph broke Rommel; ahead of him lay the dogging ill-health that is born of disappointment and frustration—desert sores, the infected liver, the duodenal ulcer. The old Rommel, that dynamic optimist, was never seen again.

Rommel's agony of mind was made worse by his clear awareness of what Auchinleck was doing.

The enemy [he wrote to his wife] is using his superiority, especially in infantry, to destroy the Italian formations one by one and the German formations are too weak to stand alone. It's enough to make one weep.

On 17th July, 1942, therefore, Auchinleck had won a historic battle. It had been as desperate, difficult and gallant as Wellington's repulse of Napoleon at Waterloo, but for Auchinleck there was no Blücher with forty thousand fresh men to come up on the flank and turn defeat into rout. Nevertheless Auchinleck had saved the Middle East, with all that this implied for the general course of the war. It was the turning point.

CHAPTER THREE

O<small>N</small> 18th July, 1942, the war in the desert had died away for a moment. It was a time to sit in the narrow shadow of a tank or truck and dream of bright clouds towering up an English summer sky; to close the mind against white light and hot dust and remember the smells of damp and growing things. But in the Axis lines exhausted, toiling men were learning the differences between winning and losing a campaign: instead of cool sea bathes, laying mines almost too hot to touch; instead of drinking iced lager, uncoiling barbed wire. As they worked, and looked back on Gazala and Tobruk, they learned that all victories are vain but the last, and *that* the generalship of Auchinleck had denied them. For the Eighth Army the day after Rommel's defeat was perhaps one of strangeness; the battle so many had thought was lost, had been won. To prosaic British soldiers, it began to appear that there were many advantages about the Alamein positions which Gazala and other places in Rommel's country had lacked: regular supplies of NAAFI cigarettes and beer, and when things were quieter, a spot of leave in conveniently adjacent Alex.

But in Eighth Army headquarters, a dusty metal mockery of a hamlet amid the stones and sand, Auchinleck could not relax with victory; he faced a new and unpleasant dilemma.

An immense German offensive was now rolling through the Ukraine; several panzer armies (each one larger than Rommel's command) formed the van of an army of more than a million men; and the Russians appeared helpless before this weight and power. Two German threats had now developed: one to Stalingrad, whose western bastions at Kletskaya and Kalach were already enveloped in German fire; and the other to Rostov, the fortress which covered the Caucasus and Auchinleck's northern flank. The Russians judged Stalingrad, covering the heart of European Russia, to be more important than Rostov and they had begun to pull their troops round Rostov back towards the Volga. Thus it was that Auchinleck received top-secret information from the British Military Attaché in

Russia that the whole of the Caucasus was expected to fall to the Germans within a month, bringing them to the borders of Persia. Troops must, then, be found for Persia and Iraq; but there were none, except those of Eighth Army and of green divisions still on ships sailing slowly round Africa. According to earlier staff studies of the time necessary to move an army from Egypt to Persia and deploy it there, such an army should have been in transit by 14th July. Clearly the troops for Persia must be drawn from Eighth Army and without delay; clearly this could only be done after Rommel had been destroyed or immobilised.

The case for an immediate British offensive was implacably put by the Prime Minister in a telegram of 12th July, hard on the heels of 'an unpleasant wire'—so unpleasant that Brooke and Ismay tried without avail to prevent his sending it, and whose contents have understandably never been made public.

> You . . . no doubt realize that it is practically impossible to send six or even four additional divisions from Home or United States to the northern theatre before the end of October. The only way in which a sufficient army can be gathered in the northern theatre is by your defeating or destroying General Rommel and driving him at least to a safe distance. If this were accomplished before the middle of September, the Australian divisions could return to their station in Palestine and Iraq . . .

Because of the time needed to transfer these troops, of which Churchill had taken insufficient account, Auchinleck realized therefore that as Commander-in-Chief he must now take a decision which as Army Commander he might judge to be rash: to launch an immediate offensive with his poorly trained and battle-worn army. Thus it was that in July, 1942, as in 1940 and 1941, the campaign in the desert was directly and fatally affected by dangers elsewhere in the vast Middle East Command.

While the troops enjoyed a brief lull after 17th July, the Commander-in-Chief was preparing his offensive. It took him—there was no more time—four days. Auchinleck proposed first to drive into Rommel's extended centre on 21st July: "We should thereby have a chance to sever his communications and roll up the northern part of his armour. . ." When this attack by 13th Corps had drawn in Rommel's reserve, a second blow by 30th Corps in the north three days later would drive the German left flank off the Miteiriya Ridge, the key to the defence; the armour would then break through before Rommel could disengage himself from the earlier battle with 13th

Corps. The whole of both corps would join in the general pursuit, with the armour in the van. First Armoured Division was to run for the Fuka bottleneck; 7th Armoured Division also for Fuka, but by another route; and the armoured cars of 4th Armoured Brigade far ahead to Charing Cross. It was not, and could not be, a set-piece battle and a sure success; it depended on Eighth Army displaying the Afrika Korp's kind of nimbleness and thrust. The doubt was there; could a British army, trained and officered in quite another, older tradition, find this élan?

Auchinleck tried hard to evoke it; Gott's orders to 13th Corps were full of thrustfulness:

> All commanders must be prepared to act with extreme vigour. Without waiting for precise orders, they must act within the spirit of these (general) orders and carry out the pursuit relentlessly to the complete destruction of the enemy forces.

Auchinleck issued his orders for the battle at a smart pace—operation instructions on 17th July, orders for the pursuit on 20th, and orders covering army-air co-operation on 21st. The pace was too fast for the slow-working staffs of lower formations (German staff work, because of greater experience and better training, was always faster and more lucid than British), and detailed organization for the offensive was poor and confused.

The 21st July passed slowly for Auchinleck, as his army moved into position. The awareness never left him that he had committed himself to a hazardous enterprise; his want of reserves to follow up initial successes was a special worry. There was the painful irony that he could best achieve his own strategic objects—continued safety of Egypt and the destruction of Rommel—by leaving Rommel in peace at the end of his stretched communications, until Eighth Army was rested and reinforced; it was not *Panzerarmee Afrika*, but the Germans at Rostov, a continent away, that had forced him to gamble.

His features were now beginning to show the effects of a month of such moral, physical and emotional strain as no other allied general in the Second World War except possibly Gort experienced. Like Wellington in Goya's portrait after Salamanca, Auchinleck had become gaunt and tense; his blue eyes gazed hollowly and implacably out of his loneliness. Above all in his mind, as he waited for the long day to pass, was the question of conscience that he asked himself before all his battles: "Are the chaps who are going to attack going

to have a reasonable chance—if not, you are just murdering them."
But this time the answer was not his to give. The possibility of
failure weighed with him least of all (it could not now endanger
Egypt, for Rommel had had all the attack beaten out of him),
although he knew that the blame would fall on him rather than on
the politicians.

Just before dusk, like a starting gun severing the tension before a
race, a rolling bombardment by his massed artillery opened his last
desert battle. Under its cover the infantry of 13th Corps went for-
ward—New Zealanders to the edge of the El Mreir depression,
Indians through the defences of the Deir el Shein box. Now it was
the armour's turn, working closely with the infantry and sappers,
to break out of the bridgeheads and to protect the infantry against
German tanks. But combined attacks against minefields and fixed
defences had been out of fashion for a year now in the desert; and
the technique had been forgotten. As 13th Corps fumbled with the
unaccustomed problem, the great flaw in Eighth Army—between
armour and other arms—cracked wider, and in an abyss of misunder-
standing and recrimination, the attack was lost.

First Armoured Division, supposed to be up with the New Zea-
landers at first light on 22nd July, was still not there in broad day-
light, despite the New Zealanders' urgent night signal that the
Mreir Depression in front of them was full of German tanks. German
artillery wrecked the New Zealanders' anti-tank guns, and then the
squat tanks rumbled out of the depression and over the helpless New
Zealanders. In the Indian sector it was the armour that was mas-
sacred. General Gatehouse, who had taken over command of 1st
Armoured Division the night before (Lumsden being wounded)
criticised the battle plan, but Strafer Gott insisted that 23rd Ar-
moured Brigade should make its attack. It was the brigade's first
action. Auchinleck had used it because there was no other, knowing
that it was physically soft, having just come off the troopships after
the long voyage from Britain; without desert training; and equipped
with obsolete 2-pounder Valentines. But it had received a thorough
training in armoured fighting in the United Kingdom and the task
given it was within the compass of this training. As it went into
action, Gatehouse too was wounded; his place was taken by Brigadier
Fisher.

The brigade's performance was a surprise and a tragedy. It began
by having a complete wireless breakdown. Out of the control of
the army command as a consequence, it charged as if it were after
a fox, full of exultant courage and devoid of tactical cunning.

Gravelled on a minefield, 23rd Armoured Brigade was shot to pieces by furious and accurate German anti-tank fire. Of ninety-seven Valentines, eleven returned. It was an astonishing indictment of the state of armoured training in Britain after three years of war.

Auchinleck took the news of this disastrous day with outward calm; but like Wellington in the Peninsula he was beginning to wonder if anybody in his army could be trusted to carry out his orders with professional competence and zeal. Clearly the army needed the most thorough weeding-out and retraining; and that would require time.

Yet the attack had achieved its object despite the confusion; Rommel had been alarmed because it had reached "dangerously far behind our front" and had "demanded the use of our last reserves". The German armour had therefore seeped away from the Miteiriya Ridge to meet the attack; and Rommel was off-balance for Auchinleck's second and principal blow. As the British tanks moved secretly northwards towards Miteiriya, the Prime Minister was drafting a telegram to Auchinleck to "hurry the Auk on to attack" and, in tranquil, air-raid-free London, "pouring out questions as to why the Auk could not have done this or that".

Auchinleck himself was facing a new crisis. General Morshead, commanding 9th Australian Division, which was to make the infantry attack on the Miteiriya Ridge, had objected to his orders.

Auchinleck was visiting 30th Corps H.Q. with Dorman-Smith after lunch on 22nd July, when General Ramsden, commanding 30th Corps, told him the news. Ramsden was a lean Yorkshireman, steady and forceful, who always wore a huge automatic taken from a German officer in the previous war. Ramsden explained that Morshead had been questioning his orders for 24th July, saying that his division had done enough attacking. "His main reason," in Ramsden's words, "was *no* confidence in our armour." Ramsden said that he had done his best "to stop this bloody-mindedness without result". Morshead, he told Auchinleck, had insisted that "he must refer to his government".

For Auchinleck, this occurrence in the middle of a carefully-timed battle was his most serious problem so far in commanding an army drawn mostly from Commonwealth countries other than Britain, where divisional commanders were subject to political pressure from home, and in turn could appeal to their own governments if they disliked their orders. It was the ultimate test of his quality as a man and a commander. At first it shattered his self-control; in Ramsden's words, "he went through the roof" in a sudden terrible anger fuelled by all the accumulated strain of a month of crisis. He ordered Ramsden to have Morshead report to him immediately. Ramsden, looking at the big man in his anger, reflected that an interview at that moment would not be fruitful. He suggested that Morshead should come up for tea.

Auchinleck thought for a moment, and in that moment the swift rage abated with equal swiftness. The Australians must be got into action and anger would not do the trick. He took Ramsden by the arm and, in his usual deep voice, agreed that Morshead should come for tea. Time passed, Morshead arrived, Auchinleck was gruffly charming, they all, in a thoroughly British Commonwealth manner, had tea. By now Auchinleck, with his usual sympathy, had seen the other man's point of view:

> Morshead was a fine fighter and had done all that he had been asked and that was a great deal. He had been asked because he had a fine fighting division—the penalty of being good. He was of course quite entitled to represent that his division had had about enough of it—particularly as an Australian commander responsible directly to his own government. His was a difficult position.

Then they walked across the sand to the operations caravan. When they were seated, Auchinleck began to persuade Morshead. He referred to "your wonderful division, comprised of the finest fighters in the world". He promised that the 69th British Infantry Brigade would be moved to Miteiriya to conduct the second and most dangerous phase of the attack. Morshead succumbed; and, rather like Wellington on his knee to Cuesta before Talavera, Auchinleck had saved his battle.

A year later he wrote of such episodes in a letter to Ramsden:

> I have often wondered since how you ever got anything going at all! The story must be told some day; it was a comedy but very nearly a tragedy!

He bore Morshead no malice; on the contrary he admired him then, and afterwards, as "a first-class soldier".

He had solved another of his problems; but the switching of 69th Brigade, as well as the time spent in talking Morshead round, had imposed a delay of two days in the attack; it was now to begin on 26th July. As Auchinleck and Dorman-Smith walked back from Ramsden's operations caravan, Dorman-Smith asked him whether the attack should be called off, as there was now time for Rommel to re-group to meet it. But Auchinleck said the attack must be put in—for reasons of a wider strategic and political kind than a mere assessment of the prospects of success on the Miteiriya Ridge. As if to confirm this decision, Rostov fell on 24th July and the Germans began to pour down into the Caucasus.

The second phase of the battle opened with one of Auchinleck's night attacks (an Indian custom) in the evening of 26th July. The Australians fought all night under the moon. By dawn on 27th they had broken into the German front and taken Sanyet el Miteiriya. South African sappers had cleared gaps in the minefields on the Australians' left, and through them the British 69th Infantry Brigade began to drive on towards the Miteiriya–Deir el Abyad track. In Ramsden's corps headquarters, Auchinleck heard the news of this promising beginning and then drove back to his own headquarters to wait in suspense for the next developments.

After two hours there was a telephone call: it was Ramsden.

> I told the Auk that it was useless to go on with the Miteiriya Ridge battle . . . because gaps in the minefields for the passage of our tanks had NOT been cleared as ordered.

While the British infantry were cutting deeper into the German defences, 2nd Armoured Brigade, which should have been up with them as both their spear and their shield, was still on the British side of the minefields. Brigadier Fisher considered the gaps not to be sufficiently cleared for his tanks. When they had been cleared, and his tanks had passed through, 69th Brigade had already been cut off and mauled by German armour and infantry as Rommel came into action with the Afrika Korps. The British armour was able to rescue the infantry eventually, but all tactical and strategic surprise was gone, and the attacking forces had fallen into that cursing confusion that the British soldier knows so well. Ramsden therefore wanted to know if he should continue the attack. Auchinleck had no reserves, nothing more to give.

"I told Ramsden to call off the battle."

The epic days were over.

* * * * *

In London, in the endless underground conferences from which men emerged white yet kippered by tobacco smoke, the Prime Minister was continuing to make those grand gestures over the map with his cigar that passed for strategy; continuing to abuse men the reality of whose difficulties he refused to acknowledge. On 30th July, "the P.M.'s impatience with what he regarded as the inexplicable inertia of Middle East Command had become uncontrollable".

For in England Auchinleck's decisive success in repulsing the *Panzerarmee*, so clear to Rommel himself then and to the historian today, had passed without notice or appreciation. This strange and unfortunate neglect is a reflection partly on want of perspicuity in high circles in London, but mostly on Auchinleck's poor sense of personal public relations. On 25th July, for example, he had written a full private letter to Brooke about the battle so modestly couched that an ignorant reader might, like the American Ambassador with Wellington's Waterloo Despatch, be uncertain whether it recounted victory or defeat.

In the desert Auchinleck, himself still full of aggression, had had to accept that he just had not the strength to beat Rommel out of his ever-stronger fixed defences.

> The weakness of the Eighth Army relative to the front which had to be held or closely watched, prevented me from forming a real reserve, in which troops could be rested, re-formed and trained for fresh assaults on the enemy; and there were no more formations in the Delta or further to the east on which I could call.

But he was not dissatisfied with the results of his month of battle, which were admirably summed up by the man he had beaten. Rommel wrote:

> Although the British losses in this Alamein fighting had been higher than ours, yet the price to Auchinleck had not been excessive, for the one thing that mattered to him was to halt our advance, and that, unfortunately, he had done.

General Bayerlein, Rommel's Chief of Staff, agreed with his chief:

> All of Auchinleck's counter-attacks were tremendously successful. If Rommel had not been beaten then, he would have advanced deep into Egypt. When Rommel lost Tel el Eisa and Ruweisat, he and all of us knew we were lost.

He significantly added:

> It is a pity that no one in Britain recognised the marvellous, though smaller, battles Auchinleck won.

On 27th July, 1942, as the gunfire died away along the Miteiriya Ridge, General Dorman-Smith submitted to Auchinleck an appreciation of the present and future prospects of the war in the Middle East.[1] After discussion, Auchinleck accepted this appreciation. It is one of the most crucial documents of the Second World War and it deserves the closest study. Yet, except in the writings of Captain Liddell Hart, it has been generally neglected. This is not strange, for it upsets the legend of how the desert war was transformed by the arrival of Montgomery; it gives the lie to those in the army who thought that Dorman-Smith was 'unsound', and Auchinleck's 'evil genius'. It forecasts the date of the battle of Alam Halfa and Rommel's plan of battle; and it describes the defence (unaltered by Montgomery) by which it might be defeated. It then looks further ahead to the Second Battle of Alamein, and describes, in outline, the offensive plan which should be adopted, which was adopted, and which was unaltered, though developed, by Montgomery.

The appreciation took into account the reinforcements which might reach Rommel in the next few weeks, and considered that

> though the Axis forces are strong enough for defensive action, they are hardly strong enough to attempt the conquest of the Delta except as a gamble and under strong air cover.

On the other hand,

> none of the formations in Eighth Army is now sufficiently well trained for offensive operations. The Army badly needs either a reinforcement of well-trained formations or a quiet period in which to train.

Therefore

> seeing that we are hardly fit at present to do any attacks, our best course is the defensive combined with offensive gestures from time to time . . . until we are strong enough to attack . . . which will not be till mid-September at the earliest.

The Second Battle of Alamein began on 23rd October.
In the meantime, the appreciation continued,

> Rommel will certainly try to attack before the end of August . . .

Rommel actually began his advance on the night of 30th/31st August.

[1] See Appendix B for the complete text.

. . . and as Eighth Army defences gain in strength and depth he will be
more than ever tempted to avoid them and seek success in manœuvre.
This may well land him in serious difficulties in the soft desert . . .
Eighth Army may have to meet an enemy's sortie developing into
manœuvre by the southern flank . . . We must therefore organize a
strong mobile wing . . . well trained in harassing defensive technique.

The appreciation now went on to sketch the plan on which
Montgomery was in fact to fight the Second Battle of Alamein:

> Eventually we will have to renew the offensive and this will probably
> mean a break-through the enemy positions about El Alamein. The
> newly arrived infantry divisions and the armoured divisions must be
> trained for this and for pursuit.

Three days after Auchinleck had discussed this appreciation and
approved it in its final form, he asked his corps commanders, Gott
and Ramsden, and Corbett (from Cairo) to come to his headquarters
for a day's conference. The instructions issued that day, 30th July,
1942, were Auchinleck's last achievement in his twelve months in
the Middle East; they formed the basis of final victory in the desert.

Firstly, Auchinleck said that there were to be no more British
attacks at present. Then he reviewed the reinforcements that were
on the way to Egypt; reinforcements on a scale and of a quality
that none of the officers in that caravan had before seen. Two new
and additional armoured divisions—8th and 10th—had arrived and
were being reequipped with Grants and the powerful Shermans for
which the Prime Minister had asked the American President. One
hundred self-propelled 105 mm. guns were also expected. The
American tanks had still to be fitted with wireless and sand filters,
and the men of the new divisions needed thorough training. All
this would take till mid-September, which therefore fixed the earliest
possible date for the offensive. Auchinleck would then have, how-
ever, four armoured divisions instead of two; and their equipment
—Grants, Shermans and 6-pounder anti-tank guns—would be for
the first time in two years in the desert vastly superior to the German.
As well as the extra armour, an infantry division—44th—had arrived
and was being trained, and another—51st—was on its way. Given
the present complete British air superiority, it would be a battle
fought on very different terms from those of *Battleaxe*, *Crusader* and
First Alamein.

Auchinleck and his officers now got up from the table and faced
the battle map on the wall of the caravan. Auchinleck pointed out

that by mid-September Rommel too would have been reinforced and that his defences would be well-laid-out, protected by mine-fields. The Commander-in-Chief explained that at the moment he favoured the set-piece attack near El Alamein itself which had been sketched in the appreciation before them. It was the kind of static, rehearsed battle in which the good qualities of a British army— endurance, steadiness and discipline—would shine, while its poor qualities—want of dash and agility—would not signify. "I considered," wrote Auchinleck later, "this operation offered the greatest chance of success." The alternative was the traditional desert plan —the armoured striking force rolling round through the southern flank and across the enemy's communications. Auchinleck ordered Gott to prepare an outline scheme for this; but Ramsden was to start immediately on detailed plans for the northern break-through.

Now Auchinleck laid down his new policy in organization and training. In his opinion, every desert battle from *Battleaxe* to those just over showed that the traditional British organization of infantry and armoured divisions was quite unsuited to modern mobile war-fare. Whether in desert manoeuvre or in close attack and defence, the co-operation of tanks, infantry and artillery was far below the standard of the easy and supple teamwork of the Germans, and often did not exist all. As Auchinleck remarked later:

> We were not as well trained as the Germans—a fault of our pre-war training. We don't really train for war in peacetime in England—we play at it.

He wanted the distinction between armoured and infantry divisions abolished in favour of an all-mobile Eighth Army made up of divisions each with its ratio of tanks, guns and lorried infantry. In this way the co-operation of all arms would be made permanent through the very structure of the division, under its divisional commander. Auchinleck thus set in motion the complex machinery of training and organizing a new model army—three days after the close of the July battles.

He concluded his conference by reviewing the measures for defeating a forlorn-hope German offensive at the end of August. The El Alamein positions were now well fortified. The west-to-east ridges of Ruweisat and Alam Halfa, which Auchinleck regarded as keys of the defence, had been already prepared with a defence zone thirty miles deep. But he emphasized to Gott and Ramsden that "the essence of the defensive plan was fluidity and mobility and the

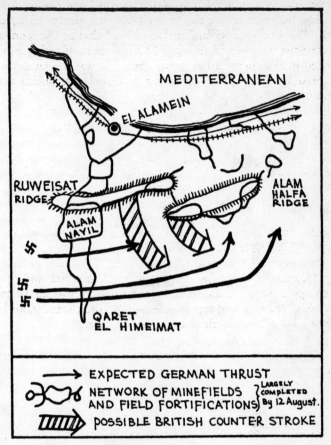

MEDITERRANEAN

EL ALAMEIN

RUWEISAT
RIDGE

ALAM
NAYIL

ALAM
HALFA
RIDGE

QARET
EL HIMEIMAT

→ EXPECTED GERMAN THRUST

NETWORK OF MINEFIELDS ⎱ LARGELY
AND FIELD FORTIFICATIONS ⎰ COMPLETED By 12 August.

▨▶ POSSIBLE BRITISH COUNTER STROKE

MAP 20. AUCHINLECK'S PLAN FOR ALAM HALFA
August 1942

maximum use of artillery fire". The bulk of the army artillery, with an escort of lorried infantry, would fight alongside the armour. If Rommel tried to drive far to the east, instead of attacking Alam Halfa, he would be struck in the flank.

The conference broke up, and Auchinleck and his officers stepped out into the sunshine conscious that at last the easier days of the war were on the way. They could reckon that they deserved some free-wheeling; they had pedalled uphill long enough.

Meanwhile there was an air of relaxing tension in the desert. The day had ceased to be composed of twenty-five hours and the headquarters mess had more time for sport: "Our chief amusement," said Auchinleck afterwards, "was fighting scorpions against tarantulas. Kisch (Engineer in Chief of the Eighth Army) had a black spider and I had a scorpion. We used to have fights in a tin box after dinner." There was time too for swimming in the Mediterranean, in whose warm embrace cares and fatigue melted away; time for him to get away from that prison of an ops room for long walks.

He took a day's leave in Cairo, and wandered strangely among the sleek civilians, along the brilliant streets; had lunch in a club where deft Sudanese in white robes of pavonine colours passed as quiet as wraiths along the marble terraces. In the Sharia Adly Pasha he turned into a bookshop, prophetically named *La Librairie la Renaissance d'Egypte*—he had always been a great reader—and bought a new copy of a childhood favourite, Macaulay's *Lays of Ancient Rome*. Perhaps the eye of the man of Alamein fell first on these lines:

> And how can man die better
> Than facing fearful odds,
> For the ashes of his fathers
> And the temples of his Gods.

A week later, after swift events and intrigues, he had been relieved of his command.

CHAPTER FOUR

AT the end of June, 1942, the Coalition Government lost a by-election at Maldon in Essex by a colossal turnover of votes. It was an expression of the heavy groundswell of public criticism of Churchill's war direction.

This was the middle year of the war, the dangerous, weary year that lay between the splendid and exhilarating defiance of 1940–41 and the victories assured by Allied superiority still to come. In Churchill's own words:

> We had had a long succession of misfortunes and defeats—Malaya, Singapore, Burma, Auchinleck's lost battle (sic) in the desert; Tobruk . . .

He was now in the greatest political danger he was to know in the course of his wartime premiership; and on 1st July, as battle was joined at Alamein, he rose in the House of Commons to answer a vote of censure that attacked him while excusing the generals; the motion was "That this House, while paying tribute to the heroism and endurance of the Armed Forces of the Crown in circumstances of exceptional difficulty, has no confidence in the central direction of the war." The Prime Minister won by 475 votes to 25, against an attack so inept as to suggest it might have been rigged as a dummy. But the groundswell of public discontent continued. "During this month of July, when I was politically at my weakest," a striking offensive victory was required. When at the end of the month Auchinleck cabled to say that he was not going to launch another offensive for at least six weeks, Churchill decided to go to Cairo in order, in his own words, to settle this issue: "Had General Auchinleck or his staff lost the confidence of the Desert Army? If so, should he be relieved, and who could succeed him?" But subsequent events were to suggest that he had already made his mind up.

Auchinleck received these tidings at his headquarters behind the Ruweisat Ridge. Dorman-Smith advised him to receive the Prime

Minister in Cairo, in full panoply of Commander-in-Chief, Middle East—before anyone else could get the Prime Minister's ear. But Auchinleck, with his complete disdain for intrigue, stayed with his army until asked for.

On 3rd August Churchill and his entourage arrived in Cairo; the Prime Minister talked with Smuts, who had flown up from Cape Town; and in the afternoon Auchinleck, having been asked for, went up to Cairo to explain the military situation. On the morning of 4th August Churchill saw General Corbett, the Chief of the General Staff, Middle East Command. In a letter to Major-General J. N. Kennedy, Director of Military Operations at the War Office (dated 5th August, 1942), Corbett described the end of his interview with the Prime Minister:

> When I was leaving, I stressed what in some ways is perhaps the most important factor. General Auchinleck has been through a great ordeal. Once again, his Army Commander has been unable to cope with the situation. All these terrible events have naturally bitten deep into his soul, and he is now busy regaining confidence in himself . . . I explained all this to the P.M., and said perhaps the greatest disaster of all would be the loss of General Auchinleck, and that he needs a helping hand to assist him back on to solid ground.

On the 4th also Wavell arrived from India; and the Prime Minister was able to play the role he loved, that of Marlborough "riding the whirlwind and directing the storm", with Wavell, Auchinleck, Alan Brooke, Admiral Harwood, Tedder, Casey (the Minister of State) and Smuts. They discussed many matters but, since Auchinleck was present, not the one uppermost in Churchill's mind—Auchinleck's relief and successor.

For, before even visiting Eighth Army, the Prime Minister had made up his mind to dismiss Auchinleck; and he first offered the Middle East to Brooke who, from *The Turn of the Tide*, seemed less concerned with the justice or military validity of the decision than with debating with himself whether he should take Auchinleck's job or not. He decided not, partly for fear that Auchinleck might think he had come to the Middle East "to work his way into his shoes".

In the early morning of the 5th August, Auchinleck stood with his staff on the airstrip near Eighth Army headquarters and watched a figure in a siren suit and topee emerge from an aircraft into the white sunshine. For a moment they faced each other—the plump, pink politician who ran the war from a cellar in London, and the lean, sun-dried soldier who had fought the battles. Then hands were shaken cordially—neither Churchill nor Brooke gave a hint of what they had already decided; Auchinleck began the unconscious but ghastly charade of showing them his army and explaining his plans.

From Auchinleck's point of view, this was above all a time for smart public relations work. The Air Force knew this, so when the Prime Minister went on to them for lunch after "a long and invigorating day with Eighth Army" [sic], he found "the food had all been ordered from Shepheard's Hotel . . . a gay occasion in the midst of care—a real oasis in a very large desert". But Auchinleck was too honest or too simple a man for press-agenting; the Prime Minister's breakfast that morning was just the ordinary Eighth Army mess issue. Before he sat down to it he had been driven round Ramsden's corps, giving his two-finger sign. An observer has described the soldiers' responses: "the last stage of the route along the ridge was thinly lined with phlegmatic soldiers who seemed to be in two minds about the warmth of the reception they were going to give the Old War Horse." Also before he had his breakfast, Churchill had another and this time detailed discussion with Auchinleck about his plans for the future. The discussion took place in Auchinleck's caravan in the presence of Dorman-Smith. Again Churchill pressed for an early offensive, "his pudgy fingers stabbing at the map, as he threw in imaginary divisions here and there." On his way to enjoy the Air Force's shrewd hospitality, the Prime Minister had a long private talk with Strafer Gott, who was his personal choice as Army Commander when Alexander succeeded Auchinleck in the Middle East Command.

Meanwhile at a lower level, certain men of the Gazala defeats were quietly telling members of the Prime Minister's entourage that Auchinleck, Dorman-Smith and other officers were responsible for *their* mistakes. This was believed.

Next evening, after consulting Smuts and Alan Brooke, the Chief of the Imperial General Staff, who agreed that changes should be made in the Middle East command, the Prime Minister sat down to make the stroke that had the effect of diverting much of the discontent at the Government's war leadership on to Auchinleck and his immediate staff officers.

Prime Minister to Deputy Prime Minister. 6 Aug. '42, 8.15 p.m. As a result of such inquiry as I have made here, and after prolonged consultations with Field Marshal Smuts and C.I.G.S. and Minister of State, I have come to the conclusion that a drastic and immediate change is needed in the High Command . . .

After giving details about the splitting in two of the Middle East Command, the Prime Minister came to the meat:

4. General Alexander to be Commander-in-Chief the Near East.
5. General Montgomery to succeed Alexander in TORCH.
6. General Gott to command the Eighth Army under Alexander.
7. General Corbett to be relieved as C.G.S. Middle East.
8. General Ramsden to be relieved as G.O.C. XXXth Corps.
9. General Dorman-Smith to be relieved as Deputy C.G.S.
10. It will be necessary to find two corps commanders for the Eighth Army in place of Gott and Ramsden.
11. The above constitute the major simultaneous changes which the gravity and urgency of the situation here (sic) require. I shall be grateful to my War Cabinet colleagues if they will approve them. Smuts and the C.I.G.S. wish me to say they are in full agreement that amid difficulties and alternatives this is the right course to pursue. The Minister of State is also in full agreement. I have no doubt the changes will impart a new vigorous impulse to the Army and restore confidence in the Command, which I regret does not exist at the present time . . .

Returning to Cairo on 21st August, after the purge, he amplified this charge:

I am sure we were heading for disaster under the former regime. The Army was reduced to bits and pieces, and oppressed by a sense of bafflement and uncertainty. Apparently it was intended in face of heavy attack to retire eastwards to the Delta . . .

It was these events, and the interpretation placed on them by Churchill, which led to a general belief that Auchinleck had been an 'unlucky' general who had been relieved of his command in the midst of disaster.

At the end of June, as Auchinleck himself had recognised, Ritchie's defeat exposed Auchinleck to dismissal. But Churchill had not dismissed him. Now Auchinleck had magnificently redeemed his errors. Thus the military case for relieving him was infinitely weaker than it had been. How weak was shown when Dorman-Smith sued Churchill for libel in respect of the phrase ". . . and restore confidence in the Command, which I regret does not exist at the present time."

The case was settled out of court, Churchill agreeing to insert a footnote in future editions of his *Memoirs*. This footnote, of the greatest historical importance, reads:

The references to the officers whose names figure in this list are factual only. Neither they nor my later remarks are to be taken as imputing personal blame to any individual. These were the principal changes in Commands and Staff when General Auchinleck was replaced by General Alexander. Major-General Dorman-Smith only became Deputy Chief of Staff on the 16th June 1942; he thus bears no responsibility for the fall of Tobruk or the defeats at Gazala. From the 25th June to the 4th August he acted as General Auchinleck's principal Operations Officer at Headquarters Eighth Army during the operations described in Chapter 24. My appreciation in that chapter of the handling of the Eighth Army is supported by Rommel's remarkable tribute.

Running deep in this sad and unpleasant affair is the memory of the fall of Tobruk. The news had broken on the Prime Minister in circumstances of the greatest personal humiliation—from President Roosevelt's own lips while Churchill was a guest at the White House.

To Churchill, with his old-fashioned way of seeing history as a procession of great names and great events, the fall of a legendary fortress like Tobruk rang louder in the mind than the complicated truths of strategy. Politically he was right; he considered the result of the Maldon election to be a by-product of Tobruk. Tobruk was the memory that he had come to Cairo to exorcise; and yet ironically the fall of Tobruk had been his responsibility.

On 7th August, Gott, Eighth Army Commander designate, was shot down and killed while flying to Cairo. The second choice had always been Montgomery; Churchill cabled to London; and Montgomery stepped on to the stage. Auchinleck still did not know he had been dismissed. In his ignorance, he thought Churchill's visit was going well for him. His first meeting with the Prime Minister had been "cordial enough", though with characteristic modesty, he admitted "one had the sense of having let him down—I was C.-in-C. and the ultimate responsibility [for the Gazala defeats] was mine". On 4th August he had discussed with Brooke, apparently successfully, the future of the Middle East Command—the strategic appreciation of 27th July, the appointment of Montgomery (Brooke and Auchinleck preferred him to Gott) under himself as C.-in-C. On 7th he sent Dorman-Smith to discuss with Brooke the question of reorganization of the divisions. Brooke acted out his part with skill; Dorman-Smith never suspected that he and his chief were already dismissed. In the evening Auchinleck went for a walk with de Guingand, the new Brigadier General Staff at Eighth Army, and discussed his plans "with great enthusiasm".

Next day, Auchinleck received the news at last, in his battle head-quarters behind the Ruweisat Ridge, but from neither Churchill nor Alan Brooke; in the Prime Minister's words, ". . . having learnt from past experience that that kind of unpleasant thing is better done by writing than orally, I sent Colonel Jacob with the . . . letter". Colonel Jacob (now Sir Ian Jacob) flew up to Alamein, drove to Eighth Army Headquarters, and walked to Auchinleck's caravan. As he wrote in his diary that day: "I felt as if I were just going to murder an unsuspecting friend. After offering the con-dolences of the Prime Minister and C.I.G.S. on the death of General Gott, I handed the C.-in-C. the letter I had brought. He opened it and read it through two or three times in silence. He did not move a muscle and remained outwardly calm and in complete control of himself. . . . I could not have admired more the way in which General Auchinleck received me and his attitude throughout. A great man and a fighter."

The letter said:

Cairo, August 8, 1942

Dear General Auchinleck,

On June 23 you raised in your telegram to the C.I.G.S. the question of your being relieved in this Command, and you mentioned the name of General Alexander as a possible successor. *At that time of crisis for the Army, His Majesty's Government did not wish to avail themselves of your high-minded offer.* [Author's italics]. At the same time you had taken over the effective command of the battle, as I had long desired and had suggested to you in my telegram of May 20. You stemmed the adverse tide, and at the present time the front is stabilized.

The War Cabinet have now decided, for the reasons you yourself had used, that the moment has come for a change. It is proposed to detach Iraq and Persia from the Middle Eastern theatre. Alexander will be appointed to command the Middle East, Montgomery to com-mand the Eighth Army, and I offer you the command of Iraq and Persia, including the Tenth Army, with headquarters at Basra or Baghdad. It is true that this sphere is today smaller than the Middle East, but it may in a few months become the scene of decisive opera-tions, and reinforcements for the Tenth Army are on their way. In this theatre, of which you have special experience, you will preserve your associations with India. I hope therefore that you will comply with my wish and directions with the same disinterested public spirit you have shown on all occasions. Alexander will arrive almost immedi-ately, and I hope that early next week, subject of course to the move-ments of the enemy, it may be possible to effect the transfer on the Western battle-front with the utmost smoothness and efficiency.

I shall be very glad to see you at any convenient time if you should so desire.

> Believe me,
> Yours sincerely,
> Winston S. Churchill.

As he read and re-read this letter his mind might well have been moved to bitterness. But he accepted it without recrimination.

> I knew as soon as Jacob arrived what he was bringing. I had guessed the night before when there was the gathering in Cairo (Churchill, Smuts and C.I.G.S.) to which I was not invited. Nevertheless, it was a shock. There was the regret at losing the finest job a general could have at the time. But it came during a lull; if it had happened in the middle of the battle, it would have been far worse. It was worse for me afterwards when I had actually handed over, and began to think about it.

He was quiet at dinner that night, and afterwards asked de Guingand to come for a walk. "He put his arm in mine and said: 'Freddie, I'm to go'."

On the following day he handed over command of Eighth Army temporarily to Ramsden, and quitted the battle headquarters from which he had won his victory. He never saw the desert again. In Cairo, he met the Prime Minister for an hour's conversation, which, in Churchill's words, "was bleak and impeccable". Auchinleck refused the offer of the Persia-Iraq command, which he magnanimously describes as "very generous of Churchill". He refused it "because I had, like another people, a certain amount of pride and I did not think that I should have the same professional control over others after having stepped down in command. Anyhow, it was difficult to start all over again." In particular he pointed out that the Commander-in-Chief of the new command would depend for troops, base facilities and even many headquarters services on his colleague in Cairo; and he did not consider the scheme would work out. As events proved, it did not.

Auchinleck now remained in Cairo to await Alexander and Montgomery; the date of transfer of responsibility was fixed for 15th August. In the meantime, the machinery that Auchinleck had set in motion on 30th July for the re-modelling of Eighth Army and for the planning of the new offensive, had been dislocated by the Prime Minister's visit and the prolonged comings and goings of various officers. Ramsden, who was planning the break-through at El

Alamein, had twice acted as temporary Eighth Army commander; Gott, the other corps commander, had first been army commander designate and then killed. De Guingand, the new B.G.S. at Eighth Army, had been there only since 3rd August; Dorman-Smith had returned to Cairo. It was the temporary dislocation consequent upon all this that was interpreted by some as a general want of leadership and purpose in Auchinleck's command. As Churchill put it:

> . . . no plain plan of battle or dominating will-power had reached the units. So serious did this appear that General Montgomery insisted on taking command of Eighth Army as soon as he had visited the front . . .

On 10th August Alexander arrived in Cairo, and on the 12th Montgomery. Until 15th August, Auchinleck was both Commander-in-Chief and in personal command of Eighth Army, though he had put General Ramsden in temporary command during his absence in Cairo. Montgomery had thus no official status in the Middle East at all; as an officer on duty in Cairo, he came naturally under Auchinleck's command. But as a matter of courtesy and in keeping with the usual custom of the service, Auchinleck took the opportunity of Montgomery's early arrival to invite him for an interview in which he could explain the general situation at Eighth Army and the plans for its future. This interview took place in Auchinleck's map room at G.H.Q. Montgomery made an odd assertion in his *Memoirs* that Auchinleck's plans at that time were of retreat into the Delta in the face of German attack, and even up the Nile. The appreciation approved by Auchinleck on 27th July, Auchinleck's conference with his corps commanders on 30th July, and his explanation of his plans to the Prime Minister and to Brooke on several occasions (in the presence of other witnesses), make it clear that Montgomery's assertion is not supported by fact. Montgomery's own chief, General Alexander, in his official despatch, disavows Montgomery's version of Auchinleck's plans:

> The plan was to hold as strongly as possible the area between the sea and the Ruweisat Ridge and to threaten from the flank any enemy advance south of the ridge from a strongly defended position in the Alam el Halfa ridge. General Montgomery, now in command of Eighth Army, accepted this plan in principle, to which I agreed.

To clinch the matter, Montgomery's publishers, with Montgomery's consent, issued a statement[1]—to be printed in later editions

[1] Reproduced as Appendix A to this book.

of the *Memoirs*—acknowledging that his account of the interview gave a false impression.

Though Montgomery was not due to take over Eighth Army for three days, Auchinleck suggested as a courtesy that a smooth transition of responsibility would be helped by Montgomery's going down to see Ramsden, the temporary army commander, and learning something of his new command. Auchinleck added, in his own words,

> Had there been an emergency, I should of course have taken over command of Eighth Army from Ramsden up to the time of formal transfer of responsibility.

On 15th August, 1942, Auchinleck handed over the Middle East theatre to his friend Alexander. At the same time Montgomery entered into command of the Eighth Army, which had technically been vacant since Ritchie's relief. Auchinleck now sent to the Eighth Army his last order of the day:

> It has been a great honour to have held direct command of the Eighth Army for nearly two months, and it is with great personal regret that I now leave you on the arrival of your new Army Commander. During these weeks you have stopped the enemy; and, in spite of your heavy losses and the inevitable disorganization consequent on a rapid withdrawal from the frontier, you have forced him on the defensive, taken ten thousand prisoners from him and destroyed or captured many of his guns, vehicles and other equipment. You will, I know, join me in acknowledging the great and glorious part our air forces have played in helping us to achieve these results. Without their aid the story would have been very different. I thank you with all my heart for the magnificent way in which you have responded to the heavy calls I have made on you and for your unfailing cheerfulness and tenacity in the worst circumstances. I know you will continue in the same fine spirit and determination to win under your new Commander. I wish you luck and speedy and complete victory.

He stayed on in Cairo for a while. The fate of Dorman-Smith and Corbett, who had fallen with him, greatly distressed him. They were not given any reason for their dismissal; the first explanation was provided by Churchill's memoirs after the war. It was against all the traditions and practice of the army for subordinate officers to be dismissed at the order of a politician; a precedent which had been resisted as long ago as Wellington's time at the Horse Guards, and which should have been resisted by Alan Brooke, as professional head of the Army. In Auchinleck's own words: "I felt terribly about what happened to Dorman-Smith and Corbett—far worse than I felt about myself. Their treatment was entirely unfair." But his subordinates were thinking, on their side, only of him. General Corbett wrote to the Deputy C.-in-C. in India:

> The grim ordeal of the desert battle ends in providing Rommel with a triumph which I prayed he would not be allowed to enjoy. I am to go, as is right with my Chief . . . I am desperately sorry for Claude. He is, as you know, as simple as he is great. . . .

Auchinleck and Dorman-Smith dined together on the terrace at Mena House. It was cool for an August night in Cairo. Two tables away a young Hussar officer was flirting energetically with a pretty young British nursing sister. It was an odd, sad occasion: both Auchinleck and Dorman-Smith looked back to that other ceremonial meal, six weeks ago, before they had flown up to Eighth Army. Then it was all about to begin; now it was all over.

A contemporary observer in the Middle East wrote:

> The over-all direction of the War does not inspire much jollity in men who have consistently been chased by superior numbers with better equipment. Besides they like Auchinleck and do not see why he should be kicked out for General Alexander and some new Army Commander from England.

General Ramsden, who served under Auchinleck and Montgomery, writes of Auchinleck as a commander:

> The Auk was being continually pressed from home, he was not given the goods, and was frequently distracted by affairs in Iraq, Syria etc.—in short, his command was too big and too much was expected of him. Yet he was a most attractive commander; with a great sense of humour, individually a born leader.

An enemy opinion was:

> If Auchinleck had not been the man he was—and by that I mean the best Allied general in North Africa during the war—Rommel would have finished the Eighth Army off.

And, now he was gone, Churchill himself could safely acknowledge that he had demanded too much of Auchinleck:

I doubt if the disasters would have occurred in the Western Desert if General Auchinleck had not been distracted by the divergent considerations of a too widely extended front. . . .

The benefits of this belated (by two years) recognition of the obvious accrued to Alexander and Montgomery, for, as Churchill put it, "I should be most reluctant to embarrass Alexander with remote cares at a moment when all our fortunes turn upon the speedy and decisive defeat of Rommel." Alexander's Middle East Command was therefore but a shrunken remnant—Egypt, Syria and Palestine —and his cares not plural, but single: "to take and destroy at the earliest opportunity the German-Italian Army commanded by Field-Marshal Rommel." In truth, the hard days of the war had gone, along with the men who had borne their heat and shock.

What must be the judgement on Auchinleck as a man and as a commander? Perhaps General Sir Alfred Godwin-Austen touches the truth:

> His outstanding fault was, I should say, his inability to believe that every soldier was not as brave as he.

COMMENTARY: PART FIVE

CHAPTERS ONE AND TWO

Montgomery's partisans have portrayed Auchinleck's counter-strokes during the First Battle of Alamein in July 1942 as random and disjointed—"a chaotic series of attacks scraped together", in the words of General Sir Charles Richardson, then a colonel on the Eighth Army staff. However, Volume II of Professor Hinsley's Official History *British Intelligence in the Second World War* makes nonsense of this view by demonstrating that Auchinleck, in Hinsley's words, "followed *Sigint* closely" in his conduct of the battle, timing and placing his attacks according to *Ultra* and other top-secret intelligence about the locations and strengths of Rommel's German and Italian units, about Rommel's fuel and ammunition shortages, about the moral and physical condition of Rommel's soldiers, and about Rommel's own plans and state of mind. Professor Hinsley tells us that in July field *Sigint* and *Ultra* "gave the C.-in-C. all the evidence he needed for the planning of his attacks by following the moves the enemy made in response to them, by locating the enemy's formations and by showing up his weak points." Of course Auchinleck's attacks were hastily mounted and launched: in the circumstances of a desperate struggle to wrest the initiative from Rommel, how could it be otherwise? It should be remembered that by British standards of ponderously slow prior organisation and rehearsal, many of Rommel's operations in the Desert over the previous eighteen months had been "hastily scraped together". Moreover, if Auchinleck were to exploit the transient opportunities revealed by high-grade intelligence, he had to attack with minimum delay.

Auchinleck took a special intelligence party with him when he assumed personal command of the Eighth Army on 25th June. By now *Sigint* was providing him with Rommel's daily report to O.K.H. at only twenty-four hours' delay. On the night of 29th/30th June decrypts revealed that Rommel proposed to attack the Alamein position on the 30th; later decrypts on the topic of fuel shortages revealed that the attack had been postponed to 1st July, and that the main German thrust would be in the north, round the Alamein perimeter itself. At the same time British Army "Y" intelligence gave the true German tank strength on 1st July: thirty-seven runners in 21st Panzer Division and seventeen in 15th Panzer. This cumulative information enabled Auchinleck to concentrate his army artillery and 1st South African Division so as to halt Rommel's thrust round Alamein by converging fire.

In the early hours of 3rd July Auchinleck learned from *Enigma* decrypts that Rommel's plan for the day was to cut the coast road behind Alamein, which again enabled the British C.-in-C. to block the enemy's path. In the early hours of 4th July a decrypt told Auchinleck that Rommel was not going to attack that day; in the afternoon of 5th July a further decrypt gave the *Panzerarmee Afrika*'s day report for 3rd July in full, dilating upon its weaknesses, the effects of Royal Air Force bombing and the supply shortages which compelled "temporary suspension of large-scale attack". It was this continuing certain knowledge of the exhaustion of Rommel's army, the fragility of its strategic position, that impelled Auchinleck to order the first of the counter-strokes which his critics regard as "fantasies"—the attacks on 2nd and 5th July aimed at Rommel's right-rear and communications. In Auchinleck's own words, quoted in this book, "The whole idea was to get Rommel over to the defensive—upon troops so long victorious and on the verge of Alexandria, the moral effect would be disproportionately great."

Auchinleck's stroke on 9th July on the coastal sector with the fresh 9th Australian Division supported by massed artillery was based on top-secret intelligence that the bulk of Rommel's German formations had been moved south (as the result of Auchinleck's earlier attacks) and that the coast was now held by Italians. The later switch of 21st Panzer back to the north, leaving unsupported Italians on the Ruweisat Ridge, was likewise revealed to the British C.-in-C. on 13th July by field *Sigint*, so leading to the Eighth Army's night attack on the Ridge on 14th/15th July which routed the Brescia and Pavia Divisions.

During 15th/17th July more *Enigma* decrypts gave Auchinleck a complete and detailed picture of the parlous state of Rommel's army: serious fuel and ammunition shortages, weakness of the Italian formations and the need to stiffen them with Germans, while field *Sigint* revealed the fact that 21st Panzer was down to ten tanks on 17th July and 15th Panzer down to thirteen on the 19th.

Our new knowledge of the contribution made by *Sigint* to Auchinleck's generalship in the First Battle of Alamein gives a fresh dimension to the original narrative of *The Desert Generals*—not only by explaining exactly how he aimed his counter-strokes so unerringly at Italian formations, but also by showing that Auchinleck *knew* that he was succeeding in gradually pulling the initiative out of

Rommel's hands. And knew, moreover, by 17th July that he had won the defensive battle and saved Egypt.

CHAPTER THREE

Precise knowledge of Rommel's desperately precarious situation thanks to the *Ultra* and field *Sigint* reports of 15th/19th July, coupled with other *Ultra* decrypts suggesting that fresh reinforcements and supplies might soon reach Rommel, led to Auchinleck's decision to launch his final counter-strokes on 22nd and 26th July aimed at driving Rommel back from Alamein in full retreat. A further motive lay in Auchinleck's anxieties as C.-in-C. Middle East (shared by London) about the rising German threat to the theatre via the Caucasus. If he could turn Rommel's rebuff into rout, it would enable him to switch forces to Iraq and Persia.

Given that Auchinleck was aware that he was fielding sixty-one Grants and a hundred and fifty Valentines against Rommel's total, revealed by *Sigint*, of less than thirty German tanks, it cannot really be contended that Auchinleck's plans amounted to "fantastic optimism", as Nigel Hamilton writes in his biography of Montgomery. Indeed it is now known that on 22nd/23rd July Rommel was seriously considering a general withdrawal from the Alamein area. The failure of Auchinleck's attacks on 22nd and 26th July were therefore not owing to any inherent unrealism in the undertaking, but to failures of staff work and execution on the ground by the 13th Corps and the divisions under its command. As the three Commander-in-Chiefs in the Middle East had jointly signalled the Chiefs of Staff on 24th June, "we are still largely an army of amateurs fighting professionals".

* * * * *

Professor Hinsley's account of the role of secret intelligence in the First Battle of Alamein serves to demolish the hostile critics of Auchinleck's generalship, and lends greater force to the contention in this book that Auchinleck had demonstrated brilliant leadership in halting Rommel's advance. As Hinsley himself sums it up:

nor does analysis of the fighting in July leave much doubt that the *Sigint* did indeed make a significant contribution to his last and greatest victory, the first battle of Alamein.

It should also be noted that the official histories, *The Mediterranean and Middle East*, Vol. III, and *Grand Strategy*, both published after the first edition of this book, pay tribute to Auchinleck's achievement in throwing Rommel on to the defensive and bringing him so close to final collapse. In the words of Major-General Playfair, author of *The Mediterranean and Middle East*, the success of Montgomery's Second Battle of Alamein in October 1942 "should not be allowed to overshadow the earlier achievements of those who made it possible".

CHAPTER FOUR

Auchinleck remains almost as much a focus of controversy as Montgomery, despite, or perhaps partly because of, the vindication of his generalship in the First Battle of Alamein by John Connell in his biography *Auchinleck*, and by myself in this book. Montgomery's partisans (including Montgomery and his official biographer Nigel Hamilton) have always sought to base Montgomery's reputation on denigration of his predecessor. They still accuse Auchinleck of being a bad picker of subordinates, of fragmenting the Eighth Army into battle groups, of having no "plan" properly so called at the beginning of August 1942 for a defensive battle in the Alamein–Alam Halfa position, but instead of intending to retreat into the Nile Delta if Rommel attacked in strength. With regard to my own portrait of Auchinleck in *The Desert Generals*, I have been accused of "listening to the sad tales of the sacked generals of the Desert" and of giving Auchinleck "a brief period of undeserved success". None of these charges against Auchinleck stand up in the light of the evidence now available.

The still continuing controversy over Auchinleck's strategic intentions when Montgomery took command of the Eighth Army on 15th August 1942 is linked to the other controversy as to whether, and how far, Montgomery's plans for the Battle of Alam Halfa were derived from Auchinleck's existing plans and preparations and both questions are discussed below in the additional commentary to Part Six.

Did Auchinleck fragment the army? And was he a bad picker of subordinates? The name still most often cited as proof that Auchinleck was a bad picker is that of Major-General Eric Dorman-Smith; and it is he who is also blamed for breaking up the traditional British division in favour of "Jock Columns" or battle groups. This charge against Auchinleck and Dorman-Smith is without foundation in evidence. In the first place Dorman-Smith only became Deputy Chief of the General Staff in Cairo on 16th June 1942, when the Gazala battles had already been lost and the Eighth Army already largely broken to pieces under the aegis of Ritchie, his staff and commanders. Secondly, it was in fact on Dorman-Smith's advice that Auchinleck sought to repair this fragmentation by massing artillery, first under corps command and later under army command, as is proved by documents now open in the Public Record Office. For instance, on 15th July 1942 the C.G.S. (Corbett) told a Commanders' Conference at G.H.Q. British Troops in Egypt, according to the verbatim record:

> The artillery is being restored to its rightful place on the battlefield. Very large concentrations of artillery fire, including, for example, the coordinated fire of the artillery of two corps, are being used with overwhelming effect. On the other hand, the lack of effect of small units of artillery used singly is being realised.

Moreover, as Auchinleck himself has borne witness, the successful outcome of First Alamein owed much to Dorman-Smith's inventive mind and to his creative use of *Ultra* and other intelligence. Dorman-Smith also proposed the defensive layout which formed the basis of Montgomery's Alam Halfa battle, while the timing, nature and course of the German offensive that led to this battle had been accurately predicted by Dorman-Smith in his 27th July appreciation. Although Dorman-Smith's ideas were uneven in quality (or practicality) and although he will clearly remain a controversial figure, and to some a suspect one, the hard fact remains that he acted as Auchinleck's personal adviser in a battle which successfully rescued the Eighth Army from total catastrophe and halted Rommel when he stood nearer to final victory than before or after. For this reason alone Dorman-Smith cannot fairly be adduced as proof of poor picking on Auchinleck's part.

It must be recalled that Auchinleck chose Dorman-Smith as his personal adviser during First Alamein partly because Dorman-Smith was an "outsider" and not part of the orthodox Eighth Army "Establishment" which had been so closely involved in the calamities of the Gazala battle, such as, for instance, Whiteley, the existing Brigadier General Staff, Eighth Army, whom Auchinleck sacked at the end of First Alamein. It is understandable that the "Establishment" at the time and ever since should cherish warm resentment of Dorman-Smith. For a more balanced view of Dorman-Smith's qualities, it is worth turning to Major-General Sir Francis de Guingand, who served both Auchinleck and Montgomery, and who knew Dorman-Smith well. In *Generals at War* he writes:

> His approach to problems was often interesting and able; sometimes unique, but, on many occasions, impracticable. Nevertheless, provided his superiors were selective in their sifting of advice given, "Chink" could be of considerable value . . . During his time with Auchinleck he made his influence felt for good in certain directions. I happen to know that he was opposed to divisions not fighting as divisions but, as was the growing practice, of fighting in "boxes" instead of using their mobility. I think it true to say that "Chink" made a definite contribution in helping Auchinleck to stem the tide at Alamein, although in certain other directions he was apt to cause friction and disharmony. To sum up, whatever weaknesses Dorman-Smith may have had, I consider it was hardly fair to lay at his feet many of the Eighth Army's shortcomings.

What of Auchinleck's other principal choices of subordinates? There can be no question that in appointing Major-General T. W. Corbett as his Chief of the General Staff at G.H.Q., Cairo in February 1942 and having him in mind as a possible Eighth Army commander in the summer of that year, Auchinleck entirely misjudged Corbett's modest professional and personal merits—as indeed this book states. On the other hand, it was Auchinleck who picked de Guingand as his Director of Military Intelligence and later as Brigadier General Staff; the man who was to be the key figure in Montgomery's wartime success. Moreover, during Churchill's first visit to Cairo in August 1942, Auchinleck, like Brooke, preferred Montgomery to Gott as the new commander of the Eighth Army; a choice which Auchinleck's critics may not think best illustrates him as a "poor picker of men".

There remain the cases of Cunningham and Ritchie. As this book points out, Cunningham seemed at the time of appointment an imaginative choice in view of his performance in East Africa, and at first he impressed not only Auchinleck but also his new subordinates. While it is clear enough in retrospect that his appointment was a mistake, it is less clear that it shows Auchinleck as a "poor picker" when it was made, given the information then available to him and the paucity of alternative talent.

With regard to Ritchie, his original appointment was intended to be for the duration of the *Crusader* offensive only, and as such had the advantage of not disrupting the Eighth Army's existing command structure. It worked well enough in that context. Auchinleck's errors of judgement, noted in this book, lay in confirming Ritchie as Army Commander in March 1942 despite warnings that he was not up to the job, and in not acceding to the War Premier's well-founded request that he, Auchinleck, should take personal command of the Eighth Army before Rommel launched his Gazala offensive in May. As this book describes, the combination of an army commander of inadequate calibre and ambiguous position, a disputatious committee of formation commanders and an advisory "uncle" in Cairo proved the worst of all possible worlds when it came to fighting a general like Rommel.

Thus out of three army command appointments and three senior staff appointments (Cunningham, Ritchie, Montgomery; de Guingand, Corbett and Dorman-Smith) Auchinleck made indisputable errors of judgement of capacity for the post in two cases only (Ritchie and Corbett). It would perhaps be fairer to dub Auchinleck a poor sacker of men rather than a poor picker.

PART SIX

MILITARY MESSIAH

Field-Marshal The Viscount Montgomery of Alamein, K.G., G.C.B., D.S.O.

> Just his conceptions, natural and great;
> His feelings strong, his words enforced with weight . . .
> View the whole scene, with critic judgment scan,
> And then deny him merit if you can.
> Where he falls short, 'tis Nature's fault alone;
> Where he succeeds, the merit's all his own.
>
> CHARLES CHURCHILL,
> *The Rosciad.*

CHAPTER ONE

WITH Sir Claude Auchinleck's victory in the First Battle of Alamein, the history of the Desert War passes into a long though sometimes bloody anti-climax. For the Axis had now lost the war in the Mediterranean. In retrospect, both Italians and Germans were to recognise that their hopeless renewed offensive at Alam Halfa and their subsequent obstinate clinging to the Alamein position were alike disastrous attempts at wish-fulfilment. Kesselring, German C.-in-C. in the Mediterranean, wrote that "given our full knowledge of the gamble, the attack ought never to have been begun". Mussolini agreed:

> When (Rommel) had twice attacked unsuccessfully before Montgomery's offensive he should have withdrawn at once to Mersa Matruh . . . I told (Hitler) we had lost the initiative from June 1942 onwards, and that a nation which has lost the initiative has lost the war.

The matter had been clinched when, on July 25th, emboldened by Auchinleck's success in halting Rommel, the British and American war leaders had decided to invade French North Africa in November with large British and American forces, an intervention which in Rommel's words "spelled the end of the army in Africa".

But if the desert fighting after First Alamein is a kind of epilogue, it is, by a paradox, also the first act of the famous career of Field-Marshal the Viscount Montgomery of Alamein, K.G.; and this is what makes it interesting.

It is not easy to look back beyond the veteran Field-Marshal, with all his honours and victories, at Lieutenant-General B. L. Montgomery, in August, 1942. Yet his performance as a Lieutenant-General in the desert, when he was unknown and untried, is the key to an objective assessment of his abilities.

The difficulty of seeing him then as he really was, rather than as a superhuman figure, does not lie in want of documentation. However, in most of this documentation the haphazard facts of real life have been pruned into an artistic symmetry.

*   *   *   *   *

Bernard Montgomery was perhaps the first individual to adopt as a personal principle of conduct and judgment the Stuart doctrine that the king can do no wrong. If he admitted to an error, it was always minor, and served, like a touch of black in a colour scheme, to throw up his general infallibility. At Sandhurst he was a member of a gang that persecuted cadets they disliked; as a climax, Montgomery set light to a cadet's clothes and burned him severely enough for him to be sent to hospital. He not only tells this story in his memoirs, but tells it with relish. Such an attitude illustrates another trait—his lack of judgment in regard to conduct outside a battlefield. It would seem that he has always been so wrapped up in himself and his own view outwards to the world that he has little sympathetic understanding of other people's minds and emotions; and the results of this want of comprehension of the reality of so many things outside Montgomery have been wild strokes of misjudgment fatal to a man less professionally talented.

At the end of a lecture to Home Guard officers he told them that he was now going to present a play he had written himself. "While the audience watched fascinated, four soldiers dressed in German uniforms entered carrying umbrellas. As they opened the umbrellas a loud report echoed through the hall, and this, apparently, was to illustrate the arrival of parachutists in England. The four soldiers then lined up on the platform and announced solemnly: 'We'll cut the throat of that bastard Montgomery'."

In France in 1940 as G.O.C. 3rd Infantry Division he published an order on troops' morals and the prevention of venereal disease so offensive that both the Anglican and Roman senior chaplains bitterly complained, and Montgomery only retained his command by grace of General Brooke, his corps commander, who required him to publish an apology.

In Tunisia the American General Bedell-Smith said in fun he would give Montgomery an American aircraft if Montgomery reached a certain town by a certain date. Having done so, Montgomery claimed his plane. The affronted Americans pointed out that the bet had been only a casual joke. But Montgomery insisted on his plane with complete American crew, got it, and could not be made to see why the Americans were furious with him.

Yet paradoxically Montgomery, though unpredictable to the point of eccentricity in his general judgement and even conduct, was in war devoted to ideals of precision, punctuality, caution and close control; his plans were shaped and explained with the exactness of a watch-maker. As an instructor at the Staff College at Camberley he "had the unique gift of making complicated matters appear quite simple". His schemes there showed a tendency towards overwhelming superiority of force rather than manœuvre; and one daring student observed that he "took a sledgehammer to crack a walnut".

Montgomery's teaching, which so embodied the clear and precise nature of his military temperament and the solidity of his knowledge, did however reveal in the professional sphere his unawareness of, or lack of interest in, other people and their reactions. A student noted that a typical scheme of Montgomery's dealt with "our side's" plans with comprehensive exactitude and elaboration; but the "enemy's" intentions and reactions were not imagined, either as a source of danger or opportunity. Montgomery was the steamroller, the enemy the gravel road. Had this tendency also roots in his profound desire to dominate; and dominate absolutely rather than conditionally?

In preparation for a call to great command, Montgomery spent his life immersed night and day in that narrow world which he knew so well and in which his understanding acted so judiciously. The world outside, except for his brief and tragic marriage, remained a world of shadows. His want of true friends, of hobbies, of intellectual interests has been noted by himself as much as by his colleagues. He wished only to fit himself for success in his profession; yet his *Memoirs* indicate that by a tragic irony he thus fixed, in a favourite word, his own ceiling, for as he moved up from the battlefield to the council chambers of the Allies, his narrow professionalism and want of understanding of humanity sometimes betrayed him.

Yet in simple ways he could be touched. When General Godwin-Austen visited him in Sicily in 1943, Montgomery gave him

> a letter to a humble girl in England with a ring. He also gave me a letter he had received from the girl. This said (I quote from memory) 'Dear Monty, I see you have changed your beret. If you still have your old beret, may I have it? My man was one of yours, who was killed at Alamein, and I send my wedding ring. But if you've not got your old beret, please keep the ring.' Monty had written a very nice letter to her returning the ring, and was insistent that I posted it in England in case it went astray. He was particularly anxious about this, and reminded me several times.

The same powerful will to dominate which informed his conduct and his military thought also drove him up in his profession for, as an able man should be, he was ambitious. But for his abilities to be rewarded they must first be recognised; and the flair for public relations was revealed early and employed constantly. The development of this flair is a subtle inter-play of his natural eccentricity (with the consequent circulation of 'Monty' stories) and the cold calculation of the battlefield-side of his mind.

To rebuffs he was cheerfully insensitive, even if he admitted their justice. In the 1930s, when Montgomery was a battalion commander in Egypt, he had a brush with his brigadier, Pile:

> Both Monty and Franklin (another Battalion Commander) had recently been instructors at Camberley. The G.O.C. in C., B.T.E., Lieutenant General Sir Jock Burnett-Stuart, carried out extensive and valuable training exercises in the desert. In one of the night exercises both sides reached a state of complete confusion, which was the time when you began to learn something. Franklin and Monty were on opposite sides in this particular exercise, and late on in the night these two Battalion Commanders conferred together and decided, without reference to Brigadier Pile, to call off the exercise and march home. When Pile heard of this he was livid. He sent for both officers and gave them a tremendous ticking-off. Monty said afterwards: "I fully deserved it . . . fully", but, quite unperturbed, turned up for a previous invitation to lunch the following day with the Brigadier and the whole proceedings passed off pleasantly.

Montgomery's first major command was 8th Infantry Division in Palestine during the Arab rebellion in 1936–39. He now showed clearly his character as a man and a commander. Though chasing elusive rebel bands, he insisted on methodical operations from "a firm base, a firm base". He also revealed a tendency to look upon the troops and operations under his command in a very personal, or even egotistical manner. An incident of the time illustrates this, as well as his genius for advertising his actions in the proper quarters.

General Godwin-Austen recalls that one day Montgomery was coming on a routine visit to the Border Regiment, part of Godwin-Austen's brigade; he, Godwin-Austen and Lay, commanding officer of the Border Regiment, met at Megiddo. Lay had just heard the news that Abdul Karim, a much-wanted rebel leader, had been killed and was lying in Sannur village. He suggested that the Divisional Commander might prefer to see this gentleman rather than carry on with a routine tour. Montgomery asked:

"Abdul Karim? Who is he? Who is he?"

Lay explained, and all set off for Sannur. The dead rebel, the flies buzzing above him, was surrounded by Palestine Policemen (who had of course identified him) and troops. Montgomery strode to the body, and then snapped:

"A notebook!"

He took one of a dozen proffered, and wrote busily. Then he announced to those round him:

"This is what I've written. Major-General B. L. Montgomery, at Sannur, to G.O.C.-in-C. Palestine and Transjordan. Today *my* troops shot and killed Abdul Karim, the rebel leader. *I* have identified the body and pronounce it to be that of Abdul Karim. . . ."

Towards the incompetent he was as ruthless, swift and remorseless as a sabre-stroke. In his area of Palestine there was a certain inefficient member of the *civil* administration. Montgomery told one of his brigadiers, Brigadier (now General) Ramsden, that he was going to sack this man; Ramsden was to be in Montgomery's office at 9 a.m. on the morrow. Here Ramsden was shown a report for the High Commissioner drawn up by Montgomery. It began:

> This civil officer is one hundred per cent wet and one hundred per cent inefficient . . .

At 9.30 the official turned up, was given the report to read, and became purple with outrage. Montgomery asked him to initial it to show he had seen the report, before it was sent to the High Commissioner. He refused.

"All right," said Montgomery, "I'll send it *without* your initials. Ramsden, you're a witness."

Montgomery's departure for England was an early essay in his technique of public relations. The night before he was due to be invalided back to Egypt in an aircraft on the first stage of his journey he sent for Ramsden and instructed him to have all his brigade officers at the airport, by the plane, for his departure. The morning came and Montgomery was taken on a stretcher to the door of the plane between an avenue of his officers while he waved his now-famous wave.

The German invasion of France and the Low Countries, that most brilliant of all campaigns in the Second World War, provided Montgomery with his only taste of action against great odds and better equipment. While it is true that the British Expeditionary Force did not feel the full violence of the German onslaught until the battle was nearing its end, nevertheless Montgomery and his 3rd Division showed what could be effected by six months of hard training and a thoroughly professional approach to war. Neither Montgomery nor his men were perturbed by disaster. Montgomery on the contrary seemed to be enjoying himself in a quite nerveless manner. The worse the news, the more arrogantly confident he seemed. At one of his last conferences before the army fell back into Dunkirk, he concluded his orders to his officers by announcing:

"Gentlemen, we'll shatter the boche—shatter the boche!"

But now there was to be no more fighting for Montgomery for more than two years. From June 1940 to August 1942, the years of desperate struggle in the desert, he commanded in the home army in England, first 5th Corps and then South Eastern Command. Apart from his methods of hard training, the chief interest of this period lies in the prototype of Montgomery's plan for an offensive battle; a prototype that failed disastrously because the essential ingredient of the later offensives—overwhelming force of guns, tanks and airpower—was missing. It was the Dieppe raid.

Combined Operations Headquarters Planning Staff began work on an Outline Plan about the middle of April, 1942. At an early stage, the Commander-in-Chief, Home Forces, delegated his authority in the matter to the General Officer Commanding-in-Chief South Eastern Command, Lieutenant-General B. L. Montgomery "who," in the words of the Canadian official history, "thereafter took the responsibility for the military side of the planning and himself attended some of the later meetings of the planners". The plan adopted had much in common with Second Alamein, with Mareth, with Enfidaville, the Sangro, Caen and Arnhem. It consisted of a main blow with tanks frontally delivered against the powerful German beach and port defences of Dieppe, with subsidiary flanking attacks designed to reach round behind the town. On 11th May, 1942, the Chief of Combined Operations submitted this outline plan to the Chiefs of Staff Committee, informing them that it had the concurrence of the G.O.C.-in-C., South Eastern Command. Only now that the master plan was accepted did Canadian officers begin work on the details.

About the middle of July, 1942, Montgomery ceased to be responsible for the military side, and on August 18th when the raid took place he was in Egypt. But the master plan remained essentially unchanged. The main frontal attack broke down before furious German fire, all tanks being lost on the beach. The subsidiary attacks made better progress but were too feeble to get inland. In any case the gullies up the cliffs were impassable to larger forces. After the disaster it was concluded, as the navy suggested beforehand, that such a frontal assault as had been made required overwhelming air and gun support for success.

The failure of the Dieppe raid was partly owing therefore to bad luck and bad management on the day, but partly owing to the nature of Montgomery's master plan, and, though he himself was not there, Dieppe must constitute in a real sense Montgomery's first defeat, and a proof that Montgomery's conception of an offensive battle as a head-against-the-wall frontal trial of strength could only succeed where the enemy could be borne down by overwhelming weight of metal.

Dieppe is also interesting as the first example of Montgomery quietly brushing himself clean of so unfortunate an occurrence as a defeat. There is no discussion in his *Memoirs* of the master plan and the reasons for its failure. He briefly suggests that loss of secrecy (the Canadian official record disagrees) and the elimination of preliminary saturation bombing, among other things, caused the repulse.

In the summer of 1942, when the war was nearly three years old, Montgomery had still to hold a high command in battle. The opportunity, to fit himself for which he had sacrificed most of the usual human pleasures and interests, eluded him. He could console himself that from June 1940 had begun "my real influence on the training of the Army in England".

But at last Montgomery's opportunity came, by the accident of the death in an aircraft crash of Strafer Gott, Eighth Army Commander designate. Montgomery flew to Cairo on 10th August, 1942.

* * * * *

In the morning of 12th August, Montgomery, incoming Army Commander, and Auchinleck, outgoing Commander-in-Chief, met in Auchinleck's map room in G.H.Q., Cairo. It was a tense interview. On one hand, there was the buoyant fellow from England who had endured no battle strain for two years, eager to enter his inheritance; on the other the man whose supreme and successful efforts had just been crowned by dismissal. The two men were utterly dissimilar in every respect but their resolution in battle. As they talked, Auchinleck big and burly, Montgomery's chin on a level with Auchinleck's decorations, the spark of mutual dislike leaped between them.

Then Montgomery went down to Eighth Army. He had a vested interest in the Prime Minister's legend that in the Middle East all was incompetence and ruin until the Cairo Purge, after which instead genius and unclouded victory reigned; and he set about propagating it with conspicuous skill by putting his own name to the best of Auchinleck's plans, while assigning to Auchinleck and his officers the blame for the hiatus in leadership and planning caused by the fortnight-long comings-and-goings of the Purge.

Personally, he made a deep and energising effect on the army, battle-worn as it was and bewildered by the apparent want of leadership since July 30th. Always arrogantly self-confident and relentlessly energetic, he was above all things fresh, and, as de Guingand wrote of Auchinleck's arrival in the Middle East in 1941, "he was like a breath of fresh air". However, it would be wrong to place too much emphasis on the moral effects produced by the new army commander: for in the words of the Official History, Auchinleck "had retained to a remarkable degree [his army's] admiration and confidence."

Montgomery heard the acting Army Commander, General Ramsden, explain the situation and future plans; then told him:

"All right, I'll carry on here. You can go back to your corps."

Montgomery was to display an increasing high-handedness that he would have been the last to tolerate in others. Now, in Eighth Army Headquarters on August 12th, 1942, he signalled G.H.Q. Cairo that he had assumed command of Eighth Army, two days earlier than he should have done and in complete disobedience of orders. This gesture was of no importance militarily—he did nothing during those two days that he could not have done as an army-commander designate—but it throws a bleak light on his character as a man. It could serve only to wound Auchinleck in his last two days of command. Sixteen years later his pleasure in his action was undiminished; he made a point of saying in his *Memoirs* that on 13th August, 1942, "it was with an insubordinate smile that I fell asleep: I was issuing orders to an army which someone else reckoned he commanded!" However, he did not issue them from Eighth Army headquarters, because he "decided to leave the H.Q. quickly in case there were any repercussions". Montgomery need not have worried; his signal never reached Auchinleck.

Montgomery set about impressing himself on his command, which now became "my men", "my army". The army headquarters staff learned that he would hold a conference at a certain time and *that air cover would be provided*, an innovation for such an occasion. Unfortunately, Montgomery was so late all the air cover had gone home.

He spent a long day with General Ramsden visiting 30th Corps, conspicuously new in long shorts and white knees. But he was full of bounce, full of an almost childlike pleasure at being in command in the desert. He showed Ramsden a new wrist watch. "See this wrist watch? New one for the desert, new one for the desert!"

Later on it was a fine picnic basket—"I bought it for the desert!"

The day's tour began at 9th Australian Division; this visit had far-reaching effects on military iconography. An Australian liaison officer saluted and remarked to him: "It's a hot day, sir."

Montgomery, in a general's red-banded cap, replied: "Quite right, it is a very hot day—a very hot day. This is quite the wrong sort of hat to wear—far too warm."

"You should have one of ours, sir."

"A very good idea—a very good idea."

A selection of Australian slouch hats was provided for him to try on. Eventually he picked one, but remarked: "No badge—I can't wear a hat without a badge." So he was given an Australian badge. At the end of the day he had collected hats and badges from the South Africans and the Indians. His *Memoirs* show that behind this apparently spontaneous acquisition of distinctive headgear lay calculated policy.

He disliked Auchinleck's battle headquarters because it had no beds, no amenities and plenty of flies; and the crisis that had caused Auchinleck to place his H.Q. behind the Ruweisat Ridge being over, Montgomery moved back to join the Desert Air Force headquarters at Burg el Arab, in accordance with the year-old custom of shared headquarters. Here, under a marquee, he held his famous 'no-bellyaching' conference. His officers listened, without coughing, to a crisp, simple and emphatic lecture delivered in a metallic voice, a nasal drawl with strongly lisped 'R's'. Afterwards Major-General Brian Horrocks, an old colleague of Montgomery's who had just arrived from England to take over 13th Corps, came up to his fellow corps commander, smiling that toothy smile later so well known to television audiences. "Ramsden," he said. "Isn't he *marvellous?*"

Montgomery had heard Auchinleck explain his plans; he had heard Ramsden repeat them; he had seen on the wall of the operations caravan a map of the Alam Halfa dispositions; and he had had long conversations with de Guingand, lately Auchinleck's Brigadier General Staff, and fully versed in Dorman-Smith's Appreciation of July 27th and Auchinleck's orders of July 30th. These now became *his* plans; nowhere, in two books and a television performance, does Montgomery hint that the Battle of Alam Halfa was fought on a plan conceived by Dorman-Smith, approved and initiated by Auchinleck, and from fixed defences largely dug before Montgomery left England. He wrote in his *Memoirs*:

I decided to hold the Alam Halfa Ridge strongly . . . It was obvious to me that Rommel could not just by-pass my forces and go off eastwards to Cairo; if he did so, I could have descended on his rear . . .

And General Alexander writes in his official despatch:

The plan (Auchinleck's) was to hold as strongly as possible the area between the sea and the Ruweisat Ridge and to threaten from the flank any and every advance south of the ridge from a strongly defended prepared position on the Alam el Halfa Ridge.

Again, Montgomery writes in his *Memoirs*:

I then decided that my extreme south flank should be mobile; the 7th Armoured Division would hold a wide front and, as the attack came, would give way before it. When the attack swung left-handed towards the Alam Halfa Ridge, the 7th Armoured Division would harry it from the east and south . . .

And in Dorman-Smith's Appreciation of 27th July:

Eighth Army may have to meet an enemy's sortie developing into manœuvre by the southern flank. . . . We must therefore organize a strong mobile wing . . . well-trained in defensive harassing technique.

On August 19th Montgomery was able to dazzle both the Prime Minister and the Chief of the Imperial General Staff with the swiftness with which he had evolved his plans for the future. He made a striking success. When he had dealt with the coming defensive battle, Montgomery turned to his own offensive and described how he wished to break through the enemy position about El Alamein. He said the offensive could not take place in under six weeks, owing to the need for thorough training and for breaking in the new Shermans. This was exactly what Churchill had heard from Auchinleck. It had clinched Auchinleck's dismissal, but Churchill swallowed the delay from his new general. Brooke said of Montgomery's performance: "One of the highlights of his military career. He had only been at the head of his command for a few days . . ." and Churchill wrote later: "A masterly exposition of the problem . . . he accurately predicted Rommel's next attack . . ." The Prime Minister's visit did much to dissolve his earlier doubts about Montgomery. Unlike Auchinleck, Montgomery had a perfect grasp of public relations. He made tremendous efforts to see that the discomforts of war in the desert did not affect Churchill. He gave up his own caravan for the Prime Minister to sleep in, and placed it near the sea for ease of bathing. There was wine and brandy at dinner in the mess.

In the fortnight that elapsed between his taking command and the opening of the Battle of Alam Halfa, Montgomery developed Auchinleck's plans in two ways; he had tanks dug in along the Alam Halfa Ridge and he ordered the green 44th Division up from the Delta. However, this division saw little action in the battle. Montgomery's main personal contribution was the cast-steel control, sure and precise, that he exercised over the battle. There was to be no loose fighting. He warned Ramsden, of 30th Corps:

"It will be an Army battle, Ramsden—an Army battle."

The Eighth Army faced an easy task. Strongly and cleverly posted, it had seven hundred and sixty-seven tanks fit for action, of which seven hundred and thirteen were in the forward area. One hundred and sixty-four were the heavy Grants. Against this array, posted defensively, Rommel could muster only two hundred gun-armed German tanks. All British armoured and infantry divisions fought for the first time equipped with the new 6-pounder anti-tank guns. The British enjoyed complete air supremacy. Rommel was so starved of fuel for his striking force that on 27th August, three days before the battle, he told Kesselring that success depended on his getting the six thousand tons of fuel promised ten days earlier. Instead he got one thousand eight hundred tons and had to shorten the radius of his turning movement. And Rommel himself was enfeebled by sickness and defeat. Rommel's doctor said that he "can command the battle under constant medical attention . . . essential to have a replacement on the spot." In fact "he was so ill with an infection of the nose and a swollen liver, that he could not get out of his truck". Gause, his chief of staff, was also sick.

In the words of Dorman-Smith's Appreciation of 27th July the Axis were "hardly strong enough to attempt the conquest of the Delta except as a gamble and under very strong air cover". And there was no German air cover.

Montgomery made much at the time and afterwards of his cancellation of all provisional orders for the conduct of a retreat from Alamein. In the face of Rommel's offensive, Eighth Army would stay at Alamein, he dramatically proclaimed, alive or dead. He sought in his *Memoirs* to convince posterity that before his arrival,

The men of the Eighth Army were looking back over their shoulders, wondering where they were going to withdraw to next. All available troops back in the Nile Delta were digging defensive positions, and the area of the Pyramids was being prepared for defence.

He claimed that he stopped all this.

Yet Winston Churchill, writing of his second visit to Cairo from 17th to 23rd August, describes in detail how he, the C.I.G.S. and General Alexander set on foot "a series of extreme measures for the defence of Cairo and the water-lines running northwards to the sea". The 51st Highland Division was posted in these defences. General Maitland Wilson (C.-in-C. Iraq-Persia Command) was to take command of the Delta troops "from the moment when General Alexander told him Cairo was in danger".

Gott, while commanding 13th Corps, had been ordered by Auchinleck to prepare detailed plans for the expected German attack on the southern flank. Before his death these plans had been largely completed and were adopted by Montgomery and by Horrocks, the new corps commander. In particular two alternative areas of ground had been selected, one north and one south of the Alam Halfa Ridge, where the British armour could wait defensively in hull-down positions and behind an anti-tank screen for Rommel's attack. Depending on the direction of the German main blow, the British armour would move from its assembly area to one of these selected battle stations. There was the question of who should give the order to move, when, and to which place. Montgomery rightly decided that he would do so personally. He has described an argument with the commander of 7th Armoured Division as to whether the armour should be "loosed at the enemy". He took the credit for preventing a possible mad charge and for introducing the conception of a defensive armoured battle.

> Monty's handling of armour [said General Leese later, speaking generally] was very different from the old British tactics—there was no swanning, but proper co-operation of armour and artillery, and close-in with infantry in attacks on fixed positions. We never, never advanced with our armour—always slowly, supported by our guns. We tried to get the Germans to attack us.

But according to General Renton, G.O.C. 7th Armoured Division, neither he nor Gott had any offensive move in mind for Alam Halfa; they knew too well the need to husband the armour and especially the Grants; it was only the matter of a move to one of the selected defensive battle stations that was in question. Gott had of course, like Montgomery himself, considered striking Rommel in his flank with armour and guns if the *Panzerarmee* should move far to the east.

For Montgomery, Alam Halfa, as his first, was a crucial battle. Although he likes to say he never worried, never lost sleep, the days that wound up to 31st August, 1942, made him taut and edgy. A few days before the battle he remarked to a subordinate:

"Couldn't sleep last night—couldn't sleep last night. Supposing he attacks in the north?"

He was especially worried about the possibility of Rommel "attacking on either side of the New Zealand Division, crushing it and throwing it away."

But the battle went as long anticipated. The sick Rommel put himself at the head of his three veteran German divisions, with the Italian 20th Corps on his left, and after dark on 30th August, the *Panzerarmee Afrika* began to work its way through the British mine-fields. These were thicker than expected; by dawn on 31st August, the German armour, instead of striking fast and deep towards the coast, had only just cleared their eastern edge. There was therefore neither strategical nor tactical surprise. As the German armour made its way eastwards, 7th Armoured Division slowly gave ground. From a British sky, an avalanche of fire swept ceaselessly over the German forces, whose progress on the ground was marked, like pins on a battle map, by tall columns of black smoke from burning trucks and tanks. Soft sand burned up the precious fuel.

By eleven in the morning of 31st August the British command knew that all of Rommel's German divisions were committed in the south; as they moved slowly on through the haze, they were watched through binoculars on the Alam Halfa Ridge. About one o'clock the Germans halted to refuel and then they came on again. For the British command there had been the uncertainty as to whether Rommel would swing far out for the centre and east of the Alam Halfa Ridge, where 44th Division was posted, or close in to attack the Ridge's western end, where there was 10th Armoured Division. Now Rommel was seen to turn sharply north, a move forced on him not by a planted 'false-going' map, but by the delays in the mine-fields and by shortage of petrol.

A sandstorm rose; and beneath the cover it gave from air attack the German armour attacked 22nd Armoured Brigade in its prepared and mined battle station just south of the tip of the Alam Halfa Ridge. Under raging field and anti-tank gunfire, the German attacks broke down. But they were not pressed with the old skill and resolution: unlucky casualties had unhinged the German structure of command. General von Bismarck, of 21st Panzer Division, had been killed; Nehring, commanding the Afrika Korps, wounded. In the subsequent re-organization, the Afrika Korps and both its armoured divisions found themselves in the middle of the battle with new commanders.

At nightfall, the German armour fell back to the south. The Ragil Depression was filled with German tanks and trucks, and all night green and orange tracer lit them up, as the British artillery and aircraft bombarded them. Montgomery now re-deployed 10th Armoured Division to cover the gap between Alam Halfa and the main Alamein defences. He took Rommel's attack seriously: a

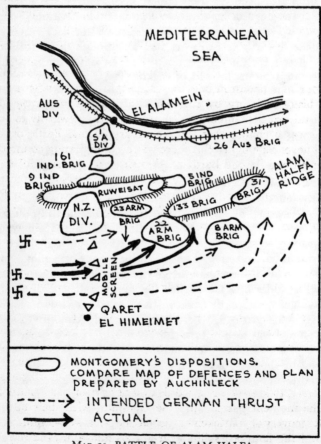

MAP 21. BATTLE OF ALAM HALFA
31 August—3 September 1942

South African brigade was taken out of the Alamein front and brought down to the Ruweisat Ridge, while a fresh brigade was brought up from the Delta to occupy the area east of the main battle vacated by 10th Armoured Division.

All through 1st September the panzers strove to break through the British defences and were each time thrown back into the soft sand of the Ragil Depression. That night 15th Panzer Division reported that it was completely paralysed by want of fuel; the rest of the *Panzerarmee* was hardly better off. On 2nd September Rommel issued orders for a retreat.

He was in a situation of the greatest peril. He lay with three divisions in a shallow depression between the powerful British forces at Alam Halfa and the Quattara Depression, far behind the main axis of the British front. He was disorganized by defeat, constantly bombed and seriously short of petrol. This was the moment for an annihilating counter-stroke in the grand style, driving across Rommel's communications to the Quattara Depression, sealing his armour in a cauldron of bombardment, and achieving a complete and historic victory by Rommel's surrender *en rase campagne*. On 2nd and 3rd September, as Rommel edged awkwardly to the west, there was a chance that the sanguinary Second Battle of Alamein need never be fought. But there was no annihilating counter-stroke. After all, the Second Battle of Alamein had been scheduled; and to Montgomery's methodical and tidy mind unexpected opportunities, however great, were, in his desert days, embarrassing. As Rommel went back, Montgomery carefully re-grouped and gingerly followed.

He later explained his failure to turn Alam Halfa into a historic victory by reference to the capabilities of his troops:

> The standard of training of the Eighth Army formations was such that I was not prepared to loose them headlong into the enemy.

This begged the question. A counter-stroke across Rommel's communications would have involved neither loosing his troops nor advancing headlong into the enemy. Curiously enough, he was later to miss another opportunity of an annihilating counter-stroke—after the German repulse in the Ardennes in 1944. Once again, he preferred to keep to his schedule and fight a set-piece battle later.

The moment passed, and the Germans, with their aptitude for swift recovery on a stricken battlefield, began a well-conducted retreat behind the familiar, skilful rear-guards and anti-tank screen. Not until the night of 3rd/4th September had Montgomery succeeded in re-grouping his forces for an attempt to interfere with this retreat. It was a half-hearted attempt, carried out by the New Zealand Division alone, and it was too late. There were two days of bitter fighting in which the New Zealanders became badly disorganised and even Montgomery had to admit that this methodical attack "did not succeed in cutting (Rommel) off".

By 6th September Rommel had brought his troops safely out of danger and into a bridgehead, bristling with anti-tank guns, on the eastern side of the British minefields. There was no attempt to turn him out. According to General Horrocks and to Montgomery himself in his *Memoirs*, Rommel was left in possession of this bridgehead, including the hill of Himeimat, in order that he might observe British decoy preparations before Second Alamein. Elsewhere, however, Montgomery wrote that he called off his pursuit because Rommel was evidently prepared to fight for his bridgehead.

Though a great opportunity had been ignored, Alam Halfa was a model defensive battle and which reflected credit on all concerned in it: the planners Dorman-Smith, Auchinleck and Gott, and the commanders Montgomery and Horrocks. It had no strategic consequences, but it was, in Montgomery's words, "very important for the Eighth Army, and particularly for me. I said what Rommel would do, and he'd been beaten . . . and it produced faith in me, in my methods. . . ." By an irony, many authorities consider Alam Halfa, with its uncharacteristic features of indirectness, deception and manœuvre, to be Montgomery's cleverest battle. General Sir Oliver Leese, who commanded 30th Corps at Second Alamein, said of it: "I always thought Alam Halfa was Monty's finest battle—I know he based Medenine on it."

Thus, in a second-hand coat of glory, Montgomery set out for the top.

CHAPTER TWO

ALAM HALFA delayed Montgomery's preparations for his own offensive by a fortnight. But he had already done much to make over the army in his image. There was the question of morale, to which he rightly attached very great importance. Here he was an innovator. He was the first British general to project himself to his public (the troops) like a politician or a crooner. Wellington and Marlborough would have found a calculated personal appeal to the army inconsistent with their professional rank. So would Montgomery's predecessors in the Middle East. Yet Marlborough and Wellington enjoyed the complete confidence and loyalty of their men, as had O'Connor, Auchinleck and Wavell, one of whom was very self-effacing and another taciturn. On the enemy side, Rommel was a most simple and unaffected man; but between him and his men existed a loyalty and a strength that recalls Nelson and his fleet. Nevertheless, Montgomery felt that to command successfully, to gain loyalty, he must embark on a publicity campaign.

The hats were the beginning, and certainly his black beret made him recognizable. Press men and photographers, kept at bay by Auchinleck, now flourished in the wartime desert as at a peacetime première. The army public relations staff burned with creative endeavour. The earliest of three years of spontaneous wayside encounters with the troops were arranged. All this would have been profoundly distasteful, even had it been necessary, to any man not abnormally vain. Montgomery actually liked all this contrived lionizing.

"I readily admit," he confided to seven million people, "that the decision to become the focus of their attention was personally enjoyable to me. . . ."

He would himself go to considerable trouble to draw a few salutes, especially in distinguished company. General Gatehouse was conducting Montgomery and Wendell Wilkie round the Alam Halfa battlefield to see wrecked German tanks. There were one or two scattered British tank units doing maintenance work. Montgomery told

Gatehouse to go over to the nearest group. Gatehouse, who thought the Army Commander wanted to show his American guest tank crews cleaning sprockets and repairing tracks, stopped some distance away in order not to disturb the men. But Montgomery had the car driven right up to them. The soldiers dropped what they were doing, clambered up and saluted; Montgomery gave them a tremendous salute in return.

Montgomery launched himself into the work of training and reorganizing the battle-worn army with an icy fire, a relentless energy. He wanted an efficient army, a professional army, above all a *tidy* army. He toured endlessly through his command, his bleak eyes seizing on the idle, the slack and the incompetent, his metallic voice questioning, ordering, denouncing and dismissing. He was like Florence Nightingale putting a hospital in order. All this was admirable.

Yet in purging the army he could be devious. After the Battle of Alam Halfa, the commander of 30th Corps, General Ramsden, asked for four days' leave in Alexandria, while remaining on constant call in case of emergency. Montgomery was genial:

"Certainly, Ramsden. Come back refreshed for the battle."

Thirty-six hours later Ramsden received an urgent call to report to the Army Commander. Arriving at Eighth Army, Ramsden asked de Guingand, the Chief of Staff, if there was a battle imminent. But de Guingand would only answer:

"General Montgomery wants to see you."

Ramsden entered Montgomery's caravan. Montgomery told him that he had been in the desert nine months and that he had decided to replace him by Sir Oliver Leese. Ramsden, dumbfounded, referred to Montgomery's remark made only thirty-six hours before; Montgomery brushed this aside by snapping irrelevantly:

"This is war—this is war."

Ramsden was an able officer who had distinguished himself in the First Battle of Alamein; he could not see why he was to go, and he said so. In justifying his dismissal Montgomery now made an odd but profoundly self-revealing remark. He said:

"You're not exactly on the crest of a wave, Ramsden."

Montgomery later claimed he made two innovations for his battle of Alamein. One was the formation of a *corps de chasse*, "mobile and strong in armour".

Because of the lack of such a corps we had never done any lasting good in our past offensives. The formation of this corps, three or four divisions, must be a priority task, and it would be to us what the Afrika Korps was to Rommel.

He described in his *Memoirs* how he put his ideas to Alexander, who approved them, and to Major-General Harding, Deputy Chief of the General Staff, who said he could organize such a corps. But this was no innovation at all; as long ago as O'Connor's campaign there had been a mobile and armoured *corps de chasse*—7th Armoured Division, which had won the victory of Beda Fomm. In *Crusader*, 30th Corps under Norrie had formed a mobile wing and had fought an armoured battle with the Afrika Korps, its German equivalent. The innovation under Montgomery lay in that the arrival of two additional armoured divisions, as well as fresh infantry divisions, allowed the formation of a third corps in the Army—10th Corps, to which was allotted the bulk of the armour (1st, 8th and 10th Armoured Divisions) and the New Zealand Division. The old *corps de chasse* now became a static infantry corps.

The second claim of innovation made by Montgomery is equally ill-founded. It relates to the placing of the main offensive effort at the Second Battle of Alamein.

> Now, in traditional desert tactics [said Montgomery on the television] it had always been to attack on the southern flank, the inland flank, and having broken in on the inland flank to swing northwards to the sea, where the only main supply route on this tarmac road hugged the coast. That had always been done, we'd always done it, and so had Rommel . . . it therefore seemed to me quite a good thing to do something else . . . *I* decided to put in our attack somewhere just north of centre.

That is, as the map facing p. 116 of his *Memoirs* shows, just south of the Tel el Eisa salient. However, by a coincidence, Ramsden had been working on just such a plan for a fortnight before Montgomery arrived in Egypt—by Auchinleck's orders.

> I ordered [wrote Auchinleck in his despatch] General Ramsden commanding 30th Corps to begin planning intensively for a deliberate attack south of the Tel el Eisa salient with a view to making a rapid advance along the coast road. I considered this operation offered the greatest chances of success . . .

It is understandable that in 1942 Montgomery would not wish to advertise the part played in his success by other generals—

especially by generals not on the crest of a wave, such as Auchinleck, Dorman-Smith and Ramsden. But sixteen years later, in the security of his unrivalled fame, it would have been generous and graceful to have shared the credit with these men, all of whom had remained unjustly in the shadows since 1942. There of course remains the possibility that Montgomery over the years came genuinely to believe his own legend; this would be understandable in view of the volume of support it has received from well-known writers.

From Auchinleck's general conception of a breakthrough on the left centre of the Axis field-fortifications, Montgomery evolved his own organization and tactics for the battle. The whole action was to be fought according to a Master Plan. It would be a methodical, tightly controlled operation, because despite the current re-training of the army he concluded that the skill of the army would not justify more ambitious manœuvres. Rommel and his officers, like Nelson and his, were so experienced, so imbued with common doctrine, so understanding of each other, that the Afrika Korps could fight a battle with an easy flexibility and local initiative. The Germans were like champion dancers—they had graduated from the set pattern of steps; all was instinctive. Under Montgomery, the British learned to lumber round the battlefield performing rigid beginners' evolutions beneath the sharp eye of the instructor.

But because of this want of faith in the abilities of his army, Montgomery had even to alter his own original tactical conception. Instead of a breakthrough, followed by a tank battle, and by the mopping-up of the enemy infantry, he now preferred an even tighter, more methodical scheme, by which the British armour would, from bridgeheads beyond the German minefields, hold off the enemy armour until the Axis infantry had been crumbled away. It was a realistic decision; it also brought the plan closer to the pattern of his own military temperament.

The four infantry divisions of 30th Corps were to smash two corridors through the German minefields, the northern towards Kidney Ridge, the southern over the Miteiriya Ridge. By an innovation of Montgomery, upon the 30th Corps front and axis of advance was superimposed a second corps, 10th, with three armoured divisions. When 30th Corps had cleared the corridors (or even if it failed to do so) 10th Corps was to pass or fight its way out and post itself defensively on open ground to the west. This cumbersome piling of three armoured and four infantry divisions on the same narrow front, but under different corps commands, took the chronic split between armour and infantry in the Eighth Army to the extreme.

It was to have unfortunate results in the battle. After the Axis fixed defences had been crumbled, and the armour defeated, 10th Corps, the *corps de chasse*, would pursue and cut off the wreckage of the *Panzerarmee*. There was some dispute as to the main axis of this pursuit. Montgomery chose the one eventually followed. The old desert hands suggested a line five to ten miles further south, where there was hard-gravel going above the Fuka Escarpment. But Montgomery, with the reluctance to stray far from the coast that most newcomers to the desert displayed, scouted these suggestions:

"No more manœuvre—fight a battle."

This decision also had unfortunate results.

There was an elaborate plan of deception to mislead the German command into thinking that the main attack was coming from the south. Thirteenth Corps, with 7th Armoured Division, was to make dummy attacks in the early days of the battle to sustain the deception.

The date of the Second Battle of Alamein was fixed with some skill. Both Montgomery and Alexander knew of course that the *Torch* landings were to take place in French North Africa in November and could conclude that the presence of a large new allied army considerably nearer Rommel's unprotected base at Tripoli than Rommel himself at Alamein, would force Rommel to fall back on Tripoli before he was cut off and crushed between two armies each superior to his own. Now Montgomery calculated that his battle would take ten or twelve days. If therefore the opening of the Second Battle of Alamein was fixed for *Torch* minus thirteen, he would be insured against defeat. Whatever happened in the battle, Rommel would have to start retreating on the thirteenth day. At first the Prime Minister urged that *Lightfoot* (an ironical code name for Second Alamein) should be launched independently of *Torch* in September or early October "on the ground that this would impress Spain and protect the flank of *Torch*". Alexander had other ideas:

> I have carefully considered the timing in relation to *Torch* and have come to the conclusion that the best date for us to start would be minus thirteen of *Torch*

which was then fixed for November 4th. October 23rd was full moon. But on September 22nd Eisenhower finally fixed the date of *Torch* as November 8th, which threw out all the delicate temporal calculations in Egypt.

But the really interesting question in the relation of *Torch* to Second Alamein is why this bitter battle, with its heavy losses, was fought at all. Of the *Torch* landings Rommel commented: "This spelt the end of the army in Africa." From that moment onward all his generalship was employed in getting his army safely back to join the German forces in Tunisia. It was the Allied forces in his rear that made him evacuate his strong defences at El Agheila. They would equally—even more so—have made him evacuate his defences at El Alamein, fourteen hundred miles away from his threatened base. Thus, it is certain that, even if Montgomery had not fought his battle, Rommel would have been out of Egypt within a month and in Tunisia within three.

The famous Second Battle of Alamein must therefore, in my view, go down in history as an unnecessary battle. Had Eighth Army held its attack until the moment Rommel had left the shelter of his fixed defences and begun to retreat, it could have completely destroyed the *Panzerarmee* at small cost. For Rommel would have been helpless, with ninety-thousand un-motorised infantry to cover with only two hundred German tanks in the face of British command of the air, one thousand one hundred tanks and a completely mechanised army of two hundred and twenty thousand men.

Why therefore was Second Alamein fought before Rommel was forced to retreat by the *Torch* landings? It was the last purely British victory in the war against Germany; it was the swansong of Britain as a great independent power. After *Torch* the British war effort from Churchill and Montgomery downwards became subordinate to the American. Second Alamein was the last chance to restore British prestige, shaken after a year of defeat, with banner headlines, with the ringing of church bells, and with any other means that might make the victory as famous as Blenheim or Waterloo. If the battle had followed the Anglo-American landings, victory would have been ascribed partly to them. Was this why the offensive could not take place at the obvious moment when *Torch* had forced Rommel to abandon the Alamein defences? The ultimate judgement of history may well be to record it as a political victory.

As fought, Second Alamein has its curious features. In view of the immense disparity of strength between the opposing armies, it is surprising not that we won the battle, but that we almost lost it. In none of the well-known British accounts of the action is given a fair picture of British and Axis strength. In round terms, the British had two hundred and twenty thousand men to the enemy's ninety-six thousand; of the Axis strength, only fifty-three thousand were

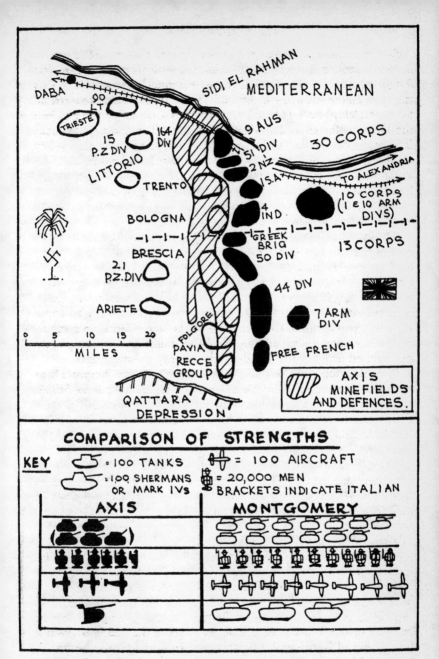

MAP 22. SECOND BATTLE OF ALAMEIN: DISPOSITIONS ON
23 OCTOBER 1942

273

German. But it was in quantity and quality of equipment that the British superiority was crushing—in tanks, guns and aircraft. Montgomery had one thousand one hundred tanks fit for action, including about two hundred and seventy of the superb Shermans and two hundred and ten Grants. Two hundred more tanks were brought up during the battle. Against this tremendous array the Axis could put into the field only two hundred gun-armed German tanks, mostly Mark III's, and three hundred Italian 'self-propelled coffins'. Only the Mark IV, with its long 75 mm. gun, was a match for the Sherman; and of these the Germans had but thirty. The Eighth Army's assault was supported by a thousand field and medium guns amply supplied with ammunition. Infantry and armoured divisions were equipped with eight hundred of the new powerful 6-pounder anti-tank guns. There were a hundred 105 mm. self-propelled guns. The Axis artillery consisted of old-fashioned short-range (five miles) Italian field guns. Of the anti-tank guns, only twenty-four were 88's. The British enjoyed total control of the air and their bombers could range freely over Axis concentrations and supply lines.

It is thus surprising that the *Panzerarmee* managed to slog it out for twelve long days with such a gigantically superior force. It is true that the Axis forces were cleverly dug in behind minefields, and British writers have made the most of these defences. Montgomery told his television audience: "His (Rommel's) position was strongly organized in depth . . . the problem was to break right through these strong positions . . ." In his *Memoirs* he called it "an immense undertaking". General Horrocks has referred to "the heavily defended minefields". Churchill wrote that "the enemy's front consisted not only of successive lines of strong points and machine-gun posts, but of a whole deep area of such a defensive system". Simple facts and calculations demonstrate that these accounts grossly exaggerate. The Axis command deployed the equivalent of six infantry divisions, or eighty-nine thousand men, along a forty-five mile front: two thousand men to a mile. On the Dyle in 1940, the forty-five thousand men of three British divisions had held a front of seventeen miles, or two thousand six hundred and fifty men to a mile, with another six divisions in reserve. Yet no-one considered that to be a strongly held front.

The entire Axis defence system (including minefields) was only five miles deep. It compares with depths of ten to twenty miles for defensive systems (German and Russian) in Russia. There was no buffer, or delaying zone. Far from being a position of immense depth, the entire Axis defences could be smothered in fire from artillery behind the British start-lines. Montgomery himself expected to drive two corridors clean through it in fewer than twelve hours, according to the final orders to 10th and 30th Corps.

The Axis command did not have a free choice in placing their armour. Acute shortage of fuel made the swift, distant concentrations of other days impossible; the armour had to be stationed where it was hoped it would fight. Therefore, instead of a loose concentration held well back, perhaps near Daba, the Axis armour was placed close behind the front; and because there was not even enough fuel to move all of it from one flank to another according to British pressure, it was split—21st Panzer Division and Ariete in the south and 15th Panzer Division, 90th Light and Littorio in the north.

Last and perhaps greatest of the Axis weaknesses was the absence of Rommel, lying sick in a hospital bed in Semmering; the *Panzer-armee* was commanded now by General Stumme.

As October wore on, Montgomery grew understandably more confident and more cocksure. No desert commander had enjoyed such freedom from nagging by the Prime Minister; no desert commander had so received accession to his every material request. Behind him in the delta, his titular superior, Alexander, bereft of wide strategic cares, fulfilled loyally the role of housekeeper assigned to him by Montgomery, who neatly said of him: "He was the perfect Commander-in-Chief to have in the Middle East, so far as I was concerned." Montgomery had now achieved a personal grip of steel on his army through his training methods and inspections and through the trusted and able friends he had appointed to high posts on the staff and in the command. Only Lumsden, of 10th Corps, was not a 'Monty' man. But on the eve of battle, Montgomery tightened further his grip on his troops by a series of addresses on the coming battle down to the level of lieutenant-colonels. These were enormously effective, for in Sir Oliver Leese's words, "he was completely convinced he was going to win the battle. He made everything crystal-clear." With Montgomery's staccato lecture ringing in their ears, the colonels returned to their battalions with the feeling that they were personally in the Army Commander's confidence and trust. These sentiments they passed on to their men. It was a brilliant exercise in calculated leadership.

During the night of 22/23rd October the assault troops moved into their forward concentration areas, and all through the following day, they lay, like O'Connor's men before Sidi Barrani, in trenches beyond the British front line. But there was no chance of discovery by German air reconnaissance; the Royal Air Force had such domination in the air that it was able to maintain standing patrols over the forward Axis airfields. At last night came to the two hundred and twenty thousand men poised in the quiet desert; they waited for the moon to rise and the battle to begin. Even history was given its task in the master plan. In a personal message to his army Montgomery wrote:

> The battle which is now about to begin will be one of the decisive battles of history. It will be the turning point of the war.

To command the battle, Montgomery left his main headquarters at Burg el Arab and moved into a tactical headquarters on the coast behind El Alamein. That evening, as the moon of battles rose, he went to bed early; and when the fire of a thousand guns lashed out at 9.40 p.m., he says he was asleep. From the Mediterranean to the Quattara Depression, the British artillery poured high explosive over the Axis line; the Axis guns were silent, for Stumme had ordered them to conserve scanty stocks of shells. After twenty minutes the barrage lifted and over seventy thousand men and six hundred tanks advanced against the twelve thousand Italians and Germans of the Trento and 164th Infantry Divisions on the Axis left centre: odds of six to one, not counting the armour. It seemed that the German line could hardly withstand such a blow longer than had the perimeter of Tobruk in June.

But, by morning on October 24th, and despite all the planning and method, the attack had already crumpled into a shambles. Because of the size of the assault force packed on so narrow a front, it had, like a swordsman in a close crowd, no room to fight. The infantry did not penetrate to the western edge of the German defence zone; the engineers did not clear through-lines for the armour; and the armour remained therefore jammed behind the infantry in the cul-de-sacs opened in the minefields. Upon this immobile mass, the Axis guns, both field and anti-tank, directed a heavy and accurate fire.

All that day the grand assault floundered in its narrow alleys in the Axis defences. And in the south, Horrocks's diversionary attack with 13th Corps had gone hopelessly astray. Seventh Armoured Division and 44th Division did not succeed in penetrating the two belts of German minefields, but were gravelled on mines which the Germans had scattered between the belts; and they remained marooned there throughout 24th October.

Chance however brought Montgomery compensation for the

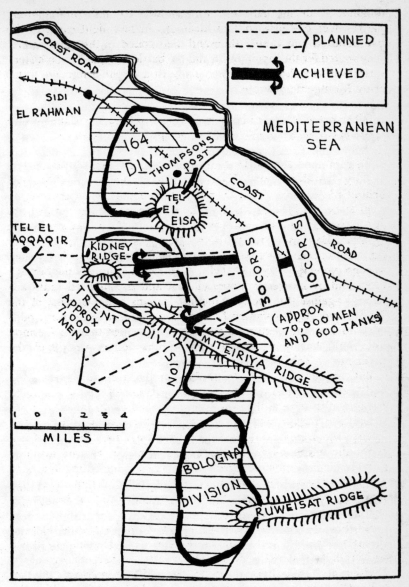

MAP 23. SECOND BATTLE OF ALAMEIN: BREAKDOWN OF MASTER PLAN
23–26 October 1942

failure of his attack to reach its objectives; General Stumme, his opponent, died of heart failure on the battlefield and was replaced by von Thoma, with a consequent dislocation of the Axis command. But to balance this good luck, Rommel, though still sick, was flying out to take command of the *Panzerarmee*.

Montgomery had made it clear in his orders that if the infantry and engineers failed to clear lanes through the minefields, the armour of 10th Corps was to fight its own way out. There were three lanes to an armoured division, each wide enough for one tank. Therefore the British armoured divisions were asked to debouch through a five-mile defile six tanks wide. If the leading tanks should be knocked out by German anti-tank fire, the defile would become a bottleneck.

During the afternoon and night of 24th October, the British assault force attempted this operation on both the main axes of the break-in. The northern attempt, towards Kidney Ridge, partly succeeded when some tanks of 2nd Armoured Brigade got clear of the western edge of a minebelt, but not of the Axis defence system. But the southern attempt, over the fireswept Miteiriya Ridge, stopped enmeshed in minefields at four o'clock in the morning of 25th October. Thus, after another twenty-four hours' fighting, Montgomery's assault had not reached the objectives assigned for dawn, 24th October. It was not to reach those objectives for another nine days. This was the first crisis in the battle.

Lumsden of 10th Corps believed that it was impossible for his armour to fight its own way out in accordance with Montgomery's orders: it was a wrong use of tanks and would result in a massacre. He wished to pull his tanks out of the corridors, re-group them behind the Miteiriya Ridge and send them back into the battle when the infantry and engineers of 30th Corps had cleared a way through the Axis defences.

Therefore Leese and de Guingand, the Chief of Staff, decided that Montgomery must personally intervene. About two in the morning, when the exhausted men of 10th and 30th Corps were still floundering forward on the Miteiriya Ridge, de Guingand roused Montgomery and in his caravan one of the most tense conferences in the history of war took place.

The dull electric light shone bleakly on Montgomery's fox-like face, with its prominent cheekbones and the nose, moustache and mouth forming a muzzle that moved, almost twitched, as he talked; on Leese, huge, bland, red-faced, a roast-beef Englishman; on Herbert Lumsden, veteran armoured commander, cavalryman, gay, charming, handsome, theatrical, highly-strung. As in Norrie's head-quarters on the Ruweisat Ridge in the July battles, Lumsden argued almost frantically that the armour must be pulled back because of its appalling casualties in an operation not suited to tanks. He quoted General Gatehouse, 10th Armoured Division, as saying that even if he succeeded in debouching beyond the minefields on to the southern face of the Miteiriya Ridge, he would be shot to pieces by German anti-tank fire.

There now followed an episode, crucially important in the history of the battle, about which there are conflicting accounts. According to Montgomery, Lumsden asked Montgomery to speak himself to Gatehouse by telephone.

> I did so at once and discovered to my horror that he himself was some 16,000 yards (nearly ten miles) behind his leading armoured brigades (sic). I spoke to him at once in no uncertain voice, and ordered him to go forward at once and take charge of his battle . . .

Then, according to Montgomery, he told Lumsden and Leese that his orders were unchanged, and that the armour *would* fight its way out. He kept Lumsden back a moment and "I spoke very plainly to him"; he warned that he would replace both him and Gatehouse if there were more hesitations.

General Leese confirms that he and Montgomery measured the distance on the map from Gatehouse's headquarters to the front line, but Gatehouse, in fact, was not at his H.Q., but up at the front. He has a very different version of this telephone conversation. Gate-house was the most experienced tank commander in the British service; he had made his whole career in armour, for his own regi-ment was the Royal Tank Regiment. He had won four decorations for personal bravery. According to him, Lumsden returned from the conference in Montgomery's caravan and told him that his attack must continue. Gatehouse replied that he was refusing the order: it would destroy that armour which Montgomery was supposed to have formed as a *corps de chasse*. Lumsden warned him of the con-sequences of such a refusal. Gatehouse therefore went back and telephoned Montgomery himself, with Lumsden's agreement, from a field telephone line far behind the forward troops. There were sharp words along the field telephone wire; Gatehouse began by saying:

"What the hell's going on?"

His manner thereafter was far from deferential. Montgomery

listened while Gatehouse told him the armour was expected to advance over the crest of the Miteiriya Ridge, through uncharted and uncleared minefields, covered by strong batteries of anti-tank guns, and be eight hundred yards down the forward slope by dawn. Because of the noise of tank tracks, surprise was impossible. Then Montgomery modified the scope of the attack from six armoured regiments to one: the Staffordshire Yeomanry. It lost all but fifteen of its tanks and the operation ended where it had started, behind the Miteiriya Ridge.

Yet Montgomery later told a television audience: "The necessary part of the armoured division got established beyond the minefields."

The real significance of the events of the small hours of 25th October, 1942, lies not in this controversy, but in that the offensive had staggered to the verge of defeat after just forty-eight hours' fighting—an amazing event, in view of the forces engaged, and one clearly, prima facie, calling Montgomery's generalship in question. However, Montgomery in both his books and during his television appearances rarely admits to major errors in generalship, although he does criticize others. The near-failure of his offensive on 24th and 25th October, 1942, Montgomery firmly blamed on alleged cowardice and want of energy on the part of the armour of 10th Corps and its senior officer. But it was illogical to blame the armour of 10th Corps rather than the infantry of 30th Corps, for 30th Corps had failed in its own allotted task.

In fact, the breakdown occurred because of the cumbersome two-tier organization of infantry and armour on the same narrow, minestrewn front, and because the armour was given a role completely unsuited to it.

The basic problem in planning Second Alamein lay in the right tactical and organizational combination of armour, infantry and artillery in order to penetrate a continuous fortified line without flanks. For the armour, it presented, in General Leese's words, "the novel task of close co-operation with infantry against fixed defences", and at Alamein was seen for the first time "this game of fighting armour and infantry on a master plan".

Clearly the armour and infantry in the corridors, dependent as they were on each other's success, must work intimately together and in perfect harmony as to timing and movement. In the German army, where all arms were trained and organized on the same system, this co-operation was natural. In the British army, despite Auchinleck's radical reorganization of the armour after *Crusader*, armour and infantry remained two separate services, trained and organized in different ways and split asunder by sectional pride. After the Gazala defeats, this gulf was widened by a profound suspicion on the part of the infantry of the armour's professional ability. Now, by a paradox, these two services had to be made to carry out a tightly dove-tailed joint operation in minefields and under heavy fire. It was like asking an estranged man and his wife to make love.

Just before his dismissal, Auchinleck had set on foot his own revolutionary solution of this chronic separatism. He ordered that all distinction between armour and infantry division should be abolished; and the army reorganised into 'Mobile Divisions', mainly motorised infantry but each with an armoured brigade under command. Trained together, all arms commanded by common divisional commanders, these divisions would have been the mobile mixed combinations similar to those Rommel had in his German troops—the entire Eighth Army, and not just 10th Corps, would have formed the equivalent of Afrika Korps, but six times as large. Auchinleck's proposals aroused enormous opposition; every conservative instinct, regimental and separatist, was against it. McCreery, the Major General, Armoured Fighting Vehicles, in the Middle East was a cavalryman; he objected strongly to Auchinleck's suggestions and was instantly dismissed. Auchinleck intended to replace him with Gatehouse. Had this come to fruition the training and organisation of the British armour would have been for the first time directed by a tank officer. When Auchinleck went, the proposals were thankfully torn up and McCreery made Chief of the General Staff to Alexander. However the New Zealand Division for the rest of the North African campaign had an armoured brigade under command, and mobile infantry and tank co-operation was so good that Montgomery used the division more and more as the spearhead of his attacks.

It was then Montgomery's turn to think of an answer.

His solution was in every way opposite to Auchinleck's and in every way wrong, for it carried the existing dangerous separatism still further. He formed 10th Corps, containing the armour, and ordered it to fight a joint battle with 30th Corps, containing infantry. Whereas before in the desert armour and infantry in combined attacks had been at least co-ordinated by a common corps commander, and whereas Auchinleck intended they should be intimately co-ordinated by common *divisional* commanders, now the Army Commander himself formed the only command link. And thus in the crammed defiles in the minefields on 24th/25th October, two corps under separate commanders made separate efforts over the same ground.

Now, in the middle of the battle, Montgomery's resolution as a battlefield commander redeemed his clumsiness as a planner. In General Leese's opinion Montgomery "was the greatest field commander since Cromwell. Only Napoleon was as good". Remembering his enormous resources, Montgomery decided to drive the attack forward, come what may.

This was the moment, with the British attack stalled and in confusion, for a crushing German counter-blow, but Rommel had not yet arrived in Africa, and the inexperienced von Thoma only put in a piecemeal attack with 15th Panzer Division against Montgomery's northern corridor; it achieved nothing, and lost many tanks.

The 25th October was another bad day for Montgomery. The New Zealand Division's efforts at 'crumbling' had failed; now the Australians nearer the coast were to crumble. First Armoured Division was to advance westward from Kidney Ridge and if possible pass a brigade into the open desert and occupy Sidi Rahman, the nodal point of German communications. The division was unable to move at all. Sidi Rahman was not occupied until 4th November. In the far south, after 4th Light Armoured Brigade had run into mines and heavy anti-tank fire, Horrocks and 13th Corps were turned over to the defensive. But Montgomery did not bring 7th Armoured Division up to reinforce the main battle: "as long as 21st Panzer Division was in the south, I required an armoured division in 13th Corps." This contradicted his favourite principle of balance, where a 'balanced' commander "need not react to the enemy move but can continue relentlessly with his own plan".

On the 26th October, the South Africans and New Zealanders made some ground on the Miteiriya Ridge; otherwise the great offensive remained stuck. Though the Master Plan had so completely foundered, Montgomery appeared unmoved.

> He was always calm; nothing disturbed him. It never struck him that anybody else could win. If things went wrong, we always had something else to put in—we were always in balance.

His orders were all personal, never written. His corps commanders saw him every morning and every evening of the battle. Some of the tired staff officers were shocked by the way his cold, glittering eyes stared out of a drawn face; by the fanatical expression; by the "surgical callousness" over the mounting casualties. All day long on 26th October he stayed in his headquarters, thinking, and the army hardly stirred. It was almost as if he had run out of ideas.

He had in fact the task of cobbling together a fresh battle.

For his existing bridgeheads had been sealed by powerful anti-tank screens; his infantry—in the Australian, Highland and South African Divisions especially—had been decimated to the point where replacements were an anxiety; he had already lost two hundred tanks, equal to the German total strength; and 30th Corps was so disorganized that it needed a pause for recuperation. Axis resistance had been unexpectedly tough, for, despite deception measures "probably unequalled in military history", the Axis Command, in Montgomery's words, "had withdrawn troops and guns from his forward positions in anticipation of our offensive, and we had therefore found him in greater depth than had been expected".

At the end of the day Montgomery decided to regroup his troops and start again in a fresh direction—towards the coast in the Australian sector. The New Zealanders went into reserve, and their sector, which had formed one of the two main corridors of breakthrough in his master plan, was turned over to 13th Corps and became purely defensive. The whole of the following day, 27th October, found the Eighth Army still stuck fast, carrying out its re-organization. All this hardly squared with Montgomery's doctrine of balance, nor with the comment in a letter to Brooke on 1st November that "I have managed to keep the initiative throughout, and so far Rommel has had to dance entirely to my tune".

Rommel had now arrived on the battlefield. He immediately brought 21st Panzer Division northwards (it took less than a day) and thus left 7th Armoured Division sadly out of balance. Twenty-four hours after leaving his hospital bed he led his concentrated armour in a counter-stroke against the British armour at Kidney Ridge, coming in with the setting sun behind him. He had fewer than one hundred and fifty tanks. Savagely bombed as he assembled and advanced, he was beaten off by the new 6-pounder anti-tank guns and by the heavy British armour with the loss of a third of his tanks. News reached Rommel at that moment that his army was almost out of fuel. Next day, 28th October, he attempted to attack again; Royal Air Force bombing broke the attack up before it reached Eighth Army.

Rommel now expected Montgomery to end the battle by launching immediately a decisive attack with massed forces. But Eighth Army was still being sorted out.

Since 21st Panzer had gone from the south, Montgomery now reacted by bringing 7th Armoured Division northwards. First Armoured Division and 24th Armoured Brigade went into the peace of reserve. Montgomery now abandoned hope of a breakthrough in the northern of the two original corridors as well as the southern; the master plan was defunct. The next attack would be on the coast. The battle had now lasted five days, and Eighth Army had been motionless for three.

"You always had a sense of time to spare," said General Leese later of Montgomery's battles. "We never went into battle unless we had enough of everything."

Now the second phase of the battle began; and henceforth the sheer weight of British resources made up for all blunders. On 29th October the grand offensive got modestly under way again with a divisional attack by the Australians along the coast that cut behind part of the 164th German Infantry Division. It is to be remarked that Montgomery's attacks in this battle were generally piecemeal, one division at a time. But Montgomery learned that 90th Light was behind the coastal front, and although of course a balanced army did not have to react to enemy moves, but ruthlessly pursued its own plans, Montgomery now changed the point of his main attack south again to the New Zealand sector.

The impending blow on the New Zealand sector was intended as the finishing stroke of the battle. It would take nearly two days to organize. In Alexander's significant words: "It was to be an operation very similar to that of 23rd October." Thirtieth Corps was to open a gap right through the remaining Axis defences; 10th Corps would pass into open country. Montgomery fixed the objectives of the operation as the destruction of the enemy armour and the disintegration of the enemy army. He christened it *Supercharge*. It was scheduled for the night of 31st October/1st November; and armoured cars were to be passing on to Rommel's communications by dawn on the 1st. On 31st October Montgomery had to postpone the attack twenty-four hours because "the stage management problems . . . were such that if launched on this night it might fail". It was a measure of the disorganization of 10th and 30th Corps.

On the night of 30th/31st October, a preliminary and diversionary attack by the Australians reached the coast and trapped part of 164th Division against the sea. In a violent counter-attack, 90th

Light and a battle-group of 21st Panzer Division rescued their comrades and destroyed eighteen British tanks.

When Montgomery first reached Egypt in August he had told his staff officers that "the policy of fighting the enemy in brigade groups, Jock columns, and with divisions split up into bits and pieces all over the desert was to cease. In future divisions would fight *as* divisions." Yet it is interesting to note that the 30th Corps force for *Supercharge* contained as many as three brigade groups: one from 50th Division, one from 44th Division, and the Greek Brigade.

Now came the last act of an exhausting, muddled and prolonged action. The Axis forces, heavily outnumbered at the beginning and without reinforcements or rest for seven days, had now fought almost to the limit of their strength.

At one o'clock in the morning *Supercharge* began; nearly eight hundred tanks, covered by three hundred and sixty guns. But once again there was furious fighting and heavy losses among the attackers; 9th Armoured Brigade lost eighty-seven tanks. Not until dawn on 2nd November did the British stagger at last out of that defensive system, into which they had broken with, in Montgomery's words, "wild enthusiasm" ten days before.

And even now the battle had still more than a sixth of its course to run; for in front of the British armour of 10th Corps was Rommel and his two panzer divisions, ninety tanks against seven hundred. At Tel el Aqqaqir was now fought the last great tank battle of the desert war, in which the odds were too grossly uneven to leave the issue in doubt. But Rommel fought one of the best actions of his career in order to gain time for the organisation of the retreat that must soon begin. His counter-attacks almost broke through the British salient: and at the end of the day, Montgomery's *corps de chasse* was still milling about impatiently in front of Rommel's guns. Though Montgomery had in his orders written that *Supercharge* "will therefore be successful", it too had been a failure—it did not achieve any of the objectives assigned to it for 1st November by Montgomery's handwritten order. The British armour did *not* occupy the Tel el Aqqaqir area by first light, did *not* develop operations from that area "as the sun rises" to destroy the enemy armour and bring about the disintegration of the enemy rear areas. As the news of failure came in, it seemed that the stubborn enemy would never break. All next day (3rd November) the 10th and 30th Corps pursuit remained largely corralled by the German armour and anti-tank guns; and behind that skilful rearguard, the Panzer Army began to slip away from Montgomery's eager fingers.

For Rommel it was perhaps the trickiest moment of his career. He had to disengage a hopelessly outnumbered and partly immobile army in country that gave no natural protection against attack by huge masses of armour and lorried infantry. This operation must be carried through under ceaseless air bombardment and in the shackles imposed by shortage of fuel. Its success must rank as a prodigious feat of arms and leadership. Rommel held his tiny army together by force of character, by the loyalty of his veterans. In trances of exhaustion these men, the same who had taken Tobruk and Gazala, unreinforced, unrelieved, served their guns with instinctive skill, taking heart from the sight of the stocky figure of the Field-Marshal as he toured the battlefield fighting his thin line of battle in person like Wellington.

Rommel even hoped he might get the bulk of the infantry away "since the enemy was operating with such astonishing hesitancy and caution".

Now however Montgomery found an unlooked for ally in Adolf Hitler. On 3rd November, the Fuehrer sent Rommel a telegram ordering him to stand and die at Alamein. It was a typical piece of politicians' interference; it carried echoes of a similar British order. Rommel obeyed. His orders for retreat were cancelled; the flow of troops ceased along the precarious road to safety; and by order of the Fuehrer, the *Panzerarmee* waited patiently for annihilation. A personal emissary was sent to Hitler to point out that retreat was the only way of saving the army. On the evening of 4th November Hitler replied that in view of the situation, Rommel might act as he saw fit. Thus at the critical moment when the battle was about to become a pursuit, Montgomery was handed a bonus of thirty-six hours' start.

During 3rd November and 4th November, in obedience to Hitler's order, Rommel tried to hold on to his front; 90th Light were deployed in front of his twenty-two remaining tanks; massing in stately pursuit to the east and south were six hundred and fifty British tanks of 10th Corps and 7th Armoured Division, supported by lorried infantry. Montgomery put in two more attacks on the flanks of the German corral and at last broke clean through into open desert; the Fuehrer's permission to retreat followed; and the Second Battle of Alamein had ended.

It ended so unspectacularly that the British Command could not make up its mind if the battle was over or not.

CHAPTER THREE

BRITISH losses in the battle totalled thirteen thousand five hundred men (killed, wounded and missing) and six hundred tanks. German losses were one hundred and eighty tanks, a thousand dead and eight thousand prisoners. Italian losses were a thousand dead and sixteen thousand prisoners.

On 5th November, as oil and blood leaked slowly into the sand of the battlefield that carried so many British dead, Montgomery held a press conference. He was in great form, bouncing with victory, and lightheartedly swapping banalities with the journalists. Then he told them, and through them the British public:

"Gentlemen, this is complete and absolute victory."

His titular superior, Alexander, signalled the Prime Minister to "ring out the bells".

As Clausewitz points out, the fruits of victory are gathered in the pursuit, but no fruits were gathered in the pursuit from Alamein. It was not therefore a 'complete and absolute victory'.

In order to gather these fruits, as Clausewitz also points out, the pursuit must be vigorous; Montgomery's pursuit after Second Alamein showed all the bustling confidence of an archdeacon entering a *maison clos* and its slow start throws a bleak light on the state to which the Eighth Army had been reduced by twelve days of murderous attacking.

Montgomery said that the good commander always thinks and plans two moves ahead. Montgomery had formed 10th Corps specially as a *corps de chasse*. His battles always went, he gave the world to understand, as planned. Yet after the British broke into open country on 2nd November it took Montgomery three days to organise a full-scale pursuit, which did not begin until November 5th, when Rommel, despite the thirty-six hours delay imposed by the Fuehrer, had already got a day's start. Why was not Montgomery's long-cherished pursuit force ready and poised for an immediate chase on 2nd November? It was because 10th Corps, which was supposed never to be involved in a static front, had been largely consumed in the 'dog-fight' and what was left of it and of 30th Corps was too disorganized and exhausted to pursue anyone. A new *corps de chasse*, under command of 10th Corps headquarters, had to be hastily cobbled together on the battlefield; and when it got under way, it included 7th Armoured Division and the New Zealand Division, which had never been part of 10th Corps. In fact this *corps de chasse* seemed to embody the "policy of fighting the enemy in brigade groups . . . and bits and pieces of divisions" that Montgomery had denounced on arrival in Egypt, for 1st and 10th Armoured Divisions had each borrowed a motor brigade from 44th Division. Here is the real proof of how badly the battle had gone, how utterly the master plan had failed, and how lucky Montgomery had been to have such immense resources that he escaped the fate of Cunningham and Ritchie.

On November 3rd, the New Zealand Division with 4th and 9th Armoured Brigades (the brigade group again) were ordered to go for Fuka. But now occurred the last mishap to be caused by the clumsy super-imposing of 10th Corps on 30th Corps front; this scratch pursuit force got hopelessly tangled with the 10th Corps supply convoys; nightfall found it only halfway to Fuka. Meanwhile routeing and traffic control were chaotic.

On the morrow of its victory Eighth Army thus lay at a standstill, paralysed by confusion as great as any seen under the predecessors Montgomery so despised. "No more manœuvre—fight a battle"— but the battle had been fought, and now there must be manœuvre. It seemed as though Montgomery's vision and will had ended with the break-out.

At last on the 5th November the full-scale pursuit under 10th Corps got under way. It was directed by Montgomery in short, tight turns to the coast, though all the experienced desert commanders advised a long march through the desert, parallel to the enemy, as far even as Tobruk. First Armoured Division cut into Daba and found Rommel gone. Tenth Armoured Division made only eleven miles towards the Fuka escarpment. The New Zealanders were held up most of the day by a wire fence, thought to bound a minefield, with German rearguards behind it. The minefield turned out to be a British dummy laid in the summer. Harding, a veteran of the desert, took 7th Armoured Division well south along the Fuka escarpment, but got tangled with the New Zealanders' supply trucks, and was delayed in a dummy minefield. The pursuit was thus highly dispersed, the mistake of which Montgomery was to accuse Eisenhower after the Battle of Normandy in 1944; Montgomery argued that the pursuit in 1944 would have succeeded if all administrative resources had been put behind one axis of advance; ironically the argument applies equally to his own advance after Second Alamein. During November 6th, Montgomery closed his principal trap at Baggush, just east of Matruh; it was empty. The sole catch of the day was a remnant of 21st Panzer Division, which, immobilized for want of fuel, was brought to action by 22nd Armoured Brigade. It held off the British until nightfall, received some fuel, and slipped away.

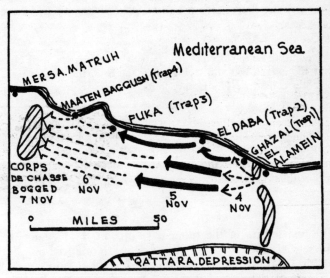

MAP 24. FAILURE OF BROAD FRONT PURSUIT AFTER
SECOND BATTLE OF ALAMEIN

On the German side, the retreat was orderly and controlled. In General Leese's words:

> The German is very, very quick about sorting himself out—forming new battle-groups. This is helped by his training, which is uniform throughout all divisions.

Now, with his further escape on 6th November, Rommel's acute danger was over. For there is a law of diminishing returns in the efforts of a pursuer to cut off an enemy, who is marching away in a straight line.

On the night of 6th November, as the disappointed pursuit headed once more inland, heavy rains fell and turned the soft sand south of Mersa Matruh into a quagmire. Now the *corps de chasse* became stuck fast. This circumstance, which took place therefore *after* Montgomery had cut into the coastal road four times and found it empty, and *after* Rommel had irrevocably increased his lead, Montgomery ingeniously used as an excuse for his total failure to catch Rommel after Second Alamein. This excuse was started on its rounds as soon as 10th November in a letter to General Brooke: ". . . what saved him was the rain; I had nearly reached Matruh and was getting in behind all his transport when torrential rain turned the desert into a bog . . ." It turns up in Churchill's *War Memoirs*:

> By nightfall on the 6th they (the pursuit) were nearing their objective, while the enemy was still trying to escape from the closing trap. But then rain came . . . The twenty-four-hour respite prevented complete encirclement.

It has been repeated in other accounts. But Montgomery's account does not even on its own premises make sense. The rain fell impartially on Briton and German; and the *Rommel Papers* make clear that the Axis retreat was as greatly hampered by it as the British pursuit.

*   *   *   *   *

With the failure of the immediate pursuit from Alamein, both armies settled down to a long march of fifteen hundred miles. Here, in mobility and manœuvre, Montgomery was as lost as a dray horse on a polo field. The Maréchal de Saxe wrote that the pursuer "must attack, push, and pursue without cease. . . . All manœuvres are good then: it is only precautions that are worthless." Montgomery disagreed. His experienced desert commanders pleaded to be allowed to race hard through the desert, in order to force Rommel to battle and destroy him. Gatehouse of 10th Armoured Division asked if he could take his division ("the strongest in Egypt and with a complete B echelon") immediately on to Sollum and Tobruk. But Montgomery said there was to be no mad rush which might expose him to a riposte. He repeated this over and over again to different audiences; that he was not going to risk at all coming back again "like the others". No initiative was allowed even to corps commanders: Montgomery kept the army tightly under his own rigid control, and Rommel was delighted and astonished that his retreat was being so little pressed. "I wonder," he said to Bayerlein, "why he doesn't hurry? But it's lucky for us."

Montgomery's caution in this long pursuit illustrates his obsession with tidiness and method. It also shows a curious limit to one of his most publicized characteristics: the belief in his own ability.

For this was not entirely a rational caution. Rommel now had only ten tanks. His tiny force was known to be intermittently paralysed by want of fuel.

Eighth Army was now traversing Rommel's old ground—El Adem, Knightsbridge, Sidi Rezegh—and the memories of thunderbolt attacks out of the setting sun, of manœuvres of astonishing speed and skill were evoked by the rusted wrecks of these ancient battlefields. Rommel! His stocky figure, with the pugnacious face under the goggled cap, was still held in awe and admiration by both armies. There was magic there; who knew what he might still do, despite his ten tanks and want of petrol? Better not go out there in the desert—*his* country—and mix it in a fluid battle of manœuvre, not even with two armoured divisions at your back. He might do something unorthodox; something not covered by the master plan. He might be twice as quick on his feet. He might be the better general. And thus Montgomery, who had seen himself on arrival in Egypt as the 'anti-Rommel', also fell under his spell; and the *Panzerarmee's* shield during that epic retreat was its commander's reputation. And this interpretation is corroborated by a senior officer close to Montgomery at the time, who agrees that "Rommel's reputation did make an impression on Monty's mind".

So through Sollum and Tobruk and Gazala Eighth Army trailed after Rommel, while its commanders chafed and grumbled and Montgomery remained, in Pope's line, "willing to wound, yet afraid to strike". Rommel went without haste, falling back from petrol dump to petrol dump with his ten tanks and ten thousand men, leaving behind extensive mining and booby-traps. Some days one or both his panzer divisions lay stalled helplessly in the open desert for want of fuel. No fresh forces reached him from Germany and Italy; none were likely to; and there was no hope of fighting any kind of general action. "Rommel was not the same as he had been against the Auk," General Leese was to say later. "He could have been very formidable had he not been made to dance to our tune." All Rommel could do was make faces at Montgomery in order to keep him to a slow pace. In General Leese's words:

In the retreat I never saw Rommel fight a real action; there was no battle crisis until Mareth. But there was a lot of fighting—a battle every day, because you couldn't take chances with German rearguards. Rommel fought every day with something.

Montgomery took Tobruk on 13th November; his eleven days for the distance from Alamein compares with Rommel's nine in the reverse direction, when he deployed for, fought and won a battle on the way. Amid the rocks of Gazala Rommel halted his men, fought a short action, and then faded into the west behind mines, blowing the road at every escarpment, booby-trapping abandoned trucks and houses; even the palm trees under which his pursuers might rest. He was receiving half his essential quantity of petrol; for a time he had no shells for the army artillery. His men had been fighting non-stop since 23rd October. It was an amazing display of military virtuosity.

Now Montgomery stood at the gates of the Jebel Achdar, where O'Connor had stood two years before. Those with him who had served with O'Connor pressed him to throw a powerful force through Msus to the coast road and there repeat the total victory of Beda Fomm. He refused, saying that he was determined he would not repeat the mistakes of the past (Beda Fomm?) and place himself in a weak position which might give Rommel a chance to launch a counter-stroke. Yet it was well-known that at this moment Rommel had not more than thirty-odd tanks—a trickle of replacements had arrived—and that he was desperately crippled by want of fuel; Montgomery was in no way exposed to the same risks as O'Connor, who had flung his tiny mobile force across the then unreconnoitred desert into the path of an immensely stronger army. But siege, not manœuvre, was the *forte* of Montgomery's exact talents: though he agreed to let a light force make the journey through Msus, the main body of the army plodded on behind Rommel's rearguards. The light force got bogged by rain and caught nothing.

Benghazi fell on November 20th after a delay that enabled the Germans to wreck the port and destroy stores, and on November 24th, Rommel halted in his old defences at El Agheila. Here he bravely deployed. There were the two divisions of the Afrika Korps, in the total strength of a brigade; 90th Light (one and a half battalions); 164th Infantry Division (three thousand men with no weapons heavier than machine-guns); a battalion of parachutists; the Italian 20th Corps in the strength of a brigade; and eight batteries of guns. Rommel had thirty tanks, twenty armoured cars, forty-six anti-tank guns and forty 88's. With this scarecrow force he prepared to defend a line a hundred and seventy kilometres long; more than twice the length of his front at Alamein. It was outrageous bluff.

It succeeded. Montgomery came up with the one hundred and twenty tanks of the 7th Armoured Division, and the infantry of 51st Highland Division; looked at El Agheila; and settled down for three weeks to prepare for a setpiece attack on this formidable obstacle. This process he describes in his *Memoirs* as 'hustling' Rommel and getting possession of El Agheila by "bluff and manœuvre". In a television performance he said of Rommel and the El Agheila defences: "Well, we soon turned him out of there." Yet elsewhere he wrote: "I decided that bluff would not remove him", and "I would be unable to start my operations against the Agheila position until mid-December".

At the back of Montgomery's mind—and of his troops' minds— was the fear of Rommel suddenly debouching in surprising strength as in 1941 and 1942. Yet the situation was utterly different: on November 8th the Anglo-American forces had invaded French North Africa, and by November 24th were nearing Bizerta and Tunis. An American airborne force was in southern Tunisia, dangerously near Tripolitania. There was thus no possible question of Rommel staging a counter-stroke from El Agheila that would take him further away from his endangered base and from the German forces now being built up in Tunisia. From November 8th, Rommel's one intention had been to effect a junction with von Arnim before allied forces could get between them. And the fresh troops and equipment which might in other circumstances have come to Rommel were being fed into Tunisia. By an irony, those forces for which Rommel had asked before Second Alamein, which very probably would have enabled him to win that battle and which the Fuehrer had refused him, were to provide as prisoners early in 1943 the Allies' greatest triumph so far in the war.

So Rommel therefore stopped at Agheila only to rest his troops, reorganize them and gain a little time before slipping away again. With a particle of Marlborough's strategic imagination Montgomery could have divined all this; called Rommel's bluff, and brought him to battle immediately with more than one hundred and twenty tanks against thirty-five.

While the three-weeks'-long preparations for a set-piece attack on the Agheila position were going on, Montgomery went back to Cairo on leave. He was a full general now: and Second Alamein had already turned on the tap of public adulation. He bathed gratefully in the resulting gush. He showed his flair for timely public appearances by reading the lesson at the Sunday Evening Service at St. George's Cathedral and recorded archly that "it caused quite a stir". Success and renown inflated his ego; he had already demonstrated, as he was increasingly so to do in the next few years, an unwillingness to hear suggestions or advice. But, with tact, ideas could still be got over to him. General Leese, who was to succeed him in Italy as Eighth Army commander, recalls how he and de Guingand would consider how tactfully to approach him with a suggestion.

> One of them would go to his caravan in the evening, and put their case. Monty would shake his head and say:
> "Can't do that, can't do that."
> Then in the morning he might say: "I've been thinking, and had an idea . . ." He would then explain the idea which would be the one put to him the night before.

The legend was beginning to be established: the caravan set apart, never to be disturbed except by an inner acolyte; the withdrawing from the society of men of his own age into the society of admiring young disciples; the sandwiches eaten in the desert during visits to lower formations so that he should not have to mix socially in the messes. There was not now a senior officer left with Eighth Army who had shown himself unmoved by his spell and critical of his genius, for both Lumsden and Gatehouse had gone.

Yet, like the right and wrong side of a mirror, all this bright glorification of self seemed to be backed by a profound and sombre self-doubt. Did Montgomery feel that his authority, his hold on the loyalty of the army, might be weakened by mixing freely in the messes of its various formations? Why did he progressively withdraw to his Tactical H.Q. and the society of young men who must always agree with him? The answer to these questions can perhaps be found in his desire for overwhelming material superiority, in his love of exact tidiness, in the artificial predestination of the master plan.

Meanwhile Rommel was now experiencing, like Auchinleck and Wavell, the benefit of advice from home. Berlin and Rome demanded a fight to the last on the El Agheila line; Rommel demanded the troops, tanks and air cover. The critics thus silenced, Rommel prepared to slip away. Montgomery's offensive was due to open on 15th December. On the night of 7th/8th December, the Italians drove out of Agheila with headlights blazing and amid stupendous uproar. The oasis of Marada was also evacuated; and Rommel and his handful of Germans were left in the vast freezing winter spaces of Agheila. Not surprisingly, Montgomery was aware that the Italians had gone and he therefore advanced the date of his attack to 13th December. By a coincidence Rommel had fixed the time of his retirement for the night of 12th/13th December. On the 12th, as a German account puts it, "Montgomery gave signs of life", by reconnaissances in force.

The winter rains fell across the bleak scene of mud, gravel and camel thorn. As the day wore on, the usual preliminary bombardment by air and artillery began to wax in weight and fury. It went on all through the night; then the set-piece mass-attack rolled majestically forward and by late afternoon was through the Agheila line. But all this dread preparation and careful onslaught was wasted; Rommel had slipped away in the night without losing a man. Only elaborate mining and booby-traps received the British. Montgomery had shouldered down an open door. In his *Memoirs* he said of Agheila: "Everything went well."

While 7th Armoured Division and 51st Division pushed cautiously along the coast road (the main blow had been, as usual, frontal), the New Zealand Division felt for Rommel's desert flank. General Leese said later:

> We did not have enough tanks for a flanking movement in addition to those we had to maintain on the battlefront as a firm base.

According to official returns, 7th Armoured Division and 4th Light Armoured Brigade had a hundred and sixty-three tanks fit for action, plus a squadron in reserve.

Now Montgomery was blessed by double luck. The fifty-four tanks of the Afrika Korps had reached Mugta on the coast road when the pursuing tanks of the 7th Armoured Division caught up with them. Harding (7th Armoured Division) put in an immediate attack with sixty of the heavy Shermans. But the German armour had no fuel for manœuvre; only enough for a direct march. At the same time, the New Zealanders (with a brigade of tanks under command) reached the coast at Merduma, on the German line of retreat. Because of the German want of fuel, therefore, Montgomery had at last trapped the Afrika Korps, and could fight a battle against his immobile opponents with about two hundred tanks to fifty-four. By a further stroke of luck, Rommel was not in command that day; General Fehn was new from Russia and had no experience of the desert. Total victory seemed imminent. Cairo Radio, who must have got it from the Eighth Army, and the B.B.C. proclaimed that Rommel was in a bottle that Monty was about to cork. But the Afrika Korps was too potent a brew for a teetotaller to hold; next morning, 16th December, both panzer divisions, fighting in battle groups, smashed through the New Zealanders and disappeared. British light forces kept a distant contact while Eighth Army halted to reorganise.

For Rommel this was a time of bitterness; he chafed under the frustration of facing an opponent for whom he had scant respect, but whom he was unable to fight because Berlin and Rome refused all reinforcements and supplies. Now he was foolishly ordered to make a last stand at Buerat, which though a naturally strong position, was not properly fortified, was easily turned, and was far too long a front to be held by a small force such as his.

On 21st December Montgomery began to advance again. It was not easy: as General Leese said:

> Clearing the two to three hundred miles of the road between Agheila and Syrte of mines cost heavy casualties among the engineers and had a strong moral effect.

Fifteenth Panzer Division and 90th Light fell back slowly from Syrte, fighting for four days a skilled, dangerous and cunning rear-guard action. On 29th December, all was quiet again; the Panzer Army deployed at Buerat; and Montgomery began to organise his long and tenuous communications so that they might support another set-piece attack. Montgomery wanted the port of Tripoli urgently, before the Germans could wreck it as they had Benghazi. He wished to attack before the Germans could anticipate him by withdrawal; and because of the need for speed he only gave himself three weeks to get ready. In his own words, "I decided to plan for the Buerat battle on the basis of ten days' fighting using four divisions." Rommel had only thirty-eight tanks, twenty per cent of his establishment in anti-tank guns, ten thousand Germans and thirty thousand Italians without transport!

Throughout the advance from Egypt Montgomery had been moving all the time a second corps one stage behind the forward troops to "preserve balance". It was 10th Corps, the *corps de chasse*.

By 15th January, Montgomery was ready to attack Buerat. On the 12th, he issued another of those personal messages to the troops: "ON TO TRIPOLI!" These messages seem closely modelled on Napoleon's orders of the day to the Army of Italy, as in fact Montgomery's *Memoirs* closely resemble in style the memoirs of the Emperor: unconscious revelation of high personal valuation.

Rommel had managed to persuade Mussolini to let him send back from Buerat those troops without transport; and once again his small force of Germans prepared to match skill against numbers.

After elaborate air and artillery bombardment, 51st Infantry Division, under Montgomery's personal command, attacked astride

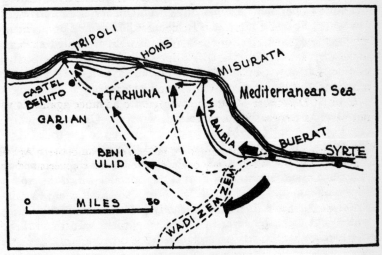

MAP 25. BUERAT TO TRIPOLI
15–23 January 1943

the coast road, while 7th Armoured Division and the 2nd New Zealand Division, under Leese, cut round Rommel's desert flank to deliver the main blow. Another armoured brigade was in reserve. For once, the need for speed determined Montgomery's plans and leadership; yet even now he was held back by his own character. His final orders for the troops making the decisive swing round the German flank "provided for a due measure of caution to be exercised . . . as I wished to avoid heavy casualties to our tanks".

Of the issue of a battle between four hundred and fifty tanks and fifty there is no doubt. Fifteenth Panzer Division, on the German right wing, fell slowly back on Tarhuna before Leese's attack, destroying fifty-two British tanks; and the rest of Rommel's command fell back in step. Montgomery's advance, which started later, made good progress; 90th Light had already withdrawn.

Now occurred an astonishing thing. This imposing offensive, whose essence was speed; which required, in Montgomery's words, "tremendous drive and energy"; which was Montgomery's one and only attempt at war in Rommel's style, moved so slowly that it lost all contact with the enemy, who was retiring in no haste. It began to seem even possible that Tripoli would not fall in time to serve as a new base port; that Eighth Army might have to retreat to secure its supplies. Doubt, nagging uncertainty, now blew coldly into the cosy world of balance and master plans; and with nearly five hundred tanks under command against fifty, Montgomery began seriously to wonder if he could succeed. He blamed the slowness on his men, and dispensed to at least one subordinate what he called an 'imperial rocket'.

His march failed in its original object. He never "crashed" (his word) through the steady, controlled retreat of the *Panzerarmee*, which held him at its own pace, and which gave up Tripoli only when the port had been completely wrecked. On 23rd January, 1943, Eighth Army entered the town and paused to re-group. The prize which might so easily have been O'Connor's; the prize to capture which Wavell and Auchinleck had built a great base out of the empty sand and rock of Egypt; the prize for which the troops of Cunningham and Ritchie had fought so gamely, was now Montgomery's. For the soldiers, however, Tripoli did not signify laurel wreaths, but cafés, boulevards, trees and gardens. To them, beer spoke louder than posterity.

The capture of Tripoli was, of course, the occasion of another personal message to the troops:

Today, 23rd January, exactly three months after we began the battle of Egypt, the Eighth Army has captured Tripoli . . . By skilful withdrawal tactics the enemy has eluded us . . . The defeat of the enemy in the Battle of Alamein, the pursuit of his beaten army and the final capture of Tripoli, a distance of some fourteen hundred miles from Alamein, has all been accomplished in three months. This achievement is probably without parallel in history . . .

Four days after the capture of Tripoli, in pouring rain, was fought the last action of the desert war. At Zuara, a force of 7th Armoured Division met rearguards of 90th Light; there was a four-day struggle for the place, and then 90th Light, who had fought with as much élan in their last engagement in defence of infamy as in their first, fell back along the dismal road of retreat. On 4th February Churchill and General Brooke visited Tripoli, and Montgomery arranged a spectacular victory parade. On 12th February, second anniversary of Rommel's arrival in Africa, the last rearguards of the *Panzerarmee Afrika* retreated across the Tunisian frontier.

The desert war was over.

COMMENTARY: PART SIX

INTRODUCTION

Although the section on Montgomery's Desert generalship occupies only a fifth of the running length of *The Desert Generals*, it was on this that hostile comment and controversy focused, and still does. To recapitulate, the book made the following charges:

1. That Montgomery was not accurate when he told Winston Churchill in August 1942 and the readers of his *Memoirs* in 1958 that Auchinleck intended to retreat from Alamein if attacked again in strength.
2. That, on the contrary, Montgomery's defensive battle at Alam Halfa was based on Auchinleck's existing plan and preparations.
3. That the Second Battle of Alamein in October 1942, far from being a brilliant victory won according to Montgomery's "Master Plan", as he made out in his *Memoirs*, stalled within the first twenty-four hours; had to be completely re-fashioned; and eventually succeeded only by a narrow margin.
4. That the initial failure was largely owing to Montgomery's faulty organisation whereby the 10th (Armoured) Corps was superimposed on the same narrow minefield lanes as the 30th (Infantry) Corps.
5. That the failure to trap Rommel immediately after the battle was owing to the chaotic state of the Eighth Army and not, as Montgomery alleged, rain turning the ground to bog on the night of 6th November.
6. That Montgomery's pursuit of Rommel from Alamein to Tripoli, and specifically south of Benghazi, at El Agheila and at Buerat, was needlessly and incomprehensively slow and cautious.

I will discuss below chapter by chapter each of these charges as they occur, in the light of fresh evidence to appear since the original publication of this book.

CHAPTER ONE

The debate over Auchinleck's and Montgomery's plans in August 1942 has become lost in semantic quibblings as to what may be properly called a "plan". It should however be remembered that the controversy would never have arisen at all if it had not been for Montgomery's statement to the War Premier on 19th August 1942, retailed to the Cabinet by Churchill, and reproduced in his *The*

Second World War in 1951, and then again repeated in Montgomery's own *Memoirs* in 1958, that Auchinleck intended that "the Eighth Army would fall back on the Delta" if Rommel attacked in strength. It was therefore *Montgomery* who set the terms of reference for the controversy, and he himself describes this alleged intention of Auchinleck to retreat as "Auchinleck's plan of operations". We are therefore discussing a matter of broad strategic designs, not detailed operation orders.

The documentary evidence now available is conclusive that Auchinleck's "plan of operations" at the time of his dismissal was to fight a defensive battle in the Alamein–Alam Halfa position which he had high confidence of winning, and then to launch a setpiece offensive of his own about mid-September. As early as 10th July 1942, Dorman-Smith, his acting Chief of Staff in the field, was writing from Tactical Headquarters, Eighth Army, to Main Headquarters:

> Long term 8th ARMY Defence Plan envisages defensive action in depth in general area El Alamein–high ground 4288 about 15 miles SSE El Alamein Station thence running along Ridge ENE towards El Hammam Station. If enemy moving on Alexandria attempts to by-pass this area he meets Alexandria defences and exposes his rear to mobile forces to be stationed East of and covered by Wadi Natrun.

Dorman-Smith's Appreciation of 27th July, quoted in full as Appendix "A" to this book, and adopted by Auchinleck's Commanders' Conference on 30th July as the basis of forward planning, amplifies the strategy outlined in this signal. By this time engineering work on the defensive layout was well in progress. On 28th July Eighth Army reported to G.H.Q. M.E.F. that minefields at Alam El Halfa, Alam El Tritriya and Alam El Khadim (making up what is usually known as the Alam Halfa Ridge) were a hundred per cent complete, while defences on the ridge to hold a brigade were due for completion by 5th August. On 10th August 1942, three days before Montgomery arrived in the Desert, 30th Corps held a commanders' conference to discuss "the method by which the battle will be fought in the main zone with particular reference to the artillery plan".

Thus the basic fact is clear, as stated in this book, that Auchinleck intended to fight a battle in the Alamein–Alam Halfa position if Rommel attacked, and had begun preparations so to do. Even Nigel Hamilton, Montgomery's official biographer, acknowledges this by devoting much space to criticising the details of Auchinleck's arrangements. Moreover, Auchinleck had also taken the first steps towards preparing the setpiece offensive outlined in Dorman-Smith's Appreciation of 27th July aimed at breaking through the enemy defences at Alamein that eventually became Montgomery's Second Battle of Alamein. For on 6th August Auchinleck visited Main Headquarters, Eighth Army in order to discuss the establishment of a training area with mock German defences "to enable formations and units to carry out exercises in breaking through the enemy defences with special attention to clearing a gap for armoured forces through the enemy minefields". Next day Auchinleck met the Chief Engineer Eighth Army to choose a suitable place for this mock German defence; on 12th/14th August siting and survey work were carried out; and on 15th August, the day Montgomery formally became Eighth Army Commander, the construction work was begun.

Employing the term "plan" in the sense in which Montgomery used it in this context in his *Memoirs* and Alexander in his Despatch—that is, a broad design—there is no doubt whatever from the new documentary evidence just cited that, as this book contended, "the Battle of Alam Halfa was fought on a plan conceived by Dorman-Smith, approved and initiated by Auchinleck, and from fixed defences largely dug before Montgomery left England". There can also be no doubt that Auchinleck's "plan" must have been evident to Montgomery from the first moment he looked at the current battle-map showing Eighth Army's existing deployment, defences and minefields in the Alamein–Alam Halfa position. The Situation Map for 17th August 1942 attached to the Draft Narrative of Volume III of the official campaign history shows the minefields on the Alam Halfa Ridge exactly as detailed by the report of 28th July cited above; and this layout is identical to that shown on the map of the Battle of Alam Halfa itself in the published official history.

Montgomery's own testimony is worthless owing to his proven trait of disregarding truth. For example, in a note dated 1962 found by his official biographer among his papers he wrote that "Alam Halfa was never in the picture at all until I took over", which is totally and demonstrably false.

Not surprisingly, Montgomery further developed the Alam Halfa defences in the fortnight that elapsed between his accession to command and the opening of Rommel's offensive. As the G.H.Q. Liaison Officer to Eighth Army reported on 15th August, "defended localities are being considerably strengthened, both in personnel and e.g. fresh minefields". In particular he brought up 44th Division from the Delta to garrison the Alam Halfa Ridge; a division earlier earmarked for the Persia–Iraq front, at the time when the danger of a German breakthrough via the Caucasus had seemed highly possible. It should be remembered that whereas Auchinleck's Middle East Command had included the Persia Iraq area, Alexander had been relieved of responsibility for this, enabling him to concentrate entirely on Rommel. He could release reserve formations to the Desert with an easy mind.

As this book freely acknowledged, Montgomery's own innovation lay in the style and method with which the Eighth Army fought the Battle of Alam Halfa. Auchinleck had intended a mobile battle pivoting on the fixed defences, and Gott, the 13th Corps Commander, had issued instructions for tactical withdrawals, in the face of enemy attack, from forward defended localities to a main battle zone or "Army Reserve Positions" such as the Alam Halfa defences. Could Montgomery have interpreted these contingency moves as an intended "retreat"? It is hard to believe so, unless he had an ulterior motive for such an interpretation. Nevertheless these tactical plans were certainly cancelled by Montgomery on assuming command, as the report by the G.H.Q. Liaison Officer with Eighth Army for 15th August makes plain: "Eighth Army's defence policy is to stand and fight in the present positions and no withdrawal is to be made. The words 'Army Reserve Positions' are being deleted from the printed maps." Because this and other relevant Eighth Army documents were then closed to research, *The Desert Generals* was therefore in error in saying that Gott's detailed plans for 13th Corps were adopted by Montgomery and Horrocks, the new Corps Commander.

Was Montgomery's new order to fight in the forward defended localities rather than in a main battle zone necessarily the improvement claimed by his partisans? It is interesting that Rommel, in planning his own defence at Alamein before October 1942, relied on just such a withdrawal from a forward line to a main battle zone, in accordance with standard German practice, and that this withdrawal proved completely successful in evading the impact of the British preliminary bombardment and initial assault.

Montgomery made much of Auchinleck's intention at all costs to preserve the Eighth Army "in being", implying that this signified an intention to retreat into the Delta if heavily attacked. Auchinleck, as C.-in-C. of a Middle East Command that included the threatened Northern Front along the Persian–Russian frontier, was certainly resolved not to allow the Eighth Army to be pinned down and destroyed at Alamein. *If*, but *only* if, he was defeated by Rommel in the Alamein–Alam Halfa position, he would retire into the Delta in order to preserve the Army, the strongest field force in the theatre. Contingency plans were therefore put in hand under Auchinleck for the preparation of a defence of the Delta, and for the transfer of G.H.Q. Middle East from Cairo to Sarafand in Palestine.

Whatever the moral impact of Montgomery's vaunted "No Retreat" order on assuming command, that order must be considered strategically meaningless, because no C.-in-C. Middle East could in the event have committed the Eighth Army to a "stand-and-die" battle at Alamein which, if lost, must have left the entire theatre wide open to Rommel. It simply is not plausible that if Rommel *had* broken through at Alam Halfa towards the coast, the Eighth Army would have allowed itself to be cut off like the Tobruk garrison. If defeated at Alam Halfa, Montgomery would willy-nilly have had to retreat into the Delta.

And indeed the danger that Rommel might outflank the Eighth Army and directly invade the Delta remained very much in the mind of G.H.Q. M.E.F. *after* Alexander took over from Auchinleck, as G.H.Q. records make plain. A G.H.Q. Operation Instruction to British Troops in Egypt on 29th August, the eve of Rommel's Alam Halfa offensive, laid down contingency plans in case R.A.F. airfields in the Wadi-Natrun–Mena-Fayum area had to be evacuated "through the arrival of powerful enemy forces . . ." It is also noteworthy that on 21st August the contingency plans for the evacuation of G.H.Q. M.E.F. from Cairo to Palestine were amended but not cancelled by the new régime.

What then is the final outcome of these historical transactions? That the new Middle East Command, like the old, saw as a worst possible case the irruption of powerful German forces into the Nile Delta and made plans accordingly. That Auchinleck and Dorman-Smith were first to anticipate Rommel's plan to turn the British defences at Alamein via the southern sector, and to conceive of a defensive battle based on a refused left flank along the Alam Halfa Ridge; and that this conception had been embodied in a layout of minefields and fortifications on the ground before Montgomery arrived. That Montgomery thereafter greatly strengthened this layout both in terms of troops and defences. That the style in which the Alam Halfa battle was commanded and fought, as well as the detailed tactical disposition of the Eighth Army formations, were entirely Montgomery's own contribution.

* * * * *

Since the publication of Montgomery's *Memoirs* and *The Desert Generals*, credit for innovations in an entirely novel direction has been given to Montgomery that also properly belongs to Auchinleck. Nigel Hamilton in his official biography of Montgomery claims that whereas Auchinleck made "pathetic" [sic] use of *Ultra* decrypts of *Enigma*, Montgomery from the start perceived its importance and based his plans on it; further, that it was under Montgomery that intelligence and operational planning were first properly integrated. Hamilton rests his claim on his own interpretation of Sir Edgar Williams's testimony in interviews with him, although he has read Volume II of Professor Hinsley's official history *British Intelligence in the Second World War* which flatly contradicts the claim. The documentary evidence in Professor Hinsley's book demonstrating how closely Auchinleck's conduct of First Alamein was based on *Sigint* has already been cited above. But Hinsley also states that it was *Auchinleck* who first created an efficient intelligence organisation and integrated it with operational planning, a reform from which Montgomery was to benefit:

> . . . the new commander took over as his intelligence staff a team that had been formed during July by the transfer of DMI Cairo to be Chief of Staff Eighth Army, and the appointment of new men to the posts of GSO1 (I)A and GSO2 (I)A. During the hard fighting between the end of June and the end of July the new team had already assisted the C-in-C Middle East to make the maximum use of intelligence. From the beginning of August it was profiting from its experience during the recent fighting by introducing further improvements into Eighth Army's intelligence arrangements . . .

These improvements were announced on 1st August, twelve days before Montgomery's arrival in the Desert.

It appears moreover that Nigel Hamilton may have misinterpreted what Sir Edgar Williams told him. For in a letter to me, Sir Edgar writes:

> Of course the Auk did not ignore *Ultra*—he was a good soldier and he wanted to stem, then defeat his enemy. He was very attentive to what one told him, much of which was of course based on *Ultra*.
>
> But *after* [author's italics] he had stopped the rot at Alamein, one began to feel increasingly that the next two stages . . . required a fresh mind and approach and that however good the Intelligence and it was really becoming quite good, it would not be put to effective operational use with the Auk still there.

Thus Sir Edgar's doubts about Auchinleck's operational use of *Ultra* do not relate to First Alamein, as Hamilton claims, but to the future. Sir Edgar further writes, with respect to Professor Hinsley's book,

> If it makes it clear that Montgomery inherited a good Intell./Ops set-up from the Auk, that would, I think, be fair comment, for Freddie de G. as B.G.S. and Hugh Mainwaring as G1 Ops were a powerful combination. I saw this as the G2 I and formed the link with especially "Y" and the Corps Intell. staffs, to tune the remarkable *Ultra* flow with the local set-up. To say that the Auk created the efficiency would be to overstate the case but Montgomery certainly inherited an effective group, I'd say . . .

Here too, therefore, Sir Edgar Williams's recollections concur with the findings of Professor Hinsley's documentary account; and neither support Nigel Hamilton's renewed attempt to found Montgomery's Desert reputation on denigration of Auchinleck.

CHAPTER TWO

The Desert Generals contended that Montgomery's Alamein "Master Plan" to clear gaps right through the German defence zone and pass the armour of 10th Corps into open country beyond within the first twenty-four hours completely failed; and that Montgomery's claim in his *Memoirs*, repeated on television, that following his further orders to the commanders of the armour "all my armour was out in the open" by 8 a.m. on 25th October was untrue. Both these charges have been since confirmed by the detailed accounts of the battle in Field-Marshal Lord Carver's book *Alamein* and Volume IV of the official history, *The Mediterranean and Middle East*.

The official history writes of the situation on the morning of 24th October that 10th Corps "had nowhere broken out from 30th Corps' partly formed bridgeheads", and of the situation on 28th October, following Montgomery's order of 25th October that the armour was to break out at all costs, that " 'Operation Lightfoot' had not achieved all that had been hoped of it; in particular, the deployment of the armour beyond the 30th Corps' bridgehead had not gone well . . ." On this day also, according to the official history, Montgomery "realised that the impetus of his offensive was on the wane . . ." The initial failure of the Master Plan is also acknowledged by Montgomery's official biographer, who writes that far from the armour being all out in the open by the morning of 25th October, as Montgomery claimed,

the British Armoured Corps was stuck—glued to both 2nd New Zealand Division and 133rd Lorried Infantry Brigade on the Miteiriya Ridge, and clinging to the eastern extremity of the Kidney Ridge beyond the 51st Highland Division's sector. Further south, Horrocks' 13th Corps had stalled too. The "Masterplan" had failed.

Montgomery and his partisans have attributed the failure of 10th Corps to break out into the open to a want of resolute leadership and fighting spirit. *The Desert Generals* argued, however, that the real cause of breakdown lay in Montgomery's own plan, whereby three armoured divisions were asked to debouch in the face of anti-tank guns from nine cleared lanes, each only the width of a single tank through the German minefields, and whereby the armoured corps was superimposed on the same sector as the infantry corps which was to win the initial bridgeheads. This analysis has since been supported by Lord Carver in his book *Alamein* and by the then Commander Royal Artillery to the Eighth Army, General Kirkman. According to Lord Carver, not only Lumsden (commanding 10th Corps) and his armoured division commanders, but also the three Commonwealth infantry division commanders, Freyberg, Pienaar and Morshead, had warned during the planning stages that to ask the armour to fight its own way through the enemy defences if the infantry failed to clear a path was not a feasible operation of war. Lord Carver also agrees that the superimposing of one corps on another led to immense muddle and disagreement. He describes the scene on 24th October as British armour and infantry formations lay crammed together in bottlenecks within the German defences:

The congestion was appalling and the confusion considerable. The whole area looked like a badly organised car park at an immense race meeting held in a dustbowl.

General Kirkman, the Commander Royal Artillery Eighth Army, told Montgomery's official biographer that it had been impractical to superimpose an armoured corps on an infantry corps in the same sector to achieve a breakthrough, "because two corps commanders can't operate in the same area. There was terrible confusion . . ."

It is thus fair to say that authoritative accounts of Second Alamein, drawing on war diaries and other documents not available in 1960, wholly vindicate *The Desert Generals'* criticisms of Montgomery's own account of the battle and also its analysis of the causes of the failure of the "Master Plan". As even Nigel Hamilton acknowledges:

> Bernard Montgomery's later insistence that everything went according to plan was not only untrue, but unfortunate . . . he thereby concealed a vital aspect of his own military stature: namely to *alter* his plan when necessary, and to impart confidence to all around him when his original plan of battle failed.

The Desert Generals paid tribute to Montgomery's calmness and coolness of nerve in the face of initial failure, remarking that "Montgomery's resolution as a battlefield commander redeemed his clumsiness as a planner". However, we now know from Professor Hinsley's *British Intelligence in the Second World War* that in the sheer battle of attrition that now followed until the enemy finally broke on 4th November, Montgomery enjoyed the priceless advantage of exact and detailed daily information about Rommel's dwindling resources in tanks, fuel, ammunition and manpower.

Even before the Second Battle of Alamein began on 23rd October 1942, Montgomery knew from *Enigma* decrypts that by 25th October *Panzerarmee Afrika* would be down to four and a half days' battle supply of fuel, of which only three days' supply was then east of Tobruk. He also knew that the *Panzerarmee*'s forward strength in manpower amounted to only 49,000 Germans and 54,000 Italians against an Eighth Army strength of 195,000. A decrypted return of enemy tank strength for 14th October gave a total of two hundred and thirty-four German tanks, enabling British intelligence to calculate that on the eve of the battle it would be unlikely to reach two hundred and seventy. On 23rd October, the first day of the battle, a decrypt of the German tank return for that same day gave totals of two hundred and thirty-eight German tanks (including thirty light Mark IIs) and two hundred and seventy-nine Italian, and provided a breakdown of the different types of tank. Eighth Army was fielding one thousand and twenty-nine tanks, with two hundred more in immediate reserve and a thousand in workshops. In view of these comparative figures known to the British command at the time, it really is impossible to understand how Hamilton can claim that "Eighth Army had enjoyed relatively greater superiority over Rommel in the 'Crusader' operations of November 1941, and at Gazala in May 1942".

Yet while *Sigint* and other sources yielded accurate information before the battle about the location of enemy units and the nature and strength of the German defences, they failed to detect the enemy withdrawal from the forward edge of his defence zone to the *Hauptkampffeld*, or Main Battle Zone, on 20th October. As a result, according to Professor Hinsley, British intelligence underestimated the strength of this main position.

On 28th/29th October, when Montgomery had begun to build a fresh battle in place of the defunct "Master Plan", *Enigma* decrypts gave him a complete picture of Rommel's fuel and other supply problems, together with the news that the enemy was now down to eighty-one German tanks. A further decrypt on 30th October revealed Rommel's shortage of ammunition; and another on the night of 2nd/3rd November gave Rommel's own report to the German high command saying that his army was at the end of its tether. Nevertheless, according to Professor Hinsley, high-grade *Sigint* made no decisive contribution to the tactical land fighting, nor directly affected the placing or timing of the final British thrusts in *Supercharge*, while Hitler's "stand-fast" order of 3rd November was not decrypted and received in the Middle East until the after-noon of the 4th, when it had lost its operational usefulness.

CHAPTER THREE

Accounts published since *The Desert Generals* have confirmed my analysis that it was not heavy rain on the night of 6th November 1942 which stalled the British pursuit and enabled Rommel to escape, as alleged by Montgomery in his *Memoirs*, but the exhaustion and confusion into which Eighth Army had fallen by the end of the battle. Lord Carver in his book *Alamein* writes of the last stages of the tank battle at Tel el Aqqaqir on 4th November:

> Little if any attempt seems to have been made on a higher level to co-ordinate the confusion that was bound to arise from so many divisions struggling to push out through the bottleneck of the salient area. It would have been hard enough if all had been under the command of the same corps: with two different corps, who were not on the best of terms anyway, both trying to carry out the same task in the same area, it was chaotic. There is no other word to describe the incredible confusion of that dark night in a sea of dust.

As a result of this chaos, Carver continues, formations ordered by Montgomery to cut Rommel off at Fuka and Galal were late starting, were heavily delayed by the problem of night movement over unreconnoitred desert, and failed to catch him. A second attempt to cut him off at Charing Cross, south of Matruh, with

Briggs's 1st Armoured Division, likewise failed owing to critical delays to the division's "B" echelon with essential fuel supplies because of the congestion of the battlefield and to bogging down in soft sand later. Carver bluntly states: "It is now clear that the sudden arrival of torrential rain on November 6th was in no way responsible for the failure to cut off more of the remnants of the *Panzerarmee*." Ronald Lewin in *Montgomery as Military Commander* also concurs. The official history, in words which closely parallel *The Desert Generals*' explanation of why Montgomery's celebrated *corps de chasse* (10th Corps) was not ready and poised at the end of the battle to fulfil its *raison d'être*, says that "because of the course taken by the battle since 23rd October there was no strong mobile formation fresh, concentrated, and poised for distant pursuit, as, for example, had been Allenby's Desert Mounted Corps at Megiddo in September 1918".

In sum, therefore, the course of Second Alamein, as *The Desert Generals* first contended, calls in question Montgomery's generalship at this stage of his career, and certainly cannot justify his official biographer's attempt to portray him at Alamein as a military genius in the burgeoning.

In accusing Montgomery of needless caution in his long pursuit of Rommel from Alamein to Tripoli, this book assumed that he could infer Rommel's weakness from the known traditional sources of military intelligence. Now, however, Professor Hinsley's *British Intelligence in the Second World War*, Volume Two, puts Montgomery's caution in an entirely new light by telling us that throughout the pursuit "General Montgomery was fully apprised by the *Enigma*, by air reconnaissance and by Army 'Y' of the state of Rommel's forces and, more important, the *Enigma* gave him advance notice of Rommel's intentions".

On 10th November Montgomery ruled that no main bodies of the Eighth Army were to advance west of Fort Capuzzo for the time being lest they outran their supplies and exposed themselves to the risk of a counter-stroke by Rommel. Instead he hoped to defeat Rommel at El Agheila. Next day air reconnaissance showed that the enemy was evacuating Bardia and Tobruk, which led Lumsden (commanding 10th Corps) and Air Chief Marshal Tedder, Air Officer Commanding-in-Chief Middle East, to urge that a mobile force should strike across the Desert to reach Benghazi before him. Nevertheless Montgomery refused, remaining fast to his plan to fight Rommel at the El Agheila bottleneck. Writes Professor Hinsley:

Nor was he deflected from this plan when he learned from the *Enigma* during 10 and 11 November that 21 Panzer Division was down to 11 serviceable tanks, that 15 Panzer Division had no tanks left and that the Panzerarmee had only one quarter of an ammunition issue and fuel for only 4-5 days.

On 15th November 10th Corps was ordered to send armoured cars across the Desert to the south of Benghazi, a mere ghost of O'Connor's daring march of 1941, while the main body of the corps followed Rommel along the coast road. Only on 18th November, when it was too late, did Montgomery order 10th Corps to advance "at utmost speed" to cut Rommel off.

From 14th November onwards, also, *Enigma* informed Montgomery that Axis reinforcements were flowing not to Rommel but to Tunisia; in other words, that he did not face the danger that had confronted his predecessors at El Agheila of a Rommel freshly strengthened and ready for a riposte. On 24th November *Ultra* decrypted an *Enigma* signal from Rommel to the German high command saying that it was unlikely that he could hold the El Agheila position for long, and other decrypts revealed that Italian formations were being sent back to Buerat. Thus Montgomery well knew that if he paused to make elaborate preparations for a setpiece assault, Rommel might slip away in the meantime. Nonetheless he still settled down to organise and stock for such an assault. On 5th December 1942 *Enigma* gave him the complete strength and supply return for *Panzerarmee Afrika* and the Luftwaffe for 1st December: fifty-four German tanks, a shortage of ammunition, no reserves of fuel. On 8th December a further decrypt revealed to the British commander that Rommel intended to retire in the face of a strong attack. Even so, not until four days later did Montgomery bring his planned offensive forward by forty-eight hours. As *The Desert Generals* pointed out, the dread British bombardment fell on empty desert; Rommel had already gone.

Montgomery's plan for attacking Rommel's fresh position at Buerat called for the dumping of supplies sufficient to nourish ten days' fighting by four divisions; a major cause of delay and of strain on British logistics. Yet as Professor Hinsley writes,

When 8th Army attacked at Buerat on 15 January with between 7 and 8 divisions and 700 tanks it knew [from *Enigma*] that it was faced by one and a half German divisions with 34 tanks and 6 Italian battalions with 57 . . . and that the enemy still lacked sufficient fuel and ammunition for heavy fighting.

Why did Montgomery so signally fail to take advantage of this astonishing flow of precisely accurate secret intelligence, which removed all guesswork from generalship? In the light of Professor Hinsley's evidence I am the more convinced that I was right when I wrote in *The Desert Generals* that "this was not entirely a rational caution", but one which illustrated Montgomery's "obsession with tidiness and method" and showed "a curious limit to one of his most publicised characteristics: the belief in his own ability". This was indeed the first book to discern "a profound and sombre self-doubt" behind Montgomery's "bright glorification of self", a self-doubt manifested in "his desire for overwhelming material superiority, in his love of exact tidiness, in the artificial predestination of the master plan". Now Montgomery's official biographer, Nigel Hamilton, with the advantage of access to all his private letters and diaries, confirms that he was a man tormented by inner insecurity springing from a harsh and loveless upbringing, "pathologically over-controlled", with "a concern for order that amounted to an obsession".

✳ ✳ ✳ ✳ ✳

In retrospect it is possible to see that Montgomery's admirers and critics alike have been blinded by his conscious and deliberate myth-making. For the best of military reasons—to give Eighth Army confidence in him and confidence in itself—he created *two* myths; that of his own infallible generalship, where all went exactly according to plan; and that of the Eighth Army as one of the élite armies of history. After the war, however, vanity impelled him to continue embellishing his own myth, for, in Nigel Hamilton's words, Montgomery "developed a quasi-paranoid streak of subsequent self-justification, a noxious insistence that his battles and campaigns were fought exactly according to plan—claims so obviously untrue that some historians . . . were bound to see him as a boastful and profoundly suspect figure . . ." It was indeed inevitable that Montgomery's account of his own generalship, not being congruent with the facts, would be challenged sooner or later by historians. He would better have secured his reputation by presenting in his postwar memoirs the truth rather than the myth both about his own generalship at Second Alamein and about the Eighth Army.

What was this truth? That while no battle goes as planned, Montgomery had the clarity of mind, the steadiness of nerve and the strength of will to fashion new expedients in the face of failure, and carry them through to ultimate victory. That the Eighth Army was, like the Grand Fleet at Jutland, a cumbersome and inferior fighting instrument, capable of winning against German troops only in a carefully rehearsed, tightly controlled setpiece operation with ample margins of numerical and material superiority. And that Montgomery, like Jellicoe at Jutland, bleakly faced this reality and tailored his battle accordingly; and did so the better because, again like Jellicoe, his own temperament leaned so strongly towards elaborate rehearsal and tightly centralised control. This is not the stuff of Alamein Reunions at the Albert Hall.

When *The Desert Generals* first appeared in 1960, admirers of Montgomery were angered by the portrait of the Field-Marshal as vain, egotistical, braggardly, careless of the truth, mixing impulsive kindness and generosity with breathtaking cruelty. Yet this portrait is borne out in rich detail by Nigel Hamilton in the 848-page first volume of his official biography, covering Montgomery's life up to the end of Second Alamein. Indeed Hamilton presents him as militarily a genius but personally an emotional cripple, going so far as to use the word "pathological" more than once in regard to his psychology.

Here too, therefore, the version of the Desert campaign first presented by *The Desert Generals*, and so controversial at the time of first publication, has been fully confirmed by subsequent research in documentary sources not then available.

NOTES ON THE SOURCES

PART I

CHAPTER ONE

With the exception of that on p. 31, all quotations from General O'Connor are from personal communications to the author. General O'Connor's comment on p. 31 on his seniors' conception of the scope of the attack is from *Against Great Odds*, by Brigadier C. N. Barclay, p. 19.

All Brigadier Caunter's comments and recollections are communications to the author, as are those from Major-General E. Dorman O'Gowan (Dorman-Smith) and General Sir Alexander Galloway. The extract on p. 33 from the letter of 28th November 1940 from Wavell to Wilson is taken from *The Mediterranean and the Middle East*, by I. S. O. Playfair, Vol. I, p. 265.

The account of the trial attack and evolution of the final tactical plan for attacking the Italian camps (pp. 31 and 32) is based on information supplied by Major-General Dorman O'Gowan (Dorman-Smith) and Major-General A. H. Gatehouse.

The references to the Italian Air Force and Luftwaffe ciphers are from Professor F. H. Hinsley, *British Intelligence in the Second World War*, Vol. I, pp. 375–6, as is the reference to the crucial information about the Nibeiwa minefield gap and to air reconnaissance.

CHAPTER TWO

All quotations from General O'Connor are from personal communications to the author, as are those from Brigadier Caunter. The figures of the result of the Battle of Sidi Barrani are taken from *The Mediterranean and the Middle East*, by Playfair. The quotation on p. 39 from a telegram from Churchill to Wavell is taken from Churchill's *Second World War*, Vol. II, p. 483, as is the interchange of messages between Mussolini and Bergonzoli on p. 40. The figures of the result of the capture of Tobruk are from Playfair, op. cit., as are those of remaining Italian strength in Libya. The messages from Churchill to Wavell and to the Chiefs of Staff on p. 44 are taken from Playfair, Vol. I, pp. 227 and 338; that on p. 45 to Wavell from Playfair, Vol. I, p. 339. The figures of results of the capture of Tobruk are also from Playfair. The account of the tent incident at Sandhurst on p. 48 was given to the author by General Sir Alfred Godwin-Austen.

Notes on Sources

All references to decrypts of Italian signals are from Hinsley, Vol. I, Ch. 12; to German signals concerning German expansion in the Balkans towards Greece from Hinsley, Vol. I, Ch. 11, especially pp. 352–3.

CHAPTER THREE

All quotations from General O'Connor are communications to the author, except for that on p. 61 about the possibilities of success of an advance on Tripoli, which is taken from Barclay, op. cit., p. 74. All quotations from General Sir Michael Creagh, Brigadier Caunter, General O'Gowan (Dorman-Smith) and General J. M. L. Renton are from personal communications to the author. The account of the sending of the victory message to Wavell on p. 56, and of O'Connor's manner after victory, was given to the author by General O'Gowan. General O'Gowan also gave the author the account of O'Connor's visit to the captured Italian officers, and of his own visit to Wavell's headquarters (p. 58). The quotation from Churchill's message of congratulation to Wavell over Beda Fomm is from Churchill, Vol. III. p. 58. The quotation on p. 58 from General Kennedy's minute of 13th December 1940 on Salonika is taken from *The Business of War*, p. 69. Churchill's remark about firing squads is taken from the same source, p. 75. The quotation from a general staff minute of 16th February 1941 on p. 59 is also from *The Business of War* (pp. 83 and 85). Field-Marshal Lord Alanbrooke's judgment on Greek intervention on p. 59 is from *The Turn of the Tide*, p. 248. Churchill's apologia for the Greek intervention is from Churchill, op. cit., Vol. III, p. 27. Wavell's telegram of 10th February 1941 to London on p. 61 is quoted from *The Business of War*, p. 75. Rommel's opinion of O'Connor's chances in an advance on Tripoli (pp. 61–62) is taken from *The Rommel Papers*, p. 94.

All references to decrypts of German signals indicating German strengths in the Balkans, and to British "guesstimates" of future German invasion strengths in Greece are from Hinsley, Vol. I, Ch. 11, especially pp. 357–8. The reference to British "guesstimates" of the effective strengths of the Greek and Yugoslav armies is from Hinsley, Vol. I p. 359, as is the quote from Hinsley. The D.M.I.'s warning of 24th, February 1941 is quoted from Hinsley, Vol. I, p. 360.

PART II

All quotations from Field-Marshal Sir Claude Auchinleck, General Sir Frank Messervy, General Sir Michael Creagh and Major-General O'Gowan (Dorman-Smith) are from communications to the author. The quotation from Churchill about destroying Rommel's army (p. 68) is from Churchill, op. cit., Vol. III, p. 197. The quotation from his signal of 12th May 1941 to Wavell about using the three hundred new tanks and the need for victory in the Desert is from Churchill, op. cit., p. 264. Wavell's signal of the same day is from the same source, Vol. III, p. 277. Mrs. Churchill's reference to the Premier's state of mind on p. 68 is also from Churchill, op. cit., p. 276. The account of the state of 7th Armoured Division before *Battleaxe* was given in a communication from General Creagh to the author. The account on pp. 70–71 of General Beresford-Peirse's confusion of 'forward rally' with 'rally forward' was given to the author by General A. H. Gatehouse. Churchill's comments on p. 73 on Wavell's responsibilities are taken from Churchill, op. cit., Vol. III, p. 217. The exchange of signals on p. 74 between Churchill and Auchinleck about an early offensive is taken from Churchill, op. cit., Vol. III, p. 324. Churchill's comment on p. 75 on Auchinleck's visit to London is from Churchill, op. cit., p. 326. Auchinleck's reaction to this visit was given to the author by the Field-Marshal.

All references to signals intelligence in this section are derived from Hinsley, Vol. I, Ch. 12. The specific reference to poor British field intelligence failing to make good gaps in *Enigma* decrypts is from Hinsley, pp. 397–9.

PART III

CHAPTER ONE

With the exception of that on p. 86 at the press conference before *Crusader*, which is taken from *They Sought Out Rommel*, p. 4, all quotations from General Sir Alan Cunningham are personal communications to the author. Auchinleck's reasons for choosing Cunningham as 8th Army Commander on p. 79 are in a communication to the author. Quotations from General Godwin-Austen and General Gatehouse are, unless otherwise noted, communications to the author. The contemporary public relations booklet quoted on p. 83 is *They Sought Out Rommel*. For the summary of British armour organisation for *Crusader*, the author is indebted to Playfair, op. cit., *The Sidi Rezeg Battles*, by Agar-Hamilton and Turner, *The Tanks*, by Captain B. H. Liddell Hart, and conversations with General Cunningham, General Gatehouse and General Galloway. The quotation from Cunningham on pp. 85–86 on British action depending on German reaction is from Agar-Hamilton, op. cit., p. 69. Churchill's comment about generals' comforts is from Churchill, op. cit., Vol. IV, p. 321; his signal to Auchinleck about the inactivity of Middle East armies on p. 87 is from the same volume, p. 425. Auchinleck's reference to the unreadiness of the South African Division on p. 87 is from his *Despatch*, p. 311; the quotation about the tight margins in supply is from a communication to the author. The reference to the chances of success is likewise a communication to the author. Churchill's message to the army quoted on p. 89 is from Churchill, op. cit., Vol. IV. p. 434. The account of Cunningham's state of mind before *Crusader* is derived from eye-witness impressions given to the author by General Godwin-Austen, General Sir Arthur Smith and others. See also Kennedy, *The Business of War*, p. 181.

Notes on Sources

All references to signals intelligence are based on Hinsley, Vol. II, Ch. 21. The specific reference to the failure of British intelligence to cast light on German equipment is from Hinsley, Vol. II, pp. 297–8.

CHAPTER TWO

Unless otherwise noted, all quotations from Field-Marshal Auchinleck, General Cunningham, General Godwin-Austen, General Creagh and General Gatehouse are from communications to the author. Sources for Cunningham's state of health are similar to those for the close of Chapter One, although in personal communications to the author General Cunningham has denied that he was at all unwell. In the author's opinion, the balance of evidence lies the other way. The figures for the losses incurred by 22nd Armoured Brigade in their attack on Bir Gubi (p. 93) is taken from the Account of the Operations of 7th Armoured Division, 18th November–27th December 1941, Secret, 31st January 1942. All orders, movements and casualty figures for the British armour are based on this document. The general account of the *Crusader* battle is based on Agar-Hamilton, op. cit.; Playfair, Vol. II; Auchinleck's *Despatch*; Liddell Hart, op. cit.; the Account of the Operations of 7th Armoured Division; *Panzer Battles*, by F. W. von Mellenthin; *The Rommel Papers*, *Rommel et l'Afrika-korps* by H. G. von Esebeck. Cruewell's orders on p. 93 are from von Mellenthin, op. cit., p. 62. Cunningham's orders to his corps on p. 96 are quoted from Agar-Hamilton, op. cit., p. 201. The references to the resistance of British artillery at Sidi Rezegh on p. 97 are from the *R.A. Commemoration Book*, p. 189. The meteorological description on p. 98 is from *Those Against Rommel* by Alexander Clifford, p. 142. The quotation from General Gott on p. 104 about a tank commander's role is taken from *The Seventh and Three Enemies*, by G. M. O. Davy, p. 144. The German comment on p. 104 on British and German panzer organisation is from von Mellenthin, pp. 52–53; the British comment on p. 105 from the Account of the operations of 7th Armoured Division, p. 102 (issued under the name of the divisional commander, General Gott). The extract from a letter from Godwin-Austen to Freyberg on p. 107 is taken from Agar-Hamilton, p. 286. The quotation on p. 108 from Auchinleck about Cunningham's reaction to the setback in *Crusader* is from a communication to the author, as is Auchinleck's own reaction (p. 108). The German opinion of Auchinleck's decision to continue the offensive is from von Mellenthin, p. 75; Churchill's from Churchill, Vol. IV, p. 445. Bayerlein's description of the battlefield on p. 109 is from *The Rommel Papers*, p. 162. The quotation from General Norrie on p. 110 is from a letter written to the South African War Histories, quoted in Agar-Hamilton, p. 291, footnote. The extract from Auchinleck's directive on p. 111 is also from Agar-Hamilton, p. 308; and the quotation on p. 111 of Auchinleck's account of Cunningham's reaction to Rommel's counter-stroke is from his *Despatch*, p. 339. The extract about the conversation in Air Marshal

Notes on Sources

Conyngham's caravan is from Eve Curie's *Journey Among Warriors*, p. 52. Major Stirling's description of Cunningham on p. 113 is taken from Virginia Cowles' *The Phantom Major*. Sir Arthur Smith's impressions of Cunningham at the time of his relief are quoted from a communication to the author.

The lack of reliable intelligence about German tank losses in the opening clashes of *Crusader* is in Hinsley, Vol. II, p. 307. The failure of *Sigint* information about Rommel's dash to the wire to reach Eighth Army in time is from Hinsley, Vol. II, pp. 308–9. The quotations from Auchinleck's correspondence with Cunningham in hospital are from Nigel Hamilton, *Monty: The Making of a General 1887–1942*, p. 512.

PART IV

CHAPTER ONE

Unless otherwise noted, all quotations from Field-Marshal Auchinleck, General Godwin-Austen, General Messervy, General Galloway and General Smith are from communications to the author. The quotation from a public relations officer on p. 118 is from *They Sought Out Rommel*, p. 33. The reference on p. 119 to the inevitability of German retreat is from von Mellenthin, p. 81. Churchill's tribute on p. 119 to Auchinleck's will-power is taken from his *War Speeches*, Vol. II, p. 136. The German description on pp. 119–120 of the state of the battle is from von Mellenthin, p. 80. The description of British rout on p. 126 is from Pitt-Rivers, *Royal Dragoons History*, p. 34; and the German description from von Mellenthin, p. 87. Auchinleck's approval of Ritchie's change of plan (pp. 127–128) is quoted from his *Despatch*, p. 317. Auchinleck's reference to Godwin-Austen's request for relief is from his *Despatch*, p. 317. The account of General Dorman-Smith's visit to Eighth Army's headquarters at Auchinleck's request, and the subsequent picnic at Fayoum, were given to the author by General Dorman O'Gowan (Dorman-Smith).

The Hinsley references to *Sigint* in the closing stages of *Crusader* and before Rommel's riposte are from Vol. II, Ch. 21, specifically pp. 311–12. Hinsley's judgement about improvements in intelligence organisation after Shearer was replaced as D.M.I. by de Guingand is also from Ch. 21. The reference to "some historians" means specifically Hamilton, op. cit., p. 652.

CHAPTER TWO

Unless otherwise noted, quotations from Field-Marshal Auchinleck, General Messervy, General Renton, General Ramsden and General Dorman-Smith (O'Gowan) are from communications to the author. General Gott's reference to future organisation of armour on p. 130 is taken from the Account of the Operations of 7th Armoured Division, p. 106. Auchinleck's reference on p. 131 to the rigidity of pre-war British organisation is taken from his *Despatch*, p. 368. Auchinleck's notification to London (p. 132) that Tobruk would not again be held in isolation is from his *Despatch*, p. 318. De Guingand's reference to the strain on Auchinleck of Churchill's requests is from his book *Operation Victory*, p. 108. The extract from Auchinleck to Ritchie on p. 136 on the necessity of using divisions as divisions is from a letter of 20th May 1942, quoted in his *Despatch*, p. 391. The German reference to what actually happened is from von Mellenthin, p. 94. Figures of British and Axis strengths on p. 138 and relative effectiveness of equipment is taken from Liddell Hart, op. cit. and Playfair, Vol. III. The account of the relaying back by armoured cars of information of Rommel's advance, and the inertia of Eighth Army formations in passing it on, was given to the author by General Renton (then commanding 7th Motor Brigade). The account of Rommel's appearance before Retma on p. 140 was given to the author by Colonel R. N. Bruce. What Renton found at El Gubi (p. 140) is as recounted to the author by the general himself. The belief of Lumsden quoted on p. 144 was a communication to the author from General Messervy. The extract from Ritchie's letter to Auchinleck on p. 144 is quoted from Agar-Hamilton and Turner, *Crisis in the Desert*, p. 39; that concerning the attack in the Cauldron (p. 145) is from a letter of 3rd June 1942, given in Auchinleck's *Despatch*, p. 392. The Eighth Army signal to Auchinleck on the results of the first day of *Aberdeen* (p. 146) is quoted in *Crisis in the Desert*, p. 46; and Ritchie's comments on the action in a signal to Auchinleck (p. 146) from the same work, p. 48. Gott's comments are from p. 51.

A full discussion of the intelligence dimension of the London–Cairo argument in spring 1942 is to be found in Hinsley, Vol. II, Ch. 22, especially pp. 350–64. References to last-minute intelligence about Rommel's *Venezia* offensive are from Hinsley, Vol. II, pp. 365–6. Auchinleck's letter of 20th May 1942 to Ritchie is to be found in John Connell, *Auchinleck*, p. 505. The Carver quote about 30th Corps' dispersion is from p. 23 of his book *Alamein*. The references to *Sigint* during the "Cauldron" battle are from Hinsley, Vol. II, pp. 372–3.

CHAPTER THREE

Quotations from General Messervy and General Ramsden are communications to the author. Auchinleck's estimate of the atmosphere at HQ, Eighth Army (p. 152), is quoted in *Crisis in the Desert*, p. 68. The extract from Churchill's signal to Auchinleck about holding Tobruk (p. 153) is from Churchill, op. cit., Vol. IV, p. 303. Auchinleck's letter to Ritchie instructing him to hold the line Acroma-El Adem and defend Tobruk (p. 153) is given in *Crisis in the Desert*, p. 78. Ritchie's signal of 14th June 1942 (p. 153) is given in same work, same page. Ritchie's summary of his policy in regard to Tobruk (p. 154) is also given in *Crisis*, p. 79. Account of conference of 14th June 1942 given to the author by General Dorman O'Gowan. Account of meeting between Ritchie and

Corbett given to author by General Corbett. Churchill's signal giving War Cabinet's expectation that Tobruk would be held for certain is taken from Churchill, op. cit., Vol. IV, p. 305. Auchinleck's reply of 16th June is given in same work, same page. Churchill's claim that Auchinleck should have fortified Tobruk is quoted from Churchill, op. cit., Vol. IV, p. 306. His claim that London had no inkling that evacuation was contemplated is quoted from the same work, p. 340. Auchinleck's Operation Instruction No. 110 is given in his *Despatch*, p. 378. The comment from Kennedy and the fact that the Instruction was passed to Alanbrooke is from Kennedy, op. cit., p. 243. The account of Auchinleck's visit to HQ Eighth Army at Sollum (p. 157) was given to the author by General O'Gowan, who accompanied the C.-in-C. The pithy 'garden roller' comment on Tobruk's anti-tank defences (p. 158) is from Sir Compton Mackenzie's *Eastern Epic*, Vol. I, p. 563. The extract from Auchinleck's signal to Ritchie about the need for urgency and all exchanges of signals between General Klopper (Tobruk fortress commander) and Ritchie are from *Crisis in the Desert*. Account of Auchinleck's visit to Ritchie on 22nd June (p. 162) given to author by O'Gowan, an eye-witness. Description of Matruh defences on pp. 163–164 is quoted from Kippenberger, *Infantry Brigadier*, p. 126.

The summary of improvements in British intelligence from early June 1942 is derived from Hinsley, Vol. II, pp. 374–5. The reference to the *Enigma* decrypt of Rommel's orders received by Eighth Army on 12th June 1942 is from Hinsley, Vol. II, p. 381. The further references to *Enigma* decrypts on 22nd/24th June are from Hinsley, Vol. II, pp. 388–90.

PART V

CHAPTER ONE

All quotations from Field-Marshal Sir Claude Auchinleck are, unless otherwise noted, personal communications to the author, as are those from General Galloway, General Corbett and General O'Gowan (Dorman-Smith). The letter from Auchinleck to Brooke on pp. 170–171 is quoted in *Auchinleck*, by John Connell, pp. 608–609. The letter from Auchinleck to Churchill is quoted from Churchill op. cit. Vol. IV, p. 320. The account of the flight from Cairo to Matruh was given to the author by O'Gowan and confirmed by Auchinleck. The account of the interview between Auchinleck and Ritchie was given to the author by Field-Marshal Auchinleck. Auchinleck's instructions before the Battle of Mersa Matruh (p. 176) are quoted from Eighth Army Operation Instruction, 25th June 1942. The description of the C.-in-C.'s journey back from Matruh on p. 180 was given to the author by Field-Marshal Auchinleck. Freyberg's 'Balaclava' (p. 180) is quoted from *Crisis in the Desert*, p. 258. The reference to the Royal Navy's precipitate evacuation on p. 183 is based on Lampton Burns, *Down Ramps*, p. 57.

Notes on Sources

CHAPTER TWO

All quotations from Field-Marshal Auchinleck, General Dorman-Smith (O'Gowan), and General Ramsden are communications to the author unless otherwise noted. Impressions of corps commanders' conference on pp. 193-194 were given to the author by O'Gowan. Impression of Gott at the time (p. 195) given to the author by Field-Marshal Auchinleck. Rommel's estimate of Auchinleck's generalship on p. 196 is from *The Rommel Papers*, p. 248, as are Rommel's exhortations to his troops on p. 196. Auchinleck's signal to his men on 3rd July 1942 (p. 197) is quoted from *The Battle for Egypt*, J. I. Scoullar, p. 175. Brooke's account of Churchill's impatience on p. 197 is taken from *The Turn of the Tide*, p. 419. The story about the 'ladies' of Alexandria was recounted to the author by O'Gowan. The quotations of the opinions of a N.Z. brigadier on the feasibility of Eighth Army plans (p. 201) are from Kippenberger, op. cit., pp. 149-150. The quotation from Rommel on p. 203 is from *The Rommel Papers*, p. 252, and those on p. 204 from p. 254. The quotation from Rommel about the possibility of his front breaking on p. 206 is from his *Papers*, p. 257, as is the extract about Auchinleck's blows on the Italians.

In the commentaries to Chapters One and Two the general references to the role of *Sigint* in the First Battle of Alamein are based on Hinsley, Vol. II, Ch. 22, and especially pp. 402-3. The quotation of General Sir Charles Richardson is from Hamilton, op. cit., p. 595. The reference to Auchinleck's special intelligence party is from Hinsley, Vol. II, p. 380; to the decrypts of Rommel's intentions on 30th June/1st July 1942 from Hinsley, Vol. II, pp. 392-3; to the decrypts of Rommel's strength on 1st July from Hinsley, Vol. II, p. 395. The decrypt of Rommel's day report for 3rd July is from Hinsley, Vol. II, pp. 396-7. The *Sigint* that enabled Auchinleck to attack the Italians on 9th July is from Hinsley, Vol. II, pp. 403-4; the later references to *Sigint* in First Alamein are also from Hinsley, Vol. II, Ch. 23, specifically p. 405.

CHAPTER THREE

The fact that the army's morale was by no means depressed by nearness to its base was noted by General Renton, who mentioned it to the author. All quotations from Field-Marshal Auchinleck, General Ramsden and General Dorman-Smith (O'Gowan) are communications to the author unless otherwise noted. The 'unpleasant' telegram (p. 209) is mentioned in *The Turn of the Tide*, p. 420. The extract from Churchill's telegram on 12th July 1942 (p. 209) is quoted in Mackenzie, op. cit., p. 584-585. The quotation on p. 209 about Auchinleck's plans for 21st July is from the *Despatch*, p. 366. The extract from Gott's orders on p. 210 are taken from *The Battle for Egypt*, p. 327. Impressions of Auchinleck's appearance at this time (p. 210) are based on eyewitness impressions and contemporary photographs. Quotations from Rommel on p. 212 are from *The Rommel Papers*. Description of Churchill's impatience on p. 212 is taken from

The Turn of the Tide, p. 433. The account of the Morshead crisis (pp. 212–213) is derived from communications to the author by Generals Ramsden and O'Gowan, and additions and amendments by Field-Marshal Auchinleck. Access to Auchinleck's letter of 1943 to General Ramsden given to the author by General Ramsden. Churchill's impatience of 30th July (p. 215) is described by Brooke on p. 433 of *The Turn of the Tide*. The extract from Auchinleck describing his shortage of men is from his *Despatch*, p. 367. Rommel's opinion of Auchinleck's success at First Alamein is from *The Rommel Papers*. Bayerlein's is quoted from an interview of January 2, 1960. The description of Auchinleck's corps commanders' conference of 30th July is based on communications to the author by Generals Ramsden and O'Gowan. The quotation from Auchinleck about the need for mobility and maximum use of artillery (pp. 218–219) is from the *Despatch*, p. 367. Description of Auchinleck's leisure activities after 30th July was given to the author by the Field-Marshal.

The references to the influence of *Sigint* on Auchinleck's decision to attack on 22nd and 26th July are also derived from Hinsley, Vol. II, Ch. 23. The quotation from Hamilton is on p. 611 of *Monty*. The quotation of the C.-in-C.s Middle East to the Chiefs of Staff on 24th June is in Public Record Office, CAB 105/18 (B) (Crusader) 4 (Final). Hinsley's summing up of the role of *Sigint* in First Alamein is from Vol. II, p. 380. The official history references are I. S. O. Playfair, *The Mediterranean and Middle East*, Vol. III, pp. 359–60, and J. R. M. Butler, *Grand Strategy*, Vol. III, Part II, pp. 614–15. The specific quotation from Playfair is on p. 377.

Chapter Four

The quotation from Churchill about the year's defeats is from Churchill, op. cit., Vol. IV, p. 322. That on p. 221 about his political weakness in July from the same work, p. 356, and the question on p. 221 is from p. 374 of that work. Dorman-Smith's advice to Auchinleck and his rejection of it is based on a communication from O'Gowan (Dorman-Smith). The account of the events leading up to the 'Cairo Purge' are based on Churchill, op. cit., Vol. IV, *The Turn of the Tide*, *Operation Victory*, and material supplied to the author by Field-Marshal Auchinleck and Generals Corbett and O'Gowan. The interpretive use of this material is the author's. Access to the letter quoted on p. 222 was given to the author by General Corbett. The reference to Churchill's offer of the Middle East Command to Brooke on 4th August (p. 222) is based on Churchill, op. cit., Vol. IV, p. 375–376. But Brooke, in *The Turn of the Tide*, pp. 439–444, says Churchill offered him Eighth Army on 4th August and the Middle East Command on 6th August 1942. Description of Churchill's arrival in desert based on photographs and O'Gowan. Churchill's appreciation of R.A.F. hospitality on p. 223 is taken from Churchill, op. cit., p. 377. The contemporary account of Churchill's reception by men of Eighth Army on

p. 223 is from Denis Johnston's *Nine Rivers to Jordan*. The quotation about pudgy fingers is from O'Gowan. The Prime Minister's letter to the Deputy Prime Minister on pp. 223–224 is quoted from Churchill, op. cit., Vol. IV, p. 328. The further quotation from a letter of 21st August 1942 (p. 224) is from Churchill, op. cit., Vol. IV, p. 421. Jacob's account of Auchinleck's reception of the letter of dismissal is quoted from *The Turn of the Tide*, p. 451.

The letter itself is given in Churchill, op. cit., Vol. IV, pp. 382–3. Auchinleck's manner at dinner that night and subsequent remark to de Guingand are from *Operation Victory*, p. 134. The quotation from Churchill on p. 228 about want of plan in Eighth Army is from a letter to the Deputy Prime Minister written on 21st August 1942, after an overnight stay with Montgomery at Eighth Army, and given in Churchill, op. cit., Vol. IV, p. 421. Alexander's description of Auchinleck's plans on p. 228 is taken from his *Despatch*, p. 841. Auchinleck's last order of the day to his men is quoted from his *Despatch*, pp. 367–368. Access to General Corbett's letter to the Deputy C.-in-C. in India, quoted on p. 230, was given to the author by General Corbett. The description of Auchinleck and Dorman-Smith's dinner together is based on an account to the author by O'Gowan (Dorman-Smith). The contemporary opinion of the higher war leadership on p. 230 is taken from Denis Johnston, op. cit., p. 43. The enemy opinion is Bayerlein's, from an interview of 2nd January 1960. Churchill's belated recognition of Auchinleck's burden (p. 231) is taken from Churchill, op. cit., Vol. IV, p. 379; Churchill's solicitude for Alexander's peace of mind (p. 231) is taken from the same source, same page. Churchill's directive to Alexander on p. 231 is taken from Churchill, op. cit., Vol, IV, p. 385.

The reference to myself listening to sacked generals is from Hamilton, op. cit., p. 609, and the quotation from General Richardson from Hamilton, p. 632. The quotation from the Commanders' Conference on 15th July is in PRO: WO 201/2050: Agenda and Minutes of Commanders' Conferences; Meeting at GHQ BTE 15th July 1942. The quotation from de Guingand on Dorman-Smith is from *Generals at War*, pp. 184–6.

PART VI

CHAPTER ONE

The quotation from Kesselring is from his *Memoirs*, p. 111, and from Mussolini from *Mussolini's Memoirs*, p. 219. Rommel's opinion of the effects of the Anglo-American invasion of French North Africa is from *The Rommel Papers*, p. 345.

Quotations from Generals Messervy, Godwin-Austen, Galloway, Leese and Ramsden are communications to the author, unless otherwise noted. Montgomery's mature reflections on setting light to fellow cadets are to be found on p. 24 of his *Memoirs*. The account of Montgomery's little play on p. 236 is quoted from *Montgomery* by Alan Moorehead. The account of Montgomery's encounter with Abdul Karim was given to the author by General Godwin-Austen; Montgomery's action over the 'civil officer' was given to the author by General Ramsden, who also described Montgomery's departure from his brigade in Palestine. The description of Montgomery's last conference in Belgium in 1940 on p. 240 was given to the author also by General Ramsden. The account of planning and mounting the Dieppe raid is based on Stacey, *The Canadian Army* (Official History Summary), and the quotation on p. 240 is taken from this work, p. 56. The quotation from Montgomery on training in England in 1940–1942 (p. 241) is from his *Memoirs*, pp. 70 and 72. Description of Montgomery's taking over from Ramsden was given to the author by General Ramsden.

The quotation from the Official History on the state of the army's morale on Montgomery's appointment is to be found in Playfair, Vol. III, p. 376. The History also denies that the army was in any way 'dispirited'. The quotation from Montgomery on p. 242 about his insubordination in seizing command of Eighth Army is from the *Memoirs*, p. 103, and of his instant retreat from the scene from p. 100. The fact that Auchinleck never received this signal was confirmed to the author by Field-Marshal Auchinleck. The account of Montgomery's first conference, with air cover, was given to the author by Brigadier E. T. Williams. The account of Montgomery's visit to Eighth Army units and collecting hats and badges was given to the author by General Ramsden, who was present. The relevant part of the *Memoirs* is p. 111. The effects of Montgomery's personality on General Horrocks were recounted to the author by General Ramsden. The quotations illustrating the similarity between Auchinleck's plans and Montgomery's plans are as follows: First Montgomery quotation is from the *Memoirs*, p. 108. Quotation from Alexander's *Despatch* is from p. 841. Next quotation of Montgomery's is from the *Memoirs*, p. 108. The quotation from Dorman-Smith's *Appreciation* is from p. 398 of Auchinleck's *Despatch*. Brooke's comment on p. 244 on Montgomery's lecture is from *The Turn of the Tide*, p. 478; Churchill's from Churchill, op. cit., Vol. IV, p. 418. Figures of relative strengths for the Battle of Alam Halfa are taken from Liddell Hart, *The Tanks*. Rommel's state of health is taken from the *Rommel Papers*, p. 270, and footnote, p. 271. The quotation about his inability to leave his truck is from Desmond Young, *Rommel*, p. 169. The quotation on pp. 245–246 from Montgomery about the preparation of defences in the Delta is from the script of his television performance on 12th December 1958. Churchill's reference to similar measures set on foot by himself and others is from Churchill, op. cit., Vol. IV, p. 468, and the reference to Wilson's taking command in the Delta from p. 424. The account of Gott's plans was given to the author by General Renton (7th Armoured Division), Gott's immediate subordinate. General Renton denies there was any idea of 'loosing the armour'. The account of Montgomery's state of mind, and comments before Alam Halfa, were given to the author by General Renton. The disorganisation of command in the *Panzerarmee* (p. 248) is detailed in von Esebeck, op. cit. Montgomery's reference to the quality of his men in the matter of a pursuit after Alam Halfa (p. 249) is from his book *El Alamein to the Sangro*, p. 8. The quotation on p. 250 on the failure of the New Zealand attack is from the same work, p. 9. General Horrocks gave the explanation referred to on p. 250 in *The Sunday Times* of 20th October 1957. Montgomery's second explanation is in *El Alamein to the Sangro*, p. 9. Montgomery's estimate of the value to him of Alam Halfa on p. 250 is from a television performance, 12th December 1958.

The quotation from Montgomery's *Memoirs* alleging Auchinleck's intention to retreat is from p. 94, as is the reference to Auchinleck's "plan of operations". The quotation from Dorman-Smith's signal of 10th July 1942 is from PRO: WO 169/3799. The adoption of Dorman-Smith's Appreciation by the 30th July Commanders' Conference is documented in PRO: CAB 44/98, pp. 415–18. The Eighth Army report of 28th July on progress on the Alam Halfa defences is in PRO: WO 201/574, as is the quote from the 30th Corps conference on 10th August. The quotation about constructing mock enemy defences to practise British troops in attack is from Rear Area 8th Army War Diary for 6th August 1942 in WO 169/3926, as are the further references to Auchinleck's interest in the project. The map of the Battle of Alam Halfa in the official history by Playfair is in Vol. III opposite p. 379. The quotation from Montgomery's papers about the Alam Halfa Ridge is from Hamilton, op. cit., p. 632. The quotations from the G.H.Q. Liaison Officer with Eighth Army is from PRO: G(O) 1482/3 in WO 169/3800. The references to contingency plans for defence of the Delta under Auchinleck are based on PRO: WO 169/3799, G.H.Q. M.E.F. Operation Instruction No. 134 of 22 July 1942. The references to further contingency plans for the defence of the Delta under Alexander are based on signals from G.H.Q. M.E.F. to Delta-force on 18th and 23rd August 1942 in PRO: WO 169/3800; to contingency plans for evacuating R.A.F. airfields from a G.H.Q. Operation Instruction to British Troops in Egypt on 29th August in PRO: WO 169/3800, DMO/1057. The amending but not cancelling of contingency plans for evacuating G.H.Q. M.E.F. to Palestine is in PRO: WO 169/3792, Supplementary Order BM/G(P)/1/9/3/2 of 21 August 1942 amending but not cancelling G.H.Q. Operation Instruction No. 137. Hamilton's references to Auchinleck's use of *Ultra* and to his own interviews with Sir Edgar Williams are in *Monty*, pp. 626–7 and 652–5. The quotation from Hinsley about Montgomery taking over an efficient intelligence/operations set-up from Auchinleck is in Hinsley, Vol. II, p. 410. The quotations from Sir Edgar Williams to me are from a letter of 28th October 1981.

CHAPTER TWO

Montgomery's admission of vanity is taken from the script of a television performance, 12th December 1958. The incident with Wendell Wilkie was recounted to the author by General A. H. Gatehouse. The account of General Ramsden's dismissal was given to the author by General Ramsden. The quotation from Montgomery on pp. 252–253 about the formation of a *corps de chasse* is from the television performance on 12th December 1958; that about the placing of the main assault at Second Alamein from the script of the same performance. The relevant quotation from Auchinleck's *Despatch* is to be found on p. 367. General Renton, General Gatehouse and others communicated to the author Montgomery's insistence on his line of pursuit. The quotation was made in the presence of Renton. The quotation from Churchill on p. 255 on the date of *Lightfoot* is from Churchill, op. cit., Vol. IV, p. 474; Alexander's view is quoted from the same source, same page. Figures for Axis and British strengths at Second Alamein are from Liddell Hart, op. cit., Vol. II. and official records. The quotation of Montgomery's about Rommel's defences on p. 258 is from the performance of 12th December 1958, and on the task of attack from the *Memoirs*, p. 116. Horrocks's comment is from *The Sunday Times*, 27th October 1957. Churchill's is from Churchill, op. cit., Vol. IV, p. 487. The figures for the British front in Flanders in 1940 is from the *Official History of the Campaign in Flanders*, p. 38. The quotation on p. 259 of Montgomery on Alexander is from the *Memoirs*, p. 118. All quotations from General Sir Oliver Leese and General A. H. Gatehouse are communications to the author, unless otherwise noted. The extract from Montgomery's personal message to his troops on p. 260 is taken from the *Memoirs*, p. 127. The reason for the absence of Axis counter-fire is given in von Esebeck, p. 137. Account of the Second Battle of Alamein is based on Alexander's dispatch [particularly interesting], on Montgomery's version in *El Alamein to the Sangro*, his versions in the *Memoirs* and on the television, on versions by Liddell Hart, op. cit., by General Horrocks in *The Sunday Times*, de Guingand in *Operation Victory*, Rommel in *The Rommel Papers*, account by von Esebeck, op. cit., on divisional and regimental histories and on unpublished material, some of it from a confidential source. Description of the difficulties of 10th Corps and its bottlenecks on p. 262 given to the author by General Gatehouse. Description of conference in Montgomery's caravan on pp. 262–263 based on de Guingand, op. cit., amplified by General Leese. Montgomery's version of his conversation with Gatehouse and Lumsden is quoted from the *Memoirs*, p. 130. Gatehouse's version is a personal communication to the author. The eyewitness account of the opening of Gatehouse's call to Montgomery is from a letter by T. Cadogan in the *Daily Express* of 6th November 1958. Montgomery's account of the results of the attack over the Miteiriya Ridge is quoted from the television performance of 12th December 1958. The quotation about not moving 7th Armoured Division on p. 266 is from *El Alamein to the Sangro*, pp. 18–19, and the next quotation is from the *Memoirs*, p. 88. The phrase 'surgical callousness' is used by Moorehead, op. cit., on p. 137. The complimentary reference (p. 267) to his deception measures is from the script of his television performance on 12th December 1958. The next quotation, about Stumme's preventive withdrawal, is from *El Alamein to the Sangro*, p. 20. The letter from Brooke is given on p. 515 in *The Turn of the Tide*. The quotation about postponement of *Supercharge* on p. 268 is from p. 136 of the *Memoirs*. Montgomery's references to 'jock' columns is also from the *Memoirs*, p. 101. 'Wild enthusiasm' (p. 269) is to be found on p. 88 of the *Memoirs*, and the reference to the success of *Supercharge* from the same source, p. 135. Rommel's comment on Montgomery's caution (p. 270) is from *The Rommel Papers*. Figures of Axis losses for Second Alamein are taken from von Esebeck, op. cit., p. 162.

Montgomery's claim that the armour did break out by the morning of 25th October 1942 is on p. 130 of his *Memoirs*. Lord Carver's account of the first phase of Alamein and the break-down of the "Master Plan" is on p. 129 and pp. 133–7 of his book *Alamein*; the official history account is on p. 41, pp. 45–6, 51–2 and p. 77 in Vol. IV of *The Mediterranean and Middle East*, whence come the quotations. The quotation from Hamilton, op. cit., on the failure of the "Master Plan" is from p. 801 of *Monty*. Carver's reference to the effects of superimposing the armoured corps on the same sector as an infantry corps, and the three corps commanders' views on the plan, are in *Alamein*, pp. 96 and 201. The Carver quotation about British confusion on 24th October is on p. 123. The Kirkman quotation is from Hamilton, p. 753. The Hamilton quotation on Montgomery's insistence that Alamein went according to plan is from *Monty*, p. 802. The details about *Sigint* information on Rommel's strength is from Hinsley, Vol. II, pp. 428–9. The Hamilton quotation claiming that Eighth Army had been relatively stronger at Gazala and in *Crusader* is on pp. 751–2 of *Monty*. Hinsley's reference to British underestimating of the strength of Rommel's defences is in Vol. II, p. 435. The references to *Sigint* information on attrition of Rommel's army during Second Alamein is from Hinsley, Vol. II, pp. 441 and 448; to the lack of influence of *Sigint* on the placing and timing of *Supercharge* from Hinsley, pp. 443 and 445.

CHAPTER THREE

The description of Montgomery's post-battle press conference is based on Moorehead, op. cit., p. 128. It may be compared with impressions of Wellington at a similar hour. The quotation about brigade groups and bits and pieces is from the *Memoirs*, p. 101. The letter to Brooke quoted on p. 274 is to be found on p. 518 of *The Turn of the Tide*. The relevant quotation in Churchill, op. cit., is in Vol. IV, p. 484. The account of the pursuit from Alamein is based on British and German sources already mentioned, and on unpublished material supplied by General Gatehouse and others. The author has also discussed this episode with General Leese, General de Guingand, Brigadier E. T. Williams and others. All quotations from General Leese are communications to the author, unless otherwise noted. The quotation from Rommel on p. 275 is from Bayerlein in an

interview of 2nd January, 1960. Figures of Axis strength during the retire-
ment on Tunisia are taken from von Esebeck, op. cit. Montgomery's
reference to bluff and manœuvre on p. 277 is taken from the *Memoirs*,
p. 146. The television performance is that of 19th December 1958. The
other quotations on El Agheila are from *El Alamein to the Sangro*, p. 30 and
p. 29. Montgomery's visit to evening service (p. 278) is to be found
on p. 147 of the *Memoirs*. The German reference to Montgomery showing
signs of life (p. 279) is from von Esebeck, p. 169. Montgomery's summary
of the attack on El Agheila on p. 279 is from p. 147 of the *Memoirs*. The
quotation about plans and quantities for attacking Buerat on p. 280 is from
El Alamein to the Sangro, p. 32. The same work, p. 35, supplies the quotation
about not risking the tanks (p. 279). The figure for British tanks at Buerat
is from *El Alamein to the Sangro*, p. 34; for German from von Esebeck, op.
cit., p. 176. The 'tremendous drive' comes from *El Alamein to the Sangro*,
p. 35. The personal message to the troops on the capture of Tripoli is to
be found in full in *7th Bn., Argyll and Sutherland Highlanders*, by Ian C.
Cameron, pp. 70–71.

The Carver quotation on the confusions after Tel el Aqqaqir is from
Alamein, p. 184; and the reference to the failure of the pursuit after
Alamein from pp. 189–90. The Carver quotation that the rain on 6th
November was *not* responsible for the failure of the British pursuit is on
p. 202. Ronald Lewin's concurrence is to be found in *Montgomery as
Military Commander*, pp. 94–102. The official history references on the
same topic are in Playfair, Vol. IV, p. 81. The quotation from Hinsley
on the timely and exact *Sigint* information enjoyed by Montgomery
about Rommel's weaknesses is from Vol. II, p. 454. The quotation from
Hinsley on Montgomery's refusal to profit from *Sigint* on 10th and 11th
November 1942 is from the same page. The further references to *Sigint*
with regard to Montgomery's setpiece assault on the El Agheila position
are from Hinsley, Vol. II, pp. 456–8. The quotation from Hinsley about
the Buerat attack is from p. 460. The quotations from Hamilton about
Montgomery's "pathologically over-controlled" nature are from *Monty*,
pp. 207 and 206. The further references to Hamilton's assessment of
Montgomery's psychology are based on *Monty*, pp. 5–7, 36–9, 151–2,
206–8, 332–4, 563–6, 606–7, 713.

ADDITIONAL SOURCES: 1960–1982

Butler, J. R. M. (1964). *Grand Strategy*, Vol. III (London: HMSO).
Carver, M. (1962). *Alamein* (London: Batsford).
de Guingand, F. (1964). *Generals at War* (London: Hodder and Stoughton).
Hamilton, N. (1981). *Monty: the Making of a General 1887–1942* (London: Hamish Hamilton).
Hinsley, F. H. (1979). *British Intelligence in the Second World War*, Vol. I (London: HMSO).
Hinsley, F. H. (1981). *British Intelligence in the Second World War*, Vol. II (London: HMSO).
Howard, M. (1972). *Grand Strategy*, Vol. IV (London: HMSO).
Lewin, R. (1968). *Rommel as Military Commander* (London: Batsford).
Lewin, R. (1971). *Montgomery as Military Commander* (London: Batsford).
Lewin, R. (1973). *Churchill as Warlord* (London: Batsford)
Nicolson, N. (1973). *Alex: The Life of Field Marshal Earl Alexander of Tunis* (London: Weidenfeld and Nicolson).
Playfair, I. S. O. (1960). *The Mediterranean and Middle East*, Vol. III (London: HMSO).
Playfair, I. S. O. (1966). *The Mediterranean and Middle East*, Vol. IV (London: HMSO).
Van Crefeld, M. (1977). *Supplying War* (Ch. 6: "Syrte to Alamein") (Cambridge: Cambridge University Press).

UNPUBLISHED SOURCES: PUBLIC RECORD OFFICE

CAB 44/98 *The Retreat to El Alamein 22nd June 1942 to 29th August 1942*. Brigadier C. J. C. Molony (Unpublished Draft Narrative).
CAB 105/17 and 18. War Cabinet Telegrams to Home and Overseas Commands.
WO 169. War Diaries Middle East Forces.
WO 201. Headquarters Papers Middle East Forces.

APPENDIX "A"

Note by William Collins, publishers of Lord Montgomery's *Memoirs*, which has appeared at the front of editions of the book subsequent to the original publication, with Montgomery's full agreement:

Since the publication of this book, the Author, in a broadcast in the B.B.C. Home Service on Thursday, 20th November, 1958 stated that he was grateful to General (now Field-Marshal) Sir Claude Auchinleck and the Eighth Army under his command for stabilising the British front on the Alamein position, thereby enabling the author to conduct his successful offensive, known to the world as the Battle of Alamein, in October 1942.

The publishers think that readers of this book, who neither heard the broadcast nor read the accounts of it in the press, might reasonably assume that, immediately before the Author assumed command of the Eighth Army, General Auchinleck was preparing to withdraw into the Nile Delta, or even beyond, in the event of a determined attack by the enemy. They wish it to be known that a number of other writers, and notably General Alexander (now Field-Marshal Earl Alexander of Tunis) in a Despatch published as a Supplement to the London Gazette *of 3rd February, 1948 makes it clear that after General Auchinleck, commanding the Eighth Army, had successfully halted the enemy's attack in July, 1942, it was his intention to launch an offensive from the Alamein position when his army was rested and had been regrouped.*

APPENDIX "B"

APPRECIATION OF THE SITUATION
IN THE
WESTERN DESERT

El Alamein, 1445 hours,

27th July, 1942.

Object

1. The defence of Egypt by the defeat of the enemy forces in the Western Desert.

Factors

2. *Comparison of Strength.* Table A[1] shows a rough comparison on a brigade group basis, based on what we now know of the enemy's present strength and his reinforcement schedule. From this it seems that the enemy will hardly be able to secure a decisive superiority over us in the first half of August, provided we fight united, since the Germans would begin any offensive with an inferiority of about three infantry brigade groups and possibly 40 per cent superiority in armour. The enemy may also be inferior in artillery. It would seem that, though the Axis forces are strong enough for defensive action, they are hardly strong enough to attempt the conquest of the Delta except as a gamble and under very strong air cover. There remains for the Axis to use one German Air Landing Division, but this is taking over I.S. duties in Greece and Crete and seems unlikely to be an asset. It might, however, be used to redress the balance at a decisive moment. Throughout August the anticipated balance of strength hardly justifies a German offensive, unless we make a serious mistake and leave an opening. He may, however, be reinforced in the second part of August, though nothing is known to be scheduled. On the other hand the Axis may make great efforts to strengthen *Panzerarmee* in the shortest time.

3. *Land Forces—Numbers and Morale.* Broadly speaking, though all our forces have been through hard times, their morale is high. German morale is probably a little lower and Italian morale not more than 50 per cent. In view of the known inefficiency of the Italian forces, any offensive action taken by the Axis forces in August would have to be 80 per cent German.

[1] Not reproduced.

4. *Material*. The Eighth Army has some 60 Grant tanks now and will receive another 60 Grant tanks early in August, but there will be no more coming until September. The deduction is that it is necessary to husband our armour carefully in view of the fact that during August the enemy may build up to between 150 and 200 German tanks.

Eighth Army's deficiencies in transport are mounting. A summary of the present state of equipment of the major formations of Eighth Army is attached as Appendix X[1]. It is also necessary to husband our ammunition resources. These stand at present as shown in Appendix B[1] attached. The enemy has, however, similar deficiencies and his reinforcing division is notably deficient in anti-tank weapons and transport.

5. *Training*. None of the formations in Eighth Army is now sufficiently well trained for offensive operations. The Army badly needs either a reinforcement of well-trained formations or a quiet period in which to train.

6. *Fighting value with reference to air forces*. At present we have such air superiority that, while our troops are relatively free from molestation, the enemy is continually attacked by night and day. Our land forces are considerably heartened by this, and a large measure of tactical freedom and security accrues from it. Unless the enemy is strongly reinforced and our air forces are correspondingly reduced, this superiority will assist our offensive or defensive and gravely impede the enemy. Our air superiority is a very considerable, if somewhat indefinable, asset.

7. *Vulnerable Points*. To us the two vulnerable points are Cairo and Alexandria. Occupation of the Cairo area by the enemy would eventually dry up the Sweet Water Canal besides securing an important area for air and land maintenance. Alexandria is useful as a naval base and port of ingress for supplies. The present position of Eighth Army at El Alamein denies direct access to either place by road and flanks any attempt to by-pass. The defences of Alexandria—Cairo—the Delta proper, east of the Nubariya canal and the Wadi Natrun area will be well forward by 14th August and should be complete in so far as defences are ever complete by the end of August. Bottlenecks exposed to air action are the Nile crossings at Cairo and northwards; these are being supplemented by two floating bridges south of Cairo and by improving the routes from these bridges eastwards. All arrangements for demolitions in the Delta are being made. The enemy has few really vulnerable points. There are bottlenecks at Sollum and about Matruh and Baggush, and his long L. of C. is vulnerable to attack by raids from the air or inland or from the sea. But otherwise the enemy is not physically vulnerable, except to direct assault. Morally his Italians are always vulnerable. The soft-sand areas of the country east of El Alamein, notably the 'Barrel Track' axis, the Wadi Natrun, the sand area to its north, are all added difficulties for the enemy's movement, particularly as they cannot be widely known to him.

---

[1] Not reproduced.

8. *Ground.* The armies are now in close contact over a forty-mile front between the sea and the Quattara Depression. Most of the area is open and can be largely controlled by artillery fire.

The front divides into three main sectors:

A. From Tel Eisa to exclusive the Ruweisat Ridge. This area is held by two divisions (five infantry brigade groups). The Tel Eisa salient has considerable offensive value, but is not essential to its defence, unless the Miteiriya Ridge is also held by us. Most of the area is difficult for wheeled movement. It is on our side strongly defended by the fortified locality of El Alamein and the mined positions to the south. This area is well supported by strong prepared localities to a depth of twenty-five miles. The enemy lies in open flat country. His positions lack any well-defined features and are covered by extensive minefields. At El Daba he has dumps.

B. From inclusive the El Mreir depression to inclusive the Bab el Qattara Depression. This area is held by two divisions (four brigade groups) supported by the equivalent of one armoured brigade. We hold the high ground in this area at Pt. 63 on the Ruweisat Ridge. This position is naturally strong and has been fortified to considerable depth. The enemy holds strongly a series of depressions which give good cover. His front has been well mined and has some wire.

In sectors A and B both the enemy and ourselves have attacked in turn without success.

C. From exclusive the fortified locality in the Bab el Qattara depression to inclusive the complete obstacle of the great Qattara Depression. The enemy is well posted on strong ground at Kelat and Taqa in positions which he has prepared for defence. The object of these positions is to protect his southern flank from being turned by our mobile troops. We have no defences in depth opposite this sector, which is lightly covered by mobile troops.

9. *Time and Space.* Had the enemy the available resources, Italy and Germany are far nearer to El Alamein than is anywhere in the United Nations. The enemy should therefore be able to reinforce quicker than we. On the other hand, apart from distant Benghazi, he has only two serviceable sea ports, Tobruk and, much less useful, Matruh. He may also make use of the railway to a limited extent. He is faced with long road hauls and a sea passage vulnerable to air and submarine attack. This affects the building up of reserves for an offensive. We are nearer our bases. Our limitation is the rate that men and material can reach Egypt from overseas. His limitation is the rate at which it can reach his troops when it arrives. This indicates the necessity of blocking Tobruk and Matruh and attacking his road and rail transport and his shipping.

10. *Political Factors.* Hardly enter into this appreciation, except inasmuch

as pressure may be put on the Axis command to press on to Egypt before their army is ready or has sufficient margin of force. Our danger lies in a politically unstable Egypt in our rear. So far this danger has not developed.

11. *The Russian Front.* The operations of Eighth Army are linked to the fate of Russia. Should the Axis penetrate the Caucasus, Eighth Army might be reduced to the lowest margin to provide reinforcements for the new front. Moreover a considerable Axis success in Russia would release air and land forces and equipment for the reinforcement of the Western Desert.

12. *Maintenance.* The enemy is experiencing great difficulty in maintaining his present forces at El Alamein. This condition may improve gradually when more heavy transport vehicles come from Italy. It is not likely to improve so much that he can maintain an appreciably larger force than that envisaged in Appendix A.[1] Our maintenance presents no real difficulties, except that our stocks of 25-pounder shells are not inexhaustible, and we could certainly maintain forces of double the present size of Eighth Army in this area if they existed.

Courses open to ourselves and the enemy.

13. *Ourselves.*

A. To continue to attack the enemy in the hope that he will crack before his army is reinforced by fresh troops. The pros and cons of attacking are:

In the northern and central sectors we have made two attempts to break the enemy's front without success. Failure has been due to lack of trained troops, rigidity of organisation and limited resources in armour and infantry and it seems that the enemy's positions are now too strongly held to be attacked with success with the resources available.

We have also attacked in the southern sector, but weakly and largely as a diversion. Our attack failed, but the enemy though strongly posted is not numerous here, and this front might go if suddenly attacked. If it did go, it offers access for our mobile troops to the enemy's flanks and rear.

The problems of attack on this front are, firstly, how to find the supporting fire without unduly weakening the northern and central sectors. Secondly, how to find the troops. The only formation which might be used is the weak N.Z. Division supported by its own artillery, the artillery of 7th Armoured Division and some of 5th Indian Division's artillery. This would have to be deployed in secret and developed as a complete surprise. Failure would probably make the N.Z. Division unfit for further operations for a considerable time. Having in mind the weakness in numbers and training of this division the chances of success can only be rated as 60–40. Failure would seriously deplete

[1] Not reproduced.

our present resources. On the whole this attack hardly seems advisable at present.

B. To adopt the tactical defensive until we are strong enough to attack, which, unless the enemy's position deteriorates, will not be till mid-September at the earliest. The obvious objection is that we give the initiative to the enemy if he is able to use it. It is very doubtful if he will be able to take the initiative till late in August with any hope of success. In fact if he attacks before, provided we have a reserve in hand including up to 100 Grant tanks, we have a good chance of defeating him seriously in the area El Alamein–Hammam. Moreover the critical period for the preparation and manning of the Delta and Cairo defences is now over. There is little danger of the enemy getting any value out of by-passing the Eighth Army on its present ground. There may be a critical period late in August before the new divisions (two of armour, two of infantry) are ready, but this might be tided over by preparing their artillery battle groups in advance of the rest of the divisions and so reinforcing Eighth Army. (This project requires further examination.) This defensive could also be mitigated by enterprises against Siwa and the southern section of his front and by seaborne attacks.

14. *Courses open to the enemy.* The enemy must resume the offensive without delay, but he is unlikely to be able to do so before mid-August and even then no real margin of superiority except in A.F.V.s, is apparent. He will certainly try to attack before the end of August and as Eighth Army defences gain in strength and depth he will be more than ever tempted to avoid them and seek success in manœuvre. This may well land him into serious difficulties in the soft desert.

Alternatively, he may have to adopt the strategical defensive because our forces are too strong and too well placed for attack. If he does, he may either stand his ground or withdraw to an intermediate position covering Matruh, which will eventually be to our advantage for he will still be in striking distance when we are again fit to attack. If he goes back to the Egyptian frontier, it is questionable whether he should not be left undisturbed.

15. *Course recommended.* Seeing that we are hardly fit at present to do any more attacks, our best course is the defensive combined with offensive gestures from time to time, including raiding. The cover plan should be such as would induce the enemy to stroke prematurely, i.e., mid-August, say, between 10th and 20th August. Meanwhile the Army front should be strengthened, and so held that at least one formation could come into reserve and train. At the same time the command of Eighth Army should be put on a permanent footing.

16. *Plan recommended.*

Intention. Eighth Army will defeat any attempt of the enemy to pass through or round it.

17. *Method.*

   (a) *Forward troops*—

      30 Corps: 1 South African Division, 9 Australian Division.

      13 Corps: 1 New Zealand Division, 7 Armoured Division.

   (b) *Reserve*—

      5 Indian Division (4 Indian Division eventually): 1 Armoured Division.

   (c) *General line of* F.D.L.s. El Alamein defences—

      Pt. 63 (eastern) on Ruweisat Ridge—vicinity of Alam Nayal. South of Alam Nayal the flank will be covered by 7 Armoured Division.

   (d) *General line of reserve positions*—

      For forward bodies, the most western line of the new rearward position.

Should it be desired to avoid the full effect of an enemy attack in great strength the above F.D.L.s can become the outpost line and the main front can be withdrawn accordingly.

   (e) *Matruh.* Should be blocked by the Navy without delay.

Tactical Technique and Future Organisation

18. In the light of the course recommended it will be necessary to adjust our tactical technique. This should be based on three facts:

   A. We have to be prepared to fight a modern defensive battle in the area El Alamein–Hammam. The troops detailed for this must be trained and exercised so as to get the maximum value from the ground and the prepared positions.

   B. Eighth Army may have to meet an enemy's sortie developing into manœuvre by the southern flank from his firm front on the general line Bab el Qattara–Taqa Plateau. We must therefore organise and train a strong mobile wing, based on 7th Armoured Division, comprising a divisional artillery, 7th Motor Brigade, 4th Light Armoured Brigade, and possibly extra Crusader units. This mobile wing must be well trained in harassing defensive technique.

   C. Eventually we will have to renew the offensive and this will probably mean a break-through the enemy positions about El Alamein. The newly-arrived infantry divisions and the armoured divisions must be trained for this and for pursuit.

19. From the point of view of G.H.Q., the organisation of our available forces in August and September might take the form, as shown on following page.

This goes further than the present appreciation, but can hardly be separated from it because, should this idea be adopted, it means that the formations now in Eighth Army will not be relieved and the new

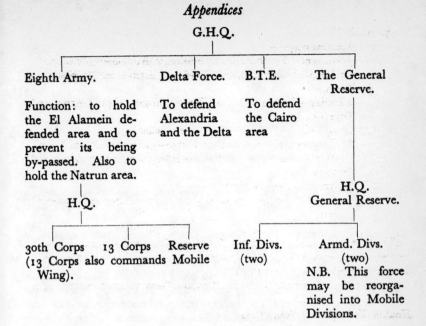

G.H.Q.

Eighth Army.	Delta Force.	B.T.E.	The General Reserve.
Function: to hold the El Alamein defended area and to prevent its being by-passed. Also to hold the Natrun area.	To defend Alexandria and the Delta	To defend the Cairo area	

H.Q.

H.Q. General Reserve.

30th Corps 13 Corps Reserve (13 Corps also commands Mobile Wing).	Inf. Divs. (two)	Armd. Divs. (two) N.B. This force may be reorganised into Mobile Divisions.

formations will be built up and reorganised irrespective of the immediate needs of Eighth Army.

20. *Summary*. The enemy now holds in sufficient strength for his purpose a front from which he cannot be dislodged by manœuvre or any attack Eighth Army can at present deliver. We are strongly posted for a defensive battle. The enemy is attempting to build up his strength and renew his attack on Egypt. Eighth Army requires re-equipment and training before it will be fit for offensive operations. During August it is unlikely that either ourselves or the enemy will be strongly reinforced on land; a successful offensive by either side is therefore unlikely. Provided the land and air situation does not change, Eighth Army can be reinforced about mid-September by two armoured divisions and two infantry divisions. This may give us a superiority sufficient to justify a direct attack on what may be by then a strongly organised front. Alternatively, we may develop a threat to the enemy's rear via Siwa. The immediate need is to reorganise present forces with Eighth Army and to rearrange the front so as to provide an army reserve. The longer-term policy is to train the newly-arrived divisions for the counter-offensive which it is hoped might begin in the latter part of September.

E. Dorman-Smith, Major-General.

[Accepted by General Auchinleck, C.-in-C., M.E.]

APPENDIX "C"

"I hope you are teaching your students that a little unorthodoxy is a dangerous thing—but without it one seldom wins battles." *Wavell to Dorman-Smith, 1940.*

In the course of this book, General Dorman-Smith's name appears at various moments of great significance, either when he has supplied military ideas of originality and success (as in the First Battle of Alamein) or when like Cassandra he has foretold woe to come (as before *Battleaxe* and the Gazala battles). His is a strange story: up to 1942 regarded as among the most brilliant and erudite staff officers in the British Army, he sank after the Cairo Purge into professional obscurity. Yet even today his name comes up early in conversations about the Desert Campaigns as a subject for praise or obloquy. His career is a fascinating example of the deserts accorded to intellectuals in British life—especially brilliant ones who forget to conceal their brilliance, who forget to tolerate the mediocrity around them.

As a subaltern in the First World War, he served with the Northumberland Fusiliers in Flanders and Italy. He temporarily commanded a battalion at Passchendaele. He received three wounds and the Military Cross before he was twenty. After the war, he returned to his regiment, was adjutant for three years, and between 1922 and 1926 instructor at Sandhurst. During the next two years he was a student at the Staff College, Camberley (passing in at his first attempt and in his second year being placed in the top four of the college). Afterwards he was Instructor in Tactics at the School of Military Engineering, a new post. In 1931 he was appointed Brigade Major to the 6th Experimental Brigade at Blackdown, under Brigadier Archibald Wavell. This was a plum appointment: it marked the general very high opinion of his capacity. In 1934 and 1935 he was in S.D.2., the department of the War Office concerned with the preparation of the army for modern war. This was another key post, wherein Dorman-Smith played an important part in the steps taken to motorise completely the British Army, as had been urged by Fuller, Liddell Hart and others since 1918. At that time a British expeditionary force in a future European war was visualised as a mass infantry body like that of the First World War. Some (like the future Field-Marshal

Montgomery) even doubted whether we should send an expeditionary force at all. Dorman-Smith at a private dinner with Duff Cooper, Minister for War, produced maps on which he had plotted a German advance through the Low Countries, proving that by concentrating highly mobile forces at narrow points of attack the Germans could break any front designed on current French or British theory. He proved conclusively that Britain was bound to be involved in major ground fighting in the next war, and added that this war was coming certainly and soon. Dorman-Smith went on to list deficiencies in organisation and equipment in the British army and plead for mechanisation. But Duff-Cooper, who had had similar ideas pressed on him by other radicals, was too lazy or too much a member of the Establishment to upset the military *status quo*.

Dorman-Smith, after serving as an instructor at the Staff College in 1936 and commanding an infantry battalion in Egypt in 1937–38 (and converting it into a mobile unit), became Director of Military Training in India. This was a prospective step towards the highest posts of the Army: Gort, CIGS, had occupied this post. In India Dorman-Smith worked closely with General Auchinleck, Deputy Chief of the General Staff. Despite severe shortages of equipment, radical reforms were carried out in the backward and hidebound Indian service; upon such fine units as 4th and 5th Indian Divisions was to depend desert victory in 1940–43. Between 1932 and 1938, Dorman-Smith obtained all possible brevet promotions—from Captain to Brigadier in peacetime in ten years. In 1940, a Middle East Staff College was opened at Haifa. Teaching here could have a decisive influence on the future armies of this important theatre. At his own request, Dorman-Smith was appointed Commandant, although the transfer from India involved demotion and loss of pay. Wavell, now C.-in-C. Middle East, had a very high opinion of Dorman-Smith's professional knowledge and inventive brain. He sent him to O'Connor's headquarters to observe the rehearsal of the tactical plan of attack at Sidi Barrani and to advise upon it. Seizing on Gatehouse's suggestion of a tank-attack on the unmined north-west corner of Nibeiwa, Dorman-Smith evolved the unorthodox and successful plan of attacking from the west with tanks and lorried infantry after an unregistered barrage ("Firing for Demoralisation", he called it) from the east. He incorporated his ideas into a paper, "Attack on a Desert Camp", reprinted as an appendix to Wavell's despatch. During the end of O'Connor's campaign Wavell sent him up again to observe and write a full report on it. As an old friend of Harding and O'Connor, Dorman-Smith took part in the discussions that led to the great march to Beda Fomm.

From April to June 1941, Dorman-Smith held temporarily the post of Director of Military Operations in Cairo. While in Cairo, Harding discussed with him the plan for *Battleaxe*. Dorman-Smith criticised it strongly, pointing out that if the flank guards supplied by the weak 7th Armoured Division were beaten by German armour, the infantry attack on the Axis frontier defences would be caught in the flank. In his view the plan was a slavish and inapt copy of the Sidi Barrani plan. His own suggestion was to establish an artillery, anti-tank and 'I'-tank screen on the plateau west of Capuzzo, behind which the infantry would besiege the Axis frontier defences. Seventh Armoured Division would draw the German armour on to the screen. Rommel would in any case be forced to attack to relieve his frontier troops. The plan thus combined, as did all Rommel's, offensive strategy with defensive tactics. It was not adopted.

While there was no question about Dorman-Smith's able mind and profound military knowledge, there was a darker side to his career, adumbrating professional extinction should he ever once fall from grace. He had had an astonishing run of quick promotion. He wore his brilliance openly on his sleeve. He was a theoretician and a perfectionist; he did not always understand how to handle the common clay of mankind. He could not and would not compromise in the comfortable British way. In his career he created much admiration, many special friendships, but also a general fund of ill-will among the hidebound, the slow and the 'Establishment'. The British prefer practical, 'liveable' men to purist brains; Dorman-Smith would have done better in the German Army. Those who bore him ill-will seized and enlarged on the fact that some of Dorman-Smith's tactical and strategic inventions were not practicable; and attempted to write him down as a military dreamer. This, too, is a characteristic British attitude to original thinkers. Both Auchinleck and Wavell were wiser: they used those of Dorman-Smith's inventions which their own practical sense told them would work, and rejected the rest. In Auchinleck's words: "To a particular problem, Dorman-Smith might produce ten solutions. Out of the ten, you could pick perhaps four that were practicable, and one that was a winner."

In February, 1941, Auchinleck sent Dorman-Smith to report on the state of Eighth Army (as fully recounted in the text of this book). In mid-May, 1942, he became acting Deputy Chief of the General Staff in Cairo, an appointment confirmed on 16th June. It was at his suggestion that Auchinleck wrote to Ritchie to advise him to hold all his armour concentrated well north astride the Trigh Capuzzo before Rommel's offensive of May 26th. Dorman-Smith had equally valuable advice to give after the fall of Bir Hacheim, when Ritchie was standing with his back to Tobruk and his communications. There was the question whether to fight on this line, or retire to the frontier, abandoning Tobruk, or fight on a third position, covering Tobruk, but giving up the exposed Gazala salient. Dorman-Smith strongly recommended the third course, which formed the basis of Auchinleck's orders to Ritchie of 14th–15th June, 1942. On June 25th, Dorman-Smith accompanied Auchinleck when the C.-in-C. took over command of Eighth Army at Mersa Matruh in the face of imminent final catastrophe caused by the failure of the 'practical' men. The full story of their professional collaboration and decisive success has been told in this book. Auchinleck freely gives Dorman-Smith credit for the tactical and organisational ideas that saved Egypt at First Alamein: the fluid, mobile defence, the avoidance of 'boxes', the concentration of the armour, the centralised army-control of artillery, the directing of British attacks on the Italians, the establishment of a defended and refused left-flank at Alam Halfa. Without the quick-thinking, imaginative and unorthodox Dorman-Smith at his side, it is possible that Auchinleck, for all his supreme qualities of resolution and leadership, might not have been able to outgeneral Rommel in the swaying First Battle of Alamein. This period was the summit of Dorman-Smith's professional career—and, it may be thought, not an unworthy height to reach. His testament as a military thinker is the Appreciation of the military situation in the Middle East submitted to Auchinleck on 27th July, 1942, and reproduced as Appendix B to this book. On August 8th he was relieved of his post (as has been recounted).

This fall was final. There was no recovery. All those in the army who bore him ill-will, who had never forgiven him his brilliance and unorthodoxy, saw to that. On reaching London he was reduced to colonel's rank, later to be appointed brigadier commanding a Welsh infantry brigade in Kent. Dorman-Smith (who of course did not know why he had been dismissed in Cairo) settled down to make a success of his new, if junior appointment. He disproved his earlier reputation of being a theorist unfit for direct command by handling his brigade in a big exercise, *Spartan*, in spring 1943, with outstanding ability. But in October General Neil Ritchie became commander of 12th Corps, of which Dorman-Smith's brigade formed a part. It was thought that the presence of the man who had helped save Egypt might be embarrassing to the man who had lost the Gazala battles. Dorman-Smith was immediately removed and spent several months in idleness. In March, 1944, his repeated requests for an appointment were granted: he went to Italy to command an infantry brigade in the Anzio beachhead. This brigade delivered a model attack on the Aquabona ridge (vide *The Tanks*, Vol. II, p. 278), after which the division was in reserve until August 1944. Dorman-Smith had now been broken twice; yet his abilities were once again beginning to rebuild his career. However, in August, 1944, as the brigade moved into the front at Florence, Dorman-Smith was suddenly and unexpectedly removed from its command by the divisional commander on the grounds that he was unfit for brigade command. No explanation was given. He was sent back to England, once more without employment and under a cloud of mystery. No explanation or justification for this third breaking of his career was ever given, despite Dorman-Smith's efforts to obtain one from the authorities. On November 1st, 1944, he was removed from the active list of the army, so ending his military career. In view of Dorman-Smith's general army record and his conspicuous success as a brigade commander both in England and at Anzio, this unexplained relief from his last command, following two earlier (and utterly unjust) reliefs, leaves the strong impression that after the Cairo Purge the word quietly filtered through the military 'Establishment' that Dorman-Smith was not to be given a chance to rebuild his career.

Most British defeats have been caused by stupidity. This continuing British military fashion, this melancholy sequence from Yorktown through the Duke of York's campaigns, through the Crimea, the Zulu and Boer wars, the two great wars to the Suez operation of 1956 is starkly illuminated by the treatment accorded to Dorman-Smith.

INDEX

Index

Index

Index

Index

INDEX FOR NEW COMMENTARY